No Silent Witness

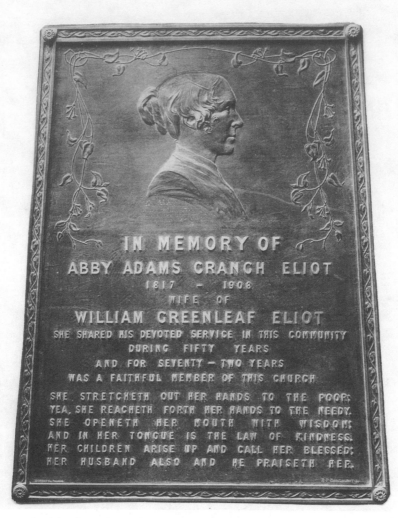

Memorial tablet for Abby Adams Cranch Eliot. Courtesy of Warner A. Eliot

No Silent Witness

The Eliot Parsonage Women
and Their Unitarian World

CYNTHIA GRANT TUCKER

UNIVERSITY PRESS

2010

OXFORD

UNIVERSITY PRESS

Oxford University Press, Inc., publishes works that further
Oxford University's objective of excellence
in research, scholarship, and education.

Oxford   New York
Auckland   Cape Town   Dar es Salaam   Hong Kong   Karachi
Kuala Lumpur   Madrid   Melbourne   Mexico City   Nairobi
New Delhi   Shanghai   Taipei   Toronto

With offices in
Argentina   Austria   Brazil   Chile   Czech Republic   France   Greece
Guatemala   Hungary   Italy   Japan   Poland   Portugal   Singapore
South Korea   Switzerland   Thailand   Turkey   Ukraine   Vietnam

Published by Oxford University Press, Inc.
198 Madison Avenue, New York, New York 10016

www.oup.com

Oxford is a registered trademark of Oxford University Press

Library of Congress Cataloging-in-Publication Data
Tucker, Cynthia Grant.
No silent witness : the Eliot parsonage women and their Unitarian world / Cynthia Grant Tucker.
p.   cm.
Includes bibliographical references
ISBN 978-0-19-539020-9
1. Eliot, William Greenleaf, 1811–1887—Family.   2. Spouses of clergy—United States—
Biography.   3. Wives—United States—Biography.
4. Children of clergy—United States—Biography.   5. Daughters—United
States—Biography.   6. Unitarian women—United States—Biography.
7. Unitarians—United States—Biography.
8. Eliot family.   I. Title.
BX9869.E45T83 2010
289.1092'273—dc22
[B]   2009039918

9 8 7 6 5 4 3 2 1

Printed in the United States of America
on acid-free paper

This book is for those who see themselves in its story and for those who will write the next chapters.

Acknowledgments

I wish to acknowledge the many institutions and individuals who made this book possible. The Radcliffe Institute and the University of Memphis provided the grants that allowed me to travel more freely to research sites, and I am grateful to them for their generosity.

My thanks also go to the archivists and librarians who welcomed me to their reading rooms and into the stacks or fielded requests from a distance. For their partnership in this adventure, I wish to recognize the late Louisa Bowen and her successor, Stephen Kerber, at the Lovejoy Library at the University of Southern Illinois in Edwardsville; Florence Gillich at the Whitney Medical Historical Library at Yale University; Lucinda Glenn at the Hewlett Library at the Graduate Theological Union in Berkeley; Theodore Hollingsworth at the archives of the First Unitarian Church of Portland, Oregon; Jane Knowles and Diana Carey at the Schlesinger Library of the Radcliffe Institute; Erda Lebuhn at the Unitarian Universalist Fellowship of Berkeley; Nancy McColl at the Chesney Archives at Johns Hopkins University; Lauren Miller at the Digital Collection and Archives at Tufts University; Frances O'Donnell and Donna Maguire at the Andover-Harvard Library at Harvard Divinity School; Jane Otte at the Winsor School in Boston; Carol Prietto at the Olin Library at Washington University; Gay Walker at the Hauser Memorial Library at Reed College; and the staffs at Harvard's Houghton Library and Countway Library of Medicine, the Knight Library at the University of Oregon in Eugene, the Massachusetts Historical Society, the Missouri Historical Society in St. Louis, and the Oregon Historical Society in Portland.

Colleagues and friends have also been vital companions and stakeholders during this project. They have cheerfully helped in manifold ways and gone the distance in spirit, never seeming to doubt that this book would someday get finished. For their loyalty and practical aid, I wish to thank Elizabeth Curtiss, Celeste DeRoche, Melanie Fathman, Alicia M. Forsey, Gordon Gibson, Mary-Ella Holst, John Hurley, Betty Hoskins, David A. Johnson, Phyllis Rickter, Ann Bryan Ruger, and Arliss Ungar.

While my notes and bibliography credit the scholars whose work was useful to mine, there are two in particular who deserve greater mention. The first is John Scott of Georgesville, Quebec, who went to remarkable pains in sharing his research into the summer camping community at Lake Memphremagog. Without this veteran journalist and masterful historian, I would never have known of the Mays' and Eliots' "other life" away from the city where radical Unitarians gathered for more than a century, nourishing future generations of feminists and freethinkers. Scott's massive knowledge and staggering generosity have been humbling.

In truth, no amount of elaboration can adequately convey my debt to the late scholar Carolyn Heilbrun, whose writings have long been my beacon and compass in navigating through academe. From her wariness of insular theory and inaccessible language, to her challenge to us who are tenured to use our security to "make noise" and "take risks," to her understanding that "women catch courage from women whose lives and writings they read," the integrity of her thought steadied my hand as I wrote this book, emboldening me to risk becoming, as she would have said, "unpopular." I credit this wonderful mentor, a woman I met only once, years ago, for the strengths of the work I am proudest of as an educator and author.

I am, of course, keenly aware of my primal debt to this book's female subjects. Women who learned to make noise and break rules and then saved the damning evidence, they inspired their dutiful progeny to make their papers available once the culture was ready to listen to women and take them seriously. For their graciousness and unconditional trust in sharing their private archives, as well as for donating larger collections to excellent institutions, I wish to recognize Alexandra O. Eliot, Christopher Rhodes Eliot III, Frederick Lee Eliot, Mary C. Eliot, Warner A. Eliot, Alice Flagg Feutz, and Eleanor Goddard May II. I must also thank descendants Tom Korson and Robbie Cranch for their interest and help.

I am grateful to Oxford University Press, all the staff who worked on this book, and above all, my editor, Cynthia Read, for recognizing the value of the Eliots' grassroots history and giving the women the audience they deserve.

Finally, I wish to thank my family—David, Hope, and Grant—for their constant encouragement, interest, and unfailing love.

Contents

No Silent Witness

1

The Unitarian Universe

I came to explore the wreck.
The words are purposes.
The words are maps.
I came to see the damage that was done and the treasures that prevail.
      —Adrienne Rich, *Diving into the Wreck, Poems 1971–1972*, 22–23

The tarnish and glow in this story are maps to the culture in which
Unitarians lived for the better part of two centuries. They are windows
into a world that was shaped from the clay of human nature and fired
in the passion of burning ideals. And they hold the keys to why women
who lived at their planet's center of gravity—sacrificing to keep
churches running and rearing the next generations of clergy—were
prone to feel like outsiders looking in from a parallel universe. From its
welcoming heaven, open to all souls regardless of income or pedigree,
to its earthly profession of tolerance, freedom, fairness, and boundless
love, their vision of what the Creator had wrought was animated by
paradox. It was both more and less than a blueprint of how its
architects actually lived.

    No natives did more to map out this world than the family of Abigail
Adams Cranch (1817–1908) and William Greenleaf Eliot (1811–87). This
far-reaching branch of one of America's prime Unitarian dynasties was
crowded with clergymen, full-throated wives, and daughters who sought
larger frames for the pastoral impulse and women's destiny. As they
stretched their ancestral roots from the East to St. Louis and Portland,

TABLE 1. The Eliot Forebears

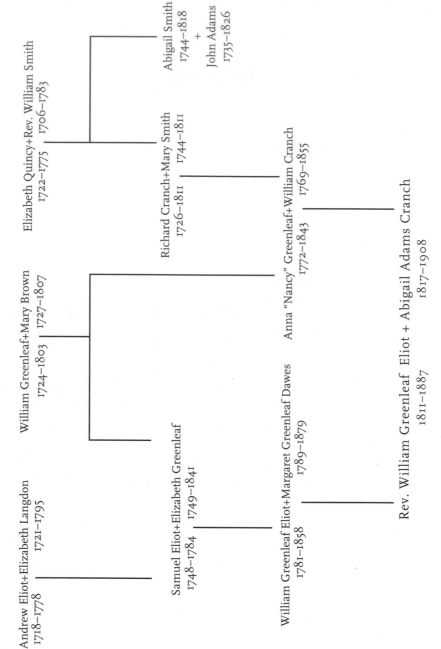

Oregon, down to Berkeley and up to Milwaukee, St. Paul, and back to Boston, Cambridge, and Concord, three generations lived through the life cycle of their denomination. The oldest remembered its quickening in the early 1800s, and the youngest, its formal consolidation in 1961 with the kindred Universalist Church of America. The men left their names on the buildings and streets of a world that revolved around public life, while the women wrote letters describing a globe that turned on the axis of family concerns and a female vocation that often seemed frozen in time while the world around them was rapidly changing.[1]

The Eliot women could simply have gazed at the record of male achievement and known that their family name would find an exalted place in history. The dazzling roster went way back to Boston before the American Revolution, when Andrew Eliot served as the minister of the New North Church. St. Louis's William Eliot brought the family further distinction, not only by leading the Unitarians' Church of the Messiah but also by spearheading Washington University, heading the Western Sanitary Commission during the Civil War, and working tirelessly for good public schools. History would remember Abby and William's oldest surviving son, Thomas Lamb Eliot, for his strikingly similar record in the Pacific Northwest. Regarded by many as Portland's greatest citizen-servant ever, Thomas served as the minister of the aptly named Church of Our Father and seeded the city's library, art museum, system of public parks, and Reed College. Grandson Frederick May Eliot, also an ordained minister, stood out as one of the most influential presidents of the denomination. His cousin T. S. Eliot, a giant in the world of letters, was part of this pantheon, too, despite his shocking desertion of the liberal faith in which he was reared.

Yet it was not in the women's nature to risk their own immortality by slipping into the future as stowaways, hidden and isolated in men's reputations. Unwilling to vanish, they kept an account of what they achieved and endured. Not everything got into the cargo, and no one pretended it did. "Some things," they shrugged, were "best said, not written," and not everything that was written survived. The women's own letters debated the question of what to commit to the scissors or flames, and to judge from the fragments and gaps, this was no idle talk. What they saw fit to save was inclusive, however, and resonates centuries later as their loyalties and integrity thread through the records. They pull together the generations, the East and the West, Christians and Humanists, sanctuaries and parsonages. They honor the same-sex partnerships along with conventional marriages; the empty cradles and pews as well as the crowded nurseries and churches; the pastorates of daughters and wives no less than traditional ministries; and the whispered doubts that muted the thundering certitudes.

———————————————— ‿ ————————————————

The outgrowth of an insurgency against the dark side of Calvinist dogma, the Unitarian world seemed born for dissent. Although its privileged New England gentry were deeply invested in social stability, Liberal Christian societies—self-governing and without binding creeds—were magnets to independent minds that quickly outgrew their hand-me-down faith. When the mavericks turned to empirical scholars and Transcendentalist mystics for truth, the Unitarian Christians dug trenches, unwilling to share their estate with false prophets. The liberal arena turned into a battlefield circled by Trinitarians where turf wars were so unremitting that three generations of Eliot men who had a genetic aversion to conflict were caught in the middle or pushed to the front.

When William Eliot first brought his bride to St. Louis in 1837, he stood well within their religion's mainstream. Repeating what he had heard William Ellery Channing preach in Boston, the young man renounced eternal damnation for all but a chosen few and threw off the onerous chains of Original Sin. His unified God was a loving Creator who made all his children essentially good and capable of infinite improvement. To show them the way to salvation, the evolving perfection of character, God had sent Jesus of Nazareth, a teacher who was less than divine but occupied an exalted place in the minds of the Liberal Christians. Channing's student went on to explain that God had equipped his people with reason and conscience to help them discern and adhere to the wisdom put forth in the Holy Scriptures. Availing himself of Joseph Buckminster's higher critical tools, young Eliot warned against reading the Bible as all of one piece and infallible and stressed the need to distinguish between its poetic and literal meanings.[2]

It was not long, however, before William Eliot's "pure gospel preaching" had gone out of vogue. By the time the Eliots' oldest son, Thomas, set out for Harvard Divinity School, his father had to caution the boy not to fall for the traps that were waiting. Nowadays, Unitarian clergy catered to every whim, he warned. They dissected obscure theological points, or expounded on social reform, or lectured on aspects of modern science and called this liberal religion! No substitute for the teachings of Jesus, their sermons were shams, and the people knew it. William's communicants told him as much when they came back from visiting friends in the East. They had only to go to the old meeting houses and hear the groans in the pews, they said, to thank God for sending St. Louis a man who was not afraid to go out of style. Defending their bastion of Christianity in the Midwest was no easy task when their radical cousins—the Ethical Basis or Unity men—were fast gaining ground. Indeed, by 1870, they had infiltrated the Eliot church, inducing a number of members to leave and start a second society. The enmity between the city's two Unitarian churches would still be palpable twenty years later at William Eliot's funeral.

Nor did Thomas Lamb Eliot find any greater comity by taking his wife, Henrietta Robins Mack Eliot, and their little boy Willy away from the cinders to plant a new church in the cool soil of Portland, Oregon. With the humanist element stalking the Christians and rapidly spreading along the West Coast, the Unitarians'

FIGURE 1.1. The Church of the Messiah, St. Louis, 1851. Courtesy of the First Unitarian Church of St. Louis.

hope of presenting a unified front in this region was doomed. For William Jr., who followed his father as Portland's pastor and tended the parish for twenty-eight years, his colleagues' profession of brotherly love would ring hollow well into the twentieth century. There was not a church in the country aside from his own, he would grieve in the 1950s, where he could really be comfortable with the Unitarian message. This in spite of the bridges his cousin Frederick had tried to build in his twenty years as commander-in-chief of their liberal denomination.

FIGURE 1.2. The Church of Our Father, Portland, Ore., ca. 1880. Courtesy of the First Unitarian Church, Portland, Ore.

Theology was not the only source of contention among the men who preached the same fundamentals but acted as if they had no common ground. During the nineteenth century, Unitarians' shared opposition to slavery had run a broad spectrum of feeling, leaving plenty of room for partisan rage. The lines in this battle were drawn as early as 1833, when Lydia Maria Child's antislavery tract—*An Appeal in Favor of That Class of Americans Called Africans*—stirred William Ellery Channing to take up the cause and the steady approach of gradual moral coercion. In doing so, the Rev. Channing incurred the wrath of conservative coreligionists, who wanted the church to stay out of it, and of radical abolitionists, most famously Theodore Parker, who censored Channing for being too timid and slow. The personal damage and setback to Unitarian solidarity was a drama that played out on countless, less visible stages for much of the century. In St. Louis, the Eliots' border-state church lost a third of its members twenty years later when William appealed to the owners of slaves to set them free as a matter of conscience.

Like his grandfather William, Frederick May Eliot served in a minefield of unresolved issues. The Unitarian landscape was pitted not only with old theological rifts but also with economic and regional chasms that seemed to grow deeper each year. Rural liberals who counted on old urban wealth in the East to help them build churches and schools resented the condescension that came with that patronage. Having sacrificed comfort to spread their faith, they were stung by the Brahmins' unmasked contempt for their lack of sophistication. The city folk in the West also bristled at how they were snubbed by Easterners. It was bad enough being statistically dwarfed by conservative evangelicals without their fellow liberals putting them down.[3]

Frederick May Eliot's moniker, "Mr. Unitarianism," was well-deserved praise for a man who rescued a battered denomination. In the twenty years under his watch, the American Unitarian Association (A.U.A) had seen church membership grow from just over 60,000 adults in 1938—only twice what it was in 1850 and runty compared to other traditions—to roughly 105,000 names. The growth in the Sunday school rosters seemed nothing less than spectacular, reaching some 58,000, an increase of nearly 280 percent. Frederick's concept of lay-led fellowships brought in another 2,000 people; and 1,700 more had joined The Church of the Larger Fellowship, a mailing list congregation for those who had no brick-and-mortar religious homes. But while the rank-and-file liberals had pulled together and ministers formed new alliances, the argumentative impulse persisted and simply opened new ruptures. By the time the 1950s arrived, Mr. Unitarianism not only embodied his cohort's progress but also displayed the destructive effects of his colleagues' continual strife. Emotionally scarred but intent on remaining in office, President Frederick May Eliot was gunning for reelection and arming himself for another hard fight when he suddenly died of a heart attack in 1958.[4]

While Unitarian women had plenty to say in these sacredly framed disputes over slavery, war, equal suffrage, and liberal theology, they had to strain to make themselves heard. A resistence to female influence in religious discourse had grown intense since the start of the nineteenth century, when New England's established church lost its state support. Stripped of the muscle and stature they had previously enjoyed, and driven as much by the politics of survival as by any scriptural doctrine, Congregational clergy saw reason to fear for their manhood.

With the men whose taxes had paid their wages no longer invested enough to show up, these pastors were left with overwhelmingly female constituencies. The feminine face this put on their workplace suited some better than others. It furnished a haven for gentle fellows who shrank from the rough competition outside. But for those whose self-confidence suffered from being cut off from the realm of male power, the female culture presented a risk that put them on the defense. Unable to brandish a rigid and fiery creed as the orthodox could, Unitarian preachers were easy targets for jabs at their masculinity. Trinitarian pulpits assailed them as spineless pretenders to real religion, effeminate frauds with nothing to show but dog-eared books and a dreamy gaze. In short, liberal ministers had enough problems without women telling them what they should preach. It was critical that females remember their place and be quiet so men could be men.[5]

Unlike the biblical literalists, who protected the separate spheres by citing the damage that Eve had caused by crossing the line in the Garden of Eden, the Unitarians argued that God's plan was written into the world he created. "Woman was *formed* to obey," as one scholar put it in 1831, and it was her duty to minister to the needs of her family at home. The publication of Horace Bushnell's *Christian Nurture* in 1847 elevated this line of defense by canonizing domestic religion. It established the home as the "seat of religion," where mothers, anointed as priestesses, tended worshipful families at table and hearth and filled the young souls with the spirit of Christ. As a charming vignette of the moral growth that began at home in a mother's arms, this iconography helped the liberals compete with the evangelical brothers, whose instant act of conversion had a proven appeal with the masses. But beyond this, by setting the home apart as the "church of childhood" and woman's preserve, it reinforced the division of precincts known as the doctrine of separate spheres, strengthening men's authority in the larger church outside.[6]

The spheres were also adaptable buffers against political forces of change that threatened the Unitarians' social order. They were used as rebukes when antebellum agitators clamored to vote, declaring their "natural rights" were being abridged and their "common humanity" trampled. The separate spheres were exploited again to check further female ambition when Unitarian brothers reversed themselves after the Civil War and endorsed women's suffrage to neutralize the Fifteenth Amendment's effect of letting the black and foreign-born men cast ballots. By voting, the argument went, white middle-class women would clean out corrupt politicians, close ungodly brothels and taverns, and end the blight of domestic abuse that ruined so many homes. In short, they could do even more in the way of looking after their families' wellbeing, and they could do it without ever leaving their orb.[7]

As it floated between the earth and the stars, women's glorified sphere also threw its shadow over the Unitarians' claim to progressive education. The Unitarian brothers had held the bragging rights to the culture of learning since gaining control of the Harvard curriculum in 1803 and naming Henry Ware to the pivotal Hollis professorship two years later. Yet it would take almost two centuries for a female to gain admission, and longer before she would see the Harvard seal on her diploma. Unitarian men in the West seemed quicker to recognize and redress this injustice. In 1868, sixteen years after starting a theological school in Meadville, Pennsylvania, they opened its doors to women. William Eliot had already created a special department for females at Washington University in St. Louis and gone on to push for a coeducational policy across the board.

Yet here, too, the ideology of the separate spheres still prevailed. Females needed good schooling so they would be fit companions for husbands and well-equipped to teach their children at home. William Eliot fully expected that as the doors opened wider for women, some "who should be at the spindle" would want to move into the men's domain, and their "small successes" would "turn their heads"

FIGURE 1.3. Divinity Hall, Harvard, ca. 1875. Courtesy of the Andover-Harvard Archives.

temporarily. They would want to be doctors and lawyers and college professors and politicians, and they should be given the chance to see whether or not they could really succeed. Still, his "old fashioned notions about such things," as he wrote in 1870, led him to think their natural instincts would soon send them back to rearing families and doing their part for the church. For the rest of the century, all the girls on the St. Louis side of the Eliot clan were enrolled in their grandfather's school as a rite of passage. They carried a partial load of courses for several years without earning degrees, this seeming a safe allotment for daughters whose future was going to be in the home. If this exceeded what most of their Unitarian sisters enjoyed, it still carried limiting ambiguities that were unknown to the brothers at Harvard.[8]

Nor did the Unitarian teachings of human worth and inclusion extend to the females who felt called to preach and lead churches. Although the denomination boasted about being one of the first to have sanctioned the ordination of women, such bragging was disingenuous for a group that had let females in by default before turning them out and changing the locks. Interest in rural and westward expansion after the Civil War had given the distaff the chance to move into areas few males were willing to plow. The majority prospered, in part by casting their work as womanly service, thus easing parishioners' jitters before their doubts could empty the pews. But they were excellent managers, too, good listeners, and inspiring preachers, who fostered strong feelings of kinship and won their people's love and respect.[9]

Away from their parishes, it was a much different story. Trinitarians cast them as demons, not homemakers drawn to a larger scale, and the liberal establishment saw them as fools, or worse, as freaks of nature. By the 1880s, this undertow had merged with a riptide of widespread concern that American culture was being emasculated. Fed by the long stretch of years without wars in which men might have proven their valor, and by the unsettling shifts in the marketplace from the farms to the cities, fears about feminization had swollen into a full-scale obsession. Craving the vigor and toughness they believed had made young America great, the public demanded more combat in sports and turned to authors and entertainers who fed their hunger for rugged, brute force. School boards sought ways to reduce the number of females teaching the primary grades, and voters elected a boxer, cowboy, and Rough Rider—Teddy Roosevelt—to ripple his presidential muscle and show the world what the nation was made of.[10]

Separately but in step with their Trinitarian counterparts, the anxious Unitarian leadership marched on the feminized church, determined to reinstate their masculine prowess. As the century turned, their settlement office in Boston was systematically hijacking ordained women's attempts to find work. The officials "forgot" to include their names when asked to recommend candidates. They suggested one sister apply to a church the members had already voted to close. From the panic, one would have supposed the pulpits were flooded with female incompetents.

In reality, a dozen or so remarkably able women had left a record of parish growth that put the brothers to shame.[11]

At a time when most of the old Eastern churches were barely solvent and poorly run, and their ministers were being dressed down by the top brass as "lazy, indifferent, and helpless," the women in the upper Midwest had organized fifteen societies and revived several others And these were not dormant organizations that looked good only on paper. Under their guidance, their congregations built handsome churches and paid the bills without asking Boston for help. Yet these were the very ministers whom the Unitarian leadership purged. Half-a-century after the first Unitarian woman received ordination, only forty-three had achieved that distinction, no more than a third had found permanent pulpits, and even fewer had lasted for more than five years. Their eviction hastened an exodus of other progressive females, who gave up their volunteering at church for more fulfilling endeavors.

As a strategy for reviving the churches, new programs designed to attract more males were no more effective than trying to stifle the females. Like their orthodox brothers, the liberal clergy were ready to build gymnasiums, install billiard tables, and organize team sports where younger fellows might find a wholesome "outlet for their animal spirits" and satisfy "the legitimate desires of their physical natures." To make the older males feel more at home, they created clubs that had the feel of business and social fraternities. After the Trinitarian Men and Religion Forward Movement's crusade for virility reached its crest with revivals in 1911 and 1912, the Unitarians took larger steps of their own to beef up the liberal church by way of a broader fraternal evangelism. The result was the National Unitarian Layman's League, which from its creation in 1919 well into the 1930s, served the denomination well as its faithful and primary fund-raising arm. This brotherhood paid to keep pulpits filled, scouted for new ministerial candidates, and built a much-needed library for the liberal seminary in Berkeley. At the local level, however, the turnouts on Sundays continued to drop. The men still stayed home as the women were drifting away.[12]

— — — ⟳ — — —

Whether or not they liked the idea of their sisters being ordained or could fathom the insult and sympathize with that cadre's professional exile, or whether they thought of themselves as Liberal Christians or radical Humanists, Unitarian women were likely to feel estranged from their cherished tradition. They rejoiced in their freedom from punishing creeds and the shackles of orthodox literalism. Their hearts and intellects reveled in the liberty to stretch out full length and study the Bible in light of their reason, optimism, and conscience. They were grateful, too, for the options they had to cling to Channing's Heavenly Father, to put their stock in Emerson's Oversoul, or to form their own "loose-leaf" amalgams of liberal religion.

Yet whatever they chose, they were likely to be disappointed by what they got from the pulpits.

In Massachusetts, Lidian Jackson and Ralph Waldo Emerson's oldest girl, Ellen, was already venting her discontent as a fifteen-year-old in boarding school. The sermons the local ministers served up as liberal religion were "frightful fare," she fretted in letters addressed to Concord during the 1850s. Dry lectures that no one could swallow, they offered her nothing of practical use, and thirty years later, the diet was even worse. The spirits of "most of the people" were wasting away on the husks of their rich tradition. Jesus was nowadays "only a man" who was "valuable to the human race, exactly as Washington was," Ellen grumbled in 1881.[13]

Not unique to New England or limited to the nineteenth-century Sabbath, the dissonance was also a trial for Ruth Irish Preston of Davenport, Iowa. Ruth was famished, she wrote in her diary fifty years after Ellen complained. Brought up on practical sermons with ethical themes, she craved the meaty religion that she had chewed on all week. Nowadays preachers were tedious scholars, so self-absorbed and aloof, she groaned, they never lifted their eyes to notice the congregation was dozing. If the pews had been cushioned, Ruth wrote in her diary, she would have napped with the others. But she was so thin that she squirmed in her seat and suffered through deadly lectures for years before she emphatically put down her pen and closed the book on the liberal pulpit.[14]

There was more to this female unhappiness than the ache of a separation from Jesus or pangs for the meat that had nourished the intellect in an era now gone. Regardless of their historical moment or theological tilt, Unitarian females who liked their pastors in other respects felt betrayed when their preaching discounted the dark side of life and the problems that weighed them down. In St. Louis, the young Sally Smith, William Eliot's scribe in the 1850s, dutifully wrote out his sermons exactly as they were dictated during the week but invariably revised them when she heard them delivered in church. Orphaned for almost a decade but still beset by the loss of her parents, Sally permitted her mind to dart off as soon as the minister started to preach. She let it compose another text that embraced her memories and pain until the organ announced the last hymn and she realized the sermon was over. Her treachery shamed her, she wrote in her diary, but it gave her the comfort she missed when the minister told her how she should feel instead of acknowledging what she felt.[15]

In a universe with neither a hell nor a recognizable world for the living, women were on their own to name the roots of their discontent. Unlike their Universalist cousins, who had a long history of fighting the devil and grappling with the evil in flawed economic and social conditions, these Unitarian sisters heard few unequivocal calls for reform from the pulpits or from the pews. Most rank-and-file Unitarians were too comfortable with the status quo and too individualistic by nature to tolerate the rhetorical whippings the clergy gave one another. Only the ministry's radical fringe were willing to preach on women's oppression, and only the most exceptional men were open to speaking of it in their homes.

The dissonance was amplified for the women who lived in the parsonages where ministers censored the conversations to fit with their positive message at church. While some borrowed Paul's words to Timothy to enjoin the women "to be in silence," the Eliot men had their own admonition engraved on their coat of arms. *Tace et Face*, translated freely as "Don't talk about it, just get back to work!" summed up the manly way of numbing one's anguish and insulating one's faith. When they suffered the death of a child or defeat in denominational politics, men doubled their workload, burned themselves out, and went off alone to recuperate. However refreshed upon their return, they were no more receptive to wifely laments. Their spouses, obliged to protect the minister's privacy outside the parsonage, typically had no one else with whom they could share the whole of their burdens.

Not easily silenced, the Eliot women protested on several fronts. For a man to say he was open-minded but not give his own wife a hearing—and then have the gall to call it a virtue—was more than a marital insult. It dealt a potentially crippling blow to their efforts as parish first ladies. Laity-one-step-removed, these wives were amphibious creatures uniquely equipped to take their community's pulse from all sides. They could offer reassurance and counsel more or less on their husbands' behalf while eliciting confidences that women would not have felt comfortable sharing with men. They developed an ear for sifting out useful suggestions, ignoring mindless complaints, and distinguishing genuine praise from hollow flattery.

Loath to let their experience go to waste when their husbands could benefit from it, these wives persisted in trying to get their attention. They wanted to tell them to throw out the halos, pedestals, and rosy lenses that cluttered their sermons and hampered the work their wives had to do on the ground. What sisterly words could they offer the women who felt left out and abandoned when preachers, vaunting the joys of marriage and family, ignored such real sorrows as unemployment, addiction, and infertility? The Eliot matriarch, who had nine of her fourteen children die in St. Louis and never lost sight of the vacant places they left, had no good answer for this. And here was a woman as well prepared as a liberal minister's wife could be.[16]

Abigail Adams Cranch Eliot brought to this role not only the dedication and wit of the great-aunt for whom she was named but also the insights unique to those who had grown up together with their religion. Abby was just beginning to walk when her fledgling tradition was getting its footing. In 1819, the year she turned two, William Ellery Channing gave it its name, redeeming the taunt *unitarian* by claiming it as the badge of a noble and enlightened Christianity. Abby was eight

FIGURE 1.4. The Eliot homestead: 2660 Washington Avenue, St. Louis, 14 March 1883.
Pencil sketch by John Cranch, brother of Abigail Adams Cranch Eliot. Photograph
of the original, courtesy of Mary C. Eliot.

when the movement assumed a denominational presence, christening the American
Unitarian Association, a loosely cobbled confederation of dissenting societies.
Meanwhile, the church in the capital city of Washington, where Abby was reared
with her second cousin and sweetheart William, had made its own place in history.
Organized by a core that included her father and future father-in-law, it was one of
the first to hoist the radical Unitarian flag straightaway. Understandably, Abby felt
"wide-awake" to the positive message her husband would preach when she followed him out to Missouri after their marriage. Yet the real awakening came only
after she settled into a role that was wedded to unrealistic expectations.[17]

After the century turned and lay sisters gave up their volunteer work at the
church for the greater rewards in fields where they were asked their opinions and
paid for their labor, the parsonage wives were left in their time warp to rue their
immobility. It would take the marriage of Abby and William's son Christopher to
Mary May to produce a new generation of females who scripted larger lives that
were nourished but unconstrained by family tradition. With their father's pastoral
ethic and their mother's feminist syntax to guide them, their daughters, Martha and
Abby, would bypass their elders' churchly employment to forge careers in public
health and preschool education. And they would skirt conventional marriage to
follow their hearts into lifelong unions with women who were their lovers, soul
mates, and colleagues.[18]

As hard as it was for the parsonage women to speak for themselves in the here and now, it was harder for them to be heard in the afterlife. The Unitarian constellations of immortal authors included few females, and those who were there appeared with disguised or redacted identities. Compromised by a double standard of literary production that mirrored the sexes' separate domains, published autobiography was a losing proposition for females. To be well received, the authors had to corset their talents and candor, show delicacy, and forfeit their complex or untidy stories to facile ideals. Those who refused were condemned as offensive and aberrant, and the treatment accorded such women as Margaret Fuller and Julia Ward Howe made it clear that the punishments did not end when the miscreants finally died. If not demonized, as in Fuller's case, they were sanctified, as in Howe's, and neither distortion honored the struggles in which they had honed a prophetic voice.[19]

While the Eliot women were not exempt from the double standard of authorship, and their few published writings had all the marks of a self-imposed censorship, their personal archives would bring them an immortality Fuller and Howe were denied. As family stewards, not public figures, they neither sought nor were subject to radical makeovers in the next life. None claimed to have conquered their culture's inherited prejudices, and those who came closest did not spare themselves when confronting their cohort's hypocrisy. Their purpose in saving their records was not hagiography, or settling scores, or replacing one truncated history with another. Their aim was to keep the family united, which is to say, honest and human. Moreover, for all the collisions in living intimately with their opposites, Eliot wives still felt the flame of their youth in advanced old age. This has made it that much easier to embrace them with all their faults and to honor the often difficult men whom they loved unconditionally.

By keeping their kindred united and recording their side of events, these witnesses also enabled their story to travel across the waters of time and bank on the strangely familiar shore of another millennium. Ministers' wives do sound different today. Emboldened by modern technology and a public that thrives on confession, parish first ladies announce to the world they are stripping away the old stereotypes. They declare they are weary of being dressed up as the virtuous wife in Proverbs, a figment whose flawless example, able and uncomplaining, has put them to shame. Even those who still find satisfaction as pastors' advisors and adjuncts in ministry go on record as feeling slighted, taken for granted, or gypped by their husbands' low pay. At odds with a view of reality their spouses proclaim as the word of God, they declare that their womanly truth has been lost in translation and abrogated by myth. Yet for all their new outlets and amplification, they broadcast the very same heresies that the Eliot women struggled to air in private.

2

Calling the Family Together

Is it not wonderful—the children counting the daughters in law and sons in law....A colony of Eliots indeed—I wish we could all meet once on earth!

—Abigail Adams Cranch Eliot to Henrietta Robins
Mack and Thomas Lamb Eliot, 25 April 1897

The matriarch of the family would never have recognized herself as the spirit who hovered above them protectively in their wishful imaginations. That blessed mother and "angel Grandma, so trustful and brave" and "the strongest" among them, was capable of heroics to which not even her husband was equal. If the venerable William Eliot was his colleague Emerson's "Saint of the West," his wife was the one their children believed could "reach up and part the clouds" to "let in the light" and keep the whole family in view. The object of this adoration knew better, and so did her female defenders. Mrs. Eliot was a remarkable woman, but she was as human as any of them. She had the lines on her face to show it before she was middle-aged. If the minister's uncomplaining helpmeet appeared to her sons as an angel, she reminded the parish ladies of the small sculpted figures at church that clung to the pillars, straining to hold up the roof. Except "Mrs. E." was no decorative fixture. She had her feet on the ground and could speak.[1]

On balance, there was more truth than projection to Abby's reputation. Descended from women who had to be patient and strong to prop up their husbands and sons, Abby had come by her storied attributes

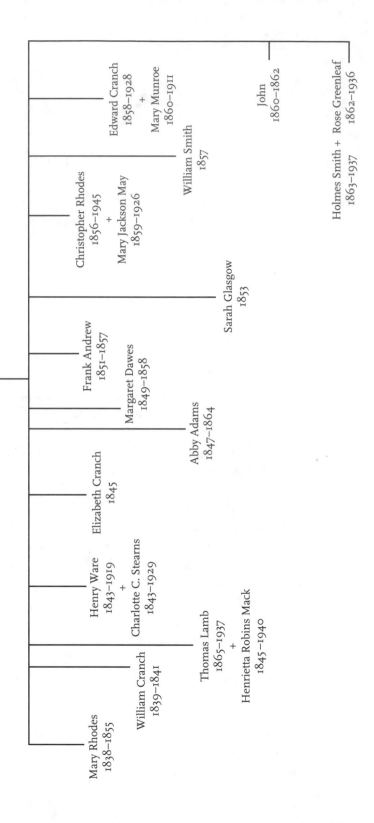

TABLE 2. The Eliots in St. Louis

Rev. William Greenleaf Eliot + Abigail Adams Cranch
1811–1887   1817–1908

Mary Rhodes
1838–1855

William Cranch
1839–1841

Thomas Lamb
1865–1937
+
Henrietta Robins Mack
1845–1940

Henry Ware
1843–1919
+
Charlotte C. Stearns
1843–1929

Elizabeth Cranch
1845

Abby Adams
1847–1864

Margaret Dawes
1849–1858

Frank Andrew
1851–1857

Sarah Glasgow
1853

Christopher Rhodes
1856–1945
+
Mary Jackson May
1859–1926

William Smith
1857

Edward Cranch
1858–1928
+
Mary Munroe
1860–1911

John
1860–1862

Holmes Smith + Rose Greenleaf
1863–1937   1862–1936

honestly. When Mary Smith, her paternal grandmother, married her grandfather Richard Cranch, she had sealed her fate with a man who was gentle, devout, and a bungler in worldly affairs. Unable to earn what his family needed by selling watches in Boston, he moved them to Braintree, ten miles to the south, and relied on the wits of his spouse to make up the deficit in their income. This she accomplished by taking in boarders and running a dairy while rearing three children. Richard, directing his own gifts to public service, represented the town in the Massachusetts legislature, stood as a justice of the peace, and served as the parish treasurer, all of which added to Mary's cares without putting anything more in her purse. There were limits to Mary's forbearance. "I am not my own," she once complained to her sister Abigail Adams. It was grossly unfair that she had to be selfless and sacrifice for everyone else. But these moments of weakness were few. She rarely protested.[2]

Mary had next to save her only son, William Cranch, from ruin. Like his father, he was tender, devout, studious, and incapable of earning or managing money. Thanks to his mother's industry, he was able to go to Harvard and then to study the law. But naive and impatient, he fell for a scheme to make a quick fortune developing real estate in the newly established District of Columbia. He purchased on credit a third of the land at bargain prices from government agents, and two years later, at age twenty-eight, he was penniless and disgraced. It was said that only the grace of God had kept him from going to jail for his debts, but the family all knew that his mother and aunt's intervention had rescued his dignity. Aunt Abigail Adams, whose husband was then the president of the United States, quickly put in a word on her nephew's behalf, and in 1800, his uncle John found him a post as a district commissioner. The position was neither glamorous nor had much in the way of a salary, but it kept William solvent until the next year, when, as one of his final official acts, John Adams named him to serve as a judge on the district's circuit court. Here William performed so well that four years later, President Thomas Jefferson tapped him to be its chief justice. This was the station he held for the next half-century.

Mary's daughter-in-law Nancy Greenleaf was also essential to William's recovery. Her "prudence" and "other excellent qualities" as Abigail Adams said, protected him from self-doubt and depression. Her bright, playful personality and unfailing deference to William's position cheered him and guarded his self-esteem, and continued to do so long after a relapse seemed even remotely possible. The children would always remember their father as s being a warm and affectionate man but never once heard him addressed in their home as anything but "The Judge."[3]

Nancy's experiences as a wife also lent particular urgency to her efforts to give her girls the footing to brace up the men they married. She had them sent to the best private day schools and kept them on balanced diets of study, church, and wholesome play. Her spirited daughter Abby, a pretty brunette with a ready laugh, was flourishing under this regimen when she turned eighteen and got engaged to the newly ordained

FIGURE 2.1. William Greenleaf Eliot, ca. 1837. Photograph of painting by his brother-in-law John Cranch. Courtesy of Mary C. Eliot.

William Eliot, who was almost six years her senior. She liked "commonsensive and unaffected" people and ridiculed female conceit and the girls in her circle who put on airs. Intent on being herself, she wolfed down seconds and thirds at Thanksgiving dinner and savored the ribbing she got from her uncle John Quincy Adams one year when he sat beside her. "Why Abby!" he teased, reaching over and patting her stomach, "I thought you were…very delicate…[but] it seems to me you are pretty solid!"[4]

FIGURE 2.2. Abigail Adams Cranch, age seventeen. Pencil sketch by her brother John Cranch, 1834. Courtesy of Mary C. Eliot.

Abby had to be solid to follow her groom to Missouri two years later. The railroads out of Washington, which had only been running a matter of weeks, had shaken them "nearly to pieces" before their car reached the end of the line. After stumbling off the train at the station in Philadelphia, they had taken a steamboat to Buffalo, then another bound for Ohio. When a caved-in canal wall would not let them through, they switched to a broken-down stagecoach only to find, when they reached Cincinnati, a river so low it was choked with sandbars. It took their steamer twice as long as expected to get from there to St. Louis. The steward ran out of provisions, and when they finally pulled into port on October 3, 1837, the passengers had been living on crackers and biscuits for more than a week.[5]

Waiting for them was a shipping port with few signs of organized civilization. Since its settlement by the French as a fur-trading station in 1764, St. Louis had moved toward becoming a major gateway to the western frontier. Expanding apace with the river traffic, the population was almost 6,000 by 1830. By 1850—still seven years before the transcontinental railroads would reach the city—the number would be more than 77,000. Here the liberals who came from the old Congregational parishes east of the Alleghenies found a mingling of rich and brash cultures entirely foreign to theirs. The French had made their way up the river from New Orleans, bringing their Roman Catholicism, a code of honor that forced men to duel, a fondness for gaming and drinking, and an open acceptance of prostitution. Baptists and Methodists, Presbyterians and Episcopalians, most from Virginia and Kentucky, had begun to arrive with their customs and slaves once Missouri became American soil in 1803. German-born Lutherans, few of whom spoke any English, would follow, seeking a better life when the 1848 revolution drove them out of their homeland. On their heels would come fortune-seekers who, chasing the glitter of gold farther west, would run out of funds or ambition or both by the time they arrived in St. Louis.

Still sparsely settled when Abby arrived in 1837, St. Louis had only a few rough roads and irregular cinder walks to coax its scattered houses into some semblance of a community. Depending upon the weather, the streets were steeped in mud or buried in dust, and in season, the potholes of stagnant water served as havens for breeding mosquitoes. With no sewerage, dry cellars, nurses, or any understanding of how disease spread, Abby found "chills and fever everywhere," especially in the shanties surrounding Choteau Pond, where the poor took their baths and then washed their dishes and clothes. Undaunted, she set out to visit the sick and to get to know the parishioners, who had just built their brick and stone meeting house for her husband's pulpit at Pine Street and Fourth. That the bride was still optimistic and ready to start her new life in such a place rather than catch the next steamer out was the stuff parish legends were made of.[6]

───────────────── ☙ ─────────────────

There was no confusing the Eliot men with the Cranches. Abby's fiancé was born with a genius for finance, and self-doubt was foreign to him. A giant soul in an elfin body, William would be recalled by a longtime acquaintance as someone whose delicate frame and short stature presented an "almost pathetic" foil to the magnitude of his influence. Disarming, too, was a slight speech defect, the result of a boyhood injury to his soft palate. It brought forth a little gasp when he tried to start words that began with a vowel. Yet what other males felt were handicaps were goads to his Eliot pride. When teased about his diminutive size, he followed the lead of his grandfather Thomas Dawes, another small man. Asked how it felt to be dwarfed in a world full of giants, Dawes was supposed to have quipped, "Like a silver shilling among copper pennies!" and that was the end of it. Although he was basically gentle and modest, William's inherited confidence was conspicuous.[7]

Born in New Bedford, Massachusetts, a thriving seaport, in 1811, Abby's groom came from two prominent lines. His mother, Margaret Dawes Eliot, was the daughter of Thomas Dawes, the architect who drew up the plans for the State House in Boston and then was elected to sit in its chambers, filling seats as a senator, councilor, and representative. On his father's side, one great-grandfather, Andrew Eliot, pastor of Boston's Old North Church before the American Revolution, had turned down the presidency of Harvard College, unwilling to leave his vocation. Another great-grandfather, William Greenleaf, sheriff of Suffolk County in 1776, had stood on the balcony of the Old State House in Boston before the jubilant crowds and read them the new Declaration of Independence.[8]

The minister of St. Louis's Unitarian church had been named for his father, a prosperous merchant who owned a fine ship until the government placed an embargo on trade and sank his entire investment by going to war with England. In need of some way to support his family, he moved them to Washington City and found a job as inspector in the postal department's auditing office. While never again a wealthy family, the parents used what they had to provide their children with culture and good educations. They sent William back to New Bedford to attend the Friends' Academy there; and thanks to his father's subscription to Washington's recently chartered Columbian College—a Baptist school—he was able to enter its four-year course and have his degree by 1830.[9]

Leaving the East had never occurred to the younger William Eliot until, after graduation from college, he worked for a year in his father's postal department as an assistant clerk. Intrigued by letters he saw addressed to "St. Louis near Alton," he studied the region, examining maps of the valley and the network of river ways, and imagining the small settlement becoming a major commercial hub. This fascination crystallized as a locus for future endeavors after Eliot entered Harvard Divinity School in 1831. There he found that the students, craving alternatives to the "corpse-cold" discourse for which Unitarian churches were famous, were turning to warmer currents stirred by the English Romantics and German philosophers. Encouraged by classmates like James Freeman Clarke, who became a lifelong friend, William Eliot tested these waters but soon backed away. He feared that too strong an attachment to speculation—be it the formal rationalism of the previous era or the transcendentalist gossamer of his own—would make him a paralyzed skeptic or else a distracted mystic. Whichever it was, he would not be fit for the practical service he deemed fundamental to any true Christian ministry.[10]

A year after Clarke received his degree and took his eclectic ideas to Kentucky, starting a church in Louisville, Eliot, who was one class behind him, accepted a call from a handful of liberals 250 miles farther west. A small band of free-thinking New England transplants, some well-to-do and some not, they had gone there to launch business ventures, to establish themselves in professions, and to buy up cheap land at one of the most fertile bends of the Mississippi River. Providentially, they now wanted a man to plant the religious society that had already taken root in Eliot's mind.

Eager to live with their St. Louis neighbors harmoniously as good Christians, the charter members did not parade their theological differences but represented their faith through good works and material generosity. Steering this course put the group at the forefront of every kind of philanthropy, educational initiative, and movement for civilizing the city. Because there were neither free public schools nor organized charity work when they came, the congregation moved quickly to set up a day school for needy children in the basement of their church on Pine Street, then added a sewing school for girls. A Boy's Industrial School and Mission House—later the Mission Free School—was also created "to rescue children and young persons from vice and beggary, to educate them, and find for them permanent homes."[11]

A decade after staking its claim to the city's religious uplift, the Unitarian body had grown too large for its small Doric temple a few streets away from the harbor. A new sanctuary was built farther west at the corner of Olive and Ninth and, after it opened for occupancy in September 1851, was formally christened The Church of the Messiah. For the minister and his trustees, it stood as a tower of Unitarian pride, a steepled monument that embodied the vigor they wanted their faith to project. They boasted about the size of "the ground plat," the height of the spire, the tons of iron, the masses of brick, and the Atlas expense of it all. When the last of the plaster and paint had dried in 1852, the magnificent pile had cost a whopping $105,000, close to tripling original estimates and stunning even the church's most affluent members. The publicists pointed out, of course, that it was worth every penny. The new pews and wrap-around galleries could accommodate 1,200 easily, almost three times the turnout the ushers seated on typical Sunday mornings.[12]

The private responses were more revealing of who these worshipers were. Although a good many seemed fully absorbed in taking notes while the minister preached, there were some who found the Gothic decor a constant, unseemly distraction. They might just as well have been worshiping with the Episcopalians, they groused. The stained glass windows, though handsome enough, so roiled one born-and-bred liberal, Anne Lane—whose image of what was appropriate was the simple, New England meeting house—she swore she would only go into the church to hear Mr. Eliot preach and then leave. Others, haunted by memories of dying parents and children, were more disturbed by the angels that were carved on the pillars under the roof. Their pitiful faces reminded them of the struggle it was for women, who were destined to be the supporting shoulders for faith in a menacing world.[13]

The minister's wife was busy both upholding the church's mission and following God's command to be fruitful and multiply. A model of alacrity, Abby was already pregnant with Mary when she arrived in St. Louis. She became a mother the following spring and other babies—William, Thomas, Henry, and Elizabeth—followed like clockwork every year-and-a-half. But neither little William nor baby Elizabeth lived to see the next sibling, a girl baby named for her mother and known as Ada. By the time the minister's wife had lost all but five of her fourteen children, this giving and taking of life had abraded her heart beyond repair.

FIGURE 2.3. Abigail Adams Cranch Eliot, Mary Rhodes Eliot, baby Abby Adams "Ada" Eliot, ca. 1848, courtesy of Warner A. Eliot.

No birthday went by without her reliving the brutal confusion "as tho it were yesterday." When she wrote Tom a note of congratulations on reaching his forty-eighth year, it was not the gray-haired son whom she saw in her mind but the "sound, fat cunning young one" whom the nurse had brought and put in her arms right after the cord was cut. Gently shifting his weight in her memory, she could still feel his warmth and how happy she was, never dreaming her "first affliction" was just weeks away. "Dear Willie," who "seemed to be strong and healthy," fell suddenly ill and died. In another two days they would have been able to celebrate his second birthday. "Before you were a month old," she reminded Tom, "he was taken," and "his beautiful large dark eyes look right at me to this day." Their father, Abby continued, accepted these separations stoically. "Papa said better to have them and see them go than not to have them at all." He was satisfied that he would "have them again" in the next world, "and then no more sorrow," Abby recalled, as unconvinced fifty years later as she had been then. She never could fathom how having children and watching them die could really be better than not having them in the first place. She knew this "old story" by heart and had yet to understand how it served any purpose.[14]

Abby guessed there was not a woman in church who accepted her husband's logic or could do what he asked of them when he preached, and the private contrition expressed by some of his most loyal members suggests she was right. Sally Smith's record of this dilemma is one of the most revealing. Orphaned before she moved to St. Louis while she was still in her teens, Sally credited Mr. Eliot with her new zest for life. While no one could ever replace her father, her minister had come close, guiding her to an upright adulthood and letting her know she was cherished. He recognized her intelligence and hired her as his scribe. Her workbox and leather-bound prayer book were evidence of his tender concern. When her wedding approached, with Abby's assistance, he made her the gift of her bridal gown, a breathtaking ashes of roses silk dress; and as she and her groom, Willard Flagg, crossed the river to start their new home, her heart was torn between the two men she considered the best in the world. No one ever wished more that she could prove herself worthy of Mr. Eliot's love. But Sally had long since resigned herself to falling short of his mark, particularly when he urged her sex to bridle their speech and always be cheerful. "I can *try*, which is all I can promise," she wrote in her diary.[15]

As attached as she was to the minister, Sally felt closer to his wife, whose sacrifices financed the pastor's benevolence. In her daily trips to the parsonage to take dictation and write out the sermons, Sally had never once seen Mrs. Eliot sit down to rest without first grabbing a basket of knitting or sewing. Her resolute patching of old clothes until they were ready to fall apart in her hands confirmed what Sally's aunts muttered under their breath. Mrs. Eliot would never have needed to go to such lengths to clothe her family had Mr. Eliot had the sense not to put the welfare of strangers first. The key to his celebrated success in raising large sums for the commonweal was that every list he asked others to sign started off with his own name and generous pledge. The pew holders paid him quite well for their day. His $2,500 a year in 1853 was more than four times what Protestant clergy were earning on average. Had he showed as much moderation as conscience in spending it, Sally's relatives said, they would have seen fewer signs of womanly self-denial when they went over. Yet Mrs. Eliot never protested, and Sally surmised that the happy children—the best behaved she had ever known—had learned from their parents to think of those who had less, not of those who had more.[16]

That Mrs. Eliot managed so well was all the more to her credit considering how much the minister traveled, Sally's aunts observed. The conscience that used her household allowance to feed the less fortunate was just as quick to send him away on business when he was needed at home. By 1852, he had organized liberal societies in Peoria, Alton, and Quincy, Illinois, and had circulated another of his subscription lists in Milwaukee. A whirlwind of meetings with brother ministers in the surrounding states had produced a Western Unitarian Conference, which he was elected to lead. All this at the cost of physical breakdowns requiring long, recuperative leaves and trips through the East and abroad. Sometimes he left his family with the Cranches in Massachusetts, but Sally's family did not think it mattered that much where a wife was parked with the children. However accustomed a woman might be to doing the parenting on her own, when her husband was gone, it was harder wherever she was. Even with Mr. Eliot home, Mrs. Eliot carried more than her share. Intent on conserving her husband's strength, she had made herself the first line of defense when people came to the door with their problems.

Sarah Lane Glasgow, Abby's best friend and one of the few women ever to hear her recite her full litany of complaints, also wondered who was defending the minister's wife and babes from the poor house. She and Abby were just like sisters, their friendship secured by their church and their families. Her father, William Carr Lane, was the Eliots' doctor, and Sarah's husband, William, was the minister's traveling buddy. As their spouses' professions limited what the wives could say in the parish, Sarah and Abby became the closest of confidants; and when one or the other was out of the city, their letters served as a lifeline.

So it was in 1848, when their husbands were traveling abroad for their health while Abby and the four Eliot children were staying in Massachusetts and Sarah was in St. Louis close to her parents. Abby was worried about baby Ada, whom Sarah had yet to see. Born in Quincy, the child had barely survived her first couple of weeks, and although at three months she was "bright and playful," her thin little body was still a reminder that she had been "raised from death." The older children had added to Abby's anxiety since their father's departure. Four-year-old Henry, nicknamed Hal, had been having bad earaches, six-year-old Tom had been troubled by nightmares, and pleurisy had been making the rounds in the house.[17]

When Sarah announced that she would also have a new baby to introduce, Abby was staggered and struggled to welcome the news. It was beyond her, she tried to jest, why two intelligent women like them "didn't keep out of such scrapes," and when Sarah's baby turned out to be twins, Abby responded with sympathy. Mr. Eliot's "highest ambition," she noted, was always for her to have two at once, which only went to show how the men underestimated a woman's work. It was hard enough to have one at a time, and their husbands had better be "precious good" and appreciate them when they got back home for taking care of so many children already. "I am sure they can never repay us!" Abby Eliot bantered lamely.[18]

Even without her confiding in them as she did in Sarah Glasgow, every woman at church could tell how Mrs. Eliot felt. They shook their heads incredulously at the sacrifices she had to make. Although she was pregnant in 1849, when cholera ravaged St. Louis, killing one of every ten residents, Mr. Eliot seemed determined to make his wife a widow at thirty-two. Disregarding the risks, he insisted on holding the hands of the sick and on breathing their breath as he leaned in to hear their last words. Not only that, he was taking in so many orphans that Abby had twenty-six children besides her own to worry about by the time baby Margaret, her seventh, was born that July.[19]

The parish was deeply affected whenever the Eliots lost a child. Little William had died just before he turned two; Elizabeth lived for only nine days; and Sarah, named after her mother's best friend, was gone in a matter of hours. Their deaths had been fearsome reminders that sorrow afflicted even the saintliest families. The loss of the Eliots' daughter Mary, not yet seventeen, was especially hard for everyone. She was taken with almost no warning the first week of 1855, when a seemingly minor indisposition turned fatal overnight. It was common knowledge that she was her father's pet, "the light of his eyes and the joy of his heart," as Sally Smith explained in her diary. Being the firstborn child and only surviving daughter, her place in her mother's heart had been particularly tender and deep, as well.[20]

Sally was one of the first to hear that Mary had died in the early hours of January 6, which happened to be the first Saturday of the new year. She was on her way to the parsonage to finish transcribing the next day's sermon when someone stopped her and told her the stunning news. Unbelieving, Sally walked faster, hoping to find it was all a mistake, but the confirmation was in the eyes of the maid who came to the door. The family were all upstairs when she entered the parlor, where neighbors were gathering. Margaret Eliot, who was spending the holidays at her son's home, was breaking the news to her grandchildren while the stricken parents were in Mary's room saying their final good-byes. Eventually, the boys came downstairs, and then their father. He held them and spoke of their sister's exemplary life

FIGURE 2.4. Sarah "Sally" Smith Flagg after leaving her work as her pastor's amanuensis to marry her sweetheart, Willard Flagg, in 1856. Photograph courtesy of her granddaughter Alice Feutz Flagg.

but seemed as bewildered as they. Mrs. Eliot never appeared, and Sally soon left, her mind flailing for some sort of logic as to why God had let this happen to folks "whose sole pleasure was doing [his] work."[21]

The cloud of Sally's despair and confusion grew heavier by the hour, and by the day's end, when she reached for her pen, she was "groping about in darkness." So was the rest of the parish, the cloud having shrouded the whole community. The church was full for the funeral service, and Sally could tell as she scanned the faces that everyone was "a real mourner." From a distance, she saw the young Eliot children, their cheeks streaked with tears. Afterward, at the burial ground, Mr. Eliot, visibly shaken himself, supported his wife, who groaned as the first clods of earth were tossed on the grave. There was no relief for the parish until Mr. Eliot ended another week of seclusion to meet with his members at church. He beseeched them to keep their minds on God so their burdens would not be carried alone, and it was a comfort to know that he was holding them in his thoughts again. Yet Sally could see he was speaking "with difficulty," and although he said he was *well*, when asked, his halting voice and uncharacteristic personal references to his "affliction" were hardly those of a man who had worked through his anguish. Nor did Mrs. Eliot's sorrow recede. Every family's bereavement brought it all back, as Anne Lane would write Sarah Glasgow fifteen years later. The minister's wife had recently been at the Sunday school picnic and "looked very sad," even more so "than usual," doubtless because Mr. Low's only daughter had died that morning.[22]

Whatever destruction and heartbreak nature had failed to inflict by mid-century, God's children seemed bent upon engineering through sectional feuds over states' rights and slavery. Even before the cholera came to St. Louis in 1849, Abby had seen the makings of a full-scale internecine war in the anger aroused by William's approach to slavery. Averse as he was to letting politics into the pulpit with Christ, he felt obliged to plead for some kind of voluntary emancipation. He was taking this stance, he said carefully, not as "the negro lover" some thought him to be, but as a friend of Missouri's struggling farmers and Free Laborites. He was someone who did not believe that a master could act humanely and still turn a profit, and he feared for the souls of the owners who thought they could or, worse, did not care. Some members walked out before he had finished, and others sat stewing but never came back.[23]

Ironically, the position that gave offense in the church as too radical was too moderate for the minister's colleagues and damaged his valued relationships there, as well. While he was convinced that the only Christian and practical way to banish slavery was to establish the Kingdom of God in each individual's heart, the Unitarian clergy's loudest voices were abolitionist. When the Western Conference, which Eliot had organized, passed a hard-knuckled resolution, he felt betrayed and severed his ties in protest. His anger extended to Boston, where the Unitarian *Christian Register* misrepresented his church as having an abolitionist policy, a distortion that seemed to usurp his local authority and free-slave approach.[24]

There were even worse trials once secession became the defining issue and William could no longer walk his fine line. When it seemed that Confederate sentiments might lead Missouri out of the Union, he started to preach against what he saw as the greater evil and pleaded for loyalty. Irrevocably offending those who sided with the Confederacy, he set off a civil war in the church and fully one-fourth of the membership left. The ensuing financial crisis compelled the trustees to retrench on its missions, and the church's remnant was left to reflect on the shame that stared back from the empty pews.

The defections left gaping holes in the Eliots' intimate circle, as well. The rage unleashed by their doctor, William Carr Lane, a man of fierce Southern sympathies, not only made things more difficult when one of the family was ill but also put a strain on the Eliots' friendship with Sarah and William Glasgow, Dr. Lane's daughter and son-in-law. Unable to choose between blood-ties and friendship, the Glasgows left town for the war's duration, leaving a void that was just as hard as if it had been forever. The falling out with Edward Appleton, William Eliot's cousin, and Kate, his wife, was another hard blow. Kate, who had been Abby's bridesmaid and met her husband-to-be in the Eliots' home, was now so "intensely secesh," she carried a pistol she threatened to use if Mr. Eliot spoke to her.[25]

The wound was deep, but there were more likely dangers than Mrs. Appleton. Like most city people, the Eliots thought that the illnesses that had taken four children in three years' time were caused by bad air that hovered over the harbor. This threat seemed so real to the population in 1856 that William decided to sell their house and move the family a mile or so farther out from the river to a property on the city's western fringe. Beaumont Place had been at one time the governor's residence, and the mansion still had its old charm, with rambling rooms and long porches that looked out on orchards, deep forest, and wide emerald lawns. It was "a sort of paradise" compared to the squalor downtown, but it was badly neglected, and neither William nor Abby was up to packing or making the property livable. With the fighting at church and the cumulative pain of having lost not only Mary but also Willie, Margaret, and Frank, they still had "no heart," as they told the Glasgows in 1859, "to do or think anything" other than what was absolutely essential.[26]

Ironically, when they finally moved in the spring of 1861, the spot they had thought a safe haven had acquired its own set of dangers. Just a few weeks before, the Confederate forces in Charleston had fired upon Fort Sumter, and now the Eliots' property was flanked by rival encampments. The clumsy maneuvers of ill-trained soldiers, who dulled their fears and boredom by drinking, terrorized Abby and William. Once, when the children were playing outside in the yard, bullets came whistling through the trees, splintering some of the fences.[27]

Within a year, Abby's twenty-year-old was also firing weapons. Tom had volunteered with the Halleck Guard, a unit of seventy men from St. Louis, whose charge was to keep the area clear of Confederate guerrillas. His parents prayed that this service would only involve basic drilling and minimal risk, which seemed quite probable from his first letters home. His days, he said, were spent "marching...hurrahing" and "singing John Brown's bones." In time, however, the Guard did less singing and more in the way of real soldiering. Tom's unit was sent to patrol the Missouri River as far off as Kansas City, and later he went to Boonville when Jefferson City came under threat. The only shot he ever got off was at a deserter, he told his parents, but by the time he was given his discharge the following June, he had seen enough of the soldier's life to be ready to leave it for good. William and Abby had seen enough, too. When Missouri's Board of Enrollment recalled their oldest boy two years later, William purchased a substitute for $350.[28]

More worrisome was the next son, Hal, who was two years younger than Tom. A sensitive and artistic lad who played the flute, had an outstanding voice, and commanded an excellent drawing hand, he desperately wanted to prove himself as much of a man as his older brother. He deeply resented his parents' objections and did his best to outfox them. After William twice purchased replacements for him at $300 apiece, Hal went through a back door to get his commission and anxiously waited for it to arrive. To Abby's relief, his father found out and had a few private words with the judge, and Hal's promised ticket to manly combat was never delivered.[29]

Abby was grateful that William, at least, was never in danger of being conscripted. His age—he was now in his early fifties—and frail constitution exempted him. The closest he came to soldiering was volunteering to serve as chaplain when older men formed a militia in 1862. When Confederate troops came within ten miles of St. Louis in 1864, this Old Guard was put on alert, but the threat was turned back and William's unit was never tested in battle. Yet Abby worried about her husband as much as if he had gone off to war. Though excused from the lines of fire, he was battle fatigued nonetheless, his body and mind exhausted by endless trials. In 1862, two weeks before Abby went into labor with Rose, their two-year-old John, who had just had his birthday, became the eighth child to die. Abby's namesake, Ada, became the ninth when she drowned in a skating accident at the age of sixteen two years later. In May of that year, with Ada's death still an open wound, the family got word from Virginia that Capt. Frank Eliot, William's younger brother, had fallen in the battle of Chancellorsville.[30]

Even before his daughter Ada and brother Frank were taken, William was so emotionally spent, he could no longer write in the journal he had been keeping for seventeen years. Still, he persisted in taking on more obligations, not simply to meet the real crises when the sectional feuding turned violent, but also, as Abby recognized, to barricade himself from his grief and defy its paralysis. She had seen him do this the decade before when the rancor was raiding the church and their children were dying in rapid succession. Then William had practically given up sleep to launch another big project, the Polytechnic Institute, later Washington University. Accepting the presidency of the board, he oversaw getting the charter, sketched out the school's future course, and raised more funds to go forward than the sixteen other directors combined.[31]

Abby was not surprised, then, to see William take on another huge job when the fighting broke out in Missouri in 1861. As there was no way for getting supplies and medical help to the sick and wounded, William set out to put such a system in place. The result was a Western counterpart of the U.S. Sanitary Commission, which was headed by Henry Whitney Bellows, the minister of All Souls Unitarian Church in New York City. Despite the protests from Bellows, who resented "a rival venture" competing for funds and staff and hurting the overall operation, his western colleague pushed ahead, raising money for army hospitals, medicines, food, and supplies for the troops, and seeing to their distribution. Abby, for her part, waited up anxiously for his return late at night, convinced he was driving himself to an early death in the name of national unity.[32]

With the rebel distrust of people with Northern connections threatening her bond with Sarah, Abby felt blessed to have William's coworker Dorothea Dix as a friend. A Unitarian who, like William, had been profoundly inspired by Joseph Tuckerman's ministry to the needy in Boston thirty years earlier, Dix was the U.S. Sanitary Commission's Superintendent of Nurses when William asked for her help in choosing the personnel for his corps in the West. Her unapproved trip to St. Louis in 1861 to assist in this effort so riled Henry Bellows, he moved her out to the margins of his operation, while the Eliots greeted their houseguest as an ally. Her maverick individualism and eccentricities, among them an almost unreadable script, were easy to overlook in a comrade who loved the Union and pulled the embattled Eliots under her patronage. If Dix's experience in the public sector served William's purpose, the interest she took in his family clearly worked to Abby's advantage. She was not above prying or scolding, and when she saw what the minister's charity had been costing his own flesh and blood, she scolded him and sent Abby money to spend on herself and the children.[33]

Abby was grateful she still had this shoulder to cry on when during the late 1870s William was stricken by headaches so bad, he lay writhing in bed for weeks. The doctors were at a loss for the cause, but not Abby. It was his stubborn idea that punishing work was a cure for an uneasy mind when obviously it only caused him more worry. One just had to look at the past ten years to see his accumulation of problems and know that he was nearing his breaking point. Officially, William's trustees had released him as pastor in 1871, but when he took his seat as the university's chancellor the following year, the business at church tagged along. Even after John Snyder succeeded him in 1873, parishioners came by the Eliots' house asking to see their pastor.

Given his genius for finance, it was also inevitable that he would be asked to generate funds for the church and broker the sale of its building after the members finally voted in 1879 to move farther west to Locust and Garrison streets. With the deep economic depression that came in 1873 having thwarted his efforts to raise an endowment and operational funds for his school, it had been unusually hard for him to round up pledges to keep the church running. The sum of all this was his crippling headaches and then the collapse of Abby's health. Sitting so long "on the anxious bench" watching him suffer had done her in, and once he improved, William's mulish resumption of all his bad habits kept setting her back. So Abby, still bedridden, wrote her good friend Miss Dix in 1880, "He fairly makes me ache to see him hour after hour sit in his chair in one position always writing."[34]

———————————————————— ❧ ————————————————————

Abby had always known that Tom would follow his father's path and pioneer a ministry far from home. Altogether unlike the rebellious Hal, who suffered the more for his brother's compliance, Tom was almost incapable of contradicting his father, so similar were their dispositions and understanding of duty. As a boy, Tom's boldest infractions had been on the order of skipping church to scavenge for booty left under the seats after Sunday school. A gleeful notation in one of his diaries indicates that the thirteen-year-old found some seventeen hymnals, ten books, three "hankercheifs," and a fan in one expedition. But his diary also establishes that these truancies were rare. Faithful in his attendance, he listened attentively to the sermons and took his father's instruction to heart as befitted a son who never questioned that he would enter the pulpit. Tom was enrolled when his father's new institute, Washington University, was ready to take its inaugural class in 1858, and he graduated with honors four years later. Then after his year in the Halleck Guard, he proceeded to Harvard Divinity School where, with his father's hand still on the leash, he stayed close to his Christ-centered faith. Avoiding the young Unitarian skeptics, Tom followed his father's lead so well that when he spoke at his Harvard Commencement in June 1865, the old-timers in the audience saw William "over again...in his son."[35]

It was Abby who realized her husband's hand would have to relax if Tom were to have an identity of his own. Especially now, when he was planning to marry his sweetheart of several years, Henrietta Robins Mack of St. Louis, he needed to make his decisions without parental interference or coaching. As it was, her husband had already sent Tom a schedule for what would come next: "I suggest," he had told the new graduate, "that you be ordained as 'Evangelist' on 13th October, in our Church. I'll preach. Also that you be married, Etta consenting, on Nov. 25th, with Hal as Groomsman, and in the most quiet manner possible." The couple would live in the parsonage, at least for the first few months. "The Husband should take the wife to his home, wherever it is, and not vice versa." There they would set up their housekeeping in the attic or in a spare bedroom downstairs. Once unpacked, they would make their first year together a time not of "over-crowded work, but only of diligence and learning."[36]

William's script was for Tom to stay in St. Louis to get his feet wet while casting about for a situation, nothing too far away, of course, where he could at last bring something out of the stream with his own line and hook. Almost everything came off as planned, with Tom gaining further experience as his father's parish associate. But as Abby had feared, after only a year, their son was looking for "some way off point" where he could step into the light and grow taller away from his father's shadow. When he got a tug on his line from Portland, Oregon—as "way off" a place as a man could find short of leaving the country—he went for it.[37]

While Tom's departure in 1867 did not cure his father's bad habits, it certainly changed his perspective. The idea of starting a family and church in an inaccessible wilderness no longer commended itself to him as it had before he became a father. Now worried that Tom was risking his health, he admitted that "working beyond one's strength" had at times been unprofitable for him and hard on Tom's mother and siblings. "Nay, verily," he assured him, one could "be as happy and useful...and as much the minister of Christ" by raising stock and farming. Were this too big an adjustment, Tom and Etta could settle in one of the old, well-oiled parishes in the East, where they could take life a lot easier and would not be out of their element. Both father and son ignored this advice, and William deadened his disappointment by plunging into more work. When he felt a twinge of loneliness, he tried to be philosophical: "We old folks will jog on and the young ones come up to take our places and the sun will rise and go down as before."[38]

Abby made no such pretense of being resigned to the separation from Etta, Tom, and their baby, Willy. In the fall of 1867, the written word traveled only as fast as the mail could be carried back east by coach, loaded on steamers, and moved to the opposite shore through the Isthmus of Panama. Still more than a year before the Transcontinental Railroad was finished, and longer still before there was land transportation to Portland from San Francisco, it took Tom and Etta's first letters as long as two months to get to St. Louis, and Abby was almost sick with worry about what the silence might mean. Nor were Etta's accounts of settling into the parish enough when they did arrive. From such a distance, the details were blurry, and Abby envied the birds that could fly out and get a good look at the nest up close. Only the vacant places her loved ones had left behind were in focus, and they were so clear, she could not even sit through a service at church without weeping.[39]

Having watched her son Christopher grow to be more like his oldest brother each year, Abby had never doubted that he would eventually be a minister, too, and take a church far away. Like Tom, he had gone from Washington University to Harvard and then surveyed the prospects for liberal ministry in the South and

Midwest. Rejecting the first as too racist and the second as too close to home, he accepted a call from the old, liberal parish of Dorchester, on the outskirts of Boston. He delivered his first sermon there in the fall of 1881, and while it was only half as far to Massachusetts as Oregon, the distance still felt immense. Abby longed to talk to his people herself to be sure they knew what a treasure they had, she told Miss Dix a few weeks before his ordination that winter. "He is to us, and always has been, a dear, affectionate loving son with so few faults that it would [be hard] to find them, but how do strangers know this?" She guessed he would be a big hit with the young ones, and older people had always loved him, but what about those in between? She wanted to go there and tell them, "Make some allowances for his age. He is not yet twenty-seven, but he will grow old fast enough, and if you are patient, he will have all the strength and wisdom a pastor needs and more!"[40]

Abby hated to sound like an infidel but refused to believe it was "naughty" of mothers "to *long* so" when children left home. It was a measure of love, she assured them, and not a lack of faith. While she vowed she had "perfect trust" that God would take care of her family wherever they were, she was ready to go anywhere anytime to make sure he was doing his job. She traveled to Portland in 1869, and the next year, when Tom took a leave, she accompanied him to Europe with his three youngest siblings in tow. A neighbor of Abby's remembered her saying that she would not let an ocean or continent come between her and her family. As late as 1891, when Christopher's first daughter, Martha, was born, Abby took the train all the way up to Boston to see the baby firsthand. Unfortunately, she could not always travel, and paper and pen had drawbacks.[41]

Both William and Tom, while vigorous preachers, were not the ready communicators their women folk desperately wanted. William's half-page missives were little more than signals that he was alive, and they left their recipients starved for reliable updates on family affairs. In fact, he was known to address the envelope and then leave it for Abby to fill. This so provoked his first daughter-in-law that Etta suggested he simply pretend that his kinfolk were some kind of corporation—"a Polytechnic," perhaps, "or a Philanthropy"—and write them regular letters. Tom's notes were even briefer than William's, so meager, in fact, they were dubbed "telegraphs." These "scraps" of news were so maddening in what they dismissed with a dash in mid-sentence that Abby was brought to begging her boy, "Dear Tom,…I want more! More!"[42]

If the brevity was a mark of their crowded schedules and fatigue, the skirting of any unpleasantness was consistent with the doctrine and temperament William passed on to Tom. It was the liberal minister's duty, the patriarch always maintained, to be "cheerful and happy, day by day," not "Calvinist and blue." He contrived "not to know the dirty things" that churchgoers tended to perpetrate under the rubric of "serving God." When they were thrown in his face, he said, he tried "not to care" or to "be disturbed," and when they got to bothering him, he did his best not to let on. Those who were closest to him knew he meant every word. Even at home, he hated so much to be thought of as anything "but 'well,'" that Abby had to be careful how she responded to questions concerning his health.[43]

With Etta's encouragement, Abby grew bolder in circumventing these inhibitions, which Eliot men had forced on the distaff and valorized. There were many translations of *Tace et Face*, the words on the Eliot coat of arms. Some read it as "Action speaks louder than words"; others as "Don't brag; just do the right thing." The subtext, however, was always the same: "If there is a problem, don't bring it up or ask me to talk about it." As Etta complained to her mother, Rebecca, and pleaded more gently to Abby, getting bad news was never pleasant but it was also a welcome sign that people were being embraced as family, not shut out as if they were strangers. Made aware of how "aggravating" it was when something slipped out and she tried to retrieve it, and that she was cheating herself of her children's sympathy and support, Abby soon mastered the art of indirection. "I cannot tell you much about Papa," she once replied when Tom inquired, and then warned him not to allude to his father's cough the next time he wrote.[44]

Abby's letters, meanwhile, were mirrors of her growing older. In 1868, her earliest postings to Portland showed her gratefully getting used to the fact that her child-bearing years were behind her at last. A year shy of fifty when Willy's arrival made her a grandmother for the first time, Abby savored the ease of being a parent, one generation removed. Just three years before, there had been no fewer than nine children under her roof. Three were her own, the youngest just two, and the rest of them "Union refugees" whom William had taken in for the war's duration. These little black youngsters of free slaves were all "real nice children," Abby had told her husband, and if she had been ten years younger, she would have been tempted to keep them indefinitely. But her "poor weak head" and painful joints had recoiled from the opportunity, and when someone "asked *solemnly*" three years later if she would be having another baby, Abby could not keep from laughing outright. Of course, she told Etta, excusing the question, "Every other woman was either holding a baby or 'in the way.'" But five-year-old Rosie had been the finale, and there would not be any encores. More than ready to turn the birthing beds over to these younger women, Abby gladly moved on to giving advice and being on call if her presence were needed. Unable to be at Etta's side when she was "kneeled up" in Portland, she coached her daughter-in-law from a distance: "Don't forget about that bandage I told you of." Two flannel strips with "Peruvian bark quilted in between" and dipped "in wet spirits" would save her a lot of discomfort and worry after the baby arrived.[45]

No longer tied down with babies at home, Abby found she was working harder than ever. She made parish calls almost daily, sewed with the women at church once or twice a week, and "kept up the steam pretty well" hosting Sunday school parties and teas.

Nonetheless, by the 1870s, she was having to make some concessions to age. She was wearing glasses and taking more naps. The spasms of an arthritic thumb had turned her nice handwriting into a scrawl, and it shamed her, she told her son Edward, her next-to-the-youngest surviving son, when she saw how beautifully all her children could write. At seventy, she still had vigor enough to travel but knew that her years were taking their toll. "Although I call myself *well*," she told Etta and Tom in 1887, "little ach-ings from head to toes need more watching and care." She had to postpone social calls when her teeth were parked at the dentist's for minor repairs. She was thankful that she was not "deaf, lame or blind," but her feet were so tender and sore that she hobbled about "like a very old woman." Sitting in church for the length of a service had gotten to be too much for her back. In her seventy-seventh year, her grandson Frank, who was ten-and-a-half, came up to her and asked if she were a hundred. "I suppose I look so to him," she told Etta and Tom, and it was no wonder, considering that with their gray hair and wrinkles, her children looked "rather old" to her, too.[46]

Her babies had seemed to grow up overnight and had full and interesting lives. Hal, who had "gagged" on too much of his father's church pudding, as he wrote in his memoir, had gone into business instead of becoming the minister William had wanted. Yet once he had drawn that line, he more than redeemed himself by lending his voice to the choir at church, superintending the Sunday school, and serving on the board of directors of Washington University. He and Charlotte Champ Stearns were married in 1868 and gradually filled up another long Eliot pew with their family of eight. Abby saw the same overnight transformation in Edward. One day he was just a little boy learning to walk, and the next, a Washington University grad-uate, lawyer, husband, and father. Before Abby knew it, her baby Rose was thirty-five and had married Holmes Smith, an art professor at Washington University. Their only child, Abigail Eliot Smith, brought to twenty the number of grandchil-dren Abigail Adams Cranch Eliot had to keep track of in 1900.[47]

━━━━━━━━━━━━━━━ ∾ ━━━━━━━━━━━━━━━

While the matriarch's determination to keep her family united in spirit inspired the loyalty and cohesion for which the clan was known, it also instilled a respect for the lines that marked out their place in the social order and set them apart as privileged Unitarians. For Abby, keeping the other kind out was as vital as holding her own together, and this required a firm understanding of who was where, and why. Abby and William had learned about people of African lineage early on. They had grown up in homes where the kindly but firm paternalism toward black hired help and the servants' deference were taken to be a model of good race relations. They had never heard anyone question the dark-skinned race's social position or their own people's place in the natural aristocracy. Darwinian theory, which entered the picture when Abby and William were middle-aged, only strengthened their generation's view of the races as separate species, some more advanced than others.

FIGURE 2.5. Abigail Adams Cranch Eliot, ca. 1880. Courtesy of Christopher Rhodes Eliot III.

FIGURE 2.6. Abigail Cranch Eliot, with youngest namesake, Abigail Eliot Smith, in her lap during a visit to Boston in 1902. Beside her are daughter-in-law Mary Jackson May Eliot and son Christopher. In front (l. to r.) are granddaughter Abby Adams Eliot, daughter Rose Eliot Smith, and granddaughter Martha May Eliot. Courtesy of Christopher Rhodes Eliot III.

This ethnology was not unique to William and Abby's emancipationist thinking. It underlay practically all nineteenth-century abolitionist arguments. When James Freeman Clarke, William's good friend and colleague, described it as "a mistake to speak of the African as an inferior race," he was not suggesting, or understood to be saying, that Caucasians and Negroes possessed the same inborn aptitudes and deficiencies, only that these balanced out. The black's poetic imagination and childlike credulity, he believed, made him superior to the white in religion as well as the arts but inferior in fields requiring mental acumen and powers of reason.[48]

And so it seemed to the Eliots. Their black help, which during and after the war included a runaway slave who tended the garden and pumped the organ at church, were treated benevolently, and they were retained because they worked hard and were grateful. William made much of the fact that some, like this gardener Archer Alexander, had more discernment and Christian nobility than the Caucasians who owned them. But it would have been unthinkable to argue that Archer's kind were their equals. His race, William wrote after Archer's death, possessed an "instinctive perception," a quick lower-level intelligence that was more like a dog's than a man's. That white people had an obligation to make concessions to this lower breed was a lesson the Eliot children were taught early on. Hal never forgot how he once dropped a brick on the foot of a black boy who taunted him. The injured lad's parents came to the Eliots' door to complain to the pastor, and Hal recalled that his punishment had been far more severe than it would have been had the foot in question been white. Such was his father's insistance on patience and decency toward a race that was thought to be slower in forming the civilized traits.[49]

As with most city folk, the Eliots also had strong ideas about Native Americans, notwithstanding their limited contact with them. When the Eliots built their first house on Eighth and Olive in the late 1830s, St. Louis had just a few stragglers left from the recently run-out Missouri and Osage tribes. Most of what William and Abby accepted as fact about its earliest residents came from James Fenimore Cooper's romanticized fictions of frontier adventure. William was fifteen and Abby nine when Cooper's *The Last of the Mohicans* was published in 1826, impressing its paradoxical stereotypes on American readers while reflecting the white population's ambivalence toward the people whom they were uprooting. Cooper's tribesmen were simultaneously naive and wise, demonic and spiritual, boastful and modest, hostile and peaceful, selfish and generous.

The Eliots' brief experience with a few who sometimes arrived uninvited and helped themselves to the family's property led them to think that the bad traits prevailed. Hal's memoir would tell of a tribesman who sometime around 1840 slipped into their kitchen while Abby was there with one of the babies. "Feathered and painted," according to Hal, he sneaked up behind her, pulled back her head, and snatched from her hair a ruby ribbon that he had spied through the window. Before he could leave with his trophy, Hal's terrified mother had scooped up the child and run for their lives to the closest neighbors for help. To her great relief, she found everything as she had left it when she returned with an escort, but this event, often reprised for the children, confirmed the perception that Native Americans, even if not always savage, could not be trusted as if they were white folk. They were "great thieves and not very friendly," Hal recalled from a distance of seventy years, and this still seemed reason enough for him and his brothers to have made sport of mocking the natives by following them to the campsites and sending up "war whoops."[50]

Abby undoubtedly tried to impart to her offspring the more benevolent view that tribal people were not inherently bad but simply a primitive race that was handicapped by a lack of enlightened religion. In debating the Indian problem, both those who defended and those who assailed the herding of Native Americans off their land believed that the pagans were morally stunted and natural candidates for Christian conversion. So it was that Abby supported the mission schools where Indian children were rescued from heathen ways by being taught to dress like

Caucasians and read the Bible. She liked to think that the next generations of red-skins would be better neighbors for knowing the Ten Commandments, the Beatitudes, and the Lord's Prayer. In the meantime, however, with Indian savagery still a real danger for whites, her sentiments were more fearful than philosophical. It was "dreadful," she told her son Edward in 1883, seven years after Custer's Last Stand in Montana, that tribesmen were spotted just sixty miles from where the Portland children spent summers. She wanted them back in the city where there were no scalpings.[51]

More to be feared than the tribesmen were the working-class whites who replaced them. At first, William's cohort of businessmen and professionals wel-comed the workers who came with the muscle and skills to develop a civilized city. They were happy to see the machinists, bricklayers, carpenters, and dockworkers putting in long days and saving to buy modest homes in orderly neighborhoods. When these laborers ceased to be satisfied and started making demands, however, forming unions and staging mass protests against low wages and unsafe conditions, it had a chilling effect on the people who hired them. William Eliot was too good a friend of the capitalists to interpret Proverbs 22:2—where rich and poor meet together—as advocating that everyone should be on an equal footing. His ideal of social arrangements was more complex, being based on *noblesse oblige*, which had always defined his family's ethic of service to the less fortunate. This required that those with superior bloodlines and educations govern the rest, and it carried the stipulation that those they assisted stay in their place.

The rumblings heard by the 1850s were preludes to the eruptions of violence that came with the massive depression of 1873. The crippling pay cuts and layoffs sent workers storming the bastions of corporate power and lining up for the city's free soup and bread in the aftermath. William's fear of the indigents' gaining the upper hand so clouded his view of their plight that he pleaded with City Hall to close the free soup lines. Giving the unemployed something for nothing, he warned, would only attract more tramps and turn the entire community into a slum. Every able-bodied pauper who wanted a place to sleep and something to eat should be made to work at half-wages and pay for it, the pastor insisted. In his overriding concern with saving the city from freeloading vagrants, he never asked where the jobs would come from, not even when people desperate for work forced the question by staging mass riots.[52]

Abby was shocked when the railroad strikes of 1877 brought the anarchy right to her doorstep on Washington Avenue. Her neighbors scrambled to lock the doors while the menfolk grabbed rifles to keep law and order. Her feelings were tangled and raw. She was proud when her boys Hal, Christy, and Ed fell in with the voluntary militia, 250 "wide awake, temperate, and cool-headed" lads who marched to the rail yards in orderly lines. But she trembled to think what the hungry strikers would do when this well-fed army showed up. Indeed, once they did, Abby wrote Etta later, the mob turned into a nightmare come true, a mass "of human demons, soul putrid, heartsick," and capable of the worst. Abby tried to keep calm but had fallen apart by the time things quieted down. Still weak in the knees a week later, she hoped she would never see anything like it again but expected the worst was not over. "Satan…in all his glory" had come to St. Louis and seemed to be there to stay, for his legions were just growing bolder as time went on. In 1885, it was the dissatisfied streetcar strikers setting off dynamite and crippling the city's businesses. The hundreds of destitute families who ended up "crying for bread" in the St. Louis streets, especially during the punishing winters a few years later, were further compelling evidence of inherent character flaws that prevented the poor from improving their circumstances. It was the same "old story" again, Abby grumbled in 1892. "The husbands went south to find jobs and bought booze, leaving their families for strangers to feed."[53]

By now, the lower-class attitude was a danger Abby took personally, its demons having invaded her home and threatened her middle-class expectations. Gone were the days, she grieved, when she had been able to keep good help for years with almost no problems to speak of. Her free black domestics were competent and compliant, God-fearing people. They had come to church on Sunday mornings and sat in the galleries quietly. They asked her husband respectfully to preside at their baptisms, weddings, and funerals. But it had become increasingly hard to find this kind of help. There were plenty of young girls arriving from Ireland and Germany looking for jobs, but these foreigners became impudent and demanding when they heard how the unionized workers were standing up to their bosses. Even if their conditions were met, they were just as likely to leave in a huff, and Abby was weary of training one after another. One week it might be an Irish girl, the next "a raw German," and none any good. Rose, who had turned twenty-five in 1887—two weeks before Abby turned seventy—still lived at home and tried to help out. But, Abby told Etta, since most of the girls were so rough, barely literate, and entirely unreliable, they needed more supervision than they were worth. Things were no better at Hal's, she went on. Poor Lotte was "always stirred up by the wretched kitchen girls," who kept asking for more and more but did less and less.[54]

What little was left of Abby's genuine sympathy with the working poor dissolved in 1888, when one of her cooks came after her with a whip of verbal abuse that sent her to bed for a week. "I kept my tongue still," she told Etta and Tom, but the impudence had cut so deeply into the core of her dignity, that her old body quickly gave way. Such was the impact, she tried to explain, of having this creature, a dumb "petted animal," snarl and attack the hand that had fed and sheltered it. Abby hated to think what kind of a future the next generations would have in a world where "the kindnesses shown to this class" were no longer appreciated. She supposed she should try "to remember their ignorance and have the patience of Job" and reach out to those who were worthy of help, but the urge to strike back kept her jabbing at them whenever she wrote the family. These girls were not only stupid and lazy, but one was "so plain, not to say ugly," that Abby expected the mirrors to break, she told Etta. Thinking ahead, Abby prayed that the lines would be better secured in the life hereafter. "If they go to a heaven," she told her children emphatically, "I don't want to be with 'em!" She only hoped that the Unitarian company she was counting on there would still be intact by the time she arrived.[55]

——————————————— ∾ ———————————————

Abby had fretted for years about the endless fight over who held the title to their religious communion. The Unitarian theists and self-described freethinking Humanists had been at each other's throats as long as she could remember, and William had been right there with them. William's persistent intolerance seemed uncalled for. His warnings about his untraditional colleagues were just as uncharitable in the mid-1880s, when grandson Will was thinking ahead to seminary, as they had been in the 1860s, when Tom left for Harvard Divinity School. The men they would meet there and have to avoid, William snorted, were godless pretenders. Utterly lacking in biblical learning and shallow, they solemnly lifted their eyes to the heavens with "nothing particular to be seen." William's contempt grew proportionately as the radical threat gained ground farther west, storming his Conference after the war with a banner for "Freedom, Fellowship, and Character in Religion," making no mention of God or Christ. Their standard-bearer, Jenkin Lloyd Jones, insisted that ethical principles ought to suffice as their glue for association, while Eliot's allies held that only their fundamental theistic belief was sufficient for someone to claim the name Unitarian. With no real movement on either side, the dispute would outlive every one of them.[56]

The lesson here was not lost on the Unitarian women who set out to forge a national group for themselves in 1889. Although sisterhood was their primary goal, they hoped that their methods would be an example from which the men in the movement would benefit, too. To minimize their differences and maximize their potential for strength, the East Coast women proposed the name, The Alliance of Unitarian and Other Liberal Christian Women. The intentional ambiguities, they explained, would allow them to open the door to the Jews as unitarians, as well as those who were raised as orthodox gentiles but had evolved and were liberal enough. "Help realize what we are working for…that we *all may be one*," they pleaded. Why repeat their brothers' mistakes? The men were "sore with bruises" from turning the liberal community into a war zone, and still the men could not agree to disagree peacefully. "We shall forget theology in our living faith and burning love," they declared, extending an olive branch to the West. It was a compelling offer, even to those in the heartlands who, fearing the impact of such an equivocal name, were reluctant to sign on at once. Abby Eliot felt the excitement in the updates she got from Christopher's wife, whose aunt Abby May in the East was a leading force behind the new organization.[57]

FIGURE 2.7. William Greenleaf Eliot, ca. 1880. Courtesy of Christopher Rhodes Eliot III.

The tension between St. Louis's two Unitarian churches would by itself have been reason for Abby to welcome the spirit affirmed by the National Women's Alliance. From the time the radical element who started the Church of the Unity called Jones's ally John Learned as pastor, William's successor, John Snyder, at the Church of the Messiah, had been determined to put the new man in his place. It was just another example, Abby groaned when she heard about it, of how "so-called liberal men" fought incessantly at the people's expense. Too narrow and dogmatic to be "at least...charitable and just," they kept tearing the Unitarian family apart by the way they treated each other.[58]

The infighting seemed endemic among the Unitarian brothers. Not even all the conservatives got along, which made it ironic that Snyder would taunt his rival by waving the Eliot banner. If, as she claimed, Abby went twenty years never knowing that Snyder and Learned were feuding, she knew what her husband thought of the man who replaced him in 1873. One had only to see William's face or to hear him muttering after a service: John Snyder lacked both dignity and the deep convictions and character essential for someone of his position. His sermons were just "atrocious" displays of "negativism," plain and simple. "Our young preacher here," he explained to Miss Dix in 1876, had busied himself "in proving that Inspiration is impossible, God 'unknowable,' Faith unimportant: Neither personality nor design nor causative power belongs to God; prayer is essentially unanswerable." This was a betrayal, pure and simple; the man had accepted the post "permitting himself to pass for conservative."[59]

East Coast liberals were just as bad, Abby complained to Tom, stabbing her finger at William's distant cousin Charles Eliot, Harvard's president. She had "never liked President Eliot." She considered him "narrow and mean" for acting as if the only religious liberals who counted were those in New England. It was outrageous how he "so *decidedly*" minimized *all* other schools, as if his own were sufficient to serve the entire United States. The rigidity she saw in his "wanting *all* money to pour in there" was a common characteristic that kept Unitarian colleagues from getting along. William's local success in charming his way into ecumenical circles whose Trinitarian members had once rejected him as an infidel was gratifying until Abby thought about all the bad blood that had come between him and his own Unitarian brothers.[60]

For a woman whose family feelings were so intertwined with her Unitarian roots, the only thing worse than internal strife was defection. To have her relatives turn away from the church that had succored them and their forebears was such a desecration that Abby was willing to cut them out rather than live with the stain. Such was the provocation in 1872 when Abby's nephew Edward Cranch not only married a woman in the Church of the New Jerusalem but also consented to have their children brought up as Swedenborgians. His new Trinitarian church was known as intensely creedal and mystical, and for Abby, this turn was as shocking as if he had gone to the Roman Catholics. Most of the family, not daring to ask for further details, assumed that he had.[61]

—————————————————— ⟳ ——————————————————

Back on his feet, William Eliot led the family well into the 1880s. His headaches were history, and he was again his old self, not suddenly healthy, but fully in charge. Neighbors confirmed that for more than a week in the autumn of 1882, he roused his entire household in the wee hours and herded them out in the yard to view the

Great Comet while it could be seen with the naked eye. Even after a friendship of forty-five years, Sarah Glasgow was flabbergasted at the ruthless enthusiasm with which he still ruled. He told her he would have been willing to go to San Francisco to witness it, and she almost expected to see him take off with his entourage any time. And this was a man who at seventy-one was too lame to cross the street without pain. Within a few years, he was losing a hard-fought battle with chronic bronchitis. December 1886 found him in bed with his final illness, still striving to be God's obedient servant and waiting to enter another life. Not willing to speak of discomfort, he said there was no need to call the doctor. On one occasion, when Abby persisted, he cut her off with a flawless recital of Wordsworth's "Ode to Duty."[62]

Abby was grateful for William's release when he died the next month, but it was a rough transition for her. "I cannot look at anything but he is there before my eyes watching me as I go about, with [his] same sweet loving smile," she told Etta. Only

FIGURE 2.8. Family reunion at 3440 Maple Avenue, St. Louis, after the matriarch's death in 1908. Seated (l. to r.): Charlotte Stearnes Eliot, Rose Greenleaf Eliot Smith; standing (l. to r.): Thomas Dawes Eliot, Christopher Rhodes Eliot, Holmes Smith, Mary Jackson May Eliot, Mary Munroe Eliot, Edward Cranch Eliot, Henry Ware Eliot Jr., Thomas Lamb Eliot, Henry Ware Eliot, Margaret Dawes Eliot. Courtesy of Christopher Rhodes Eliot III.

when she reminded herself of "his gain," did her longing ease up. The loss of two friends within months of his death made her adjustment that much harder. First Sarah Glasgow, her soul mate for fifty years in St. Louis, died in March. Then came the news that Miss Dix had succumbed to a lengthy illness in Trenton, New Jersey, ending a cherished exchange of letters that spanned almost thirty years.[63]

New engagements and babies helped move Abby's focus from what she had lost to what she still had. There was still lots of life at the family homestead at 2660 Washington Avenue during the matriarch's last twenty years. Three of the children still lived close by with their broods, and the youngsters kept coming from Portland to live in the manse while they went to their grandfather's school. Christy announced his betrothal to Mary May a year after losing his father, and soon there were grandchildren coming from all directions. What Abby saw of them satisfied her that they were all turning out well. She knew from the heartache endured by some of the church's most prominent members that having good children was something no parent ought ever to take for granted. Spared from living to see the defection of Hal's youngest son Thomas Stearns to the Anglican Church or to learn of the foolish first marriage and clandestine second of Ed's boy, Edward, she felt abundantly blessed and was sure there could never be "too many Eliots." "Counting the daughters-in-law and sons-in-law and twenty grandchildren and one *great* one," as she calculated in 1897, she had thirty-five in all, a whole "colony of Eliots." Her only remaining wish was that they "could *all* meet once on earth!"[64]

It took Abby's death in her ninety-first year to accomplish this last, best work. The telegraphs of her passing on October 20, 1908 brought the largest gathering of the clan in memory. As Tom described it to Etta, who had stayed in Portland to be with their daughter Ellen and nine-day-old grandson Frank, it was "lovely and merry besides." Hal "got up some great fun," and Rose sang *"Believe me, if all those endearing young charms."* Ed's daughter Alice accompanied her at the keyboard, and Christy's wife, Mary, was greatly impressed by how well they all got along. When they scattered, it was with a sense that their guardian angel was still looking after them, smiling and waiting patiently for the greater reunions to come. "I shall never get to heaven on my own merit," Hal would write of his mother, "but...I shall finally land there because she will never be happy until I am with her."[65]

3

The Rush of Words

I have been so used to a freedom of sentiment that I know not how
to...impose a silence upon myself when I long to talk.
—Abigail Smith Adams[1] to John Adams, 20 February 1796

When Abby Eliot's daughter-in-law Henrietta Robins Mack was born in
Amherst, Massachusetts, in 1845, sixteen ministers' wives going back to
the Mayflower Pilgrims were there in spirit to point the way to the
priesthood of wifely devotion. Yet it was soon clear to her parents,
Rebecca and Samuel, that had she been male, she would have been
welcomed, instead, by the long line of preachers. As far back as they
could remember, Etta's feelings and thoughts had come clothed in
speech. Rebecca was "daily astonished," she wrote her husband in 1848, by
the reasoning and words of a child who had yet to master the alphabet.
The blossoming woman who twelve years later dazzled the Eliots' oldest
son, Tom, had as hard a time keeping her thoughts pent up as he had
breaking the code of restraint that his father imposed on the family. The
attraction of opposite natures was common enough among Eliot
couples, but not so Etta's success in convincing her father-in-law and his
son that a minister's calling could rise or fall on the strength of a
womanly voice.[2]

——————————————— ∽ ———————————————

Rebecca Mack had been a pupil of Catherine Beecher's during the later
1820s, and once she became a mother, she sought to instill the model of
womanhood that she had learned at her teacher's famous Female

TABLE 3. The First Generation of Eliots in the Northwest

William Greenleaf Eliot + Abigail Adams Cranch
1811–1887   1817–1908

Samuel Ely Mack + Rebecca Amelia Robins
1815–1866   1814–1890

Rev. Thomas Lamb Eliot + Henrietta Robins Mack
1841–1936   1845–1940

Rev. William Greenleaf Eliot Jr.
1866–1956
+
Minna Charlotte Sessinghaus
1868–1944

Mary Ely Eliot
1868–1878

Dorothea Dix Eliot
1871–1957
+
Rev. Earl Morse Wilbur
1866–1956

Ellen Smith Eliot
1873–1971
+
Rev. Fred Alban Weil
1874–1933

Grace Cranch Eliot
1875–1973
+
Richard Gordon Scott
divorced 1933

Henrietta Mack Eliot
1879–1978

Samuel Ely Eliot
1882–1976
+
Elsa von Manderscheid
1880–1978

Thomas Dawes Eliot
1889–1973
+
Sigrid Wijnbladh
1888–1942

Seminary in Hartford. In the same tone of voice, she stressed that their sex were created not to be decorative ornaments but agents of moral uplift in their sacred domestic preserve, and it was their duty to use their schooling to meet the demands of this role. Miss Beecher's authority took on more weight when Rebecca went on to describe how her teacher had called her pupils her "children," and later, if these former students had daughters, she also claimed them as her "grandchildren." As a consequence, Etta grew up with the feeling that Miss Beecher's eye was watching her closely, holding her to her exacting standard of Christian womanhood.[3]

Nonetheless, Etta had to decide for herself what a good Christian woman believed, and had she not brought the matter before the courts of her conscience and intellect, she would never have taken her place in the Eliot family. Theological differences seemed insignificant when she and Tom became acquainted in 1861, after Samuel's business had taken the Macks to St. Louis. Etta was only fifteen and in high school, and Tom, four years older, in college. Any thoughts of marriage were still too far off and romantic for sobering scrutiny, especially when there was so much in common to cushion the lovebirds' affection. Their training had come from parents with kindred Congregational roots, a similar appreciation of Henry Ward Beecher's gospel of love, and the same favorite maxims about merry hearts, bright spirits, and Christian cheer.

The Macks and the Eliots seemed even closer when other sects were brought into the picture, as Samuel did when talking religion with Etta. While granting that no one communion had a monopoly on revelation, her father, who was a deacon in the Congregational church in St. Louis, felt a deep chasm between his tradition and the Episcopalians', whose way of "intoning" the services and other papist residue affected him "quite unpleasantly." He also drew the line when it came to the Baptists and the Methodists, whose frenzied revivals created a carnival atmosphere in which he thought the true spirit of worship was badly distorted, if not entirely lost.[4]

There is no record of how Samuel felt about Etta's romance with a Unitarian, but Rebecca was devastated and broadcast her pain when the pair got engaged. Although she admired the Eliots personally, she shuddered to think of her ancestors looking down through the clouds in withering horror. Her protests were so unrelenting that Etta, teetering on a nervous collapse, fled to her grandmother's house in Amherst to sort things out and decide for herself if she could embrace something she had been taught was heretical. Tom, who was now in his final term of divinity school, helped convince her she could. He sent her a few of the sermons he had been writing for classes and student preaching. These included a paper on the Atonement, which Etta pronounced "the most satisfactory and logical statement of the evangelical Unitarian doctrine" that she had heard, indeed, "a better encapsulation, in fewer words," than one she had read by Tom's father. In the summer of 1865,

FIGURE 3.1. Etta and sister Mary Mack, ca. 1856. Courtesy of Warner A. Eliot.

Etta was still unsettled and trying to figure out how much her logic was driven by "old time prejudice," "*new* prejudice," "intellectual pride," and "*enlightened, intelligent* faith." But while her sifting was inconclusive, within a few weeks of Tom's graduation, she was able to say that she shared her fiancé's belief. She had come to it freely by listening to her mind and conscience, convinced that these were the channels through which their Heavenly Father instructed the faithful.[5]

Etta sought to console her mother, but the effort was self-defeating. Rebecca scolded and moaned for the rest of her life that she had been left with no kindred with whom she could fully unite in prayer. She was widowed the year after Etta's marriage and felt abandoned as all four children strayed to more liberal theology. Resentful of Tom, whom she felt had been selfish in not giving up his religion for hers, Rebecca pressed Etta to think how his father would feel if he were in her position. Etta tried to point out that if "all his children turned Roman Catholics, or, (what would be harder for him to bear,) Frothinghamites, he'd *have* to accept it." Whether it was the rosary or the Free Churchers' radical thought they embraced, these "were facts of conscience," not choices one could just "alter at will, or for love's sake" alone. Impervious to reason and craving affection, Rebecca continued to mine her daughter for sympathy, planting more guilt, alienating her son-in-law, who "couldn't abide" the woman, and leaving Etta to lie about how much Tom loved and cherished her "precious" mother.[6]

For the Eliots, on the other hand, Tom's choice of a wife was a gift from God. Her devotion to him was obvious, as was her excellent character, and her liberal faith seemed stronger for having emerged from the forge of conversion. The young woman also brought with her a proven commitment to Christian education, having taught for some years in the St. Louis Congregational Church and its free mission school for black youngsters on Biddle Street. The Eliots could not imagine that Etta would have any trouble holding her own in a Unitarian Sunday school. All Bible-based lessons had the same primary function of teaching the family values that Horace Bushnell had enshrined in *Christian Nurture* in 1847. They had also heard from Tom that she was a natural teacher, someone who knew instinctively how to bring children into the lessons and had the magic words to draw the morals in ways that took hold. She had written to him while he was at Harvard about her morning scholars, a "dear little" flock that grew more delightful each Sunday. She also described her afternoons with her "little heathen class" at the mission and having to scream to compete with her rowdy bunch and the other classes. Her throat was "completely raw" by the time it was over, but there were always a few who paid close attention and seemed quite attached to her.[7]

Yet of all her credentials, Etta's command of the language was most compelling; for without it, her sweetheart's vocation would not have been possible. From the age of fifteen, Tom had suffered from a painful condition affecting his eyes. He could not read or write or do any close work for longer than fifteen minutes. Set on becoming a minister, he had pushed ahead stoically for four years, but in 1860, he finally had to withdraw from college and look past his father's reliance on faith to face the devil head-on. Despite the patriarch's skeptical view of what medical men had to offer, Tom traveled to Boston in February to see an expert and undergo treatment. When this brought no relief, he left on a sea voyage, thinking the change

FIGURE 3.2. Thomas Lamb Eliot, ca. 1862. Courtesy of Christopher Rhodes Eliot III.

FIGURE 3.3. Henrietta Robins Mack, ca. 1862. According to Earl Morse Wilbur, who married the Eliots' second daughter and wrote her father's biography, to the end of his life, "Dr. Eliot carried a scrap of this dress in his pocket-book." Reproduced from *Life of Thomas Lamb Eliot*, privately printed 1937, with the family's permission.

of routine and setting might be the elusive cure. But in fact, his growing anxiety had freer range in the long empty days, and so did the morbid brooding he had tried to subdue in his first twenty years in a family where seven siblings had died.[8]

Unlike his father, Etta was eager to talk about Tom's depression. Even before he allowed her to read the journal he kept while he was at sea, she had recognized the symptoms and known, as she wrote in the margin, that what he had gone through before they met in 1861 had left a permanent stratum of melancholia in his character. The record shows, too, that Etta's good eyes allowed Tom to finish his papers in college. The small faint notes in a diary kept by her aunt Jane in 1862 caught her walking across the campus with an armful of books to help her sweetheart catch up on lost work. While Tom was away at divinity school, his father got to know Etta better by asking her to be his amanuensis. Delighted to see how facile she was and how much she could help with Tom's sermons, William was "getting very fond and proud of her," Abby observed.[9]

------------------------------ ∾ ------------------------------

With rough seas most of the way, it had taken six weeks in the fall of 1867 for Etta, Tom, and their baby Willy to reach Portland, Oregon, via New York and the Isthmus of Panama. Etta had been sick and miserable on the long journey, and when they approached their destination on Christmas Eve Day in a steady rain, the muddy ground along the Willamette's west bank looked like paradise. The exhausted young wife, relieved it was not a mirage, was thankful to find the ground solid, if hardly a place that inspired love at first sight. While Etta and Tom had never expected that pioneering a church would be easy, they had pictured themselves as the boosters intended, plowing soft earth in the fast-emerging "New England of the Pacific Coast." The promise that there was already "a good deal of eastern leadership and tone" was enhanced by the charming account of how the city was nearly called Boston before the founders decided to name it after the city in Maine.[10]

The Portland that Etta and Tom found waiting in Oregon did have its signs of promise. Of the 7,000 residents in 1867, many were Yankee entrepreneurs who had come from New England the decade before and put their mark on the town's architecture, commerce, and government. Their houses of worship were typically small facsimiles of the old Eastern churches adapted to native materials. Three public and five private schools were serving two-thirds of the school-age children, and although the fire department and public utilities were sorely deficient, residents could stand on an observation deck near the newly domed courthouse and see two streets that were fully paved and a row of wharves and warehouses. Still, if Portland was more than a rough foreign outpost at the end of the Oregon Trail, it was not yet the place its promoters had conjured up. In the late 1860s, these boosters admitted the place was "provincial," known for "peculiarities in manners, opinions and business," and unprepared to offer a family anything better than "low-grade minstrels and vulgar comedy." As a "newcomer from the states," Etta wrote her sister in 1868, she had yet to get over the "nervous shock" of seeing the way the people dressed.[11]

Etta forgave them their lack of style after hearing the Unitarians' version of how they had stood their ground while the Trinitarian wagons were circling their tents. Etta had only to look at the skyline and count the number of steeples and crosses to calculate the courage this must have required of Liberal Christians. Tom and Etta found ten Christian churches and one Jewish temple when they arrived, and none, they were told, had welcomed the Unitarians. In fact, the open hostility had been the prod to their organizing their own religious community. After having to sit through a service where the preacher attacked their beliefs, two of the women had set out to raise the money to build their own church.

"They went about among their friends giving a summary of their views... and began their society with a dollar contribution apiece, seven in all, in the treasury," Etta wrote her sister excitedly. In two years' time, they had earned just under $1,000 by taking in sewing. With another $500 from gentlemen they induced to join the effort, and the donated labor of sympathetic mechanics, they built a sweet little chapel, furnished and carpeted it, bought a communion service, and paid for a Sabbath school library of 140 good books. Now that all this had been accomplished by the faithful core of thirty or so, others were starting to flock to the standard, filling the place from door to pulpit.[12]

To realize how blessed she was to be living among thinking people of faith, Etta had only to sit with Tom through a Presbyterian service such as the one they endured as a courtesy to a new orthodox preacher in 1868. By the end of the sermon, Etta was sure the elect were watching and waiting to see her and Tom drop dead in their seats like Ananias and Sapphira, the husband and wife who were struck down by God in the book of Acts for sinning against the community. The sermon was dreadful in every respect, she wrote her mother-in-law, a barrage of untenable statements wrapped in a sounds-good-but-says-nothing language and tied together with make-believe logic. One phrase in particular struck her: "The Eternal, Self-existent Son." Now what in the world did that mean?[13]

Whatever it meant, the orthodox messages took on an uglier tone when the new Ananias became more aggressive in trying to build up a following. The Eliots found that many of Portland's families were alienated from orthodoxy and were looking for something freer. But they could see, too, that few of these people were motivated enough to plow through the muddy and pitted roads to join the Unitarians on the far western edge of Portland. After waiting a year for the unchurched to come, Tom decided to go to them and launched a series of sermons at the Oro Fino Theater downtown. Enraged by this tactic, the press and conservative clergy went on the attack, condemning the theater services as cheap "hurdy-gurdy," "counterfeit" Christianity, and poisonous bait that was being put out to lure the drunks and "men

of loose morals." The publicity had the desired effect of filling the church on the outskirts of town, exceeding Tom's wildest hopes.[14]

Etta had meanwhile thrown herself into a role that was two or three times as
demanding as what she envisioned before she agreed to go west. She joined the Sewing
Society and lent a hand with the charity work, which the members believed was the
best reply to the insult that they were not Christians. She did her part when the interfaith Ladies' Relief Society started to broaden its aid to the destitute immigrants
streaming into the city. Together, the women raised enough money to set up free
public libraries, and when it became apparent that their mission of caring for
orphaned children could not go forward without a shelter, they built what came to be
known as The Home. Not having the right, as women, to form corporations or hold
any real estate, they enlisted their husbands as signatories to all the legal documents
and designated themselves as associates who made operational policy. Etta was not as
ready to take on a young ladies' Bible class, where she worried that she would betray
herself as an imposter. Yet the Scripture was all familiar, no different from what she
had learned growing up, and reading it in the light of history, linguistics, and anthro-
pology—the New Critical methods imported by Joseph Buckminster—was like
breathing fresh air.[15]

Once her furniture had arrived after a five-month journey around Cape Horn,
Etta rushed to her duties as hostess, arranging those social functions that strengthened and dignified parish allegiance by being held in the pastor's home. The physical
setup and Etta's priorities argued for keeping these simple. "The old brown house," as
their rental was called to distinguish it from the stately homestead they bought on
West Park Street five years later, still had a good many unpacked crates of domestic
goods stacked in the corners. It was also hard to get decent maids, and Etta, the first
to admit she had "never *aimed at completeness in household matters*," figured that what
it would cost her in time and nerves to make the place shine for her company was
simply not worth it. There was more to be gained, she told Tom, from trusting their
guests to forgive her the clutter and dust if they happened to notice. The refreshments
were ample, and what really mattered was that the people enjoyed themselves.[16]

With the Unitarians under siege, these events gave the hostess a welcome break
from the sessions with wounded parishioners who came to complain and commiserate. There seemed no end to the insults they and their minister had to endure. In
1874, the YMCA denied their pastor's request for membership, impugning his faith
as insufficiently Christian. When Tom came to the door, he changed the topic and
noted the Unitarians' strength: The chapel had only been up for a year when a
gallery had to be added to handle the overflow crowds. The Sunday school was
growing apace, and the mission work was expanding. Yet it was harder for Etta to
smile when small-minded clergy kept calling her sainted William Ellery Channing
"a bigot" and stabbing her spouse in the back. By 1870, Tom had to take a recuper-

ative leave, the first of many that came with increasing frequency. When he did not go out of state or abroad, he escaped to a parcel of land he bought at Hood River, a couple of hours east of Portland by wagon.[17]

This doubled the burden on Etta, who was left to handle the calls for Tom and, not infrequently, problems that he had created by not being candid. In one case, the injured party, a kind and gentlemanly professor, had hired a live-in maid on the strength of Tom's hearty recommendation only to find himself stuck with a girl whose crude, surly ways were corrupting his children. The man and his wife did not feel they could possibly keep her on without failing as parents, but as she had no other place to go, it seemed unchristian to send her away, especially after their minister had said she should have the position. Since the damage was done, all Etta could think of to tell the poor man was to pray that the girl would find someone to marry and leave posthaste of her own accord. As for Tom, Etta hoped he would think twice before he again distorted the truth to have it mirror his faith. The lines of communication were hard enough to keep straight without him withholding or twisting the facts.[18]

Whatever news failed to reach Etta at home caught up with her on her rounds through the parish. The people volunteered who was sick, who was drinking too hard, who was feeling neglected, who was verging on leaving the church, and how much the traitors would have to cough up to sit with the Trinitarians. (The Smiths had taken a $100 pew but would probably "craw-fish" back once they got their fill of Episcopalian homilies.) It took a good ear to know what to do with the scuttlebutt, and to block out the useless chatter that clogged up the lines. Some of the quickest informants were also the most inventive, and some of the neediest people were the most resistant to counsel. One woman, while "very brilliant and well read" in everyone's estimation, had a mind with a *"circular twist"* that tested the limits of Etta's endurance. By the end of one long afternoon with her, Etta was ready to throw up her hands. "Poor woman," she wrote Tom that night, "I doubt…she can be really helped for longer than while one is talking with her."[19]

Etta felt more and more like a war wife whose spouse had taken her to the front lines and left her while he took a furlough. She longed to creep into his arms and forget about everyone else, yet she carried on. In one breathless letter to Tom, she promised that she would find someone to fill the pulpit, would see to the "Sewing Circle, Sunday School, and Bible Class," and would probably get up "an 'Entertainment' besides the Harvest Concert to keep things going and interest alive" until the pastor returned. When he was back, Etta got in some "churching," her code word for tracking and snatching new members. The hunt, a challenge she relished, was her favorite sport and her theater. How to capture the woman who pleaded that she was too lame to come either to worship or sew? Or the one who wanted to join the church but had to wait for her mother to die? Or again, the doctor's wife who thanked her for bringing the reading matter but was obviously in an orthodox minister's clutches and likely to stay? Whether or not she made the catch, there was always a thrill to planting the bait and seeing some movement in its direction. The unpredictable, untidy nature of churching was also a jolly escape from the regimentation her husband demanded at home.[20]

The St. Louis relatives picked up the signs that Etta was driving herself too hard and urged her to pull back from parish work and concentrate on domestic duties. Her mother admonished her not to let pride and ambition tempt her out of her sphere, while her mother-in-law pleaded moderation and begged her to "keep down the steam!" Even her father-in-law was worried enough to write a long letter warning against the lure of "external work." "Let me beg of you and Tom *to put the children and each other in the first class of duties*," he wrote. By undertaking too much, they would soon reach the point of diminished returns where both parish and parsonage suffered irreparably. Confessing that he had come to regret having spent so much time away from the family, he hoped that Etta would not make the same mistake. Etta insisted that she was not "nearly so far gone" as they seemed to think, and to ease their concerns, she painted herself as the consummate, loving but sensible mother surrounded by children she rarely let out of her sight. Baby Dora—whom they had named for Miss Dix and later called Dodie or Dorothea—was "a treasure," Etta assured her mother-in-law. "I am writing with her across my knees, and the tangents of the pen are when she kicks my portfolio." As for Rebecca Mack's sharper warnings, her words of advice were all "good and true" but "not so painfully needed," Etta promised.[21]

For all her tenacity, Etta was forced to concede by the mid-1870s that she could no longer be a minister's stand-in as well as a mother and wife unless she was also given her share of sabbaticals. In the spring of 1874, finished with kidding herself and doubtful "the zest and flavor" would "*ever come back*," she let Tom know how things stood. For the past six months, she had carried a weight of "hatefulness" inside her that made her feel like "a heathen," and there was no getting around it. "Don't imagine that something has happened to set me off, for there hasn't," she told him sternly. Their members were all as earnest and loving as ever, yet everything seemed uphill. She had tried her best not to spread her gloom, but perhaps it was time to send a message not everyone wanted to hear.[22]

Unlike her mother and in-laws, who were almost too quick to see Etta's limits, the people at church were too riveted on the pastor's exhaustion to think of his wife's without her making an issue of it. Even Miss Dix was prone to lose sight of the younger woman's interests. When Tom took off for St. Louis to rest in the summer of 1870, she simply assumed that Etta would keep the church going in Portland until he got back and only realized her blunder after Etta pointed it out. Etta's directness in letting Dix know she had no intention of playing the martyr can be inferred from the older woman's apology: "If I had never personally known you,

FIGURE 3.4. Thomas Lamb Eliot baiting his line at his country retreat at Hood River, ca. 1890. Courtesy of Warner A. Eliot.

Etta Eliot," Dix wrote back, "I should not have even suggested a temporary separation from yr dear husband....This you may have thought *hard*, *unkind*, unthink-
ingly severe. It really was a result of my faith in yr power, and appreciation of yr
work in all the relations you occupy....If you felt yourself too slightly considered,
forget all that and...remember I would never wound your feelings or leave you to
suppose *yr good*, *yr* need, yr peace, are unconsidered."[23]

Thereafter, rather than wait for somebody else to suggest she take a vaca-
tion, Etta just went ahead and arranged it. She saw to it that the trip to St. Louis
came off as a family affair, affording a pleasant change of scene and company.
Again in May 1872, she notified Tom that she was about to start for Hood River,
where he was already vacationing. It was all worked out. Dear Mrs. Frazar, Mrs.
Atwood, and Mrs. Kimball had already agreed to take turns keeping Willie and
Mamie; and Etta would bring little Dodie along to share "her papa's kisses."
When Tom tried to veto the scheme on the grounds it would tire her out, she set
him straight: she was not backing down. "I'm dreadfully put out by your telegram," she wrote with it still in her hand. "I was all ready to start tomorrow
morning, and you know how I hate to be balked in what I've set out to do. I can
stand whatever Mrs. X can. I am not *bone* tired, but home and brain tired,
and...really *must* get somewhere out of Portland for a while." Once more, three
years later, when Tom took a year off to travel in Europe, Etta made sure she was
not left behind to run the church by herself. She spent the year with their children, now a herd of five, in St. Louis.[24]

One can only speculate as to Etta's success in concealing her "dumps," but if her
depression was noticeable, it would have been taken for loneliness, given how often the
minister was away. This was certainly part of it. Tom's absences had been a sore spot
with his spouse from the time he went off on business without her during her first
pregnancy. Feeling abandoned and cramped in the St. Louis manse with her in-laws,
she wished, she had scolded, that he could just once know "how horrid" it was "to be *a
wife* that has to be in the house so much and have your husband leave you."[25]

— ∾ —

Yet married life had turned out to be lonely for Etta even when Tom was at home.
Although he was still a romantic at heart and given to bringing her flowers or placing a single myrtle blossom next to her plate at the table, he was always too tired to
make conversation. "My husband don't talk, and I have no female intimates," Etta
confessed to her mother, even while trying to put the best face on a difficult
situation. Ministers' wives, she reminded Rebecca, had to maintain an appropriate
distance. This was all for the best since gossip served little real purpose and it was
exhausting. Neither woman believed this, of course. Famished for news and a good
heart-to-heart, Etta begged her sister to send her a "big dish" of chatter before she
wasted away.[26]

Etta believed she heard more from her husband when he went abroad or escaped to Hood River. On those occasions, he wrote every day, and his letters, playful and tender but also self-critical and contrite, kept her heart "pit-a-patting" the way they had in their courting days. A penitent letter in which Tom had rued his inexcusable "hardness," swearing that it did not come "from the heart" but from "an overstrained body," gave Etta the joy of absolving him. "Don't be so *wicked* as to malign yourself again, and talk about 'tyrannies,'" Etta wrote back after putting her lips to his "*kiss*" at the end of the letter. She knew she was not easy, either. Her "longing to help and comfort" him in his "hard life" was always there, but her impulse to share her interests was so strong and persistent that she could not keep from running to him "with hectoring questions and little bothers!" Nor was brevity one of her virtues. These "half-half" concerns, like most things in life, required "particularizing." Yet these long-distance conversations, however loving, were no relief from her husband's silence when he was back home or from the constraints on her talking about her problems with women at church.[27]

Etta's plight inspired the idea of trying her luck at becoming a published author and tapping into the networks of female sympathy between writers and readers. The rise of periodical literature during the century's second quarter had opened a market for women's short verse and efforts at juvenile fiction. Etta would model her stories on family events, as she often did for her children. Her poetry, which she had been writing for years, would come from her heart. If this crossed Tom's lines of propriety, she would have the means to redeem herself by paying some of the bills as soon as the publishers' checks arrived in the mail. It all seemed easy enough until Etta's first batch of material came back rejected.

Etta's only successful submission was arguably the best indication that she had missed her calling by putting her energy into juvenile fiction. This fiery essay of 2,000 words, an "'Appeal to Conscience' by H.R.E.," read like the exhortation of a seasoned evangelist when it ran in the *Christian Union*, which Henry Ward Beecher was editing at the time. Refined in the fire of indignation, it took aim at Tom's Trinitarian colleagues, whose views were as liberal as his but who cravenly failed to support him when he was attacked by the archconservative wing. Instead of the temperate phrases that came from her pen when she helped with Tom's sermons, Etta unleashed her reprimand in a blaze of Old Testament cadences. She called on those who saw themselves in this shameful hypocrisy to heed the voice that told Abraham, "Get thee out of the country and from thy kindred, and from thy father's house, into a land that I will show thee." She implored them to cross the river, no longer too cowardly to pilot their people to where they could pluck the good fruit for themselves and join in planting an honest faith. In closing, she asked her "brothers in Christ" to forgive her "roughness of speech" and not to crumple and burn her words but to see their truth and do the right thing.[28]

Etta was able to hide her identity from the *Christian Union*'s subscribers, some of whom fired off searing rebuttals addressed to her as a man, but when she learned that the Unitarians' *Christian Register* planned to reprint it, she knew the initials would blow her cover. To soften the shock, she alerted St. Louis, let Tom see her article in advance, and awaited the repercussions. Her father-in-law, once again unconditional in his praise, put her mind at rest. He had "seldom seen anything in its line" that had suited him as much as this piece, and his son was to be congratulated for having "a wife and colleague in one." Tom, however, was still too fresh from his father's stamp to go that far. He commended his wife on the sentiments but qualified this with *Tace et Face*; hereafter, he hoped, she would let her good deeds do the talking instead of her pen. Etta was stung and protested. It was just as hard for him "*to spill*" as for her "*not to spill*," yet he gained the advantage by setting a moral standard that worked in his favor. She withdrew from the fight with the orthodox clergy, putting aside a talent for preaching that she would return to in later years. But her pledge to abandon the publishing world altogether was unrealistic. If not polemical tracts, she would write more stories to focus on positive outcomes and keep writing verse as a way to befriend her humanity. A poem she called "Out of the Silence" was characteristic:

> When weary with thyself and with the world—
> For which each missile which thy hand hath hurled
> Against earth's wrongs, hath fallen on thy head,
> And each new prayer hath brought thee stones for bread—
> Go for a space apart from all the din,
> And on some lonely hill, or wrapped within
> The healing silence of the waiting woods,
> Thou shalt find medicine for thy dark moods.
> For though no voice from riven skies shall cry,
> Nor angels troop, to right a world awry,
> Though in thine outward life no change be wrought,
> The soul within thee shall be newly taught.[29]

In January 1877, when Tom was writing his penitent letters from Europe confessing his tyrannies and pleading for wifely forgiveness, Etta saw her chance to make a clean breast of her own incorrigibility and to ask not so much for his pardon as for his blessing on her offense. For almost four years she had kept her promise that she would submit nothing more to be published without consulting him first. Tom had laid down the law to put an end to the cycle of nervous anticipation, disappointment, and tears. But with him away on recuperative leave, her "quiet conscientious thought" had released her from that agreement, and she was not only sending work out but also was having a bit of success. A children's story would be in the next *St Nicholas Magazine*, and a poem of eight lines she had written for Tom would appear in *Scribner's Monthly* about the same

FIGURE 3.5. Henrietta Robins Mack Eliot at her writing desk, June 1900. Courtesy of Warner A. Eliot.

time. "I found that the writing was such a relief to my loneliness," she owned up, "that I felt…it was right to indulge in the luxury of an occasional scribble…just for its own sake." As his father knew all about it and was "*very much pleased*," Tom might as well send her a kiss and forgive her, as he had been overruled.[30]

Looking back, Etta doubted that she would have kept her sanity if she had complied with Tom's wishes. In the spring of 1878, when their oldest girl, Mamie, was suddenly stricken with meningitis and died, the breakdown she had would have been even worse had she not had her paper and pens. Already depressed from a miscarriage six months before, Etta sank to the depths of despair as she and Tom sat helplessly by, watching the illness rack their poor child. For more than two weeks, Mamie writhed in pain until slipping into a coma from which she finally passed on Easter Sunday. Incoming calls for the minister's help had amplified the misery. "Diphtheria next door," Tom wrote in his daybook as Mamie's condition worsened. "Funeral of Taylor baby" he noted along with his own "Doubts and fears." "We suppose her dying. Meeting at church, but I did not attend," he scrawled on Good Friday. With her lingering "like a babe asleep," Tom slipped away for the service on Sunday, receiving new members and baptizing several children before rushing home. An hour later, Mamie was gone, but the parents' ordeal was not over.[31]

Tom had decided to ask R. S. Stubbs to officiate at the funeral. Stubbs, an amicable and ecumenically minded brother, was the chaplain of Portland's Seamen's Friend Society and a comfortable choice for a grieving family most Trinitarian clergy had shunned. But this was not how it appeared to some of the Unitarian laity, who spoiled the service for Etta and Tom by spreading false rumors that Chaplain Stubbs was there by default as none of the orthodox ministers would participate. The other intrusion on their bereavement, however—the ongoing life of the church—was welcomed by Tom, whose father had taught him that hard, useful work was the right therapy for one's sorrow. The day after Mamie was buried, he was back at the cemetery consoling a mournful band by the side of another newly dug grave. At the end of the week, his journal showed him making his rounds with a lighter step: "Pleasant. Writing sermon. Beat carpet. Calls on various people."[32]

On the other hand Tom conceded, it was another "dark day" for Etta, whose fortitude had its own conditions and schedule. It took time and quiet for Etta's grief to solidify into the kind of "dull ache" that she could grab and shove into a corner and leave in "its allotted place, like an article of furniture" that she could acknowledge and then move on. Friends were taking the children out to the country to give her some rest, but there was no place to hide when people came by to offer their sympathy and asked when she would be back at the church and the Ladies' Sewing Society.[33]

Their answer came from 200 miles away across the state line, where Etta had fled to be with her sister Mary and brother-in-law Edward Galvin. "I feel such a runaway, leaving you at this time," she wrote Tom contritely from Walla Walla, "but I was worse than useless, and it seemed best." Her eyes were still aching from trying to hold back the tears from the children, she said, and Tom would just have to trust the maid and the cook to look after things and hope that she would "be worth something" when she got home. As it turned out, the refuge she sought was no refuge at all. Mary, herself, was on the verge of a breakdown, a crisis reminiscent of Etta's before she left the orthodox church. Mary had made her escape two or three years before when she married Edward Galvin, a Unitarian minister, and settled with him in Washington to start a new congregation. Rebecca persisted in trying to pull her back to her orthodox roots, condemning her for leaving the faith she was raised in and urging her to repent of her heathen marriage. It would be several years before Edward, unable to ease her guilt-ridden conscience, conceded defeat, took Mary back to her mother, and found a church in Chicago. But Mary's distress was already full-blown when her sister arrived in Walla Walla, desperate for steady support and a place to heal.[34]

Etta was home in time to watch Tom lay the cornerstone for a larger church that began to go up on the vacant lot next to the chapel in late July, but she was still too distracted by Mamie's death and the other children to take an interest in anything else. The following spring, when he was excitedly building not only the larger church but also their new house at 227 West Park Street, she who had always liked working up floor plans never once looked at the blueprints. Instead she was writing more poetry to keep from becoming chronically "ill and useless" by letting her feelings "run riot." "When Grief shall come," she encouraged her pen, "think not to flee…but make of her thy friend,/And in the end/Her counsels will grow sweet."[35]

In 1880, another of Etta's attempts, a story for children, appeared in The Nursery, one of only a handful that ever got into print. The market for short prose was glutted and competition so fierce that Etta had little hope that her work would make the final cut. One editor thought that her effort was "sweet and touching" but lacked "sufficient force." Another could not even take more submissions as she had no place to put them. Her closet was packed with manuscripts, and some had been waiting nine years! "They only have room for the very best, to which class my stories do not belong," Etta told her son Will, who offered to type some in 1901. While she still felt the sting when her stories came back, Etta found that the effort was worth it. The process of crafting stories with happy endings and lessons for every age was curative and all the reward she needed, she told herself. When the Lothrop Publishing Company accepted Laura's Holidays (1898), a thinly disguised account of the Eliots' escapades at Hood River, and then its sequel, Laura in the Mountains (1905), the triumph was sweeter for being so unexpected.[36]

In the 1890s, after the last of the Eliot children was born, Etta was asked to produce what became her most visible published work. This was an English translation of the fifty-three rhyming "Communings" and "Mottoes" included in Friedrich Froebel's Mutter-, Spiel-und Koselieder or Mother Play. The project was the idea of

FIGURE 3.6. A picnic with friends from the church, ca. 1865: in foreground (l. to r.),
Joe Teal, Clara Teal, Etta Eliot, Sam Eliot (in smock, standing), Tom Eliot; on far side
(l. to r.), Ellen Eliot, Sue Woodward, George Teal, Henry Teal, Grace Eliot. Courtesy of
Warner A. Eliot.

Susan Blow, an old Eliot friend and one of America's leading disciples of Froebel,
who had made a national name for herself introducing the kindergarten idea in the
St. Louis public schools in the 1870s. Blow had always maintained that these verses,
and not the playthings and guided activities Froebel called "Gifts" and "Occupations,"
constituted the centerpiece of his work and should be the main teaching tool for
drawing youngsters into a social world and an ideal self. *Mother Play* had appeared
in English as early as 1878, but Blow was unhappy with how the songs and panto-

mimes had been cast. Determined to reinstate Froebel, whose work was being eclipsed by indigenous thinkers, Blow reworked the commentaries herself and handed the mottos to Etta, whom she knew had a mastery of German, a rare poetical ear, and a grasp of the theory the earlier translators lacked.[51]

Etta was equally confident in their congruent bents of mind. Susan Blow's distillation of Froebel's supreme educational goal as "the mystic experience of God transcendent, immanent, and incarnate" had a Unitarian resonance for her. Etta heard it again in Froebel's "second great value, *Ethics*," which Blow expressed as "personal responsibility and its correlate of…real freedom." And once more in the third value, *Language*, "an objective set of shadowy forms that pointed the way to God, the realized ideal." For Susan Blow, Etta Eliot's renderings of the "The Mother at Play with Her Child," "The Flower Basket," "The Weather Vane," "The Finger Piano," "The Bridge," and "The Nest" were wonderfully faithful to Froebel's idea that genuine poets could transfigure everyday objects and acts by giving them souls.[38]

In the end, however, Etta would rank her original work as the higher attainment. Successful in placing some eighty poems in publications as mainstream as *Scribner's*, *Harper's Weekly*, *The New Age*, and *Lippincott's*, Etta found that this validation let her speak of her art as a ministry to others as well as herself. The need was never greater, she said in addressing the Portland Women's Club. People were so caught up in pursuing material wealth and hollow prestige that they could no longer feel the presence of God. As a poet, she said, she felt called to connect with these orphaned spirits and bring them back home to a loving, coherent Creator.[39]

———————————————— ✆ ————————————————

For all the gratification of getting her words before thousands of readers, Etta still envied the live connections Tom had when he spoke to a congregation. By referencing Scripture instead of himself and drawing the universal lessons, her husband could speak of the problems he shared with his congregants without blurring the line that set him apart as their counselor. Although she had stuck to her promise to relinquish the orthodox press as a pulpit, Etta had kept her preaching hand limber. One had only to see Tom groping for words when he preached without a manuscript and then to look over at her in the pew mouthing entire phrases to know she was doing more with his sermons than taking dictation verbatim. Yet not until William Eliot's death in 1887 did his eloquent daughter-in-law make her move toward the pulpit.

Etta had long been well aware of the patriarch's qualms about women who wanted to preach. As early as 1870, when the first women started to seek ordination, William had agonized over the question of females becoming ministers and had brokered an uneasy peace with the implications. As one who defended the democratic principle in his theology, he felt, in all fairness, that he was obliged to accept this flurry of female ambition. As a private person, however, he never approved, and Etta did not have to read his mind or private journals to know this. It was evident from his sermons and from remarks delivered before a congress of educators, which she was able to read in the *St. Louis Democrat*. He believed that some women would foolishly try to do more than God had intended for them, and once they had failed, they would be more content to sit quietly at their spindles. The sexes' essential differences, he went on in addressing the teachers, would effectively guard the gates and keep the spheres separate. The next fifteen years saw her father-in-law advocating for women's equality, their equal admission to Washington University's professional schools, and their unabridged right to the ballot. But Etta could tell that his old-fashioned notions still governed his personal feelings. This, alone, seemed good reason to wait until he had died before taking the pulpit.[40]

When she did, as a volunteer preacher for a newly created society, Etta's recently widowed mother-in-law was delighted. Admittedly, Abby's first, fleeting thought was that speaking in public might take the same toll on her daughter-in-law as it had on her husband and son. William had always come home feeling sick after preaching, and Tom fared no better. At forty-six, he looked sixty-four. Yet Abby could easily picture Etta in front of a congregation, energized and winning a following once people gave her a chance. Evidently they did. By 1895, the editorial staff of her district's *Pacific Unitarian* were tipping their hats to Tom's versatile wife as "not only a poetess of acknowledged merit" but also one who "occasionally drops into preaching."[41]

Tom's transition to pastor emeritus in 1893 also helped clear Etta's path. Not that his obligations or hers became lighter when he stepped down. While he turned his attention to starting the cultural institute that became Reed College, Etta kept tumbling "from one thing to another," the "big girls on the one hand and the little children on the other, and the church between," she admitted in 1895. Yet she made time to write and give sermons and justified this to herself as a vital work that did not encroach on her husband's professional turf. The warm invitations she got had as much to do with her skillful self-deprecation as with her acknowledged eloquence. She was only an amateur, she demurred, who was just filling in as best she could until the *real* preachers arrived. If nothing else, she was known to say, women in pulpits were oddities who were good for drawing a crowd. The question of whether this satisfied Tom was moot by 1902, the economy's crash having closed the churches that asked for her services earlier.[42]

FIGURE 3.7. Etta and Tom at Hood River, ca. 1927. Courtesy of Warner A. Eliot.

Etta's preaching days would have been over sooner if she had not had a son with a pulpit. But Will had followed his father and grandfather into the liberal ministry and recently taken the Unitarian church in Salem near Portland. After 1901, he was splitting his time between filling its pulpit and traveling the district to rescue endangered churches and organize new ones. Etta had often been scolded by Tom for poking her fingers in his "church pie," but Will, more relaxed, appreciated her picking up the details he let slip. From sending out notices of his next sermons it seemed a small step for her to present one, and this is what happened after an opportune mix-up. Tom had agreed to preach for Will but put the wrong date in his book, and this gave Etta her opening. Not to seem overly eager when she notified Salem that she would step in, she presented the situation as an unfortunate one that left her no choice. Since Salem's pulpit was Will's special charge, the people, no doubt, would "rather see his *wife* than his mother in it." But since the failure to meet the commitment was not her son's but her husband's, she could not in good conscience do otherwise "than bear the brunt of it."[43]

Salem appears to have been her last chance to sermonize in a church. Female preachers might still have been oddities, but they were no longer a draw. In twenty years, the American public had come to believe that the nation's problems were symptoms of an enfeebled nation whose institutional spine had been softened by women's ambition and influence. Females in pulpits were no longer just "foolish women" or novelties. They were blemishes to be shunned by both liberal and orthodox bodies alike. So it was that after Will was called to be pastor in Portland in 1906, Etta contrived to gather her own congregation by offering the women a class on reading the Bible as inspirational literature and history.

Taking the floor before Sunday worship, she lectured and guided discussion, so enthralling the group with her melding of spirituality, practical insights, and scholarship, more people came out to hear her than stayed to hear Will. The women insisted the class be continued indefinitely, and many original members were still there when Etta stepped down after twenty-five seasons. Well into her eighties and losing her sight, she could no longer manage the lectures. She was still writing, however. Although she was too blind to see what she wrote, by leaving large spaces between the lines, she was able to keep them from running into each other. Nor did the doyenne relinquish her role as the voice of the Women's Alliance. Not even a new set of dentures that felt like "a sewing machine" in her mouth cramped her style. "She talked forty-five minutes on her feet and was gay and witty and spiritual and inspiring all in one and also," one witness vouched, "her teeth didn't tattle or slip or whistle." In short, "she was marvelous."[44]

4

Where Words Fail

There will be narratives of women's lives only when women no
longer live ... isolated in the houses and the stories of men.
—Carolyn Heilbrun in *Writing a Woman's Life*[1]

Portland parishioner Kate Stevens Bingham kept Etta Eliot humble. One
of the first to have signed the church roster in 1868, when she was just 16
years old, and still in touch with the parsonage sixty years later, Kate was
a constant reminder of how bedeviled by words Unitarians were. No
matter how welcome Kate felt at the church, or attentive during the
sermons, or engaged in the cheery conversations that animated the social
hour, she had a sense of being left out, an irony Etta knew well. But even
while women as outwardly different as Kate and the minister's wife
shared this feeling and might have found comfort in telling each other,
the parish's vernacular and the pulpit's messages got in the way. Such
were the obstacles when social advantage meant more than inclusion and
a liberal ministers taught by example that hiding the truth could be
justified.

It had never occurred to the young Kate Stevens that standing apart
from the crowd might be lonely. She cultivated her social distinctions.
Her membership in the exclusive Oregon Pioneer Association certified
her, she wrote in her journal, as one of the area's leading "people of
means and culture ... not only of sterling character but also of gentle
blood." Before coming west, her progenitors had been civilizing Rhode
Island. Her mother, born Margaret Hazard, had forebears who went back

to Gideon Wanton, one of Rhode Island's early colonial governors. Kate's father, Isaac Stevens, had traced his lines to the veterans of the great wars who had formed and spread the United States to the West. Groomed at Phillips Academy and West Point, he continued in this tradition as Washington's first territorial governor. Charged with taming and dispossessing the Indian nations, he accomplished his mission and then went back to the District of Columbia to represent his white constituency in the U.S. Congress. Kate saw no limit to what her father might have achieved had there not been a war that showed him his duty leading the Union troops in Chantilly, Virginia. Her father, a general, died on the battlefield there in 1862.[2]

Unlike Kate's trumpeted ancestral history, the story surrounding her marriage to Edward Bingham in 1886 was one she would just as soon have forgotten and tried to confine to her journal. That private record, a melodrama that moved through a maze of shifting scenes, coincidences, and fateful decisions, began not in Portland, Oregon, but on the outskirts of Boston. Kate's mother had moved the family to Dorchester during the 1870s, and several years later, in 1882, the parish called Christopher Eliot, their previous pastor's younger brother, to shepherd the congregation. For sentiment's sake, they went back to attending an Eliot church, and while Kate thought the sermons were boring, she was given an unexpected incentive in 1885, when a stranger began to appear in a neighboring pew. Although he said nothing to Kate, the signs of a pending relationship—a glance, a slight nod—were unquestionable and became her obsession. Kate's ears picked up when the minister spoke of the sanctity of marriage. It shamed her, she wrote, to know that her feelings were "earthy," not those he exalted; and when she sat with her Sunday school girls before the worship service, fingering the stylish silk dress she wore for the stranger's benefit, she was mortified by her weakness in letting his presence corrupt her priorities. Finally, as Advent approached, the stranger introduced himself to Hazard Stevens, Kate's brother, and by New Year's Day 1886, the courtship was underway.[3]

Edward "Ed" Wingard Bingham, a thirty-three-year-old attorney, explained that he had some land near his mother and brothers in Portland, Oregon, and was temporarily in the East to promote a new horseshoe business. A short, thick-set fellow with thin, balding hair, rather carelessly dressed, and "a little slouchy," he struck Kate as "almost common" and a most improbable knight to have come out of nowhere and taken her heart by storm. "Dubious" was her mother Margaret Stevens's word for the whole affair. She could see that Kate, who was now in her thirties and rarely saw gentlemen socially, was "fairly starved" for attention and letting her hopes inflate what this man had to offer.[4]

Ed, who apparently had his own qualms about taking advantage of blind desperation, warned Kate that he had some character flaws that could offset his virtues and make him a trial. To give her a taste of what to expect and prepare her for who would be boss, he gave her orders to stop wearing bangs as soon as they made their engagement public. Afraid "he might dart back to Oregon" by himself if she balked, Kate complied and hated herself for sacrificing her personal taste and good judgment. She cringed when she saw how "much older and plainer" she looked with her hair pulled straight back. Yet instead of heeding this warning, she focused on planning the wedding and packed her bags.[5]

Married life was a predictable series of letdowns for Kate Stevens Bingham. The market Ed saw for his sectional horseshoes never materialized, and after two years, he scrapped his scheme and took her back to his rustic estate on the high eastern edge of Portland. Again, the reality failed to live up to Ed's promises. Kate had pictured their home as a quaint, shaded dwelling tucked into the crook of a rolling hillside, its sloping roof sparkling in the dew and looking especially lovely at dusk. But it was the "everlasting rains," not the dew, that beat down on the house, creating an almost impassable moat of mud between her and the city. Although, as he said, he had plenty of land and plans for a shed and a horse and buggy, these last two were yet to be purchased, and that would not happen until the stumps were cleared and a decent road could be opened. He had talked the railroad into putting a station nearby on their side of the river, but this was more beneficial to him than to her. His office in town, where he went into practicing law with his brother Todd, was an easy commute, but for her to go out to the church or the nicer neighborhoods to make calls and then come back to a steep incline up to her house was "quite exhausting." There was also the irritation of having to pass through the Fulton Park district, the bevy of little homes at the foot of Ed's property. It looked frightfully "common and low" to Kate. These families were decent, she wrote in her journal, but they were all "second class or even third class," a fact she confirmed by dropping in on seven of them unannounced.[6]

Kate admitted the walk up the hill would have been a lot easier had the home she came back to been happier. But Ed had let his mother move in and allowed her to challenge his wife's place as mistress. By the time the friction convinced him to send his mother to live with one of his siblings, Ed had gone back to his bachelor antics, and Kate rarely saw him at home. If not in his office, he was out hunting or carrying on with his hard-drinking brothers, and when she did catch a glimpse of him, he was staggering in after dark, sullen and bleary eyed, or asleep in his chair the following morning. To these disappointments, Kate's journal added the joyless and unproductive relations that deadened her "earthy" desire and cheated her hope of becoming a mother. As the prospects of having a family dwindled, she suffered from rounds of depression that came on each month when she started to bleed. Ed blamed her for using her monthly "horrors" to get her own way or to punish him. She was hurt by his callous indifference to her discouragement, and even more, she resented his acting as if he had nothing to do with it. Ed would regret his mistake of failing to make "a companion and confidant of the sensible woman" he chose to abandon, she wrote.[7]

With only the shell of respectable marriage to separate her from her servants, Kate found herself in a level association of struggling womanhood. She had always spoken of drunkenness as a blight that afflicted the lower class, the hired help like Maggie, her cook, whose husband Robert, the gardener, drank up their earnings. By averting her eyes, she had gone on believing her caste was somehow immune. In such cases as Ed's brother Todd, she blamed his drunken sprees on his wife. She was "common" and too "low bred" to inspire "superior qualities." Yet Todd, himself, had come to his sister-in-law about Ed and forced her to see that women of breeding could also have drunkards for husbands. The two distressed wives in Kate's household, one the mistress, the other her servant, would never sit in the parlor together and comfort each other as equals. Yet the outrage and sympathy Kate had reserved for her cook was now for them both. When Maggie, the "best girl" she ever had, came sobbing and begged her to put Robert under a curfew to keep him from drinking in town, Kate nodded knowingly, thinking of Ed at the office. "This is another case of a fine woman bound to a contemptible, utterly selfish and unreliable man," she fumed. "One might as well say it," Kate wrote of these men: "intoxicated."[8]

——————————————————— ∾ ———————————————————

For a while, Kate hoped that Ed's punishing headaches or her wifely bracing would cure him of drinking, but his hangovers taught him nothing at all, and her "sanguine and hopeful nature" amounted "to less than a row of beans." Conceding the folly of wishful thinking and weary of trying to go it alone, Kate turned to the church for whatever support she could find. Having sat in the pews in both Dorchester, Massachusetts, and Portland, Oregon, she knew she could count on an Eliot pulpit to speak against ruinous drink. Thomas and Christopher's preparation for fighting this blight on society had started in boyhood. One of the few times they heard their father break his own rule against preaching reform was when he excoriated the liquor trade. To make certain that Tom would remember that alcohol killed without mercy, William took him to see a man who was in the last throes of delirium tremens. Abby, equally conscientious, was still reminding her boys—when Tom was fifty and Christy was thirty-five—that "the great evil, *drink*," was to blame for "two thirds of the suffering" she and their father had seen.[9]

As pastors, neither son needed his mother's reminders. Their appointment books and correspondence were damning depositions of family crises where alcohol was involved. One day it might be the funeral of an eight-year-old boy, whose weeping mother stood at the grave site alone, her husband having drunk himself into a lifeless heap in town. On another occasion, the minister might be called to the home of a man who had been on a binge for ten days, leaving his wife "almost crazed with grief and worry." Found safe, he was taken to Salem to try the cure at the Keeley Institute only to go back to drinking when he got out. One of the worst was the case of a "man of good intentions but very weak," who time and again had told the pastors he wanted to join the church. He seemed to be breaking his drinking habit to meet the condition they set for him when the tragic word came that he had committed suicide. In Edward Bingham, the Portland pulpit had yet another example of alcohol's power to ruin good men and their families. The senior and associate pastors, who knew Ed as a gifted, progressive lawyer, saw the extent of his problem firsthand when Kate had them over for dinner on separate occasions.[10]

Kate was particularly fond of the senior minister. Mr. Eliot reminded her of her brother, a "high-minded soul," who received the Congressional Medal of Honor in 1863 for helping to capture Fort Huger, Virginia. Hazard Stevens had gone on to serve in the Massachusetts state legislature and later founded the commonwealth's Tariff Reform League. Claiming these two as her "noblest of brothers," Kate liked to think that her minister's words would lift her spirits as Hazard's did when she came to him with her worries. Yet her minister's sermons about the effects of intoxicants were of little help. Apart from his point that her misery had lots of company, his comments did little to ease her pain or embolden her to discuss it.[11]

When Thomas Lamb Eliot stood in the pulpit to tackle the demon drink, he sounded more like a politician or sociologist than a pastor. His was no longer the voice one had heard in 1874, when he joined the Praying Crusade, Portland's first temperance force, which the Methodists organized. He was no longer calling for personal vows of abstinence and appealing to individual will as the best approach to the problem. The emotional public displays the crusade had attracted, as Etta remarked, had made it "hard for quiet minded folk to do...what they would." Her husband had distanced himself from their mode of attack and shifted his confidence to systemic solutions through legal compulsion. While waiting for new laws to wipe out the trade, he used his pulpit to press for enforcement of ordinances that prohibited selling liquor in unlicensed bars. In effect, he preached an extravagance of statistics and expert opinions supporting the "High License" laws but nothing that salved the aching hearts of women in Kate's situation.[12]

Kate was present at church on several occasions when Eliot spoke of her husband by name, acknowledging his assistance in drafting anti-liquor bills, and she left the services feeling "doubly grateful." It boosted her standing among the church members and blunted the stabbing embarrassment of the night the Eliots came to dinner and Ed failed to make an appearance. The brotherly warmth of Eliot's comments, Kate thought, was more than her husband deserved, given his chilly indifference to churches and organized systems of faith. Although Ed supposed he was "more of a Unitarian than anything else," he distrusted all clergy and made no exceptions for this one. He warned Kate that any discussion of intimate problems with the minister's family was sure to do "more harm than good." Her "continual harping" about his drinking had already done enough damage, he said, and he told the pastor directly not to interrogate him about personal habits. One had to be careful "with such religious people."[13]

The man in the preacher's remarks at church was not the one Kate Bingham knew. He was not the rude and abusive husband and addict, nor was he the truant host of whom Thomas Eliot wondered "how low [he] had slipped" when he could not "brace up" for his guests. The man the preacher evoked was the other Ed Bingham, the commendable public servant and comrade-in-arms in his war against drink. This Ed was the brilliant lawyer whose efforts were wresting control from political bosses and putting an end to the influence that kept the vices in business; the fellow whose law office came to be a favorite stop on the minister's rounds and whose legislation he championed from the pulpit. Rather than dwell on the irony that his comrade's personal weakness just happened to be the target of their crusade, the preacher seemed satisfied Ed Bingham's work for the cause would be his redemption. As for Kate, when left to reflect on her minister's artful improvement of Ed, she wished he would now produce a real spouse who at least could be civil and "get up a little earlier in the morning."[14]

&

The satisfactions of milling among the crowd before and after the sermons were less elusive but not necessarily simpler for Kate or predictable. The pleasant faces of people she knew, all "apparently glad" to see her, gave her a boost for the rest of the day, and the small talk took her mind off her troubles. The concern of a casual friend one Sunday in 1889, moreover, lifted her idea of friendship to a new level quite unexpectedly. Rosa Frazar Burrell, who, like Kate, was one of the church's original members, had never shown any desire to move past the usual pleasantries until this particular morning when they sat together in Rosa's pew. Although she could not think of anything in particular to have set her off, just as the opening anthem began, Kate started to weep uncontrollably. Rosa grabbed her hand and held it tightly until the service was over and then insisted on taking Kate home with her so they could talk. Kate was amazed by Rosa's grasp of her problem until she met Mr. Burrell, who spoke even less than Ed and did not seem as bright. "Of course," Kate wrote in her journal, he had "the *sportula*, that is, the money," and money worked wonders, as witnessed this fossilized union. Lamentably, wealth was also the glue that stabilized friendships with people of means, and Kate came up short when she calculated the cost and tallied her assets.[15]

Twenty-five years before, when faced with the choice of yielding to Ed's demands or having him break their engagement, Kate had reluctantly transferred her personal savings to his account and then seen him drain it, build up his debts, and begin putting them in her name. Most recently, he had bullied her into signing a blank application to borrow another $10,000 to finance a larger house. Her brother, Hazard, himself an attorney, stepped in to protect her inheritance, but the rest of her dowry was gone. With Ed writing legislation *pro bono* instead of working for clients who paid, the shortfall was bigger each time she took stock of how the aristocrats lived. "Handsomely attired in [their] evening costumes," Kate itemized, the Eliot daughters presided at a punch bowl and silver service that had to be priceless heirlooms and made her own silver look "very shabby," indeed.[16]

It was flattering to have people come up and speak to her because of Ed's work, but compliments would not buy the piano she wanted, or settle her outstanding bills at the grocer's, or pay for hors d'oeuvres for her guests. Even after her husband had won the Terwiliger case, a highly publicized contest that brought him a well-deserved fee and renewed respect in professional circles, the Binghams were so strapped for money in 1896, that Kate had to let her domestics go and take on the housework herself. This was the moment it dawned on her that when women lost the financial support of the men to whom they were bound, they were no longer members of any class but outsiders. Refugees. She would have to bear up, she decided after spoiling an otherwise lovely evening by fretting about her bargain seat at a concert. "There I was," she berated herself, "privileged to hear such exquisite music, yet I was not happy." She hoped she would use this trial to atone and become a better person. "We all, I believe, need trouble to discipline us."[17]

But the real and imagined insults to which Kate's embarrassment left her susceptible were impediments, rather than stimulants, to achieving Christian humility. When she went back to dig up some plants by the house where she and Ed had first lived, the new owner's wife made her feel like a beggar and thief and sent her away empty-handed. Even Rosa Burrell appeared to be treating Kate shabbily. Invited to lunch, she was mortified to arrive just as Rosa was leaving, having forgotten and on her way to a funeral. Kate was convinced that money had caused the amnesia and ruined their friendship. "I had done nothing rude," she told herself. It was Mrs. Burrell, which just went to show how "wealth and position" caused people "to lose their heads."[18]

Nor was Kate able to see how she was a better person for having been wronged. If losing her standing among the elite had engendered a new kind of boldness in her, the pleasure she got from being perverse was brief, and she was not proud of it. When a woman she knew came to church with her husband reeking of alcohol, Kate cornered her after the service and "half unconsciously" brought up intemperance. Her victim blanched and changed the subject, and Kate went home and recorded her triumph before its spitefulness made her ashamed. Kate became warier, too, convinced that everyone had a false front and none could be trusted. For a while, this included the minister's wife, who extended herself as an ally as soon as Ed Bingham's addiction became apparent and grist for the gossip mill. Etta went out of her way to include Kate in luncheons, private receptions, and teas. When she saw her alone at concerts, she asked her to sit with her and the pastor. Kate was grateful. She liked being seen with them. She fully enjoyed the Eliot daughters and had to concede that their mother deserved her reputation for being "bright and interesting." Yet Kate was put off by the way Etta smiled and feigned distraction to dodge probing questions. It was "tiresome," "artificial," and "unsatisfactory," she complained, forgetting that she was as guarded and cagey herself.[19]

The upcoming marriage of Dr. John Bingham gave Etta a wedge to lift Kate's reserve: Did she think, she asked frankly, Kate's brother-in-law would stop drinking to please his new wife? Kate, who had wondered about it herself, blurted out, "it was hard to predict." Ed's brother was clearly a man of "strong vices" as well as strong virtues, and his behavior could go either way. As soon as she said it, Kate caught herself, but there was no taking it back. The floodgate was open, more words tumbled out, and Kate only hoped that the minister's wife would not be shocked by her secrets.[20]

--------------------------------- ☙ ---------------------------------

Had Etta been able to speak as freely, she could have put Kate's fears to rest. She had seen so many families ruined by drink, that as she confided to Tom, her constant frustration in Temperance reform was "the penalty of 'knowing too much.'" She could also have owned up to knowing the way it felt to be poor in a culture of plenty. Despite their seeming prosperity, there was never a time in Etta's marriage when money had not been a worry. In the early years, Tom had followed his father's example of leeching the household coffers to pay for his benevolent work. Miss Dix was irate and scolded him for subjecting his wife to the same "crowding cares" his father had forced on his mother. If charity—or "rather say *justice*"—were to begin at home, as it should, a man with a conscience would "*not* ignore his own *Tribe*." But the lectures in Etta's behalf had no effect.[21]

By their tenth anniversary in Portland, the minister's family had been quite comfortably fixed, thanks in part to the generosity of his father's parishioner Persis Smith. By 1880, this wealthy aunt of Sally Smith Flagg had put a total of $1,500 into a fund for Etta's personal use while the children were growing. Tom had also made shrewd acquisitions in real estate in Multnomah and Clatsop counties as well as in Portland itself. The timely sale of a choice parcel on the Willamette River before the depression provided another buffer against the hard times after land values plummeted. But while Tom felt cushioned enough in the 1890s to think of retiring, Etta, who had no idea how much padding there was, still worried incessantly. In fact, even though they had maids and a cook and a stately home in the best part of town, her scrimping was rooting itself in the tribal memory. Forty years later, her children's children—who heard the story of how Etta made little coats for the boys out of Tom's ragged suits—could not understand how their grandparents managed to send them checks on their birthdays.[22]

The letters she quietly left on his desk presenting her case for needing a budget were testaments to Tom's resistance and Etta's desperation. Had he only been willing to listen and put himself in her position, she pleaded, he would have agreed she deserved the same gears that gave him his sense of control. If he were to tell her they needed to move to a smaller house, "give up entertaining, and carriage hiring, and keep but one servant, and dress the family and set the table on so much a month," she would do it, and all with good humor. It was not in her nature to be ostentatious. She did not need lace curtains and portieres. All she wanted was peace of mind and a basis for making the best use of money and time. Ought she to give "so much brains and strength" to something as mindless as "patching and piecing" when she might be doing more good for the church and the children by reading and writing? Etta also wanted allowances for the girls to teach them to manage their money and learn to be more self-sufficient than their mother. The record does not tell us when, if ever, Etta got her concessions from Tom, but it does show that she was still waiting as late as 1892 and understood Kate's situation all too well.[23]

Familiar, too, were the pangs of conscience that Kate had started to feel when she got to thinking about her sense of entitlement. Etta knew that for all her own boasting about cheerful sacrifice and simplicity, she fully enjoyed and expected to have the advantages of the social elite. The economic depression that came in 1893 made this shameful inconsistency painfully evident. Although, from what she could get out of Tom, his side of the family was spared the worst, the penury to which her younger brother Charles Mack was reduced was proof that her battle with class pride had only begun. Charles was a hopeless dreamer, a country doctor who one day decided his calling was in the ministry. Ignoring his sisters' warnings that he would have trouble feeding his family, he took to preaching, borrowed until he had used up the last of his credit, then turned to his siblings to bail him out and left his disgrace at their doorsteps. However she looked at it, Etta told Tom, she was shamed by the situation. She was angry at Charles for embarrassing her and encumbering her with his costly ideals, and she was ashamed of being so shallow and selfish that she would react in this way. When she thought about "*all* the aching hearts and wounded prides the world over, struggling to 'keep up appearances,'" she felt "wicked in owning anything beyond the barest necessities."[24]

In times like these, the minister's wife was blessed to have in a favorite cousin a soul mate with whom she could put her remorse in perspective. Although they had gone in different directions, she and Elizabeth Robins were both introspective, compassionate women with similar bents toward apostasy. The younger and bolder cousin Bessie had scandalized the family by spurning not only their orthodox faith but also their social ambitions for her. At twenty, she left her home in Ohio to forge a career on the stage, first on the East Coast and then overseas, and finally putting down roots in England. She had made a comfortable living by publishing thinly veiled autobiography that explained how she had become a champion of the working class and women. When fictionalized in *The Open Question* in 1898, the story of Bessie's decision to leave her elders' "dignified guardianship" and their condemnation of her for claiming a public voice that brought her an income resonated with Etta's struggling dreams.[25]

As someone who had democratic ideals but enjoyed the advantages of her class, Bessie was also able to mirror the conflict that tormented Etta and to offer an explanation, if not an excuse. She confessed that despite the praise she received for her advocacy for the working class, she felt she had done very little to better their lot. Living on her own terms, as she did, with a personal secretary and maid in a beautiful old house in Surrey "surrounded by gracious ways," it was hard for her to remember those others who held the short straws in life's lottery. "Sympathy does much, but it simply doesn't generate the force that real first-hand knowledge does," she agreed when Etta confessed to a lack of commitment. Still hearing the hard-core reformers' taunts accusing her of "half-heartedness," she assured her cousin in Portland that she was too quick to applaud her small effort abroad. Without direct knowledge "goading them on," none of the "comfortable people" like them had ever accomplished enough to narrow the gulf between the haves and have-nots. If they had, "the Aegean stables of the world" would have long since been cleaned.[26]

———————————————————— ⚭ ————————————————————

Not the sort to enter such murky depths of self-scrutiny, Kate Bingham looked instead to the women's associations at church to improve her self-esteem. Several gradual steps toward modernization had transformed the Ladies' Sewing Society into the Unitarian Women's Alliance, and by the early 1890s, the group was nudging its purpose forward to bring it in line with national trends. They supplemented their fund-raising mission with cultural programs intended to stimulate personal growth without disturbing their genteel values. Desperately lonely during the dreary winter of 1890, Kate turned in her $20 for dues on a Wednesday afternoon, and within a week, she had invitations to several teas and a concert. Kate's investment also paid off with a share of the entrepreneurial power and male respect that the group enjoyed as an earning force in the church. Since the days when the founders relied on their sewing to fill the coffers, the group had become more ingenious in getting their clients to part with their wealth. Their scrapbooks bulged with the remnants of "dime socials," dances, children's fairs, theme night tableaux, costume parties, doll carnivals, flower sales, and full-scale bazaars.[27]

The church was itself a showcase of what their collective enterprise had produced. Besides a quality pipe organ valued at $2,400, the women had paid for the Sunday school's library books and piano, the services of the vocal quartet that

FIGURE 4.1. The Church of Our Father Ladies' Sewing Society, 1887. Etta Eliot at the center, third row from the top. Rosa Burrell, in the same row, is next to the last on the right. Courtesy of the First Unitarian Church, Portland, Ore.

propped up the volunteer choir, and the maintenance of the building and grounds. Most significantly, if less visible, the group had been called upon more than once to rescue the church when it found itself in arrears and unable to pay the minister. As part of this force, Kate saw her energy count for something in dollars and cents without being tainted by work unbecoming a lady.[28]

The Alliance also advanced Kate's dream of achieving the personal earning power she envied in Mrs. Eliot—whom she heard was paid something for each published story or poem—and in the Eliots' oldest girl, Dorothea, who gave singing lessons for pocket money. Kate wished that she had been taught to do something that she could convert into cash for herself, and such training seemed to begin when she was elected recording secretary. This vote of confidence from no fewer than sixty of her peers, and the chance to write and deliver reports and original papers at meetings emboldened Kate to think bigger about her potential as author and lecturer. Her minister was encouraging, too. Mr. Eliot told her he thought she had "a vocation" in what she was doing, promised that he would critique any manuscript she might want to present, and urged her to take her portfolio out on the road. This support was a deeply affecting contrast to Ed's derisive remarks. He said she was wasting her time with writing and being a fool to call it her "work."[29]

Beyond its promise of self-reliance, Kate saw in the lecture circuit her chance to "associate intimately" with the cultural elite. Such were her thoughts when she heard Harvard's president, Dr. Charles Eliot, give "a delightful lecture" on education before the Women's Alliance. Despite a distracting, purplish birthmark that covered half of his face, he was "a very scholarly, high bred looking man" and a feast for Kate's social ambitions. So was Miss Susan Hale of Boston, also worth booking despite the poor turnout in Portland. Miss Hale's presentation, a reading from Samuel Richardson's *History of Sir Charles Grandison*, was "very pleasant and amusing." and of course, Kate noted expansively, Miss Hale was the sister of Edward Everett Hale, the Unitarian minister, and the daughter of newspaper editor Nathan Hale, who was named for his uncle, a war hero during America's Revolution. Miss Hale was thoroughly "upper class socially and intellectually," and this, by itself, had made her visit worthwhile.[30]

The Alliance's programs gave Kate the perspectives from which to assess her place in the world. Along with the Susan Hales, who heightened her image of what she might yet have become, there were lectures about the conditions for women in India and the Philippines, which, according to Mr. Eliot's associate pastor, Earl Morse Wilbur, were "little better than slavery." These descriptions of how much worse her lot might have been in some backward society improved Kate's view of her own situation. Most compelling, however, were various books that were taken up by her reading group, texts that reflected her life with an accuracy found neither in lectures nor sermons. One of them, Benjamin Franklin's *Autobiography*, mirrored her story so well that her narrative and the author's merged as she read it. "He was away from his wife and family for many years...twenty, I think," Kate fumed as she added Franklin's offense to her list as another black mark against Ed. "It made me feel sad and I do not respect nor like Franklin so well for staying away." His wife was still waiting and "wishing for him" when she finally died, and Ed [*sic*] was making a big "mistake in going away so frequently." Again, when they read Henrik Ibsen's *A Doll's House*, Kate was the tragic Nora, a loving and talented wife with a selfish and utterly ungrateful spouse. The lessons were striking: Wives were not dolls and should be prepared to support themselves and to face life's hard realities.[31]

If these insights struck Ed as subversive, he was lucky that Kate's alliance shrank from the live, controversial topics explored by the secular women's clubs. As it was, the churchwomen voted to stick to their speakers on travel, the fine arts, and history. They left the discussions of poverty, labor unions, and legal reforms to the church's mixed but largely male William Eliot Society. The likelier soil for seeding rebellion was outside the church altogether, where several Alliance women helped to create the Portland Women's Club. Eager to broaden her social contacts, Kate was guardedly curious. "The trouble with clubs," she warned herself, was that they were "apt to be dominated by a few old bosses" and "composed of widows, old maids and disgruntled married women." Soon relieved of her fears, she signed their book. She was happy, she wrote, to have a club with a larger range of offerings, including political subjects, so long as she had the freedom to choose what she wanted. More telling, however, she joined the resistance against the Equal Suffrage Society when its militants wormed their way into the group and started to "spoil" it for everyone else. Their presence, Kate wrote, created factions and weakened the solidarity, a unity worth defending in a culture where female relationships seemed hard to sustain one-on-one.[32]

A spirit of sisterhood based on kindred priorities was the adhesive that sealed Kate's loyalty to the Women's Alliance in Portland. In 1904, when she left the city for good, her bond with the group was so strong she never stopped paying her membership dues. For a number of years she also contrived to keep her hand in her old role as scribe by serving as Portland's delegate to the National Unitarian Women's Alliance's yearly conventions in Boston. With the ministers also meeting that week, Kate was able to give her sisters out west some lively accounts of the "interesting personages." She had an eye for the little details the pastor left out when he gave his reports, and her write-ups were entertaining, if superficial. One year, for example, she treated them to a description of "Miss Ellen Emerson," who was something of a museum piece in her old age. Kate had not actually spoken to her, but this daughter of Ralph Waldo Emerson was "robed in a quakerish style of dress" that might have been fashionable at one time but was "strangely unlike the showy gowns worn by both high and low" in the twentieth century.[33]

FIGURE 4.2. Kate Stevens Bingham, ca. 1913, newly remarried to James H. S. Bates.
Courtesy of the Washington State Historical Society.

Kate's friendship with Etta was no more successful in helping Kate to take
charge of her destiny than the Women's Alliance was in changing her basic values.
It took a string of events beyond Kate's control to bring her the independence the
minister's wife had hoped she would gain on her own. On October 22, 1901, *The*

Oregonian's morning edition announced to the world the disgrace Kate had tried to conceal: "In a Fit of Dizziness," Portland attorney Edward W. Bingham had taken a fall from his second-floor office window. He escaped with no serious injury but was shaken and told Kate contritely that she would be better off without him until he got straightened out. By December, she was living in town with the Eliots and making arrangements to get back east to her relatives before Christmas. The minister handled the last-minute business of buying the ticket and checking the luggage, and Etta provided the words of assurance that steadied Kate as she boarded the train in a tearful farewell to her friends.[34]

Kate was away for more than a year, and when Etta next saw her when both were in Boston in January of 1903, the minister's wife hardly recognized her. "She looks twenty, certainly ten years younger than when she left Portland," Etta wrote Tom, "and I think she must weigh from ten to twenty pounds more. She looks really plump and young and pretty." Yet underneath, Kate was no different. Unsettled without a domestic partner and interesting companions, she was back to romanticizing her feelings for Ed and her wifely duty. The news that his health had deteriorated dramatically since her departure was all it took to convince her to go back to Portland and tend to his needs. "Alas, she *loves* the wretch and feels she must go to him and help him make one more try for freedom," a weary Etta wrote Tom. "Well, one can only go so far in advising, and people must lead their own lives." There were limits to what one could do for another by talking.[35]

5

The Voice Coach

Truth is the only safe ground to stand upon.
—Elizabeth Cady Stanton, speaking before the United States
Congress Committee of the Judiciary, 18 January 1892.

Had it been up to Etta, her second girl would have been Abby Eliot's
namesake, but Tom had suggested the honor go to their benefactor
Miss Dix instead. His mother agreed, never doubting that there would
be plenty of Abigails coming along and certain the children would learn
soon enough there was more to a legacy than a name. And so it was
with the child who arrived on Valentine's Day 1871. Dorothea Dix
Eliot —also called Dorothy, Dora, and Dodie—soon found that she
shared much more with the woman who pulled herself out of contention. Taking her cue from the grown-ups' comments about their similar
features—their prominent chins, their wide arched brows, and their
high rounded cheeks—the little girl sat in her grandmother's lap and
studied her face to confirm her endowment. Still gathering evidence
thirty years later, the recent bride and the elderly widow would line up
their hands and howl when they found that their fingers and nails were
identical. More sobering, they would also discover themselves in each
other's stories.[1]

Dodie was no less her mother's daughter for being her
grandmother's legacy. She had Etta's strong will, churning conscience,
and inborn respect for language and candor. Even if breaching the Eliot
rule of silence worked to her "detriment," she promised herself she would

TABLE 4. **Second Generation of Eliots on the West Coast**

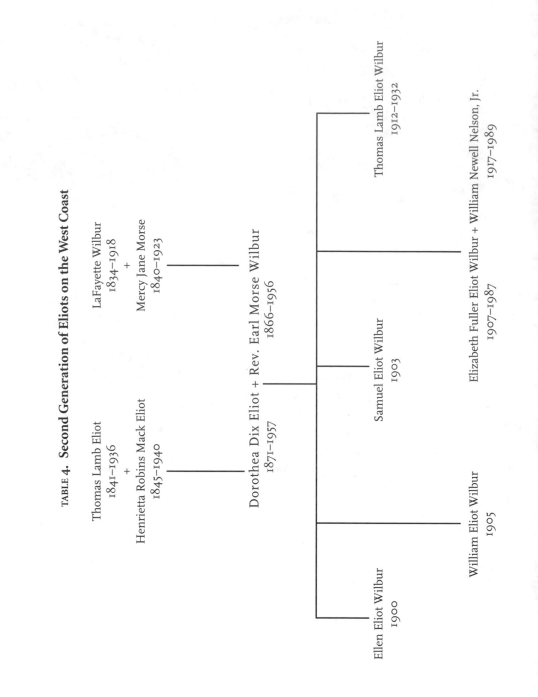

Thomas Lamb Eliot
1841–1936
+
Henrietta Robins Mack Eliot
1845–1940

LaFayette Wilbur
1834–1918
+
Mercy Jane Morse
1840–1923

Dorothea Dix Eliot + Rev. Earl Morse Wilbur
1871–1957   1866–1956

Ellen Eliot Wilbur
1900

William Eliot Wilbur
1905

Samuel Eliot Wilbur
1903

Elizabeth Fuller Eliot Wilbur + William Newell Nelson, Jr.
1907–1987   1917–1989

Thomas Lamb Eliot Wilbur
1912–1932

speak the truth and "be natural...at whatever cost." Etta encouraged these attributes as well as her daughter's good mind, striking a grudging compromise with the
child-rearing arbiter Edward H. Clarke. Clarke's *Sex in Education* (1874) had convinced American parents that rigorous study could make their daughters infertile
or damage their offspring. Etta was no fan of Clarke's. She found his view of the
female anatomy suspect and demeaning. But he was persuasive, and just to be safe,
she kept all her girls in the Portland schools until they had turned sixteen. Then she
let them go east to St. Louis, as she did their brothers at earlier ages, to live with their
grandmother Eliot while attending Mary Institute at their grandfather's university.
With their constitutions still settling, she limited them to "a half-allowance" of
classes, a prudent allotment that nourished their love of learning without encouraging any disruptive ambition.[2]

Dodie continued her education after returning to Portland by sending away for
workbooks available from the Home Study Society and taking their courses in
music history, political science, and Renaissance art. Kate Bingham admired the
young woman's interest in self-improvement, and the picture of her in Kate's diary
as bright, energetic, and versatile was consistent with what Etta told Dodie's grandmother Mack in the later 1880s. Having "thrown herself heart and soul" into "trying
to help her father," Dodie was giving some half-days each week to the Flower
Mission and Mission School, holding an office in the association for younger adults
in the church, serving as Sunday school pianist, performing as soloist in the choir,
and earning part of the fees for her music lessons—in voice, guitar, and piano—by
teaching beginning vocalists. There was also an entourage of persistent young men
to take her to operas and concerts. Etta had feared she would "topple" from all the
attention and was glad she could say that at nineteen the girl still seemed to be
"unsusceptible." The test of how long that would last was just months away.[3]

In the autumn of 1890, a new face appeared in the parish. Twenty-four-year-
old Earl Morse Wilbur, fresh from Harvard Divinity School where he and Will had
been friends, had come to assist Dodie's father. His photograph showed a clean-
shaven young fellow of middle height, with deep-set gray eyes and curly brown hair.
Will explained that he had been born in Vermont and came from a long line of
farmers, strong Scotch-Irish stock who followed the Presbyterian mandates of Bible
reading, good citizenship, frugality, and hard work. Earl's father had been allowed
to break out of the mold and become the town's lawyer. He wanted his boys to have
the same options and sent them on to the state university after they turned sixteen.
It was there that the oldest, Earl, decided that being a history teacher would give
him "the greatest influence for good."[4]

To that end, he went on to Harvard, entering through the divinity school, the
tuition being substantially less than it was in the regular college. When the history
courses he wanted did not materialize, he cut his losses by taking advantage of what

FIGURE 5.1. Dorothea "Dodie" Dix Eliot, ca. 1897. Courtesy of Christopher Rhodes Eliot III.

FIGURE 5.2. Earl Morse Wilbur, ca. 1890. Courtesy of the First Unitarian Church, Portland, Ore.

was still available. Since he had been floating away from his orthodox moorings for quite some time, he decided this might be the chance for him to get "straightened out" theologically. When he left, he would still be prepared to teach from a pulpit if not in a classroom. By the end of his studies, however, his faith had been shorn of too many miracles to get past the Congregational board of examiners. They were not in the business of licensing heretics, they informed him contemptuously, and so he decided to take Will's advice and make his home with the Unitarians.[5]

If it sounded as if he had "drifted into the ministry" almost by accident, as he feared it would when he finished his story, the Eliots were convinced that God had been stirring the current that brought them this "flat-footed Anti-trinitarian," Earl Morse Wilbur. They marveled at his efficiency in revitalizing the Sunday school and his industry in riding his bicycle out to the district's farthest reaches to bring back the dropouts and canvass the parish to put together a yearbook. His sincerity in whatever he did was endearing. Even among the old-timers, who would always consider the senior man their real minister and preferred his old-fashioned homilies to the young fellow's scholarly "lectures," Earl's boyish trust and goodness and genuine interest in others' problems opened their hearts as he had never dreamed possible. The secrets, some unremarkable, some "as deeply interesting as a romance," made him realize, he told his parents, how privileged parish ministers were to be trusted with such revelations.[6]

After seeing his dedication and talent, the older man was ready to hand his associate most of the work. Although he was in his early fifties, Thomas Eliot felt a lot older. He lacked the endurance to draw any benefit from his recuperative leaves. He could still preach "a very fine sermon," Kate Bingham observed after one of his furloughs, but it was apparent that he was "a very sick man, one completely broken down." This left the assistant to pick up the slack and forgo any lengthy vacations. There was a real danger the church would go under unless he were there, people said. Earl had two unusually good informants: his younger brother, Ralph Wilbur, who had joined him in Portland to practice law, and Ralph's wife, Alice Heustis Wilbur, a native Bostonian. Two of the most active members at church, the couple gave Earl full accounts of the outcome when Mr. Eliot had to handle the services on his own. One Sunday when Earl was away, "Dr. Eliot preached to the children 15 minutes, stretched out the notices to a great length, and had not fairly gotten into his sermon when he discovered that it was time to stop—which he did abruptly." No one had "any idea of what he was driving at."[7]

The situation was aggravated by the shifting of titles and boundaries when Eliot asked that the junior man be made pastor and he be named pastor emeritus. Dr. Eliot said he would still do a part of the preaching and help with the services, but as Earl soon complained to his parents, he invariably "proved a 'broken reed' " when his assistance was needed. One Sunday morning the older man actually waited until the processional hymn to say, as they were approaching the platform, that with his partner's "permission," he would sit in the pews, as it had been a hard week. Earl had wanted to scream that his own week had been a lot harder, what with having to do the entire services, morning and evening, which meant two fresh sermons, and teaching a Bible class, leading the weekly teachers' meetings, and all the routine miscellaneous duties expected of him. Instead, he said nothing. He tried to remember that "Dr. Eliot's presence as one of the ministers" was "both an advantage and a disadvantage."[8]

—————————————————— ✑ ——————————————————

If doing the work of two men was the penalty, knowing the Eliots was the reward. Earl's friendship with Will automatically gave him a niche in the Eliot household. Earl was always at dinner when Will was around, and the rest of the time, he took his place at the table at least once a week. Etta remarked on how well he fit in. He did not "spoil the 'home-y-ness' of things," as some people did, and she could see why Will regarded him as a brother. Earl felt the same way about the family and would have been lost without Will. When a young man was leading a liberal church in Trinitarian country, he needed a peer who shared not just his beliefs but his generational outlook. Dr. Eliot, Earl explained to his parents, was really too old to sympathize.[9]

As the Eliots were becoming Earl's "pattern by which to judge all other families," Dodie, the first of the daughters he met, was becoming his template for choosing a wife. He was charmed by her wit and candor, her beautiful voice, and the energy she put into helping her parents. Her father warned his associate that "she would be a hard fish to land" but gave his approval when Earl said he wanted to give it a try anyway. Earl delivered his first declaration of love in September 1893, and when Will got engaged to his college friend Minna Sessinghaus several months later, Earl was still years away from making his catch. Some ambitions were "not entirely within one's control," he reminded his mother, who asked him when he would follow Will Eliot's lead. They would all have to wait for the right time, he said. One could hardly "take a wife as one would buy a farm or select a horse." Earl's patience paid off. By 1894, he and Dodie were going to parties and plays together, and there was an active exchange of flowers and chocolates and thank-you cards. Dodie smiled when her father observed that his colleague displayed the ripe wisdom and gravity of a much older man. Yet it was Earl's tender sincerity and eternally youthful innocence that eventually bent Dodie Eliot' heart to his line.[10]

The summer of 1897, when she agreed to the marriage, was Dodie's awakening to Earl's fervor for planning ahead, a passion rivaled only by his love of rummaging through the past. He had his list of wedding guests ready before their engagement was publicized, and he started producing the bridal bouquet six months before the event. He dug the bulbs, put them on ice, and timed it so they would flower on cue. Dodie was touched and as much in awe of his foresight as she was impressed by his research. Yet she was also uneasy about its effect on his grasp of the present and his long-term judgment, qualms that soon proved to be justified. Earl had insisted upon arranging a twelve-month honeymoon tour of Europe; and while almost every detail worked out exactly as he had planned, down to the cost, which came to within a dollar or two of his estimate, there was one crucial miscalculation. Earl had recently written a history of the Portland church's first twenty-five years and noticed that when on at least one occasion the senior pastor had tried to resign, the board had refused and pressed him to take a leave of absence instead. Blindsided by his trust in history's penchant for repetition, Earl failed to consider how different things were in 1898. With the church in such dire financial distress that his salary had already been cut, anyone else would have known the trustees would let him walk out when he opened the door. Yet naively, he offered his resignation, and it was accepted without discussion.[11]

The finality of it did not sink in until Dodie and Earl heard from Alice and Ralph that the church was surviving without them. Dodie's father had offered to fill the pulpit so long as the church board retired its debts and found a replacement quickly. A small corps of lay readers, Ralph among them, was helping him with the services, and Alice said they were seating the largest congregations that she could remember since coming to Portland in 1894. The Women's Auxiliary also continued to cover itself in glory—its Christmas bazaar had put the Episcopalian ladies to shame—and the trustees, keeping their part of the bargain, had put out a call for a preacher.[12]

Alice and Ralph were taken aback by the newlyweds' shock and dismay that the search committee had not been in touch with Earl. Ralph, who had never approved of so long a vacation, had to explain to his brother that when a grown man gave no hint that he was ready to get back to work, he could not expect to be seen as a serious candidate. The world did not turn at his pleasure, and if he were smart, Ralph jabbed his pen, he would telegram Portland to say he was on his way home. But Earl was convinced they would gain more from traveling, and Dodie, impressed by his passion, agreed. As a consequence, while they were seeing majestic cathedrals and ancient ruins, the church in Portland called somebody else to be minister.[13]

William Lord had been in the ministry twenty years before going to Portland, and he and his wife made a promising first impression. Kate Bingham, who gave the welcoming speech when they came to the Women's Alliance found him "bright," "cultivated," "well read," and "up to date." After the pews had been full to capacity every Sunday for several weeks, Kate's sense was that everyone in the church was "highly pleased with him." Alice Wilbur allowed that Mr. Lord's style in the pulpit was "a little too lively." She found herself jumping whenever his fist came down on the cushion for emphasis. Yet she also confirmed that the Lords were both charming and making friends right and left.[14]

The only position available by the time the honeymooners returned at the end of August 1899 and Earl starting looking in earnest was with the Independent Congregational Church in Meadville, Pennsylvania, a small academic community in the northwestern tip of the state. The town was home to Allegheny College and the divinity school that had served Liberal Christians since 1844. Despite the

pittance they offered as salary and a history of tension between the church and the
seminary, the situation appealed to the scholar in Earl. It would give him a chance
to teach a few courses as well as tend the parish and preach. Dodie dismissed this as
nonsense. They were offering him a booby prize, and she would not take it grace-
fully. She refused to go when the people invited them out to get acquainted; if they
wanted to see what she looked like, Earl would have to show them her photograph!
But in the end, since Meadville was all they had and Dodie worried that Earl might
begin to have second thoughts and leave them with nothing, she yielded and
promised to be "contented with *anything*."[15]

Earl accepted the call without hesitation and never had any regrets. In a parish
as badly neglected as Meadville's, any small change made a difference, and Earl saw
attractive opportunities everywhere. By going through dusty membership lists, he
tracked down the absentees and coaxed enough of them back to the church that
people remarked on the Sunday crowds. With 125 in the mornings and 75 in the
evenings, the Sunday school was reconstituted and Confirmation classes revived.
The minister cleared out a space for a lending library in the parsonage, and by his
second year had gotten his foot through the door of the seminary. Giving instruction
in German and doing critiques for the students in "sermonizing" added to the
variety and stimulation he found at the church. In sum, even after making "deduc-
tions" for all his "natural optimism," he felt that his work in Meadville was going
"most excellently."[16]

Dodie's dissatisfaction was also predictable. The Meadville she saw was a
cultural desert where men could get by and feel they were thriving in a little oasis of
learning while women withered for lack of purpose and stimulating companionship. Dodie wondered how many of Meadville's matrons were driven to easier
deaths than this after Earl learned that one of the faculty wives had locked herself
in a closet and slashed her arms while her husband was working at school. The
wounds had been superficial, but her mental prognosis was poor, as Dodie could
well understand considering that the professor was keeping it secret. The poor
woman obviously had no one to talk to.[17]

Meanwhile, the sturdier ladies called at the parsonage "almost too much," con-
firming Dodie's impression that their lives were tragically empty. Mrs. Tyler always
came fully prepared for her overlong stay with a big bag of knitting. Mrs. Laur, who
never reneged on her promise to come again soon, was "a real bore, poor thing,"
with a talent for the most "miserably lugubrious subjects!" A typical midsummer
afternoon that Dodie described for Earl's benefit brought Mrs. Barber-Clarke and
Mrs. Gilman, arm in arm. "Mrs. G. was on one of her brilliant streaks, and O, the
things she said about people!" It was an ordeal for Dodie to stay in character,
"smiling and smiling" and holding her tongue like a pure-minded minister's wife
while "agreeing inwardly to...every word."[18]

Dodie wished these women had saved their breath for the gasping Benevolent Sewing Circle. As Earl described it, this shriveled remnant of female devotion was breathing its last, having reached "the five old ladies stage" before the Wilburs arrived; and Dodie had tried every ploy but failed to avoid being dragged to its funeral. She had pointed out that she hated to sew and pleaded that she had never belonged to a group of older women before. But since nobody else stepped forward, it fell to her to build up the numbers and try to keep the alliance out of the grave. The initial turnout of forty-three was encouraging until it was time to move on from refreshments to business, and then the women were "deader than *dead.*" Dodie practically had to get down on her knees, she wrote Earl, who was out of town at the time, and beg for someone to make a motion. Eventually, somebody would, but then only silence again except for the "stitch, stitch," the ticking clock, and the birds outside. Dodie insisted that Earl come and teach them the basics of parliamentary procedure, but this also touched a raw nerve. When he was not there to smile his approval and lead them delicately by the hand, half or more of the ladies stayed home without sending regrets. Dodie had only to look at her leftover cocoa and cake to see how little a minister's wife was worth in a backward parish.[19]

It was just as well that the ladies preferred to have Earl's instruction in speaking, since Dodie already had all she should handle teaching him how to communicate. As skilled as he was in translating Latin and Greek, he was often unable to get beyond the literal level of everyday discourse. He felt unloved, she pointed out, unless she wrote "lovery stuff" all the time, and in his professional dealings, he missed the vital nuances, the implications and irony. His years in Portland ought to have taught him to look for these subtler elements. One especially messy situation had centered on a Sunday school teacher named Power. This man, a well-regarded physician, had somehow become the object of rumors too vague to refute but disturbing enough to impugn his good reputation. When people dropped out of his class and brought their concerns to the younger pastor, Earl advised Dr. Power to let someone else teach the class and to focus on finding the source of the whispered attacks. Earl was making no charges, he told the man, and there was no reason for Power to leave, but the doctor would have no more part in it. Since the church had no mechanism for holding rumor-mongers responsible, and the pastor thought it appropriate to shift the burden to him, the real victim, the teacher had no way of clearing his name and chose to sever his ties. "By indulging in the safe practice of innuendo," he wrote in withdrawing his membership, this so-called liberal society had shown its "true mettle and cowardice."[20]

Either Earl had forgotten this episode or had never learned anything from it. Dodie had to remind him repeatedly not to let such rumors run wild or to whitewash the facts or edit the truth instead of confronting them honestly. When search committees, for instance, asked his opinion of colleagues he knew were unfit, she had to admonish him not to hold back lest his silence be misunderstood as approval. She realized Earl's motive was not to say anything he would not say to these men face to face, but frankly, she told him, his notion of fairness was selfish. By leaving things out, he was putting his comfort ahead of the church's welfare, and there was no justice in sparing the rogues and incompetents at the people's expense.[21]

When it came to aligning Earl's thought and speech with the social class into which he had married, Dodie had a more personal stake. In the farming community where he grew up, people tended to be their own bosses and got by without hired help. The social gradations that organized Dodie's identity meant little to them, and Earl's way of speaking reflected this. His lack of pretension was to his advantage in Meadville's parish politics, where the locals were rural people themselves and resented the academic elite. But when he actually boasted that he never looked down on the farmers and tradesmen, Dodie feared that their already shaky social position was sure to collapse unless she could get him to see the difference between themselves and the blue-collar class. The most important thing to remember was that working people did not have "much sense"; if they had it, she reasoned, "they wouldn't be working people." With the Wilburs living so close to the bottom financially, it was vital to Dodie that Earl understand what set them apart from the lower ranks.[22]

Dodie had known from her mother and grandmother's scrimping that ministers' wives had to make allowances for their husbands' beneficence, but she never expected that money would be the problem it was when she married Earl. Yet it soon became clear that he not only lacked the Eliots' business acumen but had an almost unqualified faith in other people that made him an irresistable target for shysters. By listening to fast-talking private investors instead of his future wife, he had lost nearly all of his assets by the time he and Dodie got back from Europe. In addition, because of his generous qualities, Earl was forever shortchanging himself. He returned the fees he received for presiding at weddings if the couples were friends or members who contributed to the church. When Ralph spoke for Dodie in saying he saw nothing wrong in accepting the money when offered, Earl objected, insisting there *was* something wrong if one happened to be minister. Was he sworn to poverty? Not by design, but a pastor could not be a capitalist. Apparently teaching divinity students was also a pastoral obligation. For when the school came up short on funds and reneged on its offer to have him teach, Earl was willing to give the courses "for love" and the pleasure of "wider influence."[23]

Dodie took the position that Earl would never achieve that wider influence until he learned to accept the rate of exchange. His willingness to render service without taking credit or asking for favors was shackling them to Meadville unnecessarily. The effort he put into helping his colleagues find posts and helping churches fill pulpits amounted to "Middle States Secretary work." If he would just see it that way, it could serve as a stepping-stone to something better. Earl protested that he was "conscience bound" to stay where he was, at least "long enough to make a permanent impression and bring the church through another well-rounded chapter."[24]

It took almost five years of prodding and pulling before Earl would turn the page, but when he finally wrote the settlement office in Boston in 1904, the timing was providential. President Samuel A. Eliot had been looking for someone to start a school to fill the need for more Unitarian ministers on the West Coast. As there were no other candidates and the man in Meadville seemed qualified, it was only a matter of weeks before the *Christian Register*'s readers were introduced to the Wilburs as "Dean and Deaness" of a new seminary in California's Bay Area, the Pacific Unitarian School for the Ministry. The Rev Wilbur would add to the scope of his previous service by shepherding scholars. His wife, having taken her place in the Eliot "line of apostolic succession," would furnish a welcoming "home life" at the new school.[25]

—————————————————   ✑   —————————————————

The shift from tending an old, yawning church to creating a home for clergy-in-training required another adjustment to Dodie's concepts of work and rewards. While the change of pace and the challenge had been inducements for making the move, the burden of what they had taken on in agreeing to start a school from scratch was only apparent after they got to Oakland. From a distance, the benefactors' proposal had sounded more generous than it was. The annual salary of $3,000 was more than twice what Earl earned in Meadville, but so was the cost of living in California. The promised space for an office and classes in Oakland's Unitarian church had sounded like a comfortable suite with the feel of a prosperous school. In fact, it was two empty rooms stripped bare to the floor. There was not a chair or a desk or a book to encourage its new inhabitants or any prospect of students who might have used them had they been there. More astonishing, still, the trustees had made no provision to hire a faculty. Not only was Earl supposed to handle recruitment and all the administration but he was to build the curriculum and teach the courses himself.[26]

Ralph Wilbur had never heard anything more outrageous unless it was Earl's determination to meet these expectations. Adamant that the undertaking was worth any sacrifice, Earl bravely set out to find the scholars to make the school more than a name. His mailings to contacts across the country brought virtually no response, but he drummed up enough local interest to meet with a dozen prospects and open the school on August 16 with all of four bona fide students. One of these four, a businessman in his early thirties from San Francisco, left after only two months. Another, a Japanese fellow of twenty-four with some credits from Harvard, would delight the recruiter by staying until he had his degree four years later. There was also a twenty-eight-year-old Berkeley undergraduate student who supported himself and his mother on what the zoology teaching assistants were paid. A Berkeley Unitarian matron, fifty-one years of age, who had once gone to Oberlin College and was back in school as a nondegree scholar, rounded out the inaugural class. Strictly speaking, the seminary was never without a student after the first was enrolled in 1904. However, recruitment was always a struggle, and there were years when, with no graduates, the commencements were ghostly occasions.[27]

The seemingly endless ordeal of finding a satisfactory site for the school was a further drain on Earl's stamina. Even before the earthquake and fire of April 1906 damaged its home in the Oakland church, it was clear that the school would never survive unless it were based in Berkeley, where other denominations had schools and easier access to students. A wealthy Unitarian couple, Francis and Sarah Cutler Cutting, had earlier bought a house for this purpose on Bancroft Way. Mrs. Cutting had also given a parcel of land for a campus on Allston Way off Dana Street, directly across from the university's property. Unfortunately, there was only money to hire someone to draw up the plans, and by the time the trustees were prepared to break ground after World War I, the university wanted to build a substantial gymnasium that required the acquisition of the school's land. These chronic problems would take their toll, but at the outset, the sheer excitement of starting a high-stake venture enabled the dean to keep going full-speed for longer than Ralph had thought possible.

Dodie was also invigorated. The growing city's faster pace and pockets of social refinement renewed her enthusiasm for helping the cause. Adapting her mother's "churching" techniques for tracking down members and bringing in pledges, she set out to find the rich liberals and charm them into befriending the school. The thrill of the hunt was intoxicating. In one three-day sweep, she made seventeen calls despite her poor sense of direction, people having changed their addresses, and not being able to rush in and out when asking strangers for money. Visiting always took longer than planned, but this was now one of her work's attractions. Dodie had only to go into San Francisco and feel the press of the crowds—a "poison bath" of sweat and strange smells and foreign accents—to realize how lucky and suited she was for the orbit in which she now moved.[28]

The downside of coming up in the world and cultivating the better class was its magnification of Dodie's financial embarrassment. While having to scrape was not new for the Wilburs, Meadville people had either been so strapped themselves or so frugal on principle that Dodie and Earl had been able to entertain cheaply, get by with made-over clothes, and offer the simplest of wedding gifts. In Berkeley, they had to be more presentable on a budget too small for the upgrade. Their wardrobes looked shabby and unbefitting their new positions, Dodie moaned, and she wanted to die when she saw "a *stunning* Japanese lacquer table" that someone had given a bride whom they had remembered by sending a "wretched check." Dodie wished that her mother had taught her the secret of taking it all in stride, but Etta was even more anxious about spending money. The Eliots' standard of living was just as elegant as the other families whose names appeared in Portland's *Blue Book* each year. Dodie's father could well afford it, too. Unencumbered by debts, he had the means to finance first homes for all his children, including Dodie and Earl. Yet Dodie had seen her mother fretting about the cost of her darning thread.[29]

In 1908, Earl's commitment to keeping the school alive crossed a dangerous line. On hearing that the American Unitarian Association (A.U.A.) needed a new district field secretary, he quietly took the position and started to moonlight. He used his vacations and weekends to travel, lengthened his workdays during the week, and had his annual earnings of $6,800 paid to the school's account. When Ralph found out two years into the scheme, he was livid. How could his brother hold up his head after letting his in-laws pay for his house while he was giving his earnings away and pauperizing his family! There was no excuse, he told Earl, not even if thousands of other clergy convinced themselves they were better people for letting their churches exploit them. Regular men did not volunteer to become indentured servants. But there was no reasoning with a man who saw no other alternative. Earl's own mental strain had to order a halt before he would listen and think of his family. When he began to be "hoodooed with various kinds of neurasthenics," he knew he was on the verge of a nervous collapse and could not go on as he had.[30]

Dodie's rage when she realized why she had been spending vacations and weekends alone all these years abated when Earl went to Boston during the spring of 1910 and wrote her that he had been offered a church that paid its ministers handsomely. "Ye, gods!" she whooped after reading his letter. "I could something like realize my ideals of housekeeping and dressing, and so could you!" As much as she loved the charm and climate of California, she knew she "could be *very* happy in Boston," and with a fat income "to oil the wheels," Dodie was ready to roll. But, again, the time was not right, and Earl pulled the brakes. He had thought it would please her to know that her husband was finally in demand, but he was not ready to leave the school quite yet. There were seven students, all of them "trumps," and he wanted to stay until the fruit of his labor was ready to harvest.[31]

In addition, the school trustees were finally going to hire another full-time faculty member. William S. Morgan of Albany, New York, would be teaching the history of dogma, comparative theology, and the psychology of religion. Morgan's appointment would generate a titular promotion for Earl, bumping him up to President and Professor of Practical Theology. His arrival would also allow Earl to focus more steadily on his New Testament course and his research and lectures in liberal religious history. Just having the freedom to concentrate on this last field of

FIGURE 5.3. The Pacific Unitarian School for the Ministry's faculty, trustees, and graduates in front of the house that served as its base in Berkeley, May 1911. Seated are Rev. Arthur Maxon Smith (far left), Professor William S. Morgan (second from left) and Dean Wilbur (far right). Standing (at center) is trustee Francis Cutting. Directly behind him (left) is Mrs. Humphrey-Smith, an unpaid public speaking instructor, and (right) trustee Sarah Abbie Cutting. Courtesy of Starr King School for the Ministry.

study was reason to stay. For as he had confided to Will, he wanted to be *the* historian of Unitarianism and hoped to receive a sabbatical to track down its roots in Poland and Transylvania.[32]

Making the best of things as she waved good-bye to the well-paying church in New England, Dodie resolved to start counting her blessings and using her assets more profitably. She decided to supplement Earl's monthly checks from the school by renting out rooms in their house, saving one for a student who cooked and cleaned and shopped in exchange for his board. She visited her family in Portland more often and counted as earnings the money she saved not having to cross the country to reach them. She was glad to be spared the northeasters and ice storms and endless New England winters. She enjoyed the reputation her side of the Eliots had in the West and the leverage this gave her to help her husband maneuver behind the scenes. In the East, Earl's name was the only one Unitarians knew when she said who she was.[33]

Dodie could not put a price on her value as Earl's chief political strategist, but her pay was no doubt commensurate with the crises she helped him negotiate. Two particularly bad situations in the earlier years of Earl's tenure were the doing of Arthur Maxon Smith. who had come to Berkeley in 1911 to shepherd the Unitarian church and who taught part-time for a term or two at the liberals' theological school. Smith had a talent for using people to satisfy his appetites. He had married a woman who financed his brace of impressive degrees and bore their four children while he found agreeable work as an academic, most recently teaching philosophy at Pomona College in Southern California. In Berkeley, he also showed his genius for gratifying his ego by rapidly jockeying into positions of influence. Soon presiding over the A.U.A.'s Pacific Unitarian Conference, Smith began using this platform to air his contempt for its theological school, citing its stunted growth and the losing battle for student retention. He put through a resolution that its operation be scrutinized, and appointed himself to head the investigation. The next thing Earl knew, Smith was pushing a plan to dismantle the institution and put its funds into training ministers elsewhere.[34]

Before Earl could mount a defense, another bomb dropped. A local reporter had learned that prior to taking the pulpit in Berkeley, Pomona's Professor Smith had indulged in a wild affair with one of his students. The couple had taken expensive trips using false names and Mrs. Smith's money until the professor had gotten the young woman pregnant. He had paid her to have an abortion and tried to cover it up, but her brothers found out and brought charges against him, and now the press had got wind of it. This revelation of Smith's double life put the skids on his campaign to bulldoze the school, but not without dragging the Unitarian name through the mud up and down the West Coast. The Berkeley Unitarian Church lost no time in pruning its records. While preserving Smith's flowery valedictory, in which he bade his people farewell and cited poor health as his reason for leaving, its stewards burned all the evidence of his disgrace. As field secretary, Earl Wilbur would have liked to have had the same luxury. But in 1915, Smith's dirty linen was being aired on the papers' front pages beneath banner headlines that stretched from San Francisco to New York City.[35]

Dodie could understand why her husband would bend over backward to reach a fair verdict on somebody who had sought to dismantle his school. He did not want appropriate discipline to be construed as revenge. He also knew the trustees were hoping to find something in his report to warrant reducing the charges and sparing the Unitarian name. Earl's initial account had therefore been muted enough to allow Dodie's father, a district trustee at the time, to conclude that Smith was indeed "an unfortunate, compromised, very foolish man," but not a guilty one. He was rather a victim, "betrayed from one mistake after another, into a miserable situation almost hopelessly embarrassing, when perhaps he meant only to do right and save others." But when Earl had Dodie look over the brief he prepared to present to the district board later, the risk, as she saw it, was not that he might seem unjust. It was that he would let the devil go free, and she was determined to block the escape. As his editor, she took a hard line, adding details and emphasis, and disappointing a jury that had been hoping for expiation. After reading his daughter's version, Thomas Eliot had to concede that Smith's was a case where a web of "guilt in a common sin" had choked the man who had spun it. It also convinced the other trustees to render the only defendable verdict: The accused was guilty and no longer fit to be part of their clerical fellowship.[36]

——————————————— & ———————————————

Whatever the gratifications of taking a fledgling school under wing, the seminary's First Lady aspired to more. Even as she embraced this institutional child of Earl's and indulged the paternal pride that inflated its progress, her fervent wish was to take her place in the age-old "Profession of Matron," which Unitarian Frances Power Cobbe extolled in her published lectures. *The Duties of Women* had run through at least seven printings by 1893, when Dodie first read and adopted it as her "guide to a better and higher life." Cobbe's traditional wisdom that females had no greater calling than motherhood had clearly lost none of its force since Abby Eliot's formative years.[37]

The announcement that Minna and Will were expecting a baby in 1895 quickened Dodie's ambition to have a big family. Suddenly every other female she knew had a child on the way, and with babies coming so "thick and fast"—her sister-in-law was soon pregnant again—Dodie confided to Minna that she had decided to have "at *least* eight." She realized that college-trained women were having smaller families these days, but she was "as much a baby-lover as ever," and her target was modest compared to the fourteen her grandmother Eliot had. By the time she and Earl got engaged, she could hear their own children, all of them musical, singing chorales after dinner in eight-part harmonies.[38]

Had confidence been any guarantee in 1899, the couple would have returned from their honeymoon holding the choir's first member and had the second in hand by the following summer. Sadly, however, the baby who was due to arrive at the end of August was lost in early July, and Dodie, pregnant again by September, had another miscarriage in March. Earl seemed to be putting this rough start behind him thanks to his constant distractions at work and his habit of seeing the bright side of things. Only the family detected what Dodie had come to know as his "minor tone," the break in his voice when he transferred his unresolved sorrow to those around him. Yet Earl was not simply projecting his grief when, after these letdowns, he wrote Dodie's parents that she was not doing well. One had only to see her puffy eyes and hear the hollowness in her voice to know that the losses "remained very vivid for her."[39]

Dodie's bouts of self-loathing became more acute with every new baby who entered the family: her aunt Rose's new daughter, Abigail, the reputed jewel of

St. Louis; and Minna and Will's "Number 4," a beautiful, healthy infant named Teddy. One would think, she wrote Earl in June 1900, that "*everyone* in the world but me was going through successfully with children." It shamed her that she could become so depressed and ill-tempered because of others' good fortune, but her pain had no conscience or heart. It shamed her, as well, that her sweet-natured Earl had to bear the brunt of her temper. His newly acquired interest in genealogical research, which kept him absorbed for hours tracing the lines onto large sheets of paper, drew fire for being insensitive. Did it not seem ironic, given their dimming prospects for adding a branch to the chart?[40]

At a time when on average a dozen of every 100 American couples lived with the unseen and largely unchronicled heartache of infertility, there was plenty of empathy with the Wilburs' misfortune. Kate Stevens Bingham identified with it. So did Alice and Ralph, still childless after five years and almost as many failed pregnancies. The news of Dodie and Earl's second loss reopened the "empty void" in their hearts, Alice assured her brother- and sister-in-law. Abby Eliot had the same empty feeling when she got the word in St. Louis. It pulled her back almost fifty-five years to when she was her granddaughter's age. At 29 she had already lost an infant and a toddler, and she would have seven more die after that, she reminded Etta and Tom. Now the same "trials of motherhood" were "beginning in earnest" for Dodie. She would have to accept this as part of God's plan and let him take care of the future.[41]

Leaving the family planning to God was not an acceptable answer, however, when Dodie's modern era had methods by which she herself might determine the outcome. For starters, she vowed to stop being the dutiful minister's wife who had jeopardized her hopes of a family by driving herself to please others. She also consulted a medical specialist and on his advice went back to Portland to give her "internal arrangements" a well-deserved rest, leaving an unhappy husband in Meadville to fend for himself for eight months. This course of treatment revived Dodie's wifely affection and patience noticeably. Earl's letters, pining and flush with romance were a reassuring boost to her ego and melted her heart, she confessed. Earl's love "was a priceless boon," and his way of expressing his feelings was just as "adorable" as it had been in their courting days. "To have you talk to me that way, my dear," she wrote, "really makes me stand up a foot higher and feel like a queen." As a therapy for preventing another spontaneous abortion, however, the moratorium on conjugal relations was ineffective.[42]

Two doctors whom Dodie consulted in Boston gave her new hope by suggesting her trouble might be "a displacement." If "*that* was the cause," and it could be remedied surgically, as they said, she told Earl, she could stop despising herself for having a "good-for-nothing-uterus!" But surgery proved of no benefit, either, and this, said the experts, left only one option: The couple would have to resort to "*real* contraception," not just separate bedrooms. Dodie knew it would be a bitter pill for a man who would not even say the word *condom*. Earl considered this method "especially dreadful," something used by degenerate men in brothels, not by devoted husbands who were helping their wives to have babies. Dodie persisted, sometimes resorting to humor to bring Earl around: With what they knew now, she promised, they would not have to go through this awful business "the next time they married each other." In the meantime, the cycle of hope and dejection continued its torment until, at last, at the end of August 1907, a healthy baby was born. Elizabeth Fuller Wilbur was the miracle for which the parents had waited for more than nine years.[43]

Surrounded by the encouraging staff at Portland's maternity hospital, Elizabeth readily took to her mother's breast and slept contentedly, her two tiny fists nestled under her chubby, pink cheeks. Earl's joy showed itself in the usual way. Returning to Berkeley, he pictured the excellent woman their daughter was going to be "with such forebears and such a home" as they would provide. Dodie was also beginning to take Elizabeth's future for granted when, after two weeks, she suddenly stopped taking milk, began losing weight, and had to be switched to a bottle. The baby quickly rebounded, but Dodie's fragile esteem was crushed. She felt reproached by the "miserable stuff" she had made and put into her precious child's body. Nursing a baby had been the "one thing" she had counted on doing well, she wrote Earl, and failing in this, she had been deprived of her birthright as a woman. While the baby improved, Dodie brooded and grew superstitious. Afraid that any positive thoughts would be an invitation to danger, she trembled to open her well-wishers' cards and regretted not ripping them up unread when Elizabeth suddenly started rejecting the formula. The doctor put out an emergency call for a wet nurse, and Dodie despaired that her mothering role was being ransomed again. Where before it had been Earl's parishioners who encroached on her time and energy, and then the medical experts who told her and Earl when and how to have intercourse, a lower-class mother was now butting in on her intimate care of her child.[44]

Mrs. Stuart, the unwelcome angel of rescue, appeared with her lusty five-week-old infant son suckling at her breast, and Elizabeth "ate like a little pig" when she was given a turn. The baby flourished, but Dodie was spooked by this unexpected crimp on her plans. The doctor wanted Elizabeth to be kept on natural milk for some months, and the Wilburs would need an affordable place where they and the Stuarts could live as a family. Not only would they have no privacy but Dodie would have the equivalent of three helpless children to watch, not just one. As she worked the equation for Earl, Mrs. Stuart, a widow of forty-five with several grown children as well as "this *illegitimate*" baby named Frank, had been left with a mental impairment after a bout with typhoid some years before. The matron of the home for dependent women where she had been found was sure Mrs. Stuart had always been a respectable, perfectly decent woman until some knave took advantage of her disability. Still, the woman had almost no recall. She could not say where Frank had been born, how old he was, or when she last fed him, and Dodie would have to do her thinking for her to make sure their daughter got fed. For that matter, she worried that her mental dullness might somehow be passed through her milk to the baby. Even if Earl was right in contending that this was not how biology worked, it gave her "the fusses" to have Elizabeth nourished by someone whose mind was defective.[45]

Dodie's bitterness at being deposed by a social inferior settled on Frank, the extra baggage who seemed to be crowding Elizabeth. The boy was "*utterly spoiled*," she complained, and with his insatiable appetite and his mother's indulgence, she feared there would not be enough milk for two growing babies. To ask Mrs. Stuart to wean him was out of the question, Dodie wrote Earl. Either she would not understand, or if she did, she would get too upset to do her best for their daughter. The only solution Dodie could see was to have the baby removed, a maneuver she easily justified as their Christian responsibility. The woman could not take care of herself, let alone a demanding baby, and they would "have done [their] duty," Dodie moralized, feeling better already. When it was presented this way, Etta offered herself as the go-between. She would try to help Mrs. Stuart see what was best, but she would not pressure her. The woman would have to feel free to do "*exactly* as she wished." The meeting took place, and as Dodie had feared, Mrs. Stuart and Frank accompanied her and Elizabeth back to Berkeley.[46]

The Wilburs' relationship with the Stuarts had all the marks of a culture that stigmatized childless, white middle-class couples around the turn of the century. Alarmed by the falling fertility rates among native-born Anglo Saxons and the sharp rise in births among immigrants and African Americans, racial purists were picking up where Edward H. Clarke had left off. They were charging that privileged women were letting the nation's best stock die out. To the ears of a liberal religious woman like Dodie, these claims were especially cruel. For their leading proponent, David Starr Jordan of Stanford University, was also a Unitarian, and his tracts were disseminated by the denomination's publishing house. A trained biologist, Jordan had seized on the theory of evolution to study the lower orders of life and draw implications for human beings. The country, he concluded, would end up like Rome unless, through selective breeding, inferior races were kept from diluting the strong Anglo Saxon traits. "The blood of the nation flows in the veins of those who survive," Jordan warned in 1899, and "those who die without descendants can not color the stream of heredity." This concoction of national pride and eugenics was Dodie's bitter cup.[47]

As early as 1902, when well along in another doomed pregnancy, Dodie wisecracked that workers were putting her race out of business, she meant every word of it. She could not find a nurse, she complained to Earl, who would help with the housework, and next, she expected the washerwomen would not want to get their hands wet. Then "a doctor's union" would come out "against attending 'deliveries' or for charging $1,000 a case!" And they accused *childless women* of moral sterility! Nothing is known of the Stuarts' fate after Elizabeth Wilbur was weaned, but clearly their critical role in the Wilburs' lives said a lot about class identity and the humbling reversals in being a parent.[48]

Again, these were lessons Earl left behind with his grief once the crisis had passed. His certainty that their daughter was over the hump and would follow his script here on out was as steady as when he had timed Dodie's flowers to bloom for her wedding bouquet. Since the child was unusually tractable, when she started to beg for a sibling, even Dodie relaxed to the point of rescinding her pledge not to risk getting pregnant again. Ready to try one more time, she succeeded and gave birth to Thomas Lamb Eliot Wilbur on November 12, 1912. The labor was long and intense and damaged her heart, but the boy was healthy, and Dodie survived a near brush with death at the age of forty-one to start learning how difficult motherhood was after all.[49]

Eliot, as they called him, disproved his parents' assumption that what they had learned the first time around would make the second child easier. Even as babies, the two were entirely different. Elizabeth always woke up with a smile and gurgled until it was feeding time. Her brother was fretful and cried so vociferously that the neighbors complained. He thrived on rebelling, a pattern his father euphemized as "taking initiatives instead of passively obeying requests." Dodie, who bore the brunt of his mischief, had harsher words for it. At the age of three, while her mother was visiting, Eliot managed to unlock the door and slip out of the house for a bit of adventure. Dodie panicked when she discovered him gone and notified the police, and when, hours later, he reappeared grinning, his grandmother Eliot was not amused. She "received him coldly," Earl noted that night in his diary. The boy's reputation preceded him to Hood River as well as to Portland, and Etta made her views evident by refusing to eat at the table with him. When Dodie's sister Grace was at camp with her family, her brother-in-law Gordon Scott—who, according to Dodie, was "so very strict with his children" that anything less was a crime—broadcast the Wilburs' disgrace of producing a little barbarian. Dodie soon noticed that fewer relatives came to camp when they knew she would be there with Eliot.[50]

Dodie did not need their help to see the problem or place the blame. Although it had crossed her mind that some physical fluke might have led to the boy's wild behavior, she felt that whatever its source, there was no excuse for her and Earl's reluctance to rein him in. They should have laid down the law early on and enforced it consistently, she told Earl. "A systematic arrangement and *carrying out* of some plan for…*duties and play*" would have rooted good habits and made for a merrier

FIGURE 5.4. Three generations of Eliots pose for a snapshot in Portland, ca. 1918, while young Eliot Wilbur (standing in front of the grown-ups) pesters a younger cousin. Standing behind him are (l. to r.) daughter Henrietta Eliot next to her father, Tom; Ellen Eliot Weil, Elizabeth Wilbur, Ted Sessinghaus Eliot, Clara Eliot, Fred Weil, Minna Sessinghaus Eliot, Etta Eliot, William G. Eliot III, and, seeking support from her brother Will, Dodie Eliot. Seated in front with Grace Eliot Scott are her children Richard, Peter, Abigail, and Henry, and their cousin Janet Weil. Courtesy of the Schlesinger Library, Radcliffe Institute, Harvard University.

family. As it was, the boy was so finely tuned to their feelings, he mirrored their anguish. With his "little unhappy expression" rebuking and clinging to her, she strained to remember when she had last seen her thirteen-year-old with a smile on his face, looking "carefree and happy." It was a great day when Dodie could finally send her parents a good report. Now a junior at Berkeley High School, their grandson stood near the top of his class. He was a standout in flute and piano, had been in some plays at school, and was turning into a gentleman. He had taken a girl to a formal dinner and dance after carefully putting aside enough money to buy his date a corsage. At his parents' suggestion, Eliot joined the Unitarian church in Portland on Easter Sunday 1929, and as he extended a manly hand to his uncle Will and grandfather Eliot, Dodie was grateful so many were there to witness the transformation.[51]

But now it was Elizabeth's turn to try her mother's endurance by breaking out of the mold to form an identity of her own. Puberty had changed the agreeable child to an insolent adolescent whose stubborn defiance persisted well beyond college. While her father as usual saw only "traits of a very sweet Christian character," her mother got nothing but "bullying and threatening." Elizabeth went to such lengths to find something to criticize or attack that Dodie pleaded with Earl to stop letting her read their correspondence. Dodie arranged a respite by having the girl start college at Reed in Portland. Then Elizabeth's preoccupation with earning the rest of her credits at Berkeley and looking beyond to becoming a certified preschool teacher helped make the next three years bearable, too.[52]

But the criticism resumed when the graduate took an internship at the highly regarded McDuffee School and moved to Springfield, Massachusetts. As if the miles had also increased the distance between their values, Elizabeth's letters berated her parents for being aristocrats. Earl's suggestion that she might be able to "raise her stock several points" by telling the headmaster who her ancestors were drew a stinging rebuke. It shamed her, she told him, that they would put so much importance on family connections when they should be thinking "less of social position and more about character." She preferred the bohemian culture, and there she soon found the love of her life, who—according to Dodie, who went east to judge for herself—was about as "unpromising a catch as there was in the water." "A common typewriter salesman," he had dropped out of high school when he was fifteen, worked in the mines in Colorado, done a lot of hard drinking, and then attended some sort of night school for drifters. Even his head was "plebeian," and his ears were "perfectly awful." Dodie just hoped this was nothing more than Elizabeth flaunting her independence and that she would find a suitable husband and get on with starting a family. The infatuation eventually passed to her parents' relief, but for the present, the girl refused to be steered. Elizabeth bridled when Dodie complained about her choice of lodgings and urged her to find something better. The YWCA where she had a room was too scruffy for Dodie's taste, and there were plenty of good boarding houses where one could mix with "the right sort" of people.[53]

None of this lessened Earl's pride in the job he and Dodie had done as parents. As he told their son the night before Eliot left for Pomona College, heredity and environment had given him and his sister a statistical edge for achieving success as adults. He knew from a published analysis of the profiles contained in *Who's Who* that having been raised in a suburb near a large metropolitan area made it eleven times likelier that Eliot would do well in life than had he grown up on a farm, and twice as likely than had he been reared in a city. As a minister's son, he was 2,400 times likelier to gain distinction than the son of an unskilled laborer, four times more than a businessman's son, and more than twice as likely as the son of some other professional. Add to this "such blood as only a long and worthy descent" could supply, and the Wilbur children had "a long lead…to win the highest prizes." They need only put forth their best. Dodie was sure it was much more complex and that luck played a big part in who would succeed. Her reading was taking her not to *Who's Who* but to books on childhood development, and their modern theories convinced her that she had been backward and "stupid" in rearing the children. She was grateful that hers had turned out as well as they had in spite of their parents' blunders.[54]

——————————————————— ∽ ———————————————————

Unlike parenting, raising a school such as Earl's got no easier over time. The Wilbur children rewarded their parents by making significant progress, by learning from their mistakes, and developing giving natures and consciences. The institution had yet to grow up and compensate them in these ways. In twenty years, only twenty-five students had actually earned a degree, and there was not yet the financial base for an adequate campus and faculty. Granted, the school had resilience. It had recovered the numbers it lost in 1917, when students evacuated the classrooms to serve in the war as chaplains and medics, leaving an almost deserted campus behind. Four years later, Earl's unflagging labor of love, collecting rare books for the institution, convinced the Unitarian Layman's League to build them a fireproof library.[55]

But Dodie and Earl's extraordinary sacrifices had paid for these gains in an otherwise disheartening undertaking, and after a quarter-century, they were ready to hand it to somebody else. The Wilburs had other work waiting for them, most notably Earl's long-postponed, definitive Unitarian history. In 1924, a yearlong sabbatical had freed them to travel and probe at the site of his subject's sixteenth-century roots, but the time was too short and had left them impatient to move ahead with his magnum opus. By September 1929, when the school had its Silver Jubilee, the Wilburs' plan was for Earl to step down at the end of the term in the spring of 1931.[56]

The collapse at the New York Stock Exchange within weeks of the Jubilee raised serious doubts in Dodie's mind that they would be leaving on schedule. The school's longtime treasurer, Leonard Cutler, a nephew of the school's founding patrons, the Cuttings, assured them the assets were safe. Yet when Dodie tallied the loss of income from plunging enrollment and lost contributions and factored in the projected expenses, the deficit was foreboding. With the university planning to take the school's property for a gymnasium, additional funds would have to be found to rebuild on the hill north of campus. In addition, the board had promised that Earl would still get his salary after he left, and this outlay would be on top of whatever they had to pay his replacement. Dodie asked where the money would come from, and nobody knew or seemed worried.

Neither Earl nor his colleague William Morgan, who would become acting president, had the temperament to go begging for gifts, especially with so little to show in the way of graduates over the years. So Dodie explained when she told her parents that she had decided to do it herself. Since nobody else had "the face to ask for money," she had made it her mission to go through their old address books and church directories for anyone who might still be willing and able to pull the spigots. Dodie found only two, and neither delivered. The first had already run through her yearly allowance of contributions, and the other died before Dodie could get to her bedside to make her pitch. Nor would her father, to whom she finally turned for advice, talk finance with her and pass on the tips he had often shared with her brothers.[57]

Dodie felt sure that if she had been tutored in business and Earl had not been so naive, one of them would have seen a red flag before they left Berkeley as planned. As it was, not until they had landed in Europe did either of them imagine that someone at school had been cooking the books all along. Eliot and Elizabeth were with them to make it a family vacation when the telegram came with the gruesome facts: The board had started getting complaints about creditors not being paid. A meeting was held to investigate, and within a matter of hours, the lifeless body of Leonard Cutler was found in a restroom just down the hall. It was suicide. The treasurer had embezzled everything he could pry loose from the school's endowment, invested it all in real estate, and seen it dissolve when the market collapsed and land values tumbled. He had not been able to touch smaller assets held in a trust by the A.U.A. Also safe were the school lot and buildings; these were unencumbered and likely to bring a good price when the university grabbed them. But there was a shortfall, and once again, the school passed it on to the Wilburs.[58]

Not only did Earl have to leave his family reunion and put off his research abroad to keep the gains of his past thirty years from unraveling in Berkeley, but the board reneged on its promise to pay him his salary as an emeritus. With the family's monthly income reduced to the $160 they netted from renting their house and drawing on Earl's ministerial pension, Dodie was frantic to find other sources of revenue. Reminded again of the handicap under which women quietly labored, she rued not having been schooled in finance and trained to provide for her family. A Guggenheim Fellowship came through for Earl, getting them back to Europe and paying their way for another twelve months, but something additional had to be found before the stipend ran out.[59]

While Earl was immersed in the archives, Dodie researched the job situation at home. On hearing from Portland that Salem's pulpit was empty, she wondered if she and Earl might cobble together a livelihood with him preaching and her supplementing his check with "some little job as parish helper or something." This from a woman who thirty years earlier laughed incredulously when her sister Henrietta declared that she wanted "to *work* at something…to be a trained nurse, or cooking school teacher, or minister's assistant!" Now that she knew how important it was that a woman be able to earn, the churches could barely afford to pay clergy and were not about to compensate wives. Will told her as much when she floated the scheme, expecting to get his approval. From what he knew of the situation in Salem, he expected that with or without a new pastor, the church would go belly-up by year's end.[60]

Also doomed was Dodie's suggestion that Earl be hired as Will's ministerial partner. The resignation of Portland's associate pastor, Harvey Swanson, a fellow whose youthful energy had revitalized the Sunday school there, seemed to open that door when it was announced after New Year's Day 1934. Earl seized on the possibility, but Will was also about to resign. The church had grown tired of having its one attenuated old man, he said, and it was not in the market for yet another. Bitter at having no future in Portland, the scene of their courtship and happiest years, Dodie gritted her teeth and proposed to Earl that they go into exile abroad as her cousin T. S. Eliot had. Could Earl get a job as a cataloger in one of the libraries there? It was just another idea that failed to get traction and slipped away.[61]

--------------------------------- ∽ ---------------------------------

Two years earlier, Dodie's investments had finally started to pay her real dividends. She was proud of having stayed close to Earl, going back to Berkeley with him to deal with the Cutler catastrophe, and returning to Europe after the crisis had passed. After thirty-five years of marriage, she was sure he would never have held up alone, so prone was he to depression when she was not with him. Most rewarding of all was that she and their son, who had stayed overseas to travel, were finally making a "lovely" connection as carefree and jolly companions. While Earl went on to Berlin for his research, mother and son took side trips together, and "for the first time in many years, the channel of confidence" between them seemed "to be at last open." It was really a wonderful act of grace, Dodie wrote her husband from Copenhagen in April 1932, but she was also taking some credit for "trying in every way possible to make it a happy trip" for the boy. At the end of the summer, Eliot left to go back to Pomona College, and a postcard from him a month or so later signaled that he was settled and well.[62]

But on Sunday, October 16, a cable arrived informing the Wilburs that Eliot had died in the campus infirmary. He would have been twenty years old in three weeks, and his parents had planned to put a letter and gift in the mail the next day. Now, instead, they had a funeral to arrange and no way of being there. Will had to preside at a simple service containing no Scripture or homily, just music, the boy's favorite pieces by Handel and Bach. The guests were invited to let their affections speak silently from their hearts, while 6,000 miles away, the parents, keeping watch at that hour, asked God for the strength to live with the loss of their son. Beyond the calm of the moment, their prayer brought little if any relief. Etta mentioned months later that Dodie still spoke of the boy in the present tense, and Dodie acknowledged that she was still clinging, unable to let her son go. She hated herself for having

FIGURE 5.5. Taken in Lucerne, Switzerland, on 14 August 1931, this photograph was one of the last to capture the Wilbur family of four. A week later, word of Cutler's embezzlement came, and Eliot died the next year. Courtesy of Mary C. Eliot.

pampered Earl and his work when she should have been where she could get to her son when he needed her. She blamed herself, too, for not taking the time to break through the wall between her and her daughter by lecturing less and listening more, maybe learning to see through Elizabeth's eyes. "People like Mrs. John Adams, who stayed at home and raised her family while her husband was years in Europe, had the right of it." They might not have seen as much of the world, but "at least their children were not sacrificed," Dodie wrote her mother remorsefully.[63]

By 1933, Earl's refusal to see what was happening in Europe had sharpened Dodie's feeling of dislocation. While the rest of the world was hearing that Hitler's Nazis were terrorizing the Jews by roughing up their professional people and vandalizing their stores, Earl, who was right there in Munich to watch it, was telling the family that it was not so. The coverage, he said, was pure propaganda, inflated to blacken the new regime. Dodie's queasiness grew with each letter from home. A skeptical Alice Wilbur challenged her brother-in-law to explain how he could be "living in peace and quietude" when every paper and broadcast reported unmistakable turmoil and horror. She and Ralph wished that Dodie and Earl would get back on safe ground without further delay, and so did the rest of their skeptical family and friends.[64]

While Dodie tried to write cheerfully, too, so as not to add to her family's worries, her restiveness was apparent. From Hungary she wrote that the atmosphere was oppressive and unnerving. She and Earl were surrounded by totally unreliable people who no doubt were passive aggressive. The town was also "*swarming*" with soldiers, and everyone seemed afraid. Reading their letters in Berkeley, Lillian Burt, the librarian and office manager at the school, wanted to take her old boss by the shoulders and shake him out of his stupor. Not even the staunchest doves, she snorted, minimized what the Nazis were up to. Surely it took the most "Spartan qualities" for his wife to be passing the days without a project like Dr. Wilbur's to block these things out, she sympathized.[65]

In truth, Earl was faring no better than Dodie, just bearing his sorrow more patiently. His project no longer absorbed him, and the scholarly meetings that he had once relished had lost their zest. An international congress to which he had greatly looked forward for over a year was tedious, he wrote Dodie. None of the papers amounted to much, and the whole affair was merely "a pretext" for herding the scholars into a hall to "take one another's measure." Reluctantly, Earl accepted a Hibbert Fellowship for another twelve months as an onerous obligation to trudge ahead with his scholarly work.[66]

Dodie, however, decided her stint was over and nonrenewable. After more than a year since Eliot's death, she had yet to learn the details. She wanted a full accounting to get past the gnawing questions that kept the wound open. Home by Thanksgiving, she spent the better part of a week at Pomona confronting officials, grilling the doctors and nurses, and quizzing her son's campus friends. Their testimonies confirmed what she had suspected all along: The attending physician had made a false diagnosis. His initial notation, "acute nervousness," was never revised on the chart despite the signs that his patient was gravely ill and rapidly losing ground. In other words, Dodie informed the school, the real cause of death had not been pneumonia, as stated, but criminal negligence, a lethal combination of laziness and incompetence. Despite these verifiable facts, which only refreshed her outrage, there were too many contradictory statements for Dodie to feel that the case had been closed. There was no consolation or closure, either, only a sickening irony, in reading a month or so later that another young man had recently died in the college infirmary. He was under the care of the same physician Dodie blamed for Eliot's death, and this time, the student's grieving father was Charles K. Edmunds, Pomona's president![67]

Elusive, too, was the solace Dodie was hoping to find with her family in Portland. Her father was no more approachable now than when she had gone to him in the past for some strengthening word only to hear, "O, don't talk to me about it, my darling." After a series of small, silent strokes, his mind was traveling all over the map, and when he was lucid, there always seemed to be somebody else in the room to keep her from speaking intimately. Dodie had also misjudged in thinking that she would repair her neglect of her siblings. By now, they were all pre-occupied and preferred to get by without her assistance. Henrietta was too used to running the household and taking care of their parents to carve out a place for a walk-in, Dodie wrote Earl. She could not even get Henrietta to take the few dollars she offered to help with expenses, which made her feel more like a freeloading, meddling guest than one of the family. As for Grace, who was also back in the city since filing for a divorce, she had signaled that she did not want any unsolicited shoulder to lean on. Too raw from the break, she would only discuss with Ralph— who had offered to serve as her lawyer—what exactly had ended her twenty-five years of marriage.[68]

Dodie was happy to see her mother still spunky at eighty-seven, especially after having been struck by an automobile the year before. Etta was thrilled to be out of a wheelchair and able to flap her wings, but this meant that Dodie could not help her, either, without becoming a nuisance. In short, she had lost her place in a household where hearts were still warm and caring enough to be watching her "every mood and tense" but were too encumbered to to offer her any sympathy.[69]

The collapse of this fortress sent Dodie tumbling into the depths of despair. She wanted to "smash the universe" and bury herself in the rubble; for as she told Earl, she expected no more from the years ahead than the same pointless struggle to which she had given her last sixty-five. Appalled, Earl begged her to come to her senses and measure her life's importance by his. Everything in his record—the "work accomplished, reputation made, distinctions achieved, honors won"—was her doing as much as his. "God knows that you have been a co-worker in it all," he beseeched. If it had been possible, he would have happily stayed in the wings and yielded the limelight to her. Only custom had kept him from doing so, but they still had a mission to finish, and he was now counting on her to help see it through.[70]

As Abby and Etta had always said, no one recovered from losing a child. Dodie's longing for Eliot found a permanent niche in her conscious makeup. Always within easy reach but off to the side so that she could pass unimpeded, it took the place of her love for the God who governed an orderly universe. It was Earl's affirmation, not Dodie's old faith, that enabled her to recover her will and push the boundaries of her domain across the lines of family tradition. Determined that nothing would stand in his way and slow him down if she could prevent it, she vetoed Earl's thought of returning to teaching and took on the role of their sole provider.

Dodie went back to running a boarding house, now as a one-woman operation, renting out rooms to five lodgers, doing the cleaning and cooking herself, and working up to the radical step of demanding institutional justice. In 1938, sixty-seven years old, living with a weak heart, and exhausted, she felt it was time the divinity school made good on her husband's pension. She was no longer up to the punishing work and would have to stop driving herself "like two slaves," she told her brother Will, enlisting his help. If she had to grab the powers that be by the throat, she was ready to do it. Of course, there was little chance of it coming to that. Their cousin Frederick was now the president of the A.U.A., and if ever there was a time to pull strings, this was it. Writing their cousin separately, Dodie and Will explained the straits the Wilburs were in, and by November, she had her assurance the long-delayed checks would be coming.[71]

Dodie needed her spunk on the home front, too, where Earl's physical setbacks conspired against him completing his magnum opus. Just as his first volume's last batch of page proofs arrived, he had to have surgery. Then a series of minor strokes left him feeling as if he were dragging "a sled on bare ground" as he tried to build a smooth-flowing narrative out of disjointed facts. "That he should now be so balked" after sacrificing so much for this work was "maddening," Dodie confided to Will in 1949. Earl was too weak to sit up for long, she reported after his surgery, but she had devised a way for him to type on a low table next to his lounge. She continued to prop up his confidence, too, more a cheerleader now than a coach.[72]

When the second volume turned out to be shorter than volume one by a hundred pages, Earl felt rebuked by its puny size and worried that it would tattle on him. The readers would guess he had petered out before he could build to a grand finale. Dodie assured him that he had done wonders even if he had just sketched out the end. The denomination agreed. Even the young generation of Unitarian scholars—who confessed they had no idea what the old man was up to until the first volume was published in 1945—and those who would notice the narrower scope in the sequel in 1952, would grant Dr. Wilbur his place as their senior historian.[73]

Dodie's happiness for her husband was mixed with regret at his tapering interests in life. He had given up trying to make a place for the radical Unitarian shifts away from the Christian structures in which he had settled. Elizabeth's wedding in 1942 was a rare appearance for him at a Unitarian function. Two years later, his brief return to the Oakland pulpit to preach his Jubilee sermon provided another exceptional sighting for liberals who seemed not to notice or care that he had withdrawn and secluded himself on the outskirts of the denomination. As he mentioned to Will eight months later, as casually as he could, despite his poor health, he had not been visited by Oakland's pastor for quite some time before the event and not at all since. "Not that I care," he added in the minor key Dodie detested, "though I cannot refrain from passing a mental comment." Retrospection, no longer mere scholarly practice but also a buffer, let him escape from a world that was changing too fast for him. Keeping current, he said, led to nothing but endless worry and loss of sleep, and so he contented himself "on the shore," sitting quietly, translating old Latin texts, and letting "the stress roll by."[74]

Dodie had serious doubts that she would have Earl's companionship ever again, so fixed was his posture sitting bent over a manuscript. As far as she was concerned, retreat, like silence, was inconsistent with living, and Earl was happy to vouch for this with a chuckle. She kept herself "deeply absorbed, and continually stirred up," he told her brother, by reading the Manchester Guardian's flaming attacks on America's cold war agenda. Engaged in a conversation with the perplexities of the modern world, she could honestly say in the 1950s her interest had never been greater.[75]

The never-ending profession of motherhood also kept Dodie immersed in the currents. Increasingly conscious of what she had lost by not having a paying profession, she no longer asked her daughter to think about being a stay-at-home wife and mother. In time, Elizabeth also began to see her perspectives and Dodie's converging. Her choice of a husband, William Newell Nelson, a chemist from Berkeley, pleased everyone; and the bride's "trying" mother-in-law, as one of the uncles described her, improved Dodie's standing considerably with Elizabeth. The challenge of rearing four children, two of them twins, after World War II, also increased her appreciation of Dodie. Able at last to commiserate, mother and daughter could talk about where they went wrong, forgive themselves and each other, and pat themselves on the back. They would just have to live with their flaws, Dodie guessed; for she had never met anyone, not even a Unitarian, who was perfect! The best they could do was try to make progress, not by insisting on resolution or unanimity in all things, but by keeping the lines of communication open.[76]

6

Reduced to a Whisper

You can never imagine what it is like to have a man's force of genius
in you, and yet…it must be pressed small, like Chinese feet.
                                    —George Eliot, *Daniel Deronda* (1876).

Minna Sessinghaus hated the photograph she had planned to send with
her news that she and the Eliots' grandson Will were engaged. She had
sent a copy to Will in Seattle, where he was serving a church, and his
assurance that it was "just fine" made it worse. It might have been *fine* as
a parody, but that was not the idea! He was talking "real foolish" when he,
of all people, knew perfectly well what was wrong. For months now, he
had been pleading with her to stop brooding about their future together
and not to worry about her lack of credentials for being a minister's wife.
It was there in his letters: "No more frowns"; and no more "borrowing
trouble!" Considering how he had seen her scowl all the way from the
state of Washington, it was stupid of her to have thought she could sit
just a couple of yards from a camera and pass herself off as a radiant
bride-to-be.[1]

   Of course, Minna sulked, her greatest mistake was thinking that
love could somehow make up for their differences. The contrast
between her past twenty-five years and Will's twenty-seven was morti-
fying. He had been carefully shaped to a template passed down through
a line of ministers. She was the product of freethinking Prussians who
put their religious baggage aside as soon as they came to St. Louis to
build a large flour mill around 1850. Her grandparents severed their

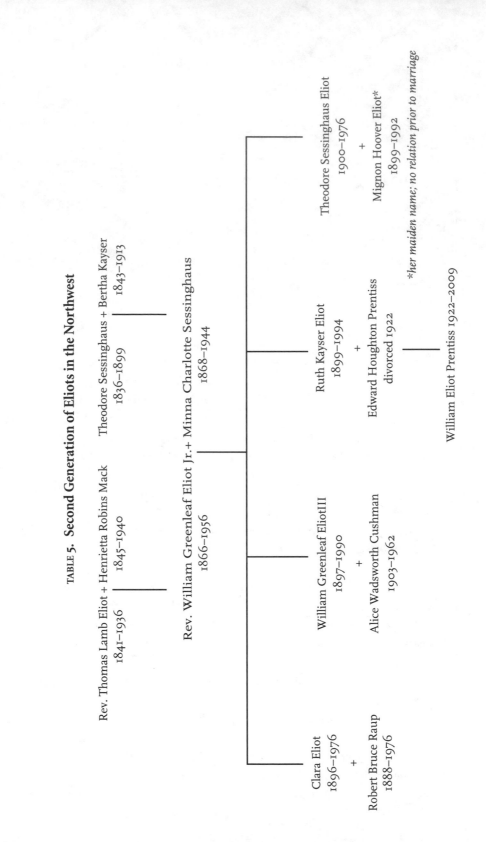

TABLE 5. Second Generation of Eliots in the Northwest

Rev. Thomas Lamb Eliot + Henrietta Robins Mack
1841–1936   1845–1940

Theodore Sessinghaus + Bertha Kayser
1836–1899   1843–1913

Rev. William Greenleaf Eliot Jr. + Minna Charlotte Sessinghaus
1866–1956   1868–1944

Clara Eliot
1896–1976
+
Robert Bruce Raup
1888–1976

William Greenleaf Eliot III
1897–1990
+
Alice Wadsworth Cushman
1903–1962

Ruth Kayser Eliot
1899–1994
+
Edward Houghton Prentiss
divorced 1922

William Eliot Prentiss 1922–2009

Theodore Sessinghaus Eliot
1900–1976
+
Mignon Hoover Eliot*
1899–1992

*her maiden name; no relation prior to marriage

previous ties to the Evangelical Church and joined the city's *Freie Gemeinde*, an ethical culture society. Minna's parents, Bertha and Theodore Sessinghaus, followed in this tradition, taking over the mill and teaching their offspring to think for themselves. They gave them good secular educations and let them explore higher realms, if they wished, without the church telling them how.

If this lack of a decent religious dowry was awkward for Minna in light of Will's legacy, so were the differences in their personalities. Although she could easily see his father and grandfather's imprint in many respects—from his choice of vocation and boyish good looks to his way of repeating people's names, as one might use commas, when speaking to them—when it came to emotional makeup, Will was his mother's and grandmother's boy. He had the same playful nature and ability to relax that softened the starch in their husbands' rectitude. Will's whistling, an indulgence the older men's censure had failed to suppress, brightened his mother's and grandmother's homes from the time he perfected the art as a boy.

The contrast when Minna took stock of her own traits unnerved her. An introverted perfectionist, she spoke her mind and was overly critical, unforgiving, and ill equipped to feign tolerance. She worried that Will, with his ready, droll humor, would rue his choice of a serious wife. She had no ear for jokes and she hated games. "Easy ones I grow weary of," she warned, and with "difficult ones…I lose patience." Furthermore, she feared she was spoiled, so accustomed to having her way without considering anyone else, that Will's thoughtful manner would emphasize her selfishness. Dodie had warned he was always "so everlastingly considerate" and "so mortally afraid" of hurting somebody's feelings or disturbing the harmony of a group that he almost never asserted his wishes or talked about what he was feeling himself. She sometimes wanted to tackle him and wring it all out, his sister confessed. Minna could understand why, with so many strong-willed females around, Will had never learned to pull rank or puff himself up. Although her own household included an older and younger brother and three younger sisters, Minna grew up feeling none of the crowding that might have taught her the art of accommodation.[2]

Minna's litany of remorse also cited a shameful domestic incompetence, the penalty of her ambition to have a life outside of the home. Her parents had humored her scorn of sewing and cooking, Minna explained, and allowed her to follow a radical bent that was being encouraged at school. Some of Mary Institute's female instructors, alumnae of colleges in the East, had been quietly turning the school in St. Louis into a feminist breeding ground. Minna's younger sister Bertie's Class of 1894 had so many seniors who wanted to speak on women's advancement at convocation, the teacher in charge of the program had to impose a quota to keep it balanced. Now that Minna's ambition had changed and she was no longer exempt from homely duties, she only hoped that her two greatest strengths—an orderly mind and the will to succeed—would make up for some of her glaring domestic deficiencies.[3]

Minna had met her fiancé at his grandfather's university. He was two years ahead of her, but they had many mutual friends and saw a good deal of each other. They had corresponded so little after he left for divinity school, however, she never thought that their friendship would come to anything more. What she knew of his progress she learned from their mutual friend Norman Flagg, the son of the former Sally Smith, who had been his grandfather's scribe years before, and Norman's information was incomplete. In the meantime, Minna received her diploma summa cum laude in 1890 and happily entered the world of professional women. Her job teaching German at Mary Institute brought her into a culture of "very bright women" whose motivation validated her larger ambitions. Avowing that womanhood did not require attachments to men or the bearing of children, these colleagues had chosen careers over marriage, deeming the two incompatible. Their intimate partners, as Minna told Will, were women with whom they could travel and work and live fully and happily on their own terms. Eager to join them, Minna was saving her money to study abroad when Will reappeared and asked for her love, and her heart, caught off guard, had said *yes*. The vigor with which she defended her colleagues' independence belied her insistence that she no longer wanted their life for herself.[4]

Will wished he had spared his fiancée the shock of proposing out of the blue, but he blamed himself less for her nervousness when she told him the rest of her story. She had a history of falling apart when situations spun out of control. It went back to high school where she and a girlfriend had fallen in love. They planned to be partners for life and sealed their pledges with passionate kisses. They pined for each other when they were apart, but then other students grew jealous. Minna became so confused that she fled the relationship and for weeks could not eat or sleep. Still, she told Will, she had no regrets. The experience taught her the difference between mature love and childish infatuation. "I was too young to understand it all, to keep my balance of mind." Her friend had been older and no doubt had found other girls to whom she was just as loving.[5]

Another derailment occurred during college when Minna began having second thoughts about the career she had always wanted. Her studies no longer excited her, but neither did the alternative, and she knew of no place in between where she would be happy. With rest, she got back on her feet and thought she was straightened out for good until she started teaching at Mary Institute. The symptoms returned in a matter of weeks. There seemed no reason for it. She enjoyed her students and colleagues, and she felt that what she was doing had value. Yet she became anxious again, stopped eating, lost weight, and wept uncontrollably, and this time did not have as quick or complete a recovery. In fact, she was still convalescing in the spring of 1894 when her wedding invitations began to go out.

Minna's physician treated these bouts of illness as nervous exhaustion. No mention was made of hysteria, the female complaint of the day. Most of the medical literature on hysterics focused on married women whose breakdowns were seen as a means of escaping the overwhelming demands of large families. Although Minna's symptoms were strikingly similar, no one who saw her spoke of her illness—as both clinicians and scholars would later—as being an unconscious way of avoiding an unsatisfactory choice between conventional womanhood and a career. Nor would this diagnosis have changed the treatment. Extended rest and mineral syrup were standard for all these conditions, and any further analyses would have made even less an impression on Minna. She had her own explanation for why she got sick.[6]

Looking at it in the context expanded by Will's declaration of love, Minna believed that her problem had come from an unhealthy intellectual pride and a limited knowledge of life. Too headstrong and smug to consider that the conventional path might be right for her, if not for every bright woman, she had charged down a less-traveled road and then wondered why she was lost and miserable. But now that Will had opened her eyes to a higher purpose, she told him, she was sure that preparing to be a good wife would be the first step back to health. Hence, during their months of engagement, while Will was completing his stint in Seattle, she put aside all intellectual work, except for her study of Middle High German, and started to learn how to do "the things that other women did." Her letters to Will reported her triumphs in mastering basic recipes. She sent him a monogrammed laundry bag to show him the strides she had made as a seamstress. She also made a real effort to show a more Christian concern for the needy and kept Will informed of her visits to help several destitute families, something she never had done before. For the first time, too, as additional training for future responsibilities, she offered to help in the Sunday school of her church and practiced holding her tongue when she saw how poorly the program was managed. It made her "a little blue" to be so at odds with the way things were done, but she tried not to dwell on what this might portend for her future.[7]

It was all about pride, Minna thought, as she looked for ways to temper her drive for perfection, counter her self-absorption, and develop a sense of humor. It pained her to think of the glee with which she had shown up the other strong students like Will by graduating from college with higher honors. For a while, Minna tried out a humbler persona, petitioning Will as her *"Father-*confessor." "Will you preach to me on this or that and help me, my dear Minister?" "I shall be so happy when you will watch over me and be my guide," she wrote. It was a terrible script and worse acting, and Will was embarrassed for both of them. He told her again that she was already fit for their life of joint service, and if she would only relax and be herself, she would do them both proud.[8]

Will took it as a good sign when Minna began to set limits on how she would change. Drawing a line at theology first, she told him not to expect her to bring her religious perspective in line with his, as this would be asking a lot more of her than his father had asked of his bride. His mother's conversion had not dismantled but liberated her true beliefs. When she searched her soul, his mother had realized that she had already moved on to the Eliots' freer faith, but with Minna, this kind of adjustment would cramp her broader position, not free it. Will could talk to her about God all he liked, and she would give him a hearing, but he would not find it easy to change her opinions. "I love my mind's independence," she warned, and it would not "think a certain way simply" because she "loved the thinker."[9]

Even as Minna defended her freedom to find her own way in these matters of faith, she worried about being at the far opposite end of the liberal spectrum from Will. She wished they had both somehow ended up on a comfortable middle religious ground, but their fate, as she kept reminding herself, had been set in motion before they were born. With no tradition to guide her, Minna had not given serious thought to having a soul or a life of the spirit until she was into her teens. Only after a teacher in high school introduced her to Emerson's essays did she start to fashion a modest unorthodox faith.

By the time she moved on to college, Minna believed "unquestioningly" in some permanent, transcendent power. It manifested itself as eternal progress and natural harmony, and as some impersonal sort of immortality. Beyond this, she claimed no belief. She refused to engage in what sounded to her like wishful speculation when people debated life after death or whether the Overarching Soul could protect the universe it informed. Minna's views had eventually taken her to the Church of the Unity, where John Calvin Learned preached an inclusive Unitarian message. With a principle of association that welcomed all who would work without creeds to hasten the Kingdom of God, the church fit well, and Minna was happy to add her name to the roster. Considering where the Eliots stood in the radical-or-thodox argument, she wondered how much of a recommendation her Unitarian standing would be when Will's family realized which membership book she had signed.[10]

For Minna, the theological tensions were incidental to these societies' different cultures and models of womanhood. Her minister's wife, L. W. Learned, was "so well-read and keen and ready" that Minna felt Will would be lucky if she could achieve a fraction of what she accomplished. For years, she had shared the load equally with her husband, and when Mr. Learned died suddenly in the autumn of 1893 Mrs. Learned also took over the preaching. In fact, she had handled it all so well, there was talk of installing her permanently until she decided to leave to be nearer her children, who lived in the East.[11]

In the meantime, lest anyone think that a woman's only way into a pulpit was widowhood, Mrs. Learned called on the network of ordained women whom Jenkin Lloyd Jones had encouraged to take command of the Western Conference. Minna was awed by their presence. The Rev. Celia Parker Woolley was wonderfully bright and versatile. In addition to being a wife and the mother of several grown children, Minna told Will, Mrs. Woolley was a published "authoress," a well-known club woman, and minister of the Unitarian church in Geneva, Illinois. "Her discourse" on the ethics of people's relationship to nature was "very able, indeed," and well received by the congregation. The Rev. Caroline Bartlett, who came from her Michigan church in Kalamazoo, was equally impressive, Minna thought. With a minister's silver tongue and a social scientist's pragmatic eye, she spoke eloquently on the topic, "The Kingdom of Heaven."[12]

Not to give her fiancé the wrong idea, Minna quickly assured him that she was not tempted to join the rush to the pulpit. She would be satisfied listening from an inconspicuous seat down below, although she could understand why there were others who wanted more voice and authority. Mrs. Learned invited such women to speak at the Women's Alliance, too. Some described their social settlement work, others their efforts with organized labor. Minna studied them carefully, hoping to learn the secret to their audacity, and she forgave them the "different look" that came from neglecting their grooming and wardrobes. Their appearance, graceless gestures, and outdated clothes, she wrote Will, only showed they had more important concerns than making themselves presentable.[13]

Of all the speakers, the one who stirred Minna the most was Jenkin Lloyd Jones, who came from Chicago to lecture on Ibsen's *A Doll's House*. Illuminating the dangers inherent in patriarchal marriages, Jones put an end to Minna's extravagant promise of wifely submission. As she listened to him explain the ground rules essential to healthy relationships, she took back her offer to leave all financial and legal affairs to Will. She was not about to live in a doll's house and end up like poor Nora Helmer, the patronized and self-loathing wife in Ibsen's masterpiece. Will, who had always intended that Minna would be an equal partner, was also grateful to Jones for this awakening. He had seen his mother and grandmother Eliot agonize needlessly because their husbands refused to reveal how much they were worth or had in the bank. Will's very next letter to Minna gave her a detailed account of his assets and put her in charge of their budget beginning in June.[14]

These lecturers also emboldened Minna to represent her church at the all-city Unitarian Club's spring meeting in 1894. The program in May was traditionally an all-female production, with ladies delivering papers by and about Unitarian women. When Mrs. Learned first asked in September if she would participate, Minna declined. By March, she was fully immersed in the life of Harriet Martineau, drawn to a subject who not only earned her living by writing, but who wielded her pen with the strength of men twice her size. Minna knew that this woman was not a saint. The sharp tongue that riled her detractors disturbed this biographer, as well. But Minna was willing to overlook such disagreeable qualities in someone who stood up for principles despite many personal trials. She identified with the woman's distrust of orthodox churches and creeds and with her proportionate reverence for natural law. She admired Miss Martineau's fearless assaults on economic injustice, slavery in all its forms, and sexist oppression.

Minna sympathized with the young Harriet whose father's business collapsed and who later redeemed the family's hard times by speaking out for the poor. Minna felt for the struggling author who was turned away any number of times before she found a publisher for her work. The abuse she took from her brother James, a Unitarian theologian who spoke contemptuously of his sister's positions on slavery, religion, and government, strengthened Minna's sisterly bond with her subject. The scholar's heart ached for the Miss Martineau whose sweetheart had suffered a breakdown, ending their plans for marriage and leaving her to face life on her own. Minna also knew something of mental illness, not only because of her own fragile nerves, but from having a brother whose demons would drive him to suicide.[15]

By the day of the presentations, Minna's sympathy was so complete that she took it as an attack on herself when the Rev. John Snyder rushed up afterward and excoriated the "wretched creature" that she had seemed to applaud. That woman came "over here and expressed her opinions even if they were not asked, and scolded against her brother," Minna remembered him shouting at her. If she had any doubts about it before, this assault convinced her that women's problems were brought on by men like Snyder, and that the world needed more females like her "most remarkable" Miss Martineau.[16]

Minna was grateful that Will got a slow start in getting a church of his own. It would take a while to develop the grasp to handle a good-sized parish, no less to adjust to the double bind of an overworked woman who felt "underused." For their first two years as a team, Will assisted Horatio Stebbens, the senior man at the First Unitarian Church in San Francisco. Minna was perfectly happy, she said, as a smaller queen in her lord's "smaller kingdom." With a new baby princess keeping her busy in 1896, her feelings were mixed when Will accepted a call from a church in Milwaukee. The position would bring him onto the board of the factious Western Conference, requiring frequent travel and adding significantly to Minna's load. Her leisurely reign was over before she felt ready.[17]

Milwaukee's people were friendly enough but hibernated most of the year. For Will to tell Dodie and Earl that Minna had triumphed in rousing the Women's

FIGURE 6.1. Minna's mother, Bertha Kayser Sessinghaus, holding new granddaughter
Clara; Minna, and Minna's maternal grandmother Charlotte Tebbe. Courtesy of Warner A.
Eliot.

Alliance, he had to be speaking in relative terms. While attendance had picked up
"superbly," most of the parish was still asleep. Will had to work twice as hard in
Milwaukee to stir half the number of men who turned out when he introduced the
idea of a "forward movement" in San Francisco. After two years of knocking on
doors, he also wrote off as "somewhat a failure" his effort to beef up the Sunday
school class for adults. Only women attended, and not very many at that.[18]

Meanwhile, the Eliots' six years of marriage had brought them four children,
two girls and two boys, all winsome, bright, and demanding. Like Will, who was
thoroughly charmed by their acquisition of language, Minna loved reading to them,
teaching them songs, and hearing them laugh, but these were the highlights on
good days. The others were marred by tantrums and spats, and fevers and coughs
that were passed back and forth, and at night, someone calling for her after she was
in bed. It was hard to find help, and while church people offered to come in and give
her a hand, they had a way of forgetting. When after five years, a colleague in Oregon
asked for Will's help, she was ready to go.

It was the Rev. George Stone, the American Unitarian Association's field officer
on the Pacific Coast, whose SOS to Milwaukee on New Year's Eve 1900 opened the

way for the Eliots' departure. His flagship church was about to go under in Portland, and Will was desperately needed to save what was left of the district's coastal fleet. Unable to raise the $900 they owed their minister William Lord for his first six months' service, Portland's trustees were talking about suspending the regular services. Stone had asked them to hold off to let the people reflect on the consequences and try to dig deeper into their pockets. Given more time, Stone said, he would turn things around. His plan was to carve up his sprawling domain into three tighter sections and bring in the younger Eliot to take charge of the North Pacific. To make it financially viable, he would also need Will to fill the pulpit in Salem, thirty miles south of Portland, but Minna and Will were game. By 1902, Will was planting new preaching stations in Oregon City, Hood River, Woodburn, and Troutdale, as well as scouting for possible sites in Idaho and Washington. Then he set up a base for his district work in the Portland church, and with his parents on hand to help and Minna holding the fort in Salem, he felt for the first time in years that something worthwhile would come from his efforts.[19]

Minna wished she had felt as positive, but her job seemed as hard and thankless in Salem as it had been in Milwaukee. She had wasted most of a precious week, she complained of a typical setback, arranging an afternoon of music and short dramatic readings to give the Ladies' Alliance members some culture. After sending out postcards, making the phone calls, giving a full day to cleaning the house, and another to getting refreshments in order, she found that everyone she had enlisted was planning to stand her up. "It now turns out that they have no program," Minna wrote Will, still smarting. One of the women had actually laughed when she called to say she had made other plans. It was the same story on weekends when the minister happened to be out of town, and most of the Sunday school teachers vanished, just as they had in Wisconsin. With her own class, a large one, to supervise and all the others to handle, it was simply "too much," she wailed. She had gotten back to an empty house, and a cold stove, and no dinner started, and four famished, ill-tempered children tugging at her. For "all the hard work, the girls' sour looks...the boys' bolting, and the teachers' excuses of 'having to do their cooking,' and 'nothing of [the] afternoon left,'" her only reward was the "little cry of vexation" she permitted herself when she finally had a moment alone and was able to shed a few tears.[20]

Minna hated to sound like a chronic complainer, but Will was the only person she trusted to listen without thinking less of her. Parishioners were inclined to assume the worst of the pastor's wife. One of them took offense at her telephone manners, unwilling to make allowances for the four noisy children at Minna's end. It was natural that she would raise her voice and ask the caller to speak more distinctly, but this one hung up and went around saying how rude Mrs. Eliot was. This after Minna had dropped everything to run up the stairs when the telephone rang. In a world with so many briars to snag her feelings and trip her up, she told Will, she counted on him to give her a shoulder to weep on and not let it go any further.[21]

Most especially, Minna did not want her in-laws knowing how much she complained. Not that she thought she would fall from grace if they did. They had never been anything other than patient and generous, and she was certain they loved her as unconditionally as they loved their own children. Her father-in-law never failed to commend her on how she was organizing Will's church or on the results he saw from the children's homeschooling. Minna knew he was being sincere in this, too. Her mother-in-law made a point of repeating the nice things he said in her absence: Will had been blessed by his choice of a wife. She was a "wonderful manager." She was working "a sort of miracle" reviving the parish in Salem. If she sounded a little disheartened, Will's father would put an arm around her and gently whisper into her ear, "But courage!"[22]

Etta sympathized with her daughter-in-law by leaving the miracles out of it and calling the hard work and sacrifices and worry by their familiar names. She pleaded for "more self-regard" lest Minna grow old in the prime of life and assured

FIGURE 6.2. The Eliots on their front porch in Salem in 1902. Seated on top step are young William Greenleaf Eliot III, his uncle Samuel Ely Eliot, and his aunt Henrietta Mack Eliot. Below are Clara, Theodore, Minna, Ruth Eliot (largely hidden), and William Greenleaf Eliot Jr. Courtesy of Warner A. Eliot.

her that she had not forgotten what it was like to be a young mother. Portland had been as primitive a city as Salem back then, and when she recalled the lack of good housing, transportation, and any real culture, she was not fooled by her daughter-in-law's cheerful letters. Behind their selective reporting and forced enthusiasm, Etta could "*feel* the *tired*" in every line and every word. It made her heart ache, she told Minna, to see her "persistently overtaxing" her strength and using the last of her energy trying to keep up a happy facade. It was "all very well to say, 'put it out of your mind,'" she went on, hoping that Minna might level with her and feel better; but mothers and wives rarely could.[23]

Minna agreed with everything Etta's admiring relatives said. She was one of "the world's rare women" and as sweet and unfailingly thoughtful a mother-in-law as a woman could want. But privately, Minna still wished for a less conscientious mother-in-law whose fort was not so "well-*wo*maned" that she could take off at a moment's notice. With three highly capable daughters at home, Etta was ready to go to the aid of her oldest son's wife any time, and when she did, Minna's efforts to prove she could go it alone were undermined. While recognizing her good intentions in wanting to lend a hand, Minna pleaded with Will to stop giving his mother encouragement in this direction.[24]

Minna knew that her fears about being upstaged seemed strange to a man who had grown up assuming that parsonage mothers and sons were meant to collaborate. In a sense, Will and Etta had served their apprenticeships simultaneously. Will's grooming for parish relations had started with Etta bouncing the child on her lap while perfecting her leadership skills in a room full of women. Soon he was getting his feet under him as the little delivery boy who appeared at parishioners' doors with his mother's messages. As their minds turned in similar grooves, mother and son were synchronized, too, in their contemplation of life's eternal mysteries. Many a summer night at Hood River, after the others had gone to bed, they had sat on the "little shelf of a porch" and pondered the wondrous display of stars, a jigsaw puzzle spread out on a vast sable sky. Etta never forgot those special nights, when they finished each other's sentences and talked about how the world had emerged from chaos. Having tackled these cosmic problems, the two thought nothing of working together to smooth out the minor snags in Will's obligations. Etta had countless "little suggestions" for him to use or ignore as his liked. They came rushing at her so fast, she explained, that it seemed impossible, even wasteful, not to keep "spitting them out." His father had turned these morsels away too often for his own good, and she was glad she had reared a son who expected her help and was grateful.[25]

～

While Minna feared that her mother-in-law would eclipse her, Will worried his father would dwarf him. He suspected that people still thought of him as the boy of fifteen who was sent to St. Louis, there to be shaped in his grandfather's mold, as his father had been before him. His training there was demanding, but, in fact, it had made Will as much his own man as it had made him an Eliot. St. Louis's pastor emeritus had done his best to leave his brand on his namesake, making sure that the young man was "up to his ears" in "piles of committees" at church and that, like his father, he went through the rigors of teaching the Mission Sunday School boys. Will's pocket diary documented the drama this last duty brought to his life. One entry shows him trying to teach his scholars about the prodigal son when one of them lets a small circus of grasshoppers out of his pocket to riotous cheers. If Will drew a lesson from this, it showed in the care he later invested in civilizing his churches' Sunday schools.[26]

On the other hand, the patriarch's strictness when they were at home led Will to break out of the pattern. Just holding a deck of cards in his hand, or being a minute late for dinner, or making a little toy horn from a letter that came in the mail for one of the uncles drew such dark looks that these lapses never recurred in the old man's presence. As Will told his children years later, the only profit he drew from this rigid austerity was a grasp of the root of his father's painful reserve and formality. Having learned from his grandfather how not to act, when he had a tender brood of his own, he put an end to the Bible reading at breakfast, let the children sleep later, and fostered their playful natures. He was also relaxed enough in the church that he happily preached while the ladies knit mittens and socks for "the boys" during World War I.[27]

As with Minna's fear of his mother's encroachment, Will's concern about being his father's clone became more intense the closer they got to Portland. The Church of Our Father had always regarded him as the heir presumptive, an image impressed on Will from a very young age. His earliest memory took him back to a morning when he was no older than four. His father was leading him by the hand like a prince to the front of the small Portland chapel where other children were seated and waiting for Sunday school to begin. Since his father's retirement, he had been mentioned whenever morale in the church bottomed out, and now and then, he returned to preach in the pulpit. Yet Will was determined to be his own man and go slow in reintroducing himself. Preaching was not his strong point, and by waiting patiently in the wings, he would give the people a chance to forgive his rough edges.[28]

—————————— ⟡ ——————————

The story of how a couple of misfits smoothed the way for Will's installation was one of the chapters the Portland people were happy to put behind them. As a window onto the mind-set and social dynamics waiting for Minna, however, this difficult interlude certainly bears revisiting. The two men who followed Earl Wilbur in Portland were earnest and seasoned clergy who simply were at the wrong church at the worst of all times. William Lord, whom A.U.A. headquarters characterized as

a "high-minded gentleman" with twenty years of "industrious, and intelligent service" to Liberal Christians, was blamed for the hopeless decline that had gone on for
five years before he arrived. By the time Portland called him, the country was
gripped by a deep economic depression, and the church had hemorrhaged so much
of its money and membership, it was barely alive. With people too strapped to write
checks and too embarrassed to show up without them, the pool of experienced
Sunday school teachers and skilled organizers was badly depleted. When the gutted
programs collapsed under Mr. Lord's watch, he was held responsible.[29]

Even so, William Lord might have lasted longer had he kept his politics to himself. But in 1900, the nation was brandishing arms in the Philippines, and Lord had
intense pacifistic convictions. Diplomacy was not possible. Although his conservative congregation of businessmen and professionals had heard enough preaching
on peace to have grasped its place in a Christian sermon, they did not come to
church to be told that America's rush to arms was unchristian. According to Ralph
Wilbur, Lord had offended so many of them by September that it was assumed he
would leave at the end of the year. Alice Wilbur thought it a shame that a man who
was "so charming socially" should be "so bigoted" as to imagine that he had carte
blanche in the church. There were limits, at least in Portland, and this was something
the Eliots knew. While Lord was excoriating territorial expansion, Will, who was
still in Milwaukee—and ignoring his grandfather's rule against bringing politics
into the pulpit—was "whacking away in favor of a decisive and radical" hand in the
world.[30]

As Will was not yet available when the Lords returned to the East, the church
had to take what there was, and there was not much. Social work was claiming the
vigorous men who would have been candidates ten years before, and none who
were settled in viable churches were willing to pull up their stakes. Grace Eliot got a
taste of the dregs while visiting her sister in Meadville. One of the two she and
Dodie heard preach had so "ordinary" an intellect, she hated to think what his fate
would have been in a congregation of thinkers. The other, "lanky, half-starved,"
with a "dangly black tie," was a virtual caricature of "the hypocritically pious" shy-
ster one saw in the melodramas. He liked to pose with his head on his hand, and he
looked so "creepy" and "snakey" that Grace could not bear to shake hands with him
after the service. His sermons, nothing to brag about either, were philosophical
exercises in turning "the mitten inside-out." The word that came down to the
Portland trustees from the Unitarian placement office confirmed her impression
that only the rejects would take the position they had to fill.[31]

Under the circumstances, Portland's Church of Our Father was willing to take
a risk with the Rev. George Cressey. This forty-five-year-old native of Maine had a
PhD, fifteen years in the ministry, and a New England manner that seemed awfully
stiff. Still, considering that the church was itself approaching the stage of rigor

mortis, any sign of life helped, Alice Wilbur told Earl, and the Cresseys' "compelling ways" did bring that. They soon got the slackers working again and feeling good about the results. They spruced up the church and pulled off "a very successful" spring gala replete with a Maypole, dancing, refreshments, a candy table, and Ping-Pong. Unfortunately, Dr. Cressey's sermons were so academic and convoluted that people stopped coming on Sundays. In the meantime, Will was becoming more visible. George Stone had taken his place in Salem, and Will, now working full-time for the district, was using a desk in the corner of George Cressey's study at church as his base. Everyone seemed to know what was coming.[32]

No one imagined that preaching would be Will's strong suit. The "sanctimonious look and manner" that irritated Kate Bingham in the summer of 1898 were still there six years later. But now it was only the children who whispered and smiled at his "monkey faces." Their elders, who had not heard any spirituality for years, accepted Will's quirks as the signs of a deep, intense faith. They were grateful, said Alice, to be reminded of what a real worship service was like. More than two years after Will's installation in Portland, Tom Eliot still found his pulpit delivery too "boiled up" when something less "strenuous" would have served just as well without rattling nerves. Yet every so often, Will would produce what his father called "one of his 'born preacher' sermons." "Recovering from Defeat," delivered in April 1908, was one of these poignant reminders of what a pastor could bring to the pulpit. Licensed by personal trials at home that were unnamed but clear to the congregation, Will's eloquence reached such heights that Tom bowed his head and thanked God that Etta had "born him."[33]

---------------------- ✌ ----------------------

Minna was glad to leave Salem for Portland a few years before Will was called as its pastor. With him doing most of his field work from a desk in a corner of Cressey's office, she saw him during the week again and had the whole family together. Then, too, the city had come a long way in the thirty-five years since her in-laws arrived. The schools were much better, and there was a new public library, a small art museum, and a plan in the works for public parks where families could walk and the children could play. There were also whispers that church member Mrs. Amanda Wood Reed had left an endowment for adding a cultural center or college to Portland's amenities. Will's father was meanwhile using his contacts and fungible real estate to finance a home for Minna and Will in the Irvington district east of the river. Surrounded by shade trees and stately homes owned by wealthy professional men and merchants, the house at 681 North Schuyler would rapidly triple in value and give Will's family a street address as prestigious as 227 West Park. From Minna's standpoint, the greatest advantage of having a place several miles from downtown was not the cachet but the distance this put between her and the church and her in-laws. It gave her some breathing space and her own domain. A trolley line had already been laid by developers as a lure to new buyers and stopped two short blocks from Minna's front door, putting Portland's hub within easy reach. When she wanted to be out of sight, it would be a lot easier living in Irvington.[34]

Setting boundaries was foremost in Minna's mind as she got adjusted to Portland. She had come from Salem fully intending to heed the appeals, which came from all sides, that she limit her outside commitments and try to go easier on herself. With restraint, she was told, she could break the cycle of headaches and sleepless nights that had made not only her own life, but Will's, so much harder in recent years. The question of whether or not to continue homeschooling for the two older children was settled by Oregon law, which mandated public schools at their age. During the evening, Minna would still give her nine-year-old Clara and eight-year-old Willy their lessons in music and German, but that would be all, unless it turned out that their teachers did not meet her standards. Since five-year-old Ruth and four-year-old Teddy were not quite ready for structured tutoring, Minna would limit her goals for them. She would read to them at night and take them on trips to the library, but she would also accept people's offers to take them for part of a day so she could rest or go into town unencumbered.

Predictably, Minna soon let down her guard. Hungry for intellectual stimulation and worthwhile activity, she offered to read an original paper before the Women's Alliance, dropped hints that she would be interested in running the Sunday school, and almost agreed to serve as vice president of a women's service club. Minna's excitement in seeing "so many prospects for usefulness" set her up, as it had in Milwaukee and Salem, for the letdowns inherent in working with strictly volunteer organizations. Minna was complimented to be recruited to fill the vice president's post until she learned this was a strategy to appease the woman who headed the slate. An inveterate traveler, the president-designate rarely got to the meetings, but she and everyone else insisted that she deserved the top slot. As Minna told Will, she would do all the work while the phantom got all the credit, and this way of doing things spoiled the appeal of the women's stated mission. Nor did it bode well for Minna finding a group of workers whom she could respect.[35]

Even so, Minna overloaded herself and was back in bed by Christmas 1904. Will moved his headquarters out of the church to his private study in Irvington and became a nanny and live-in nurse as well as the family provider. Still unable to leave her alone three months later, he sent his district colleagues regrets that due to his wife's extreme "nervousness and anxiety" he would not be at the business meetings that spring.[36]

Although he believed that God would eventually see to Minna's recovery, Will's fear that she was becoming an invalid spurred him to take stronger action himself. Just a year after being made pastor, he had the church hire a parish assistant. Officially someone who worked in the office and helped in the Sunday school, she was really there as a buffer to shield the minister's overtaxed wife. The idea was to have her move through the parish and catch all the daily complaints and requests before they could fall into Mrs. Eliot's lap. Will also did everything possible to ensure that the family's escapes from the city were real vacations for Minna, not dreaded ordeals. For a couple of summers, he rented a place at the ocean for her and the youngsters and split his time between them and his work in Portland. Minna's pleasure was gratifying. When Will read her letters describing her days with the children—sunning themselves on the rocks by the water, feasting on fresh bread and berries, and tossing the foam like water sprites—he found it remarkable how she bounced back whenever she left the parish.[37]

When renting a cottage became too expensive, the Eliots built a retreat at Hood River, where Minna fell in love with the moss-covered riverbanks and the flowering trees. Her happiness was also a tribute to Will's success in teaching the children the art of benign deceit. When others their age were exaggerating their mishaps and small disagreements, these youngsters learned to cover them up so as not to upset their mother. Only Will got the story about the hive of yellow jackets the boys had upset the day that they ambled into the house still breathless but trying to whistle.[38]

Etta also took pains to tread lightly after the family came up from Salem. Her goal was to help unobtrusively, not encroaching on Minna's preserve but not appearing stand-offish, either. Tom's tactic for not cramping Will after he was installed, a six-months family vacation through Europe, also served Etta's concern that Minna be ceded her place as first lady. After the traveling party returned and started spending more time at Hood River, a warm correspondence between the two women lessened the chance of their feeling either neglected or neglectful.[39]

There were limits, of course, to what others could do to keep Minna happy and well. There was no easy way to bring up four minister's children without having laypeople watching like hawks for any flaw or deficiency. While Minna could honestly say that her children were angels compared to most others, it took time for them to grow out of their natural devilry. Eighty years later, Ruth Eliot Johnson would still remember her mother's despair at the antics the foursome contrived in the family's front pew. Ruth's big brother, Willy, a showman, had once snatched a stack of straw hats from the vestry, smuggled them up to the front, and piled them on top of his head for all to admire. After Minna discovered the cause for the laughter behind them, she kept them corralled in the back. There they had pencils and paper and books to amuse them and still they found ways to make mischief. They pulled at the pledge card holders attached to the back of the pews to make them buzz. They giggled whenever an usher's shoes squeaked or a woman's beads broke and rolled down the aisles. Ruth had to be hushed when she saw her father closing his eyes in his chair on the platform. No matter how often her mother explained that the light was too bright for his sensitive eyes, Ruth fretted that he might have fallen asleep and would miss the cue for his sermon.[40]

The children eventually came around, but not the hired musicians. The vocal quartet was hopelessly out of key with the church's theology and belted out the most lurid anthems about divine wrath and the Crucifixion. The tenor sat in the choir stall reading and rustling his newspaper during the sermons. And Minna, silently playing her part for her husband's sake and the children's, cried inwardly over her sacrifice on the altar of wifely devotion.[41]

Portland had several organizations that promised higher standards and greater rewards. Its chapter of the American Association of University Women gave Minna the chance to associate with other college alumnae, organize programs she saw as worthwhile, and at one point serve as vice president. She also belonged to the library system's oversight coalition, which put her in contact with book-loving patrons and dedicated librarians. They set a high bar, understood the importance of acting professionally, and had Minna present a paper at a regional library conference. Reprinted in *The Sunday Oregonian* in 1910 for the benefit of parents who wanted to be more involved in their children's reading, her essay was crammed with titles of books for youngsters from kindergarten through high school. The harvest of Minna's experience and years of thwarted ambition, it was clearly the offering of someone starved for an audience.[42]

Minna had little time or strength for these sidelines after her church work, however. Indeed, by 1916, as the tenth anniversary of Will's installation approached, her family and friends were afraid that she would be too exhausted to celebrate. In June, she looked awful, haggard and frail, and when she started to talk about leaving Hood River a few weeks early to get a head start on her load of fall chores, Will begged her to stay put and rest. If she did as he asked, it was hard to see any benefit. Three years later, a church member was so alarmed by the way Minna looked that she sat down and wrote her a letter "of love and warning." She implored her to ease up and start out by handing the Women's Alliance to some other sister. The job would undoubtedly not be done nearly as well, but for everyone's sake, she must let the ladies get by with less than perfection.[43]

Minna could see no point in divesting herself of official duties in June when replacements were bound to renege and drop their obligations by fall. She figured no matter how much she gave up, she would still have her hands full, and sure enough, September found her pushed to the limits with "other people's work" on top of her own. Another three years changed nothing. She was still in charge of the Women's Alliance, for which she was planning a big social function and hoping to round up enough reliable women to pull it off. She had tried to cut back, she explained to her daughter Clara in 1919. She had turned down the chairmanship of a committee involved with the needs of immigrant families, and she had agreed to

FIGURE 6.3. The family in 1917. Standing behind their parents (l. to r.): Clara, Ted, Ruth, and William. Courtesy of Warner A. Eliot.

sit on a board related to education only to keep it from folding. Nor did she have the heart to abandon her sewing for the Red Cross. Hands for the war recovery effort were scarce with so many having gone AWOL. The chairman, herself, had left town, and Minna would gladly have skipped out, too, had she not been afraid of giving the church's detractors more grist for their mill. She was therefore doing the sewing of ten volunteers and neglecting her backlog at home.[44]

Minna's greatest sense of accomplishment would come through her children's successes. Will always said that they had her to thank for their exceptional minds and that all they achieved was yet "further proof" of how bright a mother they had. Minna did not dispute this or downplay the care she took to foster their growth. She judged every place they had lived by what it provided to help them be high achievers. In gratitude for the progressive spirit her father-in-law had fostered in Portland, Minna forgave the Northwest its "rheumy" weather and lack of refinement. Reed College's timely opening in 1911 allowed all the children to get their degrees from a school that carried an Eliot imprint without their having to leave the state to keep up the family tradition. At home, Minna's careful attention to what the children read and her tutoring sessions filled in whatever the public classrooms left out.

After graduating from Reed, Clara went on to Yale and then to Columbia, earning a doctorate in economics and starting a forty-year teaching career at Barnard, Columbia University's college for women. While still a doctoral student, she married a classmate, honed her teaching skills, had her first baby, and turned out a publishable dissertation. Minna's oldest boy, Will, went from Reed to Harvard to earn an M.A. in economics. Then he took a job with the Bureau of Public Roads in Washington, D.C., and joined the Unitarian church that his great-great-grandfather helped to establish. Ruth also took graduate work, earning a Master's degree from the University of Oregon, and then taught English at one of Portland's best high schools. Ted went into the natural sciences, earned two advanced degrees, and joined the teaching faculty at the University of Tennessee Medical School in Memphis. All four of the children married and made Will and Minna proud grandparents thirteen times over.[45]

There is no way of knowing how much Minna's feelings of being trapped by the life she had chosen contaminated her satisfaction in seeing her children turn out so well. But there was some curdling of motherly pride as her daughters grew up and made the choices that shaped larger futures. Clara's enviable ability to combine a career and a family not only aroused her mother's regrets but personalized the loss of respect for women's volunteer service in an era when women were being paid for their work.

This simmering generational conflict came to a boil right after the war, when Minna answered a call from the local Associated Charities office. Their overwhelmed staff needed volunteers with a speaking knowledge of German. Hooked by the brain work involved in this venture, Minna was soon spilling over to Clara, describing with gusto the challenge of setting up budgets and getting her clients to understand the importance of saving and thrift. Not the least of her satisfactions, she noted, was having the firsthand experience to refute the know-it-all experts, who treated these charity cases as blameless unfortunates. She had to lecture her clients on sloth and waste, inexcusable sins that enraged her now when she and Will were feeling the pinch. The church was behind in sending Will's paychecks, the cost of domestic help had gone up, and she was having to practice the strictest economy. Yet these welfare families got $50 a month on top of their rent, clothing, food, wood, and medical care. Who said they needed more handouts?

Clara's response to Minna's appeal for sympathy was hard to take. Missing her cue, the young economist rushed to explain how the system worked. These allocations were set by the Bureau of Labor Statistics, which calculated the annual income and needs of "representative" families. Minna was outraged and said so. However the bureau came up with these figures, her own, evidently irrelevant survey told her the experts were missing the mark. The allowances were exorbitant, and worse, they did not assign any real value to the homemaker's thrift and hard, unpaid labor.[46]

This last, especially roiling omission reflected the modern world's low regard for what her generation of women had actually done with their lives. That her daughter would even appear to accept this injustice was the last straw. "If your 'typical household' had made over garments as I have done for these 25 years, there would be no need of over $500 for clothing the family. I know you modern workers consider my doings pitiful, and now that I have served my term, I shall presently do less; but some things were surely gained." It was only because she had been an ingenious and careful accountant and manager that her family, she reminded her daughter, had lived like people with much larger incomes. And what of her children's work? Should that not be counted as part of her contribution?[47]

There was plenty of blame to go around, and Minna accepted her portion. "I know I have spent too much time on little things," she admitted, "perhaps too tired to see the big ones, when the little ones were in front of my eyes." Until recently, she had still thought that she could do better and have some kind of career, perhaps as the "Household Management Expert" for one of the popular magazines. The *Ladies' Home Journal* might hire her to write a column for mothers. The readers would send her their problems and get the benefit of her experience. But from what she was hearing from Clara and others, she doubted her kind of advice would now sell. Out of step with the times, she had missed her chance.[48]

While Clara's larger attainments and allegiances as a modern woman pulled Minna into an undertow of old doubts and discontent, Ruth's ill-chosen marriage at age twenty-two roused the ghost of lost opportunities. The record does not say how Edward K. Prentiss came into Ruth Eliot's life. He was neither a college classmate at Reed nor a member of the Eliots' church. His parents, who farmed in Vancouver, had seemed decent enough from that distance, however, and he was well mannered and groomed and strikingly handsome. Ruth's great-aunt Rose Eliot Smith envied Minna and Will such a "lovely faced son-in-law" when she first saw his picture before the young couple married in early September 1921. But it quickly became apparent that Ruth had known the fellow too short a time to glean that neither his looks nor his word could be trusted. Instead of providing the home he had promised, where she would be mistress of their domain, he brought her back to his parents' farm and ceded her place to his mother.[49]

Ruth had never imagined someone could be as controlling as Mrs. Prentiss, or any man as ready as Ed to stay on his mother's leash. Instead of releasing him graciously, Mrs. Prentiss strengthened her grip. She demanded Ed's full attention, his time—day and night—and his income, and he submitted, becoming her puppet and mouthpiece. Soon Ed was complaining about the small sum he was giving Ruth for household expenses. He warned her not to think she owned anything other than what she had brought from Portland. When the cold weather came, he refused to get wood and keep the house warm, even after they learned Ruth was pregnant. She became suicidal and told Ed she wanted to drown herself and the unborn child. He watched her walk down to the river and made no attempt to stop her. By the grace of God, she told her parents, she found the strength to hold on, and by Valentine's Day, 1922, her father had rescued her.[50]

Ruth's baby, a boy, was born in Portland in August. He was christened William Eliot Prentiss but known to his doting family as Billy, and he, in turn, soon gave the oldsters new names: Etta and Tom became Gammer and Gaffer. Minna and Will became Nana and Bap. Ed wanted his wife and son back, he demanded, but Ruth refused and the family agreed there were grounds for ending the marriage. Ed's actions and those of his mother, they said, were a whole lot worse than adultery. Ralph Wilbur was ready with legal assistance, and fourteen months later, Ruth had her divorce. Embraced by the family, Billy Prentiss became a favorite at church while Ruth, more grateful than ever to be an Eliot, rode out the scandal and moved ahead.

Unlike the sordid details Will kept in his diary to bolster Ruth's case in court, his record of how the immediate family scurried to insulate Minna would not have surprised their close circle of friends in the least. Minna had an "uncanny way of worming the truth" out of people, and it was a wonder Will kept her from hearing the terrible things Mrs. Prentiss was saying: Ruth Eliot was just like her mother, too hardheaded and impatient to get along with *her* mother-in-law! And protecting Minna from gossip was easy compared with trying to keep her from combing two papers a day for bad news and inflating it.[51]

Will's difficulties with the Ku Klux Klan in the early 1920s, for instance, were scary enough without her pumping them up. The Klan's vigilantes had come to the

FIGURE 6.4. Billy Prentiss with his adoring family in 1922: great-grandfather Tom, grandfather Will, mother Ruth, and great-grandmother Etta. Courtesy of Warner A. Eliot.

city to reassert their supremacist claim. Riding the anti-immigrant wave, they were terrorizing the foreign-born workers who flocked to the factories during the war and stayed on. While their tactics were different, most Protestant clergy in Portland were of the same mind as the Klan and were throwing the weight of their prejudices behind a ban on parochial schools. They objected that these facilities were supporting transplants from enemy soil whose Catholic devotion to papal authority flew in the face of democracy. Will was one of only a handful to reject this "pure Americanism" and openly fight its jingoist initiative. He was speaking at public meetings and had started to use his monthly church mailings to make his position clear in the larger community.[52]

Not surprisingly, then, when he got to his church the first Sunday in May 1922, he found two masked Klansmen distributing anti-Catholic tracts in the vestibule. Will knew, he wrote in his diary, that the hooded intruders were there to "injure the church" and intimidate him, but he would not allow it. Approaching the one who was closest, he looked "through the holes in his hood squarely into his eyes," and warned him that he would remain his opponent, forever unmasked and unbowed.

Will's father, now eighty-one, was not as restrained when he walked in a few minutes later. On seeing the hoods, he raised his cane, "expressed himself very defi-
nitely," and instructed an usher to show the two reprobates out. Will was thankful
that Minna was not there to see it although it would get in the papers.[53]

Minna relished the name and status her grandson Billy had given his Nana. She
treasured his charming inventions with words as he learned to talk and then read.
She could still be as caring and warm with him as she was with her children when
they were young and she happened to have a good day. But Minna's efforts to make
him a scholar began to wear everyone out. Soon she was having to take to her bed
and was letting the burdens, as well as the joys, of parenting settle on Will. His hasty
diary entries could barely keep up with his newly expanded activities: marketing,
writing sermons, preparing for funerals, transporting Ruth back and forth to
school, picking up Billy's birthday cake, taking the boy to the park to feed ducks. By
the time he turned seven, the youngster had come to think of Bap as his dad, and
Nana as the taskmaster who was sick a lot and needed to rest.

A series of crises in 1931 drained the last of Minna's resilience. Will was hospi-
talized for three months with pneumonia, and he was still convalescing when the
family began to see the effects of the stock market crash on their base of support.
The minister's paychecks grew smaller, and Minna short-circuited every time they
were cut, and almost any expenditure, however small, set her off. A dreadful blow-
out occurred when Ruth bought some simple supplies for making hooked rugs. In
reality, while their losses were real, the family was not going hungry. They were still
getting monthly dividends of $700 to $800 from stocks and bonds; Will's checks
from the church leveled off around $1,200; and Ruth was also earning something by
teaching. This was not a bad income for ministers' families in 1934, but Minna could
no longer do the accounting objectively.[54]

Still, her calculus was compelling when she tallied her years of work for the
church, looked at the psychic payments received, and saw that she came up short.
The old respect for parsonage families had long since become obsolete, it seemed,
and even as they were going the extra mile just before Will retired, the insults
aimed at the couple were some of the worst. Will had wanted to step down as soon
as he finished his twenty-fifth year but had stayed at the helm at the board's behest
until the financial boat could be stabilized. Minna, while rarely seen at the church,
was still sending cards and notes to everyone in the parish directory. Whether or
not she convinced them that she was still part of the minister's team, she thought
of herself in that way; and any mistreatment of Will, and there was a lot, was a slap
at her, too.[55]

In addition to all the chronic problems the people had laid at his feet—the
organist's feuds with the choir, the youth group's complaints about chaperons and
vice versa, the unhappy parents and overworked staff—Will was now getting the

blame for the church's financial embarrassment. When it got to where the trustees, who had fairly recently hired a young man named Harvey Swanson to be Will's associate, could not pay one full-time minister, much less two, they punished them both. After Swanson announced that he was leaving to take a better-paying position, the board started "dragging him through the mud" even as they were trying to get him to stay. Meanwhile, in making a counteroffer, they smeared the senior man, too, dismissing Will's methods and sermons as out of date. Some of the trustees talked secretly about trading him in for the younger man, and when the whole board was convened, it was hopelessly fractured. "Pounding on table," Will wrote in his diary, after attending the session with men who by now had lost all civility. The meeting began with them bickering over the purchase of new cups and saucers, and the board's grudging vote to give Will emeritus status with $1,200 a year felt more like a reprimand than a reward for his twenty-eight years of service.[56]

As Minna went over the balance sheet, she remembered a sermon her mentor L. W. Learned had preached at her church in St. Louis shortly before Minna's marriage to Will. Mrs. Learned had said that pretending and dreaming were valuable as practice sessions for what the future might hold. A little girl learned from playing with rag dolls, a little boy from building "a house," and a pastor's fiancée (as Minna had thought to herself), from imagining how she would shine as his capable help-meet. Once the illusion had served its function of fostering courage and purpose, it was left behind for the true rewards of doing the real thing well. All this had seemed plausible then, and it still did for women who, like Mrs. Learned, were born with the constitutions to thrive in their work as ministers' wives. But for Minna, whose makeup and background had never been suitable for the role, the transition from "making believe" to real life was a false one. Her reality was also a fiction, a niche too small for her nature and dreams. With no getting out, she had been an imposter and satisfied neither herself nor the ingrates. Will's trying last months at the church seemed a fitting end to a thankless team effort.[57]

When Dodie paid her a visit in Portland just months before Will announced his retirement, Minna, now sixty-five, was plainly "miserable." Dodie noticed a drag in her right arm and leg, and tremors, not constant but brought on by even the slightest exertion. These symptoms were not entirely new. They had first appeared in 1910 and lasted about a year. The doctors had found no organic cause then, and they were as baffled now. Their tests turned up nothing to indicate a specific disorder such as a stroke or multiple sclerosis. The best they could do was give Will and Minna a broad diagnosis of neurasthenia, a generalized "fatigue of slow yielding." It was not a progressive condition, as such, but most likely the cumulative effect of years of strain on the patient's system.

The family was willing to leave it a mystery, largely in deference to Will. He saw no profit in sifting through sediment left by events in the past, he said, alluding to

Freudian therapy, a "risky business at best." The flow of time could not be reversed, and one's history could not be changed. The children respected his wish to rely on the higher forces for healing—those powers that lay at the heart of his liberal religious belief, as he said—to bring Minna's mind and body back into harmony. Yet while they refrained from psychobiography when recounting their mother's life, the children did not rule out a connection between Minna's illness and intellect. They knew when she said she "felt underused" that she meant she had wasted her mind. Looking back from the 1980s, Ruth could see how "a very able person" like Minna "would have had more of a life" if she had lived fifty years later. With "women's lib and ... different traditions" to push out the walls, she would have been able to spread her wings and soar. Bill Prentiss remembered his grandmother as "somewhat dour in manner." A classic "perfectionist" who wanted the best from everyone, she had taken it as a personal insult when he was slow to "catch on." She "did not have an easy sense of humor," and while he could "not fine-tune the impression," he sensed there was tension when she became frustrated with the women at church.[58]

With the children leaving him to his own thoughts, Will's view of their mother's illness was cautious. By the mid-1930s, he knew her condition involved something more than excessive work and the pressure she put on herself. He could see that the farther away she was from the parish, the better she felt. He had noticed that after the children went off and started to have their own families, she had no problem crossing the country alone, going out to see the sights, and helping take care of the babies. She flourished in 1929, when she and Will celebrated their thirty-five years of marriage with a sixteen-week second-honeymoon tour of Europe. Yet even when she was in Portland, her symptoms had come and gone mysteriously, and when they were in remission, her strength was amazing. This pattern, he told her sister Clara in 1934, convinced him that Minna was harboring something that she had yet to "work through." Yet this was as far as he ventured. The likelihood—which studies of medical history and gender would later propose—that invalidism gave Minna a way to escape her impossible bind—was inconceivable to a man surrounded by women of mythic resilience.[59]

Will's mother, approaching her ninetieth year, was no longer the woman of sixty-seven, who justifiably likened herself to Milton's "Satanic Majesty, 'going up and down the Earth and running to and from upon it.'" With a fractured leg on the mend and still feeling the trauma of having been hit by a car, she was hobbling on crutches and hesitant to cross the streets by herself. Yet her toughness, as one family member observed, was still there and "simply miraculous," inspiring much younger women to ask how anyone could "keep going like that?" Will's sisters Ellen, recently widowed, and Dodie, bereft of her only son, had also been rocks in difficult times and shown amazing persistence. If his mother and sisters could do this well, so could Minna. Whatever her problem, Will told himself, she would manage to root it out once she learned how to rein in her doubts and keep them from blocking her inner resources. But for now, she required around-the-clock care, and he and Ruth were on rotating shifts as he logged in their long and tiring days with the patient: "Rubbed, stroked her forehead to calm and relax her." "Warm baths." "Ruth nearly exhausted," he wrote in his diary, and he himself was having "slight mental confusion" from time to time.[60]

Minna was last seen in public at the memorial service when Etta died early in 1940, bringing an end to a long and remarkable era. To those who were there that January, it seemed nothing short of miraculous that by sheer force of will, after years of seclusion, Minna had come to pay her respects. Back home, she could not hold a book anymore, or sit up, or turn pages. Yet she seemed to listen intently when Ruth and Will read from the recently published journals of Maud Rittenhaus, who had been in St. Louis studying art when Minna and Will were just friends. Now fifty years later, Ruth and her father laughed at Maud's wicked accounts of the Unitarian church where Maud disagreed with the Rev. John Snyder, and how she sized up the dashing young William Eliot from afar. As for how Minna felt as they journeyed back half-a-century, it was hard to know. She had not held a pencil or pen for some years and could barely mouth words when she died in April 1944.[61]

7

Talking Back and Taking Flight

Lengthen thy cords, and strengthen thy stakes....For the LORD
hath called thee as a woman forsaken.

—Isaiah 54:2, 6

In the Roaring Twenties, the years when technology first put religion
on wings, Will Eliot's doubts about broadcasting Sunday services were
quieted by the letters and cards from his pleased, if invisible, audience.
Writing from Monmouth, Oregon, Mrs. J. A. Ackerman testified that
the program had sounded "so perfectly real," she had bowed her head
when the prayer began. Beulah Patterson, too, could have sworn she
was sitting directly in front of the pulpit when she closed her eyes and
listened to Will from her rocking chair in Big Timber, Montana. As far
away as the Mexican border, proud radio owners like E. E. Clark were
tuning in religiously and reaping astonishing benefits. Of the four
churches asked by the radio station in Portland to test their command
of the airwaves, none drew a more eclectic and interested audience
than the Church of Our Father. Will's messages were sufficiently
Christian to satisfy mainstream Protestants yet inclusive enough to
engage Unitarians, Jews, and combative agnostics. Almost an equal
number of women and men appeared to be listening. Yet having the
power to lift up God's word in a voice that was amplified 4 million
times, and being equipped to reach lonely souls who were hundreds of
miles away, were bittersweet consolation for a man who preached in a
half-empty hall.[1]

Far from unique, Portland's problem of dwindling membership was a creeping shadow that covered the whole Unitarian map by the end of World War I. Truancies that had earlier mirrored the drift from the liberals' theistic roots had turned into permanent transfers to mainline communions by 1900. As Trinitarian Protestant churches embraced a softer, more practical gospel, liberals put up with their liturgy in exchange for more social prestige. Women's departures had made the defections more visible, still. Tired of having a limited voice and seeking greater autonomy, a significant number stopped going to church altogether. Rather than trying to operate the churches more democratically, the leadership's cure had focused on trying to loosen the women's grip and beefing up the ordained fraternity's image. Spotlighting one of its warriors in 1893, *The Pacific Unitarian* featured the Rev. Samuel A. Eliot as the rugged "young man who [had] unsheathed his maiden sword" in the church in Seattle. The church's culture was likewise refurbished to replicate the appeal of fraternal lodges and merchants' organizations. On Sundays, the pulpits elevated physical potency, business success, and shrewd marketing skills to the level of sacred virtues, and during the week, new programs were launched to promote them. The effect was a modest rise in male numbers, though largely in ancillary activities rather than Sunday worship; and for every additional man, several once-loyal women faded from sight, dissatisfied with the shift to a skewed Christianity that neglected their interests.[2]

Earl Wilbur had parlayed his love of the mountains into a climbing program for boys and started a Channing Club for their fathers while he was on board with the program in Portland. In 1901, George Stone and George Cressey had tried to infuse a fraternal spirit by forming the Oregon Unitarian Club, with dinners and programs reserved for the men, except on occasional "Ladies' Nights." Will Eliot also did what he could to show that religion was not just for sissies. While field secretary, he held up one parish's "Boys Brigade" as a model program, explaining how the youngsters were drilled by an army captain, who taught them to sing the great martial hymns while parading in front of the church in formation. As Portland's pastor, he added a Laymen's League and carefully tailored his sermons to fit the interests of practical men, dressing his themes in the entrepreneurial language they understood. He spoke of "spiritual savings" accounts and "portfolios" of good works, of bonds that would "never default," of banks that would "never fail," and of checks that would never bounce and come back stamped "insufficient funds." Still, the men's empty seats on Sundays remained an embarrassment.[3]

One first-time visitor to the old building at Broadway and Yamhill was puzzled. The sermon, he wrote in the *Portland Spectator*, made its appeal "directly to men" and did it so competently, he was sorry so few had been there to hear it. Addressing the need for "Practical Progress toward the Decrease of War," Mr. Eliot had made an appeal for deliberate and strenuous action. His delivery was confident, pitched to the intellect, not the emotions, and showed him to be the kind of preacher a regular male could respect. Here was "a strong, able, logical" thinker who knew his way around in the world; and so, this visitor wondered, where were the brothers? The mortification was magnified in 1924, when the church moved to larger quarters at Salmon and 12th. By the end of the decade, when fewer than 90 people were pledging, the average turnout on Sundays was even smaller, and this in a hall that could hold 450.[4]

⁓

The question directed to male absentees might have been asked of the women, instead, and arguably to greater advantage, given how much their dominant ranks had thinned since their peak in the 1880s. By the 1920s, the answer should have been obvious. As early as 1890, a rash of conversions to Christian Science had signaled the hunger the distaff had for greater control of their lives This exodus was not unique to their parish or Unitarians. Since the publication of *Science and Health* in 1875, Mary Baker Eddy's system of mind cure had captivated thousands of educated middle-class women. The core of this thought, which the founder summed up in her Scientific Statement of Being, was that matter contained "no life, truth, intelligence, or substance." Since God was perfect and omnipresent, nothing existed but "infinite mind and its infinite manifestation." Poverty, sickness, injustice, and other human afflictions only seemed real to people whose understanding was unevolved. Those who grasped the truth through prayerful study of Mrs. Eddy's writings would demonstrate their right-mindedness by "reflecting" God's presence and thereby enjoying prosperity, happy homes, and good health.[5]

Although Unitarians were, as a rule, uncomfortable with its cultic nature, they tended to give Christian Science a good looking-over before passing judgment. Its leader's explicit rejection of the harsh Calvinism in which she was reared, her concept of an androgynous God who was both a heavenly father and mother, and the Emersonian tone of her call for harnessing higher powers for good were congenial enough to warrant closer inspection. Denver's Unitarian minister, Thomas Van Ness, had gone so far as to travel to Boston in 1886 to question the founder about her applied metaphysics.

Attracted by the affinities with his own tradition's implicit belief in communion between the human spirit and Universal Soul, Van Ness was hoping the interview would give him the ballast he needed to float a healing ministry in Unitarian waters. His assessment, however, recorded in the notes he made at the time, was that here was a woman "of one idea almost to weariness." Mrs. Eddy displayed "little knowledge of books and authors" and even less interest in logic; she was usually vague and got lost in her twisted sentences. Her visitor had to concede that her simple, literal reading of Emerson—by which she equated the Universal Mind with health and prosperity—freed her to tap into forces shunned by his more cerebral communion. But granting this, Van Ness was unable to swallow her other assertions. Her claim that *Science and Health* was "the key" and as such could supplant the New Testament was to his mind a ludicrous figment of a wildly inflated ego. Even more disturbing, after her "ramblings" about the all-powerful One Divine Mind, she allowed that there was something akin to the devil: M.A.M. or "malicious animal magnetism." Too spooked by this dark metaphysical stalker in Mrs. Eddy's entourage to wrestle with an additional inconsistency, Van Ness gave it up, returned to his parish, and looked for other ways to bring healing into the Unitarian churches.[6]

Also typically Unitarian was women's rights advocate Susan B. Anthony's inquiry at about the same time as Van Ness's. Based in upstate New York, where she worshiped with Rochester's Unitarian congregation, Anthony was intrigued by the seemingly feminist overtones of the Eddy organization. That it was led by a female and gave women "readers" new status as worship leaders—as well as access to paying professions as healers, teachers, and lecturers—suggested that here was a kindred movement from which her cohort might profit. But a short course in Mrs. Eddy's religion put an end to her interest. The doctrine was too abstract, and the statements about women's rights not substantial enough for a serious feminist. The smug, systematic disregard of real human problems was troubling, too.[7]

In light of her dubious logic and vilification of rational thought—to which she applied the name "Mortal Mind"—Mrs. Eddy's alternative seemed an improbable lure for Unitarian women. They had, after all, traded mainline respectability for a liberal church because of its basic concessions to reason and conscience. Moreover, the thrust of their outreach was to eliminate sickness and social corruption, not human conditions ascribed to invisible devils. Their goals of good health and clean living were more compelling than disembodied salvation. Yet, given their dissatisfaction with the existing medical therapies and the uncertain efficacy of prayer, their defections were understandable. Here wrapped in the mantle of science was a self-proclaimed Christian faith that put the power to heal and improve their circumstances in women's hands. Portland's membership book shows that during the 1890s, at least a dozen officially transferred to Christian Science, and the parish correspondence suggests this was only the tip of the iceberg.[8]

Such was the situation Earl Wilbur walked into when he arrived in Portland and rented a room from an elderly widow from church. Bettie Farmer had fallen into the hands of three Christian Scientist friends, who took on her case and closed ranks around her when she became gravely ill. The woman was soon in such pain that a boarder summoned a doctor for opiates, and when her protectors found out, they stormed the house. Dragging the nurse from the bedroom, they barricaded themselves inside, and the lodgers could hear the three telling the patient that she was not sick anymore. After they left, Mrs. Farmer was found propped up in her bed like a dummy, dressed for an outing, and barely responsive. The only real miracle here, all agreed, was that she had not yet died in their hands. The next time they came, Earl wrote his parents, the doors were securely locked.[9]

The rookie pastor found more than the Scientists' mischief to worry about. The Spiritualists were also beguiling a number of women who wanted relief from their mental and physical problems and a more active hand in the cures. Here the hook was the idea that spirits, or guides, were concerned for the health of the living, and their healing powers could be engaged by a go-between. Claiming that mental activity was closer to spirit than matter, the medium directed the "astral energy" and positive thoughts by moving her hands suggestively over the patient. After Earl Wilbur was dragged to a session by one of the curious members at church, he pronounced it a "transparent piece of imposture" and hoped this would be the end of it. But soon another parishioner wanted to share her good fortune in finding a psychic, a wonderful Unitarian healer in no way involved with the Eddy school. She used only her "gift of see-er-ship," and her visions were so remarkable, the convert would not elaborate. Mr. Wilbur might think they were "crazy," and in truth, he was already rolling his eyes. Lost on him was her explanation that hearing about divine power was one thing, and being able to give God a hand in wielding it, quite another.[10]

Unable to grasp women's discontent with having to practice their faith by proxy, the clergymen missed the signs again when others left for ministries of their own making. Portland's Unitarian Jennie Viele moved north to Vancouver, opened her home as a halfway house, and served as a chaplain, tutor, nurse, and job counselor to "fallen women." The need was immense, she told her old pastor. When a man got down on his luck and strayed and then wanted to make a fresh start, "how ready everyone [was] to assist him, but not so with the poor woman." Moreover, as she had told a local minister who had come calling, these girls needed "something besides prayers and reading the Bible." They needed "love and sympathy and patience and something to eat…and work!" Now when a prostitute wanted a different life or was ill, she had someone to call. Mrs. Viele was willing to give Mr. Wilbur the credit for leading her into this work. When she heard him preach that the only way to love God was to love as God loved, she had felt he was speaking directly to her and encouraging her to try harder. Before that, she always "felt delicate" and pampered herself, but no more. Once she had decided to take on as much as the Almighty put in front of her, she had not only found the strength to do it but also felt stronger each day.[11]

The success of the Post Office Mission might also have served as a warning that women were not as content with their limited voice in the church as the ministers liked to think. Since 1886, when Portland women picked up the idea from a sister in Cincinnati, a group had been finding appreciative audiences by writing personal letters to tuck in with published sermons and tracts that were sent on request to households who had no liberal church to attend. Using their kitchen tables and desks as their pulpits, this corps mined the Scriptures for insights and dilated them for the scattered souls in their congregations-at-large. Addressing them from a level plane, they presented their work in disarming terms. Their "gospel," they liked to say, was just a "religion of household duties," one that promoted "the consecration of…parentage, the holy mission of homemaking," and the "calling of training the future generation to holy living." If their mission was seeding confidence in a new way of going about religion, it hardly appeared to be planting a female rebellion.[12]

By the twentieth century, most Unitarian women in Portland were too realistic to dream of being ordained or too comfortable to greet a break with convention. Increasingly hostile to female disruption, denominational papers, reflecting the muscular leadership, had for decades been playing on readers' sentimentality. Flying a masthead proclaiming "A Virile Optimism in Religion," the *Unitarian* lauded women who stayed in the background, adopting God's way of hiding his hand when bestowing his visible gifts. The periodical's "Home Page" became a forum where priestesses of the hearth were enlisted to caution their sisters not to trade in their aprons for clerical robes. "We can be evangels to souls within our reach," one evangelist wrote, but "we cannot all be preachers."[13]

Any Portland female who questioned this had her nemeses waiting in Alice Wilbur's cohort. Cared for by prosperous husbands and jealous of their positions at church, they resented the competition of ordained women, such as it was. A shameless detractor of female clergy, Alice had gloated over the poor reception Lila Frost Sprague had received when the Spragues, both ordained, were preaching in San Francisco in 1894. "Not wildly enthusiastic, was it?" she thrilled when writing the Wilburs in Berkeley after the paper announced that the missus was going to give a sermon.[14]

Single women who shared Mrs. Sprague's sense of calling would soon be coaxed into worse situations. In 1907, the chief denominational officer Samuel A. Eliot launched his scheme for protecting the pulpits from further female intrusion. Describing it as a response to ambitious young women who wanted careers in the church but needed appropriate training and proper credentials, he created the Tuckerman School for producing professional parish assistants. Much like the program the Methodists offered aspiring deaconesses, its curriculum would effectively funnel the restless female energies into a safe and "appropriate field of service": Graduates would visit parishioners in their homes, do office work, and serve as Sunday school superintendents and teachers. The institution would form close ties with area schools of social work to keep its own students in step with modern-day trends. Once the school was in operation, however, the leadership showed its true backward bent. It repeatedly warned the young women not to disturb their domestic moorings, not to involve themselves with "conspicuous agencies" for good works, and not to be led astray by "the folly of the Woman's Movement." The enrollment figures and number of graduates—only some forty diplomas were awarded in fifteen years—confirmed what critics had said from the start: The school's underlying assumptions were way out of touch with the changing times.[15]

Addressing the editor of the *Christian Register* from the upper Midwest, where her network of sister ministers had set a record for growing new churches, the Rev.

Mary A. Safford excoriated the A.U.A.'s top brass for being either ingenuous or naive. Surely President Eliot knew that the clergy had always been propped up by unpaid women who, having been mentored by mothers and aunts, did not need a school or certificate. It was the worst kind of deception and waste to put talent where it was not needed while churches were folding for want of capable ministers.[16]

The conceptual flaws were just as apparent to Unitarians in the Northwest. Already reluctant to bring more staff onto the payroll in Portland, the people there paid Will's parish assistant Anna Warner so poorly she had to leave after a year for a job that would pay her enough to live on. Nor was a church that was trying to build up more programs for men in the market for female staff. A rugged young fellow was what they wanted to work with the Laymen's League and inspire its next generation of members by leading the Boy Scout troop. It was twenty years after Miss Warner left before another female was hired from outside the church to help Will. And that woman's tenure, rocky and brief, was a further setback to any female who might still have dreamed of a pulpit.[17]

The Rev Julia Budlong, one of the few of her sex to attain that title in the new century, came up from San Francisco early in 1927. At thirty-one, she had sterling credentials: degrees and scholarships from the State University of Iowa (the University of Iowa), the Pacific Unitarian School of Religion, and Harvard Divinity School. She had also made a good start in applying her training in western Michigan, where she was called to The People's Church in Kalamazoo in 1920. For the feminists who remembered the glorious days three decades before when the Rev. Caroline Bartlett, now Mrs. Crane, had preached her prophetic sermons, the new woman's ordination had been an oasis of hope after years in the desert. Tragically, in her second year, Julia Budlong contracted polio, and after a long convalescence, found it impossible to get a new parish. Eventually gravitating back to her old stomping ground in California, she found a job as a housemother at Mills College in Oakland.[18]

When it came, Portland's offer to bring her on staff was the closest thing she could get to a pulpit, and she was the best the trustees could do in finding a low-paid parish assistant. Out of respect for her training, she was called the "assistant minister," but her duties—running the office, overseeing the use of the building, and lending a hand with the church's "religious and social work"—were hardly commensurate with her preparation. Will Eliot later admitted that the board, "in their zeal" to find him a helper, had failed to consider "the nicer points" in screening the candidate, and that he, himself, had been as remiss. He had seen signs of trouble but gritted his teeth and said that he thought he could make it work.[19]

Nothing in Julia Budlong's appearance suggested that she would cross swords with a man. With her tiny frame—she stood under five feet—and her tidy hats and gloved hands, she looked as safe as the Sunday school teachers, but none of the women were fooled. Her status as clergy and much-discussed wage were affronts to their history of thankless service. Glad as they were to have the woman take over their tedious tasks, they resented that she had been put on the payroll and treated as if she could do their work better. Moreover, her recent marriage to an actor and writer named Paul Veley, and her grating insistence on using her maiden name, belied the threatening tendencies hidden behind her conventional dress. If the parish assistant felt under-rated, the people got more than they bargained for once she started to flaunt her rad-ical politics. The relationship ended after six months, to everybody's relief. A smug Alice Wilbur, surprised that it had lasted even that long, predicted that "Mrs. Veley's" "awfully funny" bohemian affectations, working-class bias, and feminist stance would go over better in coffee houses than churches.[20]

────────────── ∾ ──────────────

Not all of Portland's women accepted their second-class citizenship as quietly as they gave up their freedom to answer a call to the pulpits. While Alice's cohort stood firmly against it, a growing number were starting to see why they needed their full constitutional rights and were doing so without the help of their ministers. Thomas Lamb Eliot's backing of suffrage had more to do with the bondage of drink than with the legal enslavement of women. When the state's franchise bill was roundly defeated in 1884, he shifted his hope for closing saloons to the Bingham ballot reform and backed away from the local feminist clamor. Keeping this distance had taken some fancy footwork under the circumstances; for Abigail Scott Duniway, the Northwest's preeminent suffrage crusader, had ties to The Church of Our Father going back to 1870. When she and her children arrived in the city, the Unitarian preacher had been the only one of the clergy to back her agenda openly and welcome the family to town. Her doubts about formal religious traditions had kept her from joining officially, but she still wrote checks to the church and was glad when one of her five adult sons decided to sign the membership book.[21]

The problem for Thomas Lamb Eliot was that Mrs. Duniway's driving concern was women's second-class citizenship, and she was afraid that making her issue "a tail to the prohibitionist kite" would "arouse the ballot-armed opposition" and kill any chance for her cause. She deeply resented the National Woman Suffrage Association's Susan B. Anthony and Lucy Stone coming onto her turf with their broader appeals to women's interests as mothers and wives. The suffrage crusader and Unitarian preacher remained on good terms. But their paths to reform had diverged too sharply for him to give her his strong support, and he let his congre-gants make what they would of his silence. Women who secretly knew they were in the same "terrible fix" as Kate Bingham, and who cautiously hoped for a broad-based rescue could see why the preachers would waffle. Kate wanted control of her dowry and legal protection against her husband's debts, but she lived too close to the curse of addiction to buy Mrs. Duniway's argument that sobriety was a distrac-tion from what mattered most. Others ascribed the Unitarian preacher's equivoca-tion to Mrs. Duniway's militant tone, assuming he shared their discomfort with it.

FIGURE 7.1. The Revs. Julia Budlong and William Greenleaf Eliot Jr. on the steps of The Church of Our Father, 1927. Courtesy of the First Unitarian Church, Portland, Ore.

Whatever the case, Thomas Eliot's lack of clarity in the pulpit had let the antis gain the advantage by the end of the century.[22]

Earl Wilbur was no more successful in making the case for the ballot stick. Taking a line he regarded as foolproof in 1894, he made a succinct and logical case for how women's votes would safeguard the home. But seeing no need to keep hammering something he thought was already nailed down, he left it at that, and the bill was defeated in 1900 to the cheers of many he thought had been allies. It pained him, he told his father-in-law, that a cause they were "so deeply interested in" had been blocked by close friends like Mrs. Burrell and his sister-in-law, two loyal and hard-working pillars of the church. Yet only someone as guileless as Earl could have failed to see what was coming. Alice had told him and Dodie at least a year before that she had agreed to head up the Oregon anti-suffrage campaign. She had been splitting her time, she had said, between dressing a doll for the Christmas bazaar and writing appeals for the public's help in defeating the legislation. Evidently it made no impression on him, so convinced was he that her family affection would bring her around to his camp in the end.

Nor had either woman yet realized what camp the men in the family were in. Dodie swore that she had no idea that her father or Earl might approve of the franchise until she read Alice's printed tract, "Woman Suffrage Not Wanted in Oregon," and told her father how much she enjoyed it. He had listened without saying much at the time, but for weeks thereafter made "caustic remarks" until Dodie began to glean she had said something wrong. "Papa," she sulked, seeking Earl's reassurance, "is evidently…disgusted with me because I am 'wobbly'…'woman-suffrage'-wise." Was she really that "narrow"? If so, Earl would have to "enlighten" her. Whatever her father and husband had said on the record or off, it had failed to illuminate where they stood, much less to inspire incipient rebels.[23]

With Will in the pulpit, the lack of effective guidance on suffrage came more from his saying too much than his saying too little. His broad-based discussions of franchise reform were so even-handed that both sides were able to find a place on the level ground he laid out. In 1908, a suffrage sermon he preached both delighted his pro-franchise father and made such a hit with Alice that she asked for a copy to add to the antis' national propaganda. A first-time visitor might well have taken this waffling as a natural effort to minimize dissension among the members, but Will had not let this concern inhibit his passionate pulpit defense of America's recent imperialistic policies. Those closest to him would have recognized in his tepid endorsements of feminist action a visceral aversion to females who pushed too hard for equality, who spoke from platforms without invitations, and ran their "yaps" in the name of justice.[24]

Will's mother had also contributed to his quandary. Suffrage had always sent Etta into a paroxysm of moral confusion, pitting her fundamental belief in parity against her distrust of the means being used to attain it. Her aversion to public row-diness and displays of emotion had roots in her father's lampooning of frenzied revivalists and her mother's dislike of the women who agitated for equal rights. An admonishing Dorothea Dix no doubt had an impact, as well, to judge from her horror when Etta let on that she hoped to have Susan B. Anthony over for tea if her Northwestern tour in 1870 happened to bring her to Portland. Such "self seeking restless women" were ruining families, Miss Dix had warned her young friend. The minister's wife must always stay on "the dignified paths of feminine worth" and not let the rabble-rousers disturb her foundation. These social "convulsions" were more to be feared than the earthquakes in California, said Dix; and although Etta probably smiled at the image, it added to the distrust she had of feminist agitators. While Etta berated herself for not being more sympathetic with those who most desperately needed their full civil liberties, her talks with her cousin Elizabeth Robins also helped her make peace with her conscience. Both Etta's failure to be a standard-bearer for women's rights and Dodie's complete lack of sympathy with the cause, Cousin Bessie maintained, reflected their "not knowing *how* hard" life pressed on thousands of other women, and to that extent, their disengagement was really beyond their control.[25]

While the pulpit's lame stand kept the radical females from reaching a critical mass in the church, there were always a few who demanded their rights and mustered the courage to talk back to power. One of this group was Louise B. Lee, whose neighbors, a fine young Canadian family, were being threatened with deportation. They had not been legally married at the time they came into the States but had since had a baby and filed for a proper license. Instead of receiving the document, they were given their orders to leave for allegedly crossing the border under false pretenses. Appalled that the system could be so unjust, Mrs. Lee phoned a federal agent whom she knew was a friend of Will Eliot's. Thinking that any friend of her minister must be a man she could reason with, she was shocked by his ill-tempered arrogance. He said he had every "right to throw immigrants into prison or over the border without a trial," and people like her had no business getting involved. Now it seemed to her, she told her pastor, that when a U.S. official thought he had the "Divine Right of Kings" and could play fast and loose with people's lives, it was time to expose them for what they were. Furthermore, when a minister befriended a man who courted his favor but did not extend the same respect to the regular folk in his parish, that churchman needed to hear the truth and take appropriate action. Mr. Eliot's dubious pal had thought he could shut her up by bullying her, but he picked the wrong woman. She knew her rights and was ready "to fight to the end."[26]

—————————————— ✄ ——————————————

Mrs. Lee's mettle was part of a new defiance. A palace rebellion that neither the preachers, first ladies, nor female crusaders could foment had been provoked by a small group of men who had their hands deep in the church's business. The circumstances were so convoluted, a legion of devils were in the details. But basically, it was a case of neglect and manly ambition gone bad and a lesson to ladies not to cede power and purse to the opposite sex. It was during the final phase of the struggle for equal suffrage by federal mandate—and five years after Oregon's state constitution was altered to let women vote—that Portland's Unitarian sisters were roused to claim and assert their full rights.

The awakening came with a drama that started behind the scenes in 1911. This was the year Xarifa Faling, a wealthy widow, had written a will in which she left practically all of her $700,000 estate to an orphanage that was one of the Unitarian sisters' prize missions. Established in 1871 as The Home, it had slowly evolved from the Ladies' Relief Society's interfaith efforts to rescue the immigrant waifs who were brought in on ships and let loose in the city. In desperate need of a decent receiving facility, the women had turned to the Unitarian minister, Thomas Eliot. He, in turn, had called on his friends, a galaxy of Portland's most influential and wealthiest citizens, to bankroll this work of Christian benevolence and to serve as trustees. The women were not yet legally able to form corporations or hold real estate, but other than that, they were clear about having complete control as directors. They would set the policy, draw up the budgets, hire the staff, and screen the cases.[27]

The executive officers tended to come from other denominations, but the Unitarians' presence was always critical. From the moment their own Mary Frazar had supervised raising the start-up funds to the point where their pastor emeritus left the board of trustees after fifty-two years, The Church of Our Father considered it one of its missions. Unitarian friends had paid more than their share. Miss Dix sent a $112 check for The Home along with a bit of advice about thinking ahead as they figured the costs. Tom's father, who thought it a promising scheme and liked the fellows Tom named as trustees, also sent them a generous check. William's only concern was that Etta would end up as "Matron and Minister at Large, Secretary and Treasurer and Buying and Distributing Agent!" His fears were unfounded. Already in place was a team of women who managed The Home so effectively that years would go by without their consulting the seated trustees, and then it was only to have them sign deeds when facilities were expanded. By force of tradition, the women continued to have the men keep the key to the safe even after the laws had been liberalized to allow them to buy and sell property.[28]

All this changed after Mrs. Faling died in 1917, and it became clear that Muscular Christianity had not spawned a culture where every trustee did his Father's business as Jesus had. When a will was submitted for probate and showed just $3,000 marked for the orphanage and $670,000 for the estate's two executors, red flags went up. A distant cousin got wind of it and filed suit, claiming the will was a phony. The Home's directors concurred and predicted the case would be open and shut. Indeed, once it finally went to court, the evidence of a crime was all there, laid out unambiguously by the culprits themselves. One of the rogue beneficiaries, Thomas N. Strong, admitted under sworn testimony that he had destroyed the original document while his codefendant, C. Lewis Mead, had drafted another in 1915. In addition, the prosecution had found the original stenographic notes in which the bequest to The Home was plainly recorded.

But rather than rule for conviction, the probate judge, who was known to take kickbacks routinely, upheld the defense. Compounding the bench's corruption and the dastardly acts of Strong and Mead, the trustees refused to challenge the will even after Xarifa Faling's intentions were proven beyond a doubt. The emeritus Unitarian pastor, reputed saint that he was, voted not to be part of the suit from which The Home, strapped for funds, stood to gain so much. In short, when faced with rocking the boat in which the most powerful men in the city—some honest, some crooked—were fellow commuters, this clutch of elite civic leaders showed where their genuine loyalties lay. Before the ladies would see justice done, they would have to appeal to the state's highest court.

As usual, the minister's family knew nothing more of these sordid details than what they read in the papers. They were used to him keeping them "in the dark" and "doing the ostrich act," as his youngest son, Thomas Dawes Eliot, griped in frustration. Rather than have it "irritate" him to see the mess that his cronies had made, the pastor emeritus buried himself in his books. Henrietta was not as hard on their father but did make a mental note of the fact that his deafness "practically disappeared" when he got away to Hood River. The family could well understand his desire to shut out the facts of the scandal, for it was as much a personal as a public tragedy for them all, and the series of trials dragged on for five years, twisting the knife in their hearts. The Eliots and the Strongs had shared half-a-century of warm memories. The defendant's father, William Strong, once a justice of the Supreme Territorial Courts of Washington and Oregon, was the man Thomas Eliot trusted to draw up the legal documents at the time of The Home's incorporation. Strong's grandsons Stuart, Robert, and Fred had been special pals of the Eliot youths, and the parents had spent many evenings together sitting on each others' porches while the children chased after the fireflies and chattered like katydids. Etta knew them to be "a *lovely* family...each and every one of them," and her feelings were hard to reconcile with the revelations about Thomas Strong.[29]

Determined to make his parents proud, the accused had followed his father into the legal profession after a false turn to engineering. There he gave every outward sign of being a highly principled fellow. Even as he was rewriting the will with Mead, he was pushing a new city charter intended, he said, to keep the crooks out of government. He had seemed so manly and sure of himself as he followed his father's path, one would never have guessed he had lost his moral compass along

FIGURE 7.2. The Unitarian Women's Alliance on the steps of the Church of Our Father at Seventh and Yamhill, Portland, Ore., 2 May 1923. In the front row (l. to r.) the Rev. Emeritus Thomas Lamb Eliot, his wife, Henrietta Robins Mack Eliot, their son the Rev. William Greeenleaf Eliot Jr., and his wife, Minna Sessinghaus Eliot. Photograph by Charles Butterworth. Courtesy of the First Unitarian Church, Portland, Ore.

the way. Once the truth came out, Etta's unhappy lot was to forward the calls for emergency meetings to Tom at his Hood River hideaway and to have some "long 'heart-to-heart'" visits with Mrs. Strong. As for The Home's directors, this assault on the myth that manliness could be built from the soft clay of money and charm cured them of abdicating their rights and authority ever again.[30]

To be sure, there were women like Alice Wilbur who clung to the separate domains. Still dressing up dolls for the holiday fairs and making their social calls in the city, they cast their ballots begrudgingly after the suffrage crusaders prevailed. However shaken their trust that the men would guard women's interests according to law, they trusted their sex even less. Others, drawing a lesson from the disastrous reliance on men to protect The Home's interests, prepared their ballots as carefully as they did their Sunday school lessons. Etta Eliot always rushed out to be first in line on Election Day, explaining that she had a lot to get off her chest. For the women who served as The Home's directors, however, it took more than equal suffrage to satisfy their sense of justice and duty. When the treasurer's books were opened, they found that the forgery was only one thread in a much broader pattern of blatant neglect. The unpaid bills, sloppy bookkeeping, dubious loans, and bad investments made it obvious there was no sense in asking the board of trustees to do anything more.[31]

It was February 1923, six years after Mrs. Faling's death and eight months after her 1911 will was upheld by the state supreme court, when Thomas Eliot finally noticed that many "small problems domestic and church wise" had snowballed and set the world "rocking." He had felt the tremors as far away as Hood River he said, and he thought it was time to yield to the new social order by giving the fairer sex more representation on The Home's board of trustees. At eighty-one he had sat there for half-a-century, and now he was ready to vacate his seat with the recommendation that henceforth, it be set aside for a female. His associates were amenable and agreed among themselves to announce their largesse at the upcoming annual meeting.

Thomas Eliot said he was confident that out of it all "some great souls" would emerge "with messages and examples of inspiration." And that is, indeed, what happened, though not the way he imagined. Having quietly hired a lawyer to disincorporate and write a new charter, the ladies, playing their trump card, removed every one of the men and replaced them with women. The look of the seated assembly at the Unitarian church changed, as well. The emeritus pastor, seldom seen in his pew on Sunday mornings, was out in the country listening to his son leading services over the radio. Gone, too, were the women whose active and vocal discipleship had outgrown the church.[32]

8

A Larger Syntax

Let us hear no more of "woman's sphere" either from our
wise (?) legislators beneath the gilded dome, or from
our clergymen in their pulpits.
—Louisa May Alcott to Maria S. Porter, 1873

Decades before there were radios to serve as a measure of last resort,
Abby's daughter-in-law in the East, Mary Jackson May Eliot, had the
solution to shrinking attendance at church. Unwilling to wait until
Christopher grabbed a bullhorn to round up the truants, she taught
him to broaden the definition and reach of their work as a clergy
couple. Their friends would say that the hand of God had set this
process in motion by dropping a heavy blanket of snow over Boston in
1882. It happened to be the first Sunday Christopher preached in the
Dorchester parish, where Mary's family had lived for years at the foot
of Meeting House Hill. Normally, the Mays would have taken their
horse and carriage into the city to worship at the Unitarian Church of
the Disciples. But with the roads impassable, they decided to trudge up
the hill to give the new man in town a good looking-over. Thus had the
twenty-five-year-old pastor met a woman of twenty-two who was ready
to change his perceptions of parish ministry and women's domain.[1]

Mary's kin were all ardent crusaders for social justice. Her father,
Frederick Warren May, had helped grease the wheels of the Underground
Railroad and put his wealth into penal reform, public schools, and

TABLE 6. **The Eliots in Boston**

Joseph May + Dorothy Sewell
1760–1841   1756–1825

Samuel May + Mary Goddard
1776–1870   1787–?

Rev. Samuel Joseph May
1797–1871

Louisa May + Amos Bronson Alcott
1792–1828   1799–1888

Louisa May Alcott
1832–1888

Rev. Samuel May
1810–1899

Frederick Warren Goddard May + Martha Rand Morse
1821–1904   1827–1894

Abigail Williams May
1829–1888

Christopher Rhodes Eliot + Mary Jackson May
1856–1945   1859–1926

Rev. Frederick May Eliot
1889–1958
+
Elizabeth Berkeley Lee
1888–1967

Martha May Eliot
1891–1978
+
Ethel Collins Dunham
1883–1969

Abby Adams Eliot
1892–1992
+
Anna Eveleth Holman
1892–1969

women's rights. Frederick's cousin Samuel Joseph May, a Unitarian minister, was both reviled and revered for his out-and-out feminist sympathies and abolitionist sermons. Willing to sacrifice caste and popularity for his convictions, he welcomed sister free-slaver Angelina Grimké into his pulpit to argue their case in front of a scandalized audience. Outside the church, where the gatherings were less civil, the preacher was rushed by the mobs and burned in effigy more than once. A second paternal uncle of Mary's, "the other Reverend Samuel," had left a Unitarian pulpit to take a top post in the Commonwealth's Anti-Slavery Society.[2]

The willingness to challenge oppression ran through the women's blood, too. Author and older cousin Louisa May Alcott impressed her nieces with novels that showed that girls "could amount to something" when they became adults. Like the thousands of other "tripping maids" who read *Little Women* (1868–69) when it came out, ten-year-old Mary saw herself in Jo March. Jo bridled against the customs that shackled their sex and retained her subversive ideals even after the author reluctantly married her off. The image of Jo and her husband running a boarding school at the end of the book and teaching the boys to value good hearts and minds over brawn and wealth led Mary to hope that her daughters would also be teachers. Cousin Louisa's real choices in life gave her stories a special validity. Mary knew that, like Jo, who cut off her tresses to help pay the bills when her father was ill, the author had supported the family after her father Bronson Alcott's utopian schemes left them penniless. Louisa had worked as a governess, actress, and seamstress before being able to eke out a living by writing. Inspired as much by the author's life as by the delightful heroines who shared her resourcefulness, industry, thrift, and faithful devotion to family, her nieces ensured that her stories would have a much larger shelf life than fiction.[3]

In Abby Williams May, Frederick's daughters had further proof that young females like Jo did exist and could go on to make a difference by bucking convention. At a time when women of breeding wore tightly-laced corsets and long, heavy gowns and considered themselves incomplete without marriage, this energetic paternal aunt, like Cousin Louisa, wore plain, tailored clothes and exemplified the androgynous spirit that ran through the May endowment. During the Civil War, Aunt Abby had headed the Massachusetts work for the U.S. Sanitary Commission and afterward helped its transition to the American Red Cross, the institution from which the female profession of nursing emerged. She pushed for creating the Boston Latin School for Girls and ran for a seat on the Massachusetts Board of Education. Not easily swindled, she won the elected position on appeal after the city solicitor ruled her ineligible because of her sex. With Mary A. Livermore, Julia Ward Howe, and Frances E. Willard, Abigail May was also a guiding force behind the American Association for the Advancement of Women.[4]

This unmarried aunt, whose wardrobe and public crusading amazed her nieces, was also a model parent. When Frederick lost his first wife in childbirth and felt he could not rear his daughter alone, Aunt Abby became both father and mother to Eleanor Goddard May. Although she despaired that her time was "cut up," and that it was "almost impossible…to be sure of an uninterrupted half-hour," the nieces could see from the seamless devotion that ran through her public and private concerns that her unconventional life was all of a piece.[5]

The family's progressive community at the Church of the Disciples prodded the May girls to actualize this inheritance. Member and lay preacher Julia Ward Howe, a close comrade of Abigail May's, insisted their sex were as fit as young males to follow God's bidding, wherever it led. While she brought no official credentials, nobody doubted that she was ordained to preach when she stood on the platform and spoke of their secret ambitions as sacred commands. Her Woman's Ministerial Conference, while frail from the start and short-lived, met often enough at the church in the years when the May girls were coming of age to embolden the middle sister, Anna, to see herself in a pulpit. By her twenties, Anna was privately preparing herself for the ministry, first at home and then as a special student at Radcliffe College. During the academic year of 1893–94, she enrolled to study philosophy under Josiah Royce and William James. Neither an ill-advised marriage that led to a drawn-out and messy divorce, nor the strain of rearing two daughters alone distracted her from her ambition. It was only after being ignored by every church she hoped would ordain her that Anna realized just how advanced Mrs. Howe's vision was and conceded defeat.[6]

Aunt Abby's friend Mary Livermore, meanwhile, convinced the youngest May sister, Sarah, that she should become a physician. Their sex's unique "mother heart," Mrs. Livermore said, would equip a young woman like Sarah to minister just as "divinely" to broken bodies as Anna would mend broken spirits. As for Mary's vocation, temperance reformer Frances Willard crystallized it by describing the vital work of homemaking on a larger scale: Women like Mary would carry their moral authority into the public arenas and make "every place on this rounded earth" more "Home-like." Mrs. Livermore's lectures enlarged on this call to maternalistic reform in posing the question "What shall we do with our Daughters?" She challenged mothers and wives to be bolder in setting their goals and to bring up the next generation to do the same. As described by these eloquent advocates of egalitarian marriage, this syntax of womanly service fit easily into the life that Mary May envisioned with Christopher Eliot.[7]

The news of the couple's engagement in April 1888, and the plan for a wedding that fall broke through the gloom that had clung to Abby since losing William the year before. Now she made it her "one all-absorbing interest," and everything she was able to learn about her new daughter-to-be delighted her. The Mays, of course, were excellent stock, she wrote the children in Portland. They had deep Unitarian roots, an outstanding record on temperance and slavery, and a faithful association with William's beloved colleague, James Freeman Clarke. Mary, now twenty-eight, had not been to college but she was smart and well read. By all accounts, she was also a wonder at helping her parents at home and at organizing committees at church. Obviously she had all the equipment for being a minister's wife.[8]

Abby was glad, too, that Mary, like Etta, did not shrink from giving advice but claimed a license long overdue in Eliot parsonages. During their courtship, Mary encouraged Christopher to adopt what he could of her minister's work at the Church of the Disciples. While it might not be realistic to bring in the sort of progressive courses and lectures for which Mr. Clarke was famous in downtown Boston, Christopher's fossilized country parish, where little had changed in 200 years, could profit from an infusion of active religious intent that was democratic, inclusive, and socially relevant. At Mary's suggestion, Christopher altered Dorchester's order of worship, weaning the people off silent consumption and making them real participants. He taught the puzzled assembly to read from the psalms responsively and to join him in saying the Lord's Prayer aloud, as Mary's family was doing in Boston. Then came the storied Communion Sunday when Christopher pulled off a sleight of hand, changing the wine into water in the interest of total abstinence. This was followed by what he considered his most "revolutionary" reform, which broadened the church's voting body from owners of pews to anyone who contributed $5 or more a year.[9]

The womanly nudges that got the Dorchester pastor to push his church to reconcile its polity with its theology eventually spurred the couple's decision to leave for a parish that needed less prodding. Bulfinch Place Church in Boston's West End had been ministering to the down-and-out for the better part of the century when the Eliots arrived to take over the work. In 1834, the Unitarian minister-at-large, Joseph Tuckerman, had pulled it under the auspices of the newly created consortium of sturdier parishes known as the Benevolent Fraternity. His successor, Samuel H. Winkley, had been faithful to Tuckerman's purpose of reaching out to every kind of human condition, rendering practical aid, and providing a place where rich and poor could be led to a higher life through worship. The building itself was a modest brick structure that stood on the corner of two narrow lanes in the run-down district above Pinkney Street. Later known as the North Slope of Beacon Hill, the area now had only a few of the Negro families who colonized there before the majority migrated to the South End and Roxbury neighborhoods. By the 1890s, it was mainly a mixture of Polish, Irish, Italian, and Jewish families, all speaking a common, heavily accented language of poverty.

In 1894, when the opportunity came for someone new to tend this anomalous parish, the Eliots were in the right place to take a long view and change direction. The family, which now included five-year-old Frederick, three-year-old Martha, and eighteen-month-old Abby, had pulled up their anchor in Dorchester and sailed to Oxford, England, where Christopher had decided to take a sabbatical. While there, he and Mary had gone to the slums to see what the settlement houses were doing, and they had begun to wonder if they could find something similar back in the States. When Winkley, approaching his fiftieth year at Bulfinch Place, put out a call for a right-hand man who would go on to be his successor, Boston became the Eliots' next destination.[10]

FIGURE 8.1. Christopher, Frederick, baby Abby, Mary, and Martha, 1893. Courtesy of Mary. C. Eliot.

Improbable as it seemed to the Brahmins that anyone bearing the Eliot name could be happy in Boston's West End, Mary was sure they were in the right place when she saw her husband greeting the people and watched the well-dressed sub-urbanites sharing worn hymnals with locals in threadbare jackets. She saw here the same potential for friendships between folks who rarely mixed that she had enjoyed at the Church of the Disciples. With Christopher's down-to-earth preaching and

FIGURE 8.2. Looking down Bulfinch Place toward the Unitarian church at the intersection with Bulfinch Street, ca. 1890. Courtesy of the Andover-Harvard Library Archives.

Mary's genius for hospitality, Bulfinch Place Church showed remarkable growth while the big churches in the Back Bay were looking emptier every year.[11]

More significantly, the numbers Mary and Christopher saw at their chapel on Sundays were only a fraction of what their nonsectarian welcome brought during the week. By 1904, the demand for classes in sewing, cooking, and carpentry, and the lines for the exercise rooms, clothing closet, and medicine pantry so strained the worn facilities that major renovations had to be made. At Mary's suggestion, the carpenters first reduced the size of the main auditorium, leaving a hall that seated 300, and then used the freed space to carve out a larger, more clearly defined parish house. New club rooms were added as well as industrial workshops, music and art studios, a third-floor gymnasium, lockers and dressing stalls, showers and tubs, and an upgraded kitchen. The newly equipped institutional church had never been more committed to bringing its neighbors on to a plane where there were no ranks or castes.[12]

The Eliots had only to leave the parish, however, to be reminded how tenuous an ideal such equality was. The well-heeled patrons on whom they depended but never saw anywhere near the West End acted as if the mission church was a warehouse for charity cases. Christopher's efforts to change this perception were sadly counterproductive. The more he insisted that Bulfinch Place was "in no outward sense" a charity but a church where each person had dignity and the concept of classes did not apply, the more he could feel the same condescension directed at him and his family. This had always gone on among ministers, but it nettled and took getting used to. To work with the poor seemed "discreditable" to a shocking number, he warned younger colleagues who also felt called to the slums. If they were really committed to going where they were needed the most, he advised, they would have to be ready "to lose all personal social standing" with "the more snobbish" people.[13]

This was but one of the jolts that brought the Eliots back to reality whenever they thought they had freed their relationships from the intrusions of class. Although their regular income was low and the monied elite looked down on them, their gentry blood gave them access to comforts unknown to their West End constituents. With a tidy bequest from the Eliot side, a generous check from the Mays, and several choice contacts, the family was able to buy a fine home on the quiet, elm-shaded South Slope of Beacon Hill. Two West Cedar Street was a prime location. The golden-domed State House was just out of sight, and everything was convenient. The Boston Common and Public Garden were only a stone's throw away, as were the fine shops and the newly built trolley lines, Mary could tell her in-laws. The church was also an easy walk up and over the flat of the slope. If their quarter was not as exclusive as the neighborhoods in the Back Bay, their six-story brownstone—with indoor plumbing and space for three children, two maids, and guests—was palatial compared to the West End tenements only ten minutes away. The wide psychic framework it took to sleep in a neighborhood built from old wealth and power while spending one's days in a parish that was worlds apart demographically, allowed for a view of humanity few Unitarians ever had.[14]

If, as Christopher claimed, he could no longer draw a clear line between social work and the ministry, Mary could make no distinction between her work for maternalistic reform and her duties as mother, wife, and parish first lady. Having managed to set the terms for her own egalitarian marriage, she worked to secure the same parity for women throughout institutional life. In 1909, with the Woman's Ministerial Conference nearly defunct and its guiding spirit, Julia Ward Howe, with less than a year to live, Mary was part of the remnant that met at her sister Anna May Peabody's house in a last-ditch attempt to rescue Mrs. Howe's dream. Her work with the Unitarian Women's Alliance was more rewarding, both during her terms on the national board and her years overseeing the Bulfinch Place chapter. No less religious in working for women's full complement of political rights, Mary also gave time to the Women's Municipal League, helped to promote the agenda of the Good Government Association, and often appeared with a monitor's badge at the polls on Election Day.[15]

With Christopher's even temper and humor serving as Mary's balancing wheels—as one of the family described the secret of her success as a feminist—the minister's wife had a stabilizing relationship from which to take aim at the issues that called for reform. But her natural grace and domestic bent were invaluable assets, as well, as they softened her radical edge and made her less threatening. Even her activist children thought of her first as a consummate nurturer. She was the warmhearted neighbor who appeared at the door with hot chocolate and soup when the carolers came by on Christmas Eve, the intrepid hostess who served hardy luncheons to hundreds of clergy in Boston each May, and the minister's wife who carried big baskets of fruit and staples to indigent families. She took charge in the kitchen and nursery at church, and her lobbying for better schools, sanitation, and decent housing came under the arc of her womanly work. A devoted wife and a mother of three cunning youngsters, Mary defied the stereotype of the angry feminist bent on reform.[16]

Mary's persistence in tending her family and running to meetings was all the more striking because she was diabetic. Insulin, which revolutionized how the disease was managed, would not be discovered until she was into her sixties. After years on the standard regimen of "compensatory eating," she was close to a hundred pounds heavier than the average woman by the time she married, and every step was hard work. The children's image of her directing the yearly May luncheons at church, her freshly starched shirtwaist and skirt limp with sweat and her scarlet face glistening, said it all. Why couldn't she "train up some nice young thing to do the heaviest part of the work?" her worried family kept asking. "Angels don't have to stay in the kitchen *always*, you know," they pressed. She had earned the right to "sit on the platform and entertain" the distinguished guests, but it was years before she would make that concession. Mary was uncomplaining again when Dr. Elliot Joslin, a leading clinician, took over her case in 1914, outlawed the rich, frequent meals, and put her instead on his "starvation treatment." The regimen was so spartan that her daughters wondered how she would survive, this being a woman who kept her foot on the throttle after the tank was empty.[17]

─────────────── ☙ ───────────────

The power of female hegemony left its mark not only at Two West Cedar and Bulfinch Place Church but also at the summer retreat that became the Eliots' heaven on earth. Nestled among the emerald groves on the northeastern shore of Memphremagog, a magnificent lake of thirty-two miles that straddled Vermont and Canada, the Eliot campsite grew up with saplings that got to be towering cedars, and generations of goldfinches, warblers, hermit thrushes, and loons. On the outer circle, the peaks of the ageless Green Mountains stood guard against civilization, and after dark, the stars staged spectacular fireworks overhead. It was "a mystic experience" to see an aurora borealis; and the children "loved the thunderstorms," too, "and were not a bit afraid." This answer to Portland's Hood River quickly became the Bostonians' temple and home "more…than any other place," and continued to be for eighty years.[18]

The Eliots had their good friends the Barrowses to thank for this sanctuary. Isabel and her husband, Samuel—who went by his middle name, June—had preceded Mary and Christopher as Dorchester's ministerial team. In the summer of 1878, several years before June stepped down to become the *Christian Register*'s editor, the couple had got up a party of six and made their first foray into the wilds of Quebec. Billed as a "Unitarian Raid on Canada," the scouts had discovered the little cove by a sandy beach that was later called Birchbay.[19]

It was natural that the Barrowses' site had inspired the Eliots' Camp Maple Hill, so similar were the two couples. June, eleven years older, was a craggier version of Christopher. A tall, lanky, sweet-tempered man with a deeply religious side and a droll sense of humor, he championed any reform he believed would redeem or dignify life. His crusades, especially temperance, suffrage, prison reform, and world peace, were the younger man's causes as well; and the adjectives used to describe the one—gentle, steady, hardworking, patient, devout, and down-to-earth—were also the words most often assigned to the other. The men were also alike in having married their comple-ments: warm-hearted, deep-feeling partners born with insurgency in their veins.[20]

Isabel, a wiry woman who barely came up to June's chest, bore the stamp of a long procession of nonconformists. Her grandfather had been roundly condemned as a her-etic in his native Scotland for advocating the education of women. Her father, who swore by Sylvester Graham's high-fiber vegetarian diet, was to blame for the dishes his daughter attempted to force on her unhappy friends, and the inspiration for her becoming a doctor. Isabel's mother, who liberated herself from fashion's stranglehold by sending away for Amelia Bloomer's pattern, was likewise responsible for the scandalous outfit her daughter adopted in 1865, when, at twenty, she entered the New York Medical College for Women. Unfazed by the spitballs and taunts from the men with whom the women attended lectures, Isabel earned her degree as an oculist and set out to repair the effects of discrimination against the most vulnerable groups. While June was employed as Secretary of State William Seward's assistant, Isabel joined him in Washington and practiced at Freedman's Hospital, one of the few facilities anywhere that accepted free blacks as patients. Within a few years, the couple was back in New England, June at Harvard Divinity School and Isabel with their baby Mabel, cultivating the radical circle who summered with them in Quebec.[21]

Isabel was a woman inclined "to direct those with whom she came in contact," so there was no question that she would take charge and rule the camp with a ruthless benevolence. Running the place as a cross between boot camp and playground, she banned women's corseted clothing in favor of bloomers and shirtwaists. She called the campers to meals with a bugle and tried to convert them to high-fiber diets to keep them in shape for her picnics and hikes, climbing and boating, dances and games. However despotic, her methods relaxed and rejuvenated the older set while teaching the young that women could lead and have the respect of confident men.[22]

By the summer of 1900, when the Eliot children were old enough for their par-ents to use their rain check and visit the Barrowses' camp on the lake, every cabin and path had a tale to tell about Isabel's guiding vision. None told the story more vividly than the campsite's first permanent building. This cedar structure stood as a monument to the enterprise of nine females who answered the summons when Isabel hollered for help in 1890. Her plan was for them to build a log cabin before "the protective men" arrived with other ideas and got in the way. For city women to tackle a project like this was almost unheard of, but this was no run-of-the-mill construction team. Every one of the crew had been training on the front lines of feminist action and was ready to work off the tension through physical exercise and laughter.

Along with Mabel and Isabel Barrows, the workers included Alice Stone Blackwell, coeditor with her parents Lucy Stone and Henry Blackwell of the leading women's rights paper, the *Woman's Journal*. Anna Howard Shaw, who had earned degrees in medicine and theology and was lecturing now for the National Woman Suffrage Association, was also there. Her personal secretary and lifelong companion, Lucy Anthony, Susan B. Anthony's niece, accompanied her. These were joined by Zilpha D. Smith, a regular with the Barrowses at the *Christian Register*'s office lunches and general secretary of Boston's Associated Charities. Florence Buck, a science teacher from Kalamazoo, was the only new face. She was planning to be a minister like her partner, Marion Murdock. Marion was unable to come and was counting on Florence, who brought her guitar, to have enough relaxation and fun for them both. Once the team was assembled, their foreman, Isabel, trudged through the woods marking trees to be felled. As the logs were made ready, her gleeful companions lifted them into place, working their way up the walls, leaving spaces open for windows and doors. Determined that no one would have to stoop—for this was against their religion—Isabel measured meticulously before giving the signal to hoist the rafters.[23]

As June Barrows wrote in a piece for the *Christian Register* later that summer, his wife and her friends were building a cabin but not a separatist culture. By early August, the women had realized "that men were too useful to be ignored" and had ordered them back, quickly put them to work, and forced them to stay for the "cabin warming." Yet even when all the men were there, the current that powered the camp that summer and every year was generated by a female dynamic. For the battered troopers like Anna Shaw, who was still having migraines her first week at camp, the sympathetic companionship was a blessing, if not a cure. Florence Buck, who had come to the lake with her own share of suffering, would have been grateful just getting away from the bigots, she told her hostess. But actually being able to pour out her heart to others who understood and needed no explanation for why, "at whatever cost or pain," she continued to live by her principles, was a gift she would never forget.[24]

Isabel Barrows was still taking captives a decade later when Mary and Christopher herded their children onto the train to Newport, Vermont, and from there took the steamer across the Canadian line to the Barrowses' camp on the northeastern shore of the lake. It was love at first sight, and the romance filled every line of Mary's reports. "Camping out," she explained to the relatives, meant sleeping in tents, taking baths in the lake, and eating one's meals at a rugged table set up "on a sort of piazza." The girls wore "bloomers" instead of long skirts and went bare-legged just like the boys and the grown-ups. They all liked to fish, could handle a rowboat, knew how to swim, and had wonderful times.[25]

Mary left it to Alice Stone Blackwell's vignettes in the *Woman's Journal* to fill in the color that set it apart from the family retreat at Hood River. Blackwell's account of a Sunday morning worship service in 1902, when Christopher happened to be the speaker, captured a motley company of campers and native residents who came from around the lake and settled themselves on tarpaulins, rocks, and the trunks of some old fallen trees. Among them were Greeks and Armenians, "a dark-eyed Jewish girl side by side with…a young Canadian maiden; a French girl and a German Fraulein." At least as many Americans were distributed here and there, including "several little girls of distinguished Boston families," who ran around "in divided skirts" and no stockings. Isabel sat at her portable organ, keeping the service moving along, and when she gave the signal, the group—representing a half-dozen different religions—began singing heartily out of the "little Unitarian hymn-books." During the sermon, a cluster of girls shelled a hefty basket of peas, while Burnet, the Barrowses' teenage son, sat knitting intently nearby.[26]

When the hymnals were not in use, the gatherings hummed with the buzz of reform, something Mary thought best not to mention when writing to Christopher's side of the family. The Wilburs, who visited briefly in 1903, had no advanced warning that one of the favorites at camp would be the notorious William Lord, whose call to The Church of Our Father in Portland had dashed Dodie's hopes for Earl's reinstatement. Here in this enclave of Eastern liberals, the spoiler, who then lost his own place in Portland by airing his liberal politics, was much beloved and respected for what he believed. The leftist consensus became even more pronounced after 1905, when the lakeside wedding of Mabel Barrows and Henry Mussey—the presumptive managing editor of the progressive weekly *The Nation*—exposed their radical friends to the magic of camping out in the wilds. This group began to come back every year, ensuring a constant stream of discussion about how to better the world. In 1909 and 1912, when Mabel hosted two colloquies, she had no trouble getting some thirty or forty social workers and writers to come up to Birchbay to rough it and talk for the better part of two weeks.[27]

In the summer of 1903, their third year at Birchbay, Mary and Christopher purchased the site for Camp Maple Hill, a neighboring parcel of 54 acres of forest and 900 feet of lakefront, for which they paid $500. The following summer, as they and the children cleared ground for the tents, marked trails, planted gardens, and put up a cedar log cabin replete with a fireplace, kitchen, and dining porch, their respective roles also took shape. While Christopher, the surveyor and sexton, gently befriended each "stick and stone," Mary, commander-in-chief, adopted Isabel's routinized methods. She served as head housekeeper, ran the kitchen, fed the family and guests, and sent frequent convoys with homemade desserts to the neighbors. The picnics she held for the local farming families became a tradition that had her feeding a hundred additional mouths at one sitting each summer. Under Mary's regime, the camp came alive with spontaneous singing, rousing camp cheers, and impromptu theatricals. There were bravos, too, as Mary read from their favorite ballads of Sir Walter Scott, breathing the wild enchantment of Scotland into the grandeur of Memphremagog.[28]

While Mary relinquished the colloquies to the neighbors' primarily masculine discourse, she cultivated her own camp's potential for serious womanly talk. From its maiden season in 1904, when Christopher, Frederick, and Thomas Stearns Eliot had little chance against nine noisy females, Camp Maple Hill was the distaff's domain. In addition to Mary, Martha, and Abby, Anna May Peabody and her girls Mary and Helen were there for the opening. So was Etta and Tom's youngest girl, Henrietta, who passed up Hood River to sample the life her aunt Mary described in her letters. At twenty-three, Henrietta had dreams that her Portland family thought foolish. Not interested in becoming a bride, she wanted "to *work* at something" that paid. She hoped for more understanding at Camp Maple Hill and was not disappointed.[29]

Henrietta's ambitions to be a nurse or a teacher of home economics seemed tame to these Eastern women, whose female circle was aiming much higher. The youngest May sister, now Sarah May Stowell, had realized her goal of becoming a doctor, and Anna had not yet abandoned her hope of becoming an ordained minister. Nor did they need any justification for Henrietta's reluctance to marry. Although things were still going reasonably well for Sarah, who was practicing medicine with her husband, also a licensed physician, while doing the lion's share of rearing two sons, Anna's dreams of domestic happiness with Frederick W. Peabody had quickly turned into a nightmare for her. Blindly in love, she had fallen prey to an unbalanced, debt-ridden lawyer, an unscrupulous predator who pocketed most of Anna's small fortune before they had even taken their vows. When she realized that he was embezzling part of her father's estate and confronted him, he bullied her into silence and went into rages in front of their girls. Although she had yet to file for divorce, she had left with the children and taken refuge with Mary and Christopher's family. This had cut off the verbal abuse, if not the lying and reckless spending; and Anna's relief to be even this free of the scoundrel was heard for miles around as her lusty yodels went echoing through the hills as she paddled across the lake.[30]

Back in the city, the Eliots' bumpy commutes between the haves and have-nots broadened the children's understanding of caste and social inequities. On Saturday mornings, the girls and their brother were royally fetched by their grandfather's coachman and taken to play on his sprawling estate in the Dorchester countryside. By Sunday, the youngsters were headed again for Bulfinch Place and their Sunday school classes

FIGURE 8.3. Mary and "Chum" at Camp Maple Hill, 1923. Courtesy of Mary C. Eliot.

"with children from poor, uneducated homes." This was followed by after-church duty helping prepare the food for the hoboes who showed up for coffee and sandwiches and "some little entertainment." Mary's efforts to find the best schools for her brood also kept them shuttling back and forth between the vantage points of those who had every advantage and those who had few. A gift from their grandfather paid for their years of kindergarten on Beacon Hill where they mixed with children from affluent homes. Then they attended the public Prince School on Exeter Street, where, their mother explained, the girls and boys would be "more akin" to their "type." These were children from working-class families, including the sons and daughters of coachmen and other educated servants employed in the plush Back Bay mansions.[31]

After his years on Exeter Street, Frederick fit easily into the rhythms of Roxbury Latin, a public high school. Competitive academically, it was excellent preparation for Harvard without the intense social pressures one found at academies for the rich. Martha and Abby's high school years were less comfortable for them socially, but also more valuable as a result. Mary P. Winsor, a girlhood friend of their mother's, ran the high school of choice for the daughters of Boston's best families at 95 Beacon Street. Eager to have more diversity, she was looking for girls from homes that were cultured but not well-to-do, and she offered to waive the tuition if Mary would let her two daughters be part of the mix. The pudding never congealed as far as Martha or Abby could tell, and each spent five years at the Winsor School as part of the social runoff, the marginal group who were treated kindly but never accepted as after-school friends. As a consequence, they acquired not only the best Boston had academically but also the sensitivity to follow their own family's model of social relations after they left.

Mary, who never forgot the injustice of having no access to college, had decided before her daughters were born that they would be going to Radcliffe. She had nursed this ambition, first for herself and then for her girls, since the year she turned twelve and her minister, Mr. Clarke, who was sitting on Harvard's Board of Overseers, petitioned the university to institute coeducation. His wife, Anna Clarke, who had also helped launch the Women's Education Association (WEA) in Boston, had added her voice to the protest against Harvard's policies. But all such complaints and appeals were firmly rebuffed. Not until Mary turned twenty did her missed opportunity start to take shape. Albeit without degree-granting power or formal ties to the school, the WEA's embryonic Harvard Annex began to stir. By the time her daughters were born in the early 1890s, the Annex was looking more like a college and kicking to leave the womb. Long overdue, Radcliffe finally opened in 1894, and Mary was able to show her girls where they would be getting diplomas.[32]

Neither Martha nor Abby adhered to the program quite as their mother envisioned. Mary had hoped for at least one Jo March to emerge from their training at college, but neither chose classes with the intention of having a teaching career. Nor, for that matter, was either committed to staying the full course at Radcliffe. Martha, always rebellious and hungry for new adventure, startled the family and rankled the dean by insisting on spending her sophomore year at Bryn Mawr. Abby's poor grades and her talk about dropping out at the end of her junior year were unexpected, as well. Yet both girls completed their studies at Radcliffe, graduated along with their classes, and, most important, showed they had learned and would live by the precepts of right relations.[33]

At Radcliffe, where having a Back Bay address was not a requirement for inclusion, social skills and talent brought Martha and Abby a new popularity. Their yearbooks showed Martha as head of the play committee, a member of the basketball team, chairman of the Junior-Senior Luncheon, and secretary of her Class of 1913, in her senior year. Abby held several student government offices and was head of the Guild, the religious and philanthropic organization. In addition, and not in the yearbooks, both Eliot sisters belonged to The Club, an exclusive and problematic secret society. This covert organization had existed since 1898, when its founders had impishly crowned themselves "the social queens" of the college. As the roster had

FIGURE 8.4. A gathering at the May estate in Dorchester, Mass., just before the turn of the century. In the wagon (l. to r.): Anna May Peabody holding one of her daughters; grandfather Frederick Warren Goddard May; Maria May; Frederick Goddard May Jr., driving; Frederick May Eliot, standing in front; and on the porch to the left of the flag, Abby and Martha Eliot with their parents, Mary and Christopher. Courtesy of Eleanor Goddard May II.

never surpassed 25 at a school of roughly 500, and most Cliffies came from the best Boston families, the members prized their inclusion as the acme of social success.[34]

Martha and Abby had obviously not gotten on any imperial nerves—which was all it took for one Clubber to blackball a girl named Winnie in 1909—before the

autumn of 1911, when they were informed they were "in." Since no one had ever betrayed her vows and there was no pledging or "punch" procedure, the Eliot sisters had no idea that the organization existed, no warning that they would be asked to join on the spot, and no time to reflect on the implications of doing so. If they had any qualms, they curbed them for more than a year and enjoyed what the group had to offer. The chaperoned weekends in upscale neighborhoods featured the same sort of harmless amusements Martha and Abby had overheard their Winsor classmates relate. There were silly nicknames and rowdy games of shadow tag, "a grand walk-skip-and jump expedition," "a wild and violent Virginia Reel," charades, and composing and putting on skits. Lampooning the "bothersome" feminists was part of the repertory, as well.[35]

The Eliot sisters were sporting at first, giving the Clubbers the benefit of the doubt when they parodied suffrage crusaders and joked about women's rights. As new inductees, they wrote these off as part of the wicked but harmless humor that went with the group's playful tone and assumed that it did not reflect what the members believed. But by 1913, the sisters had not only ceased to find it amusing but also realized that they could no longer condone the rules of association. Right before The Club met in November, Martha and Abby and high school friend Mary Burrage alerted the officers not to expect them again. They were dropping out for good. The rest of the group was astounded, for no one had ever complained, much less resigned in protest against their policies. But this bomb-shell now brought up misgivings that a number of members had buried. There was "heated discussion" before a vote released those who wanted to sever their ties. Nor did tempers cool down after that, or newly awakened scruples relax to allow the queens to go on as they had before. The controversy the Eliot girls had set off was the Clubbers' swan song. There was never another initiation after that school year was over.[36]

Although the recording secretary wrote nothing of what was behind the rebellion or what the offending principles were, one can glean from the larger record that the insurrection was bound to have come, with or without a last straw or a sudden epiphany. A speaking tour by militant suffragette Emmeline Pankhurst in 1911; the Bread and Roses mill strike in Lawrence, Massachusetts, the following year; Radcliffe's courses in economics, political theory, and social reform; and Martha and Abby's firsthand acquaintance with poverty in Boston's West End; all these challenged the Eliot sisters to square their elitist ties with their sympathies on behalf of the disenfranchised rank and file. That The Club was covert as well as exclusive compounded the problem for them. James Freeman Clarke, Julia Ward Howe, and others whom they and their family admired emphatically singled out secrecy as the most pernicious cause of social injustice. Elizabeth Cady Stanton had pleaded with women to speak out against secret groups.

Mary Eliot's girls came away from this chapter more careful of their inherited values. The Club would remain their touchstone for gauging future associations, for knowing which to avoid and which had promise. It kept them alert to the machinations of secrecy, the bogus silence whose only purpose was putting a wall between those in the know and those kept in the dark. When as a student at Johns Hopkins Medical School in 1915, Martha would be invited to join its local sorority, she would make no commitment until she was sure it was neither covert nor elitist. "I don't think much of secret societies, as you know," she would write her mother, but everyone got invitations to this one, so it was no secret at all. The Zeta Phi sisters appeared to be "broad and democratic" in how they behaved, and with "so few girls" at Hopkins, it would be good to have their own group.[37]

9

New Rules of Engagement

You can join the professions and yet remain uncontaminated by them;
you can rid them of their possessiveness, their jealousy, their pugnacity,
their greed. You can use them to have a mind of your own.
— Virginia Woolf, "Three Guineas" (1938).

Martha May Eliot had the equipment to take women's fight to another
level. The Eliot ring on her finger, with its masculine motto, *Tace et Face*,
kept her close to her foremothers' stifled complaints, and the mouth she
inherited from the Mays was ready to give them a voice. It was a
commanding mouth, "straight and firm. Just like George Washington's,"
cautioned a witness who saw it at work on Capitol Hill. Invaluable too,
although not in the hall to lend his support at congressional hearings,
was Martha's brother, Frederick, whose sense of entitlement taught her to
handle resistance to female authority. His story of manly success was also
a cautionary tale that cured her of any desire she had to act like one of
the boys.[1]

A gifted speaker whose magnetism drew large congregations while
others were shrinking, Frederick would come to be known as the voice of
his family's denomination. After Harvard Divinity School and a stint as
associate pastor at First Parish, Cambridge, he went on to Unity Church
in St. Paul to serve as the senior minister. For the next two decades, the
city showcased his leadership and charisma, positioning him for a
twenty-year tour of duty as president of the American Unitarian
Association (A.U.A.). Martha was not surprised by her talented brother's

stellar ascent or by the emotional price he paid for his rise to the top of a muscular culture. She had observed that men who confused a combative thrust with a fighting spirit were prone to be lonely and scarred by the time the medals were handed out. Frederick's injuries taught her to disregard the rules of the dominant culture and to phrase her own mission in terms of inclusion instead of conquest and turf. That she could move through America's turbulent channels of public health, defend a world of many faiths and colors from killer diseases, and emerge without her brother's permanent injuries was a testament to the rules under which Martha Eliot chose to fight.[2]

Feminist though she was, Martha's mother had haplessly reared a male chauvinist. Each year on his birthday, September 15, Mary would ask the family to listen again to the story of Frederick's grand entrance in 1889. From the start, he had seemed to be larger than life, weighing in at a hefty eleven pounds, too big for the dainty gowns that Mary had labored over all summer. Sometimes she read from the record she kept of the boy's early signs of greatness: Two months and two weeks before his first birthday, he babbled something enough like "Amen" to persuade her that he had a pulpit waiting. He was "reading aloud" from a prayer book a year-and-a-half before he could recognize words. At three, he came to his mother clutching a roll of paper, his sermon, he lisped, the one he had just been writing at his "dex"![3]

Frederick loved the applause and knew how to play to an audience. During the Eliots' year in Oxford, he strutted about in a small cap and gown, a gift from a friend who had seen his eyes follow the scholars who passed them on campus. When back in the States he was given the lead in the Sunday school play, *The King and the Child*, he balanced the crown Mary fashioned for him with the ease of a boy who was born for the part. The only dissent would come from Martha, who stole his scepter and shoved him aside.[4]

The year that began with Martha's arrival on April 7, 1891, was remembered as the family's proverbial calm before the storm. Her grandmother Abby, who came from St. Louis to help, found "a model baby" who slept through the night like an angel, cried only when she was hungry, and, for the present, was ceding the limelight to Frederick. Coming after so verbal a brother, his sister seemed "backwards in conversation" at first, but even before she acquired the speech to allay her parents' concerns, she was ready to give the orders and have them obeyed. If her baby commands had not escalated to tantrums when they were ignored, her officiousness would have been funny in such a young child. At Dorchester's Sunday school picnics the toddler forced her way to the front of the line and pulled her small weight in the tugs-of-war that pitted the girls against the boys. When they heard that the pastor was taking his family to England for his sabbatical year, the people ventured that magisterial Martha would be a match for the queen![5]

With the birth of a second girl, Abby, on October 9, 1892, Frederick's chances of pulling rank became nil and Martha's sovereignty absolute. Endowed with the same "aggressive" and "dominating" May traits as her sister, Abby was just as capable of correcting adults, especially those who made the mistake of thinking her birth name was Abigail. As competitive as her sister, too, when the family made its maiden ascent up Owl's Head Mountain when Abby was seven, she was the first on the crest that towered over Lake Memphremagog. Inevitably, the girls had collisions, not mere verbal scuffles, but "real fights…with fists." Yet they were also best friends and natural allies in grappling with males for position. When the sisters went walking in Boston's rough neighborhoods, Martha, feeling her age and protective, took an umbrella, rain or shine, and kept it unsheathed to fend off the boys who teased her sister and blocked their way. Back home, with Martha taking the lead, they worked as a team to humble their brother and covered their ears when he boasted about winning prizes at school to show up the girls. Again, it was Martha who had the last word when the family made plans or debated an issue. From her perspective, the others were too polite or wobbly to make up their minds, while from their point of view, they were just speeding up the inevitable.[6]

Frederick's position of being outnumbered by forceful and capable sisters bore an unfortunate likeness to that of his uncle, his mother's brother, for whom he was named. Neither Mary, nor Anna, nor Sarah May had needed or wanted their brother's help; and as one of his granddaughters testified later, this only son spent the rest of his life feeling "swindled" out of his role as the family's "protector and master." Trapped in his adolescent frustration, the older Frederick, by this account, became an "obsessive manipulator who either wormed or bulldozed his way" into every kinswoman's business while harping on her inadequacies as a woman. Worried her boy might turn out the same way, Mary indulged his male vanities, his top hat and tails, his watch chain and fobs, his stylish pipes and the other props that engendered his peers' respect and shored up his confidence.[7]

The requisites for respectable manhood weighed heavily, too, in the younger Frederick's selection of a career. While taking a year after Harvard to travel abroad and consider his options, he worried that it would be "very hard" to hold up his head like a man in either one of the fields to which he was drawn: education and ministry. Especially back in the States, where physical prowess and action "meant everything," schoolrooms and churches were generally viewed as safe havens for the effete. He had always had qualms about this, he confessed, but had managed to keep them at bay until meeting a British professor who validated his fears. This scholar had recently taught at Harvard and seemed to be speaking objectively when he noted the bias Americans harbored against intellectual men. Any bright fellow who shut himself up with his books was "considered a loafer" or spineless despite the obvious need for more "really great thinkers" to root out America's problems.

The idea of being branded a limp academic was so repugnant to Frederick that when he was offered a contract to teach at Reed College, he hesitated, averse to committing himself to more than a year. The school withdrew its offer, and the question of his vocation was settled.[8]

Martha believed it was all for the best. Frederick intended to follow their father's example of parish ministry, using the church as a neighborhood center and stressing its nonsectarian mission. If he was taking this path to show he had muscle and not the "soft hands" of a sissy, so be it. More practical good would come from it than from being cloistered in academe. The only red flag, as she saw it, was the constant dissension among the clergy and Frederick's illusion that he could step in and mediate a lasting peace.[9]

Within a few years of his installation at Unity Church in St. Paul, the Unitarian theists and liberal ethicists were fighting again, and the conflict was centered in Frederick's Western Conference. The Humanists, he told his family, were on the defense and edgy, and the orthodox men had put up their own "strong barrier of reserve." By 1922, Frederick had learned that trying to play the peacemaker was not only futile but also lonely. With no one to sound out about his professional problems, he wished every day he were able to "run into Bulfinch Place and talk things over." Martha guessed that his overly cautious nature contributed to the problem, as did his concern with being liked and seeming fair to all sides. She had seen this in chess games and family discussions where Frederick was so slow in weighing his options that everyone else left the table before he looked up. With neutrality proving impossible, loyalties brittle, and battle lines shifting, Frederick had only the language of warfare to give him a sense of engagement and power. And while his military conceits would lubricate his advancement, they would also belie the unease of a man who saw enemies slipping "the buttons off their foils" wherever he looked.[10]

Frederick had not, like his father, chosen a partner whose interests and roles were so meshed with his own that he naturally sought her support and advice in these matters. Elizabeth Berkeley Lee was entirely unlike his sisters, mother, and aunts in her reticent nature and limited focus. A graduate of Radcliffe College's Class of 1910, Elizabeth had belonged to The Club, undisturbed by the implications that prompted Martha and Abby's insurgency. The records show she was still taking part as a gracious alumna in 1912, hosting a get-together for the secret society's members. Gentle and bright, she was nonetheless a lovely sister-in-law and a real catch for Frederick, who wanted a stay-at-home wife, not another adviser.

Elizabeth had been studying jewelry design at the School of the Boston Fine Arts and showing great promise when Frederick announced their engagement in 1914. Deeply in love and eager to have her own family, she readily gave up this interest to be the best possible minister's wife and looked forward to bearing the next round of Eliot preachers. As newlyweds, the couple bragged of being won-

FIGURE 9.1.   Newlyweds Elizabeth Lee and Frederick May Eliot with their mothers,
25 June 1915. Courtesy of Mary C. Eliot.

derfully matched. He was her "model husband," and she was "very quiet but
strong." Indeed, as his "elfin from fairyland," she was the perfect accessory for a
minister who likened himself to Sir Walter Scott's "young Lochinvar." While he
rode through the West in his shining armor to save the Unitarian kingdom,
Elizabeth waited for his return, lonely but uncomplaining. If it made for delightful
poetry, the dynamic seemed "really horrendous" to egalitarian family and friends
who saw "how completely Elizabeth waived her identity to submerge herself in
Frederick's huge aura." Frederick paid for this, too, with a loneliness that lay
beneath his dashing veneer.[11]

Martha's sympathy for her brother would have been greater if he had been satisfied scripting his life and Elizabeth's and not meddled in hers. But as soon as she
told the family about her own goal of becoming a doctor, a disclosure that she had
thought best to postpone until she was ready for college, he tried to steer her into a
sphere more compatible with his prerogatives. Although her mother, who hoped
she would teach, was surprised and no doubt disappointed, only Frederick objected
and did all he could to dissuade her. Martha pushed back, enlightening him on

women's place in the healing arts and their progress since 1849, when Elizabeth Blackwell became the first female to earn a degree in medicine. Admittedly, women had since found acceptance mainly in caring for women and children and earned the much lower fees of a low-status specialty. But still, their number had grown to where close to 5 out of every 100 physicians in practice were females. Frederick was unimpressed and persisted in trying to lower the bar after Martha went on to medical school. As late as her senior year, when it looked as if she might be taking top honors, he counseled a more relaxed pace and questioned her need to push quite so hard. It was, after all, a much "bigger thing to be in the first twenty than in the first five." It was a telling calculation from a Harvard summa cum laude who would not himself have been happy with anything less than first place in his class.[12]

Frederick's reaction was not unique among men who heard about Martha's ambition. While she was at Radcliffe, Massachusetts General Hospital's Richard Cabot had tried to convince her that she should forget about medical school and go straight into social work. Likewise, MIT epidemiologist, William T. Sedgwick, whom Martha consulted, had automatically taken her sex's alleged deficiencies into account and scaled down her prospects in medicine accordingly. She should be a research technician, he thought. She had already taken most of the courses that she would need for the job and would not have to bother with getting advanced preparation. Not surprised, Martha deftly rephrased her question: What would Dr. Sedgwick tell a young *man* who came to him for advice? His answer was all she needed to send in an application to Harvard, "just for the sake" of "being turned down" and getting that into the record. Then she applied to Johns Hopkins Medical School, as she had planned all along. Ahead of its time, this institution had opened in 1893 with the stipulation that women and men be admitted on equal terms.[13]

———————————————— ⁍⊘ ————————————————

Martha described her professional path as part of her family inheritance. Her yearning to travel and be on her own was her "Eliot ancestry coming out!" Her grandfather Eliot had the same longing to make his own way when he left the East Coast for St. Louis; and her uncle Tom had felt this way, too, when he took her aunt Etta and cousin Will out to the wilds of Oregon. Then, too, Martha noted, an interest in learning and schools, so pronounced on both sides of the tribe, must also have been in her blood, for she knew from the start that education would have a place in whatever she did. Inherited, too, was her goal to become a physician. Her wish to save lives and prevent needless suffering had come directly from hearing about the uncles and aunts who had died in St. Louis as babies and toddlers; about her grandfather May's first wife, who had died right after Aunt Eleanor's birth; and about her own mother's close brush with death after losing a third baby girl. As for Martha's plan to attend a coeducational medical school, this was part of her Eliot grandparents' vision for Washington University.[14]

Mapping out a vocation was also a matter of sorting through this inheritance and discarding what no longer fit. The tradition of ordained ministry was easy for Martha to put to the side, not because her aunt Anna's experience showed that its door was now closed to their sex, but simply because she had nothing to say from a pulpit. Martha valued the ceremonial side of the church as a family custom but increasingly found theological discourse irrelevant and distracting. Not even her father's plain Christian gospel took root as religious belief. She made do with her "loose-leaf religion," nothing fancy or "hard and fast," but a simple reverence for life and a confidence that the world could improve. If she had to sit through a sermon, let it be concrete and applicable. Let it call for engaged benevolence, and move at a clip to the closing hymn.[15]

On the other hand, Mary and Christopher's practical mission in the West End was a major piece of Martha's vocational blueprint. The minister's daughter had seen the many faces of life's "seamy side," with their human features of hunger, addiction, sickness, abuse, and despair. Glazed eyes had stared from the alleyways and some twenty saloons as she walked to the church. The faces and names of tearful children from broken families became real to her when she took over writing the postcards her father sent out to his child-placement board. Once having absorbed these early impressions, however reluctantly at the time, Martha knew that social work would be as germane to her medical focus as neighborhood service was to her mother and father's collaborative ministry.[16]

Martha was staking a claim to a medical specialty that was still too young and amorphous to fit into any existing slot. It took a year of volunteer work before enrolling in medical school for her to find a name and a mentor for what she was aiming to do. Massachusetts General Hospital, which served the residents of the West End, had recently launched a social service department. It was headed by Ida M. Cannon, a trained social worker and visiting nurse whose stint in the slums of St. Paul had convinced her that doctors were too provincial. The neighborhood's complex and wide-reaching problems called for collaborative efforts between physicians, experts in mental health, and social workers. Fresh insight into the social environment was especially vital, as this was still a serious blind spot for biomedical science and hospital-based clinicians. To encourage this teamwork, Miss Cannon was running a demonstration study of how patient-centered holistic methods could benefit the community. She was certain that Martha would take to it naturally and feel she was on the right track for becoming the "social doctor" she wanted to be.[17]

Martha was passed on to Ada Hawes Hinton, one of the most experienced staff, who showed her the ropes and supervised her assignments. The volunteer's job was to visit the places where patients who came to the hospital lived and to fill in the pictures the doctors had sketched from seeing them in the clinic. In recording the mundane details that clinicians ignored as irrelevant to their assessments, Martha would note the sleeping arrangements, a family's cooking procedures, the water supply, and situational stresses, all of which could be keys to a good diagnosis and therapy. She was also to be an ambassador for an agency that put an embargo on moralistic pronouncements. She would have to choose her words carefully to avoid the slightest suggestion that the racial or national backgrounds of people who lived in the slums were to blame for their plight. Martha's clients included both citizens of African descent and immigrants who had recently come from Europe.[18]

The intern had come to the project thinking she knew what these cases were like from seeing the poor families milling around the church. Now she realized how flat her impressions had been. In their homes, these were three-dimensional folks, individuals who had names and addresses and unforgettable stories to tell. Moreover, in tagging along with her supervisor, Martha was getting to see these clients through the more practiced eyes of a woman whose racial history deepened the insult of how they were having to live. Mrs. Hinton, a former teacher, was African American, as was her husband, a highly regarded Harvard-trained immunologist. These two were the first professional blacks whom Martha had ever known well, and they quickened a sense of outrage against America's history of racial oppression.[19]

For the medical student from Boston, whose Bible classes and public schools had always been integrated, the intense racial bigotry Martha witnessed in Baltimore was new to her, too. "The southern feeling showed plainly in the audience," she wrote her parents after going to see *The Birth of a Nation* in 1916. Although, as best she could tell, there had been "no hissing at the Negroes," "the enthusiasm" for the Klan was unbelievable, what with "applause and shrieks and whistles and stamping every time they appeared." These offensive displays were further incentive as Martha prepared to redress the shameful treatment of blacks and other oppressed Americans.[20]

Since there was no time except in the summer "to keep attached to the social end," Martha looked for community work in the Boston vicinity during those months, weaseling out of her family's vacation plans if necessary. Negotiating a compromise for the summer of 1915, the best she could do was accompany them on a trip up the West Coast in August. This was the price of wanting to be "some kind of a 'social doctor,'" she told them. Working with different sorts of people and situations early on was the only way she would know that this was what she wanted to do later on. It was not until she had earned her credentials and opened a private practice in Boston that Martha had any reason to doubt her decision.[21]

From the moment she hung her shingle on Marlborough Street in 1920, announcing her specialty in "the prevention and treatment" of children's diseases, Martha dreaded the business of charging for care families needed but could not afford. If her language of diagnosis was scientific, her motivations were pastoral, fed by the same idea of compensation that kept her father from ever requesting or accepting a raise in his salary. This put her directly at odds with her field's growing ethos of private enterprise. Martha refused when a Boston physician representing his fellow practitioners sent her a list of the going rates and pressured her to adopt them. Yet she still had the heartbreak of having a mother who barely had money for food force her last dollar into her hand as payment for coming to see her sick child. There was intermittent relief at the Baby Hygiene Association centers, where mothers brought healthy children for checkups and basic preventive advice, and the organization, not the parents, handed the doctor her fee. With this outside work and a timely call from one of her former professors, Martha survived her foray into private practice and made her escape.[22]

Dr. Edwards "Ned" Park, under whom she had studied in Baltimore, had since joined the medical school at Yale to form a department of pediatrics. He wanted Martha to come to New Haven and be his first resident doctor, an appointment that would begin in the summer of 1921. The timing could not have been more opportune for this social doctor-to-be. Within a matter of months, Congress passed the Sheppard-Towner Act, promoting the "welfare and hygiene of maternity and infancy." The funds released by this landmark bill would let Martha take on a host of projects, including the first, a study that got her name in the medical books.

A demonstration study of the cure and prevention of rickets, Martha's maiden undertaking virtually wiped out a childhood disease that was rampant in urban centers. Research with rats had convinced Ned Park and his colleagues that vitamin D would prevent the crippling condition, but private practitioners had to have proof before making it part of their well-baby care. Setting up shop in a small storefront office in one of the poorer parts of New Haven, dispensing cod-liver oil and instructions on how to give babies sunbaths, and getting to know the families who came by "as neighbors," not clients or customers, Martha redeemed her failed attempt at being a "people doctor" in Boston.[23]

Thanks to the Sheppard-Towner Act, Martha would never again have to charge a mother who could not afford to pay, or to put a price on a service whose impact seemed sufficient reward. Since darker-skinned babies and children were the most prone to get rickets, running the demonstration in a primarily black, disproportionately neglected district made perfect sense. Although the infant mortality rates for African Americans were more than twice what they were for whites, welfare stations for infants did not exist in the black neighborhoods. In addressing this tragic inequity, Martha was finally keeping the promise that she had made to herself and Mrs. Hinton a decade before.[24]

———————————————— ∞ ————————————————

If it seemed that the independent and single-minded Martha Eliot had achieved a career with a life of its own, the assumption was easy but false. She, herself, had once thought of her future this way, but that was before she met Ethel C. Dunham, her soul mate, colleague, and partner for fifty-nine years. The two had discovered each other in 1911, when Martha, restless at Radcliffe, insisted on spending her sophomore year at Bryn Mawr. Until then, she had never dreamed that she could become so attached to someone that she would defer to her wishes, whatever the sacrifice. Yet since they had met, neither she nor Ethel had made a professional move without Martha trying to work it out first—often paying the greater cost at her end—so they would be able to work as a team or at least come home to each other at night.

Eight years older than Martha, Ethel had grown up in Hartford, Connecticut, on a compound of seven houses owned by the Collins and Dunham clans. Romping about in a social climate remarkably free of rivalries, she and her five younger siblings and fourteen cousins had gained a self-confidence that could stand on its own. Comfortable with their abilities, they did not need to prove themselves better than others in order to thrive as adults. The only problem was that the grownups expected less of the girls than the boys. While the males were prepared for professions or business, Ethel was sent to a finishing school and spent a number of aimless years traveling, playing tennis, and going to teas. Starved for a purpose, at twenty-six, she returned to high school to pick up the courses to enter Bryn Mawr with an eye to a future in medicine.

Over six feet tall and muscular, Ethel's warrior frame was deceptive. Although she was known as a crackerjack athlete, her Amazonian gaze disappeared as soon as she left the courts. Her gentle congeniality won the affection of teachers and classmates; her humor and warm generosity melted the icy distrust of competitive men; and her steadying calm had the same effect on Martha as Christopher's had on Mary. Ethel was both an emancipating and sheltering spirit for Martha. With Ethel, there was none of the claustrophobia she felt with her family, and none of the competition and passive aggression she seemed to bring out in her brother. Gone, too, was the inclination to run others' lives, which she realized was hard on her sister.[25]

While Martha had not overstated her interest in getting a feel for social work, there was more to why she had waited a year after college before starting medical school. Ethel still had a year to go, and Martha was giving her time to catch up. Their plan was to enter Johns Hopkins together and share an apartment in Baltimore. Again, four years later, when Martha qualified for an internship there but not Ethel, she turned it down, "frightfully disappointed" but set on finding two slots somewhere else. Ironically, after Martha committed herself to a place at the Peter Bent Brigham Hospital in Boston, the wartime shortage of men in the States freed a slot for Ethel at Hopkins. Then her "wonderful plans" for residencies in the same location were also thwarted, as Martha ended up joining the staff at the Children's Hospital in St. Louis while Ethel signed on as a house officer in New Haven. Desperately lonely by 1920, Martha had gone back to Boston and hung up her shingle, hoping that Ethel would find employment there, too. Instead, the for-tuitous call from Ned Park had brought them together at Yale.[26]

It had been equally vital that Martha close the distance between the fact of Ethel's primacy in her life and her parents' expectations. Nearly a decade after their daughter and Ethel had met, Mary and Christopher took it for granted that Martha would come back and live with them or find a husband, whichever came first. Clearly Martha had not been explicit enough about her long-range intentions, but she had not been deceptive about her attachment to Ethel, either. Her weekly letters from medical school had radiated the pleasure she took from keeping house with her special friend. Yet Mary continued to scour her letters for hints of significant beaux and waited for something to come of the males who took her daughter to tea and the theater. Martha had hoped that her tone of amused condescension in trot-ting these escorts out would eliminate them from the field of contenders, but no. Martha's warning that Mary had better not count on her to provide the excuse for a sequel to Frederick's engagement party was yet another attempt that fell on deaf ears. Dry humor was no more effective than Martha's roundabout explanations for why she was not spending summers at camp but with Ethel's folks in Keene Valley, New York.[27]

It is easy to understand why Martha had not been completely transparent. As a rational matter, she had good reason to know that her parents would welcome Ethel into the family as warmly as they had Elizabeth. Boston was, after all, the epicenter of female emancipation, and Mary counted among her friends any number of women who lived together and worked for reform through the busy, interconnected feminist networks. In such an environment, sexual preferences were immaterial, not something that drew special notice or tolerated debate—except to refute the misogynists who blamed all manner of social problems on women's sexuality. When Martha took jabs at medical men for denigrating the female libido, she knew that her parents agreed they had "got it all wrong." But intensely personal love has always resisted publication. Even if there had been the "coming out" language lesbian cou-ples had later, same-sex partners were no more comfortable pulling the veil from this side of their lives—least of all for their parents' perusal—than heterosexual couples were.[28]

That her parents had started looking to her to make them grandparents for the first time had complicated the situation for Martha by 1920. Frederick and Elizabeth had been trying for five years without success; and Abby, currently living in Europe, showed little interest in marriage or men. Once Martha's residency at the hospital brought her into their orb, the St. Louis relatives scolded her for leaving her mother and father alone in an empty nest with no fledglings in sight. Their prying gave Martha the push she needed to make a clean breast of where things stood by writing her parents before she returned to Boston.[29]

Martha's coming-out letter was generous, loving, and firm. It announced that she would no longer be living on West Cedar Street with her parents. As much as she loved them, her values had changed. Her "whole interest" was now of "a different mold," and Ethel was central to everything. They were going to live together under one roof for the rest of their lives. Unbridled, too, in her gratitude, she thanked them for all they were giving up. "You are so good to let us all gang our own gait," she wrote, "and I appreciate full well the sacrifice it is for you both. You spent thirty years bringing us up only to have us all clear out at once." Yet now she must trust them to understand that conventional marriage, which worked for them, was not for every woman. To spare them any additional hurt, there was no hint that she had stopped going to church or acquired a taste for drinks before dinner (a glass of sherry for her and a bourbon for Ethel).[30]

While Martha's appointment at Yale had put her in reach of setting up house with her partner, one hurdle remained on that front. Ethel, whom Park had also recruited to split her time between teaching for him and supervising the nursery for newborns at the New Haven Dispensary, could live wherever she liked. But the resident doctor had rooms at the hospital and was required to sleep there at night.

FIGURE 9.2. Department of Pediatrics faculty at Yale Medical School, 1921–22. Seated second from left is Ethel Dunham; at center, Edwards Park, chairman; and second from right, Martha Eliot. Courtesy of the Cushing/Whitney Medical Library at Yale University.

Had it not been for this final wrench in their plans, Martha might not have made the most crucial decision of her career. The rickets study allowed her to live off campus and keep house with Ethel. After taking it on, as much for the freedom as for the study itself, its historical outcome gave her the means to broker future appointments where she and Ethel could be together while moving ahead professionally.[31]

——————————————————— ∽ ———————————————————

The rickets study did not put an end to Martha's teaching or clinical work, but it did steer her main trajectory into public administration. The federal board with which the enabling legislation resided had passed the funds and their management to the U.S. Children's Bureau (CB), an office started in 1912 to investigate and make recommendations on matters affecting child welfare. This gave Grace Abbott, the Bureau's Chief, a chance to watch Martha at work and to realize that she was the person to head up a Child Hygiene Office in Washington. By agreeing to it, Martha entered the government's employ part-time. At least once a month, she came down from New Haven, staying for three or four days at a time, directing the projects under her charge, and drafting proposed legislation based on her findings from work in the field. The commute ended after five years when Ethel was called to the Children's Bureau as head of its neonatal studies, and she and Martha changed their address to Washington.

If the Sheppard-Towner Act was Martha's boon, it was also her trial by fire. From its very inception, the measure had fanned the outrage of medicine's private sector and scorched the women whose funded programs would take a bite out of their business. It was clear from the hearings that public health women had lost the legitimacy and goodwill once bestowed on their corps by the late nineteenth-century's ideal of womanly influence. Suspending all rules of good taste and civility, lawmakers representing the private doctors made sure that the victors would pay for crafting a bill that invited a government agency to infringe on their turf. James Reed, a senator from Missouri, played for big laughs and got them by probing the logic of giving "spinsters" the main advisory function "on infant bearing and care." These were ladies, he grinned, "who had never had babies" and obviously never would. They were much "too good to have husbands," "too refined" to sleep with the opposite sex. What "expert" advice could they possibly offer real mothers?[32]

The basic offense behind these attacks on the women's personal lives, of course, was not the insult to potent manhood. It was their methodology. Martha and her creative associates spurned the conventional boundaries between professional disciplines. So long as the Children's Bureau had stayed in its orbit of gathering data and sending out vast amounts of instructive literature, it had managed to coexist with the private health circles in relative peace. But the two collided as soon as the CB began to define education more broadly and introduced methods that stopped just short of actual medical treatment. Increasing the tension, these "grasping intruders" were unapologetic.

Fueled by the Sheppard-Towner Act, Martha's staff was able to send funds all over the country for vital services. Its grants permitted some forty-five states to have classes in hygiene and prenatal care and to institute drives to register births. Thirty-one states offered training for midwives. Many also sent public health nurses into the backwoods, making their literature and screenings available to rural Americans. For public health women like Martha, who regarded distinctions as artificial, combining prevention and therapeutics seemed natural and efficient. From the standpoint of private practitioners, though, Martha's well-baby clinics, health fairs, and prenatal screenings were unfair competition, a charge the voices of organized medicine amplified and portrayed as subversive. Conflating the current political prejudices with the old misogyny, the goliath American Medical Association accused the CB of being unpatriotic and mediocre: As brokers of socialized medicine, its staff was no better than Bolsheviks and was running its shabby clinics with second-rate doctors. The assaults on Martha's division became so erosive as the decade advanced that when Sheppard-Towner came up for renewal in 1927, it barely got through, and its reprieve was just for another two years.[33]

Allowing the bill to expire in 1929 was but the first strike in an all-out campaign to eviscerate the Children's Bureau. The following year, a more lethal assault on Martha's division was aimed at removing it from the Labor Department, where the agency had always enjoyed a safe harbor. President Hoover's advisors wanted Martha's all-female team of directors lodged in the less cordial Public Health Service. Their hands were tied if they tried to hold on to their programs for mothers and babies there. The White House Conference of 1930, purportedly held to assess and advance the care and protection of children, was to have been the theater for this disembowelment. Luckily, word got out: The meetings were rigged to pillage Miss Abbott's agency by anointing the private medical sector as heir to its public health patronage. From all over the country, supporters converged on the hall where the plenary session was held and staged a rebellion. It kept Martha's operation intact well beyond what its most sanguine allies expected.[34]

The victors, now working on borrowed time, would have their revenge and a new lease on life when it was President Herbert Hoover who had to turn in his keys after losing his bid for reelection in 1933. With comprehensive relief now the operative word under Franklin D. Roosevelt, the Children's Bureau was not only asked to help draft the Social Security Act, but was practically given carte blanche in creating new benefits for its constituency. Along with Grace Abbott and her successor, Katharine Lenroot, Martha crafted the Act's Title V, creating new child and maternal health services, including vital assistance to dependent and crippled children. These provisions would still be lifelines for families in the twenty-first century.[35]

The Roosevelt White House enabled Martha to broaden her service in other ways, too. In 1940, Eleanor Roosevelt's civil defense committee wanted someone with her credentials to work out a plan for protecting the youth should the U.S. seaboards be hit. This got her a berth on a team of observers dispatched to England to see how the British were handling the problems during the Blitz. Aside from the captain, who "zig-zagged" the vessel to lessen the danger of being torpedoed—rather than taking "the straightest and…quickest way," as she would have done—Martha was happy to see that the men were receptive to female advice. The team was a pleasure to work with, collaborative and productive. Upon their return, Martha drafted her first legislation of national scope, the plan for safeguarding U.S. children and minimizing the strain on their parents in the event America's coasts were attacked.[36]

Unfortunately, such committees were the exception. The typical government strategists were like those who, after Pearl Harbor, sought to secure the homeland without bringing public health specialists or females of any stripes into the process. Until a contact in California tipped her off about the conditions in Santa Ana, Martha knew nothing about the "horrors" unleashed by the "ill-begotten" scheme that was victimizing thousands of innocent Japanese-American families. What she found when she took it upon herself to fly out was a "dreadful place," a natural breeding ground for all kinds of disease. This center for holding the crowds until they were shipped out to camps farther inland was a cavernous space beneath the racetrack for which the city was famous. There were sunny, dry stalls with fresh air for the horses but nothing this grand for the people. Families were packed into 10' x 10' curtained-off pods on bare, muddy ground, and by the time Martha arrived, dysentery was rampant. The story was much the same in all thirteen camps she then visited, the only differences being that some had terrible heat and shacks, and others dust storms and drafty barracks. Martha was able to implement simple procedures to stop the epidemics, but it was beyond her to undo the government's damage to human rights.[37]

Martha's bureau itself would be victimized by the "military" mentality, her term for the government bureaucrats who were "set upon having [their] way." Hungry for power, these men had been eyeing her agency's New Deal dollars for years, and in 1946, the long-dread raid was pulled off in a takeover by the Federal Security Agency (FSA). Brought under its burly arm, Martha's programs became the hostages of a tightly controlled bureaucracy altogether unlike the Labor Department, where they had been housed before. The CB staff was no longer respected or trusted to manage its grants, and Martha, herself, was "prohibited from going on the Hill" and talking with members of Congress, as she had done in the past. Her lines of communication with Cabinet members were also shut down, and she was ordered to take her proposals to functionaries who lacked the background to represent them intelligently but "had a great urge to be in charge." Clogging the channels with misinformation, they trebled her workload and squandered the chances for innovation and growth.[38]

Unsparing in her demands on her staff and herself, Martha tried to make up the lost ground by stretching her days. She was always the first to get to the office, sometimes arriving at sunrise, and typically, when she left in the evening, "a bulging briefcase" went with her. This was the warning, one aide recalled, that they would find long lists of detailed instructions waiting for them the next morning. Give her a three-day weekend, and the memorandums were "murder!" The boss's idea of a break was to take on additional projects outside the office where there were no leashes and muzzles, less waste of time, and far-reaching minds. Martha especially welcomed the chance to assist the war-torn people abroad, both for the breathing space of the freer environment and for the insights it gave her into the needs of America's foreign-born.[39]

While Washington bureaucrats blocked Martha's access to Capitol Hill, the global network opened the way to welcoming groups where she gained a new visibility. Her work with the think tank that seeded the idea of UNICEF—the United Nations International Children's Emergency Fund—caught the eye of George Brock Chisholm, then head of the World Health Organization (WHO). He asked her if she would become his Assistant Director-General, based in Geneva, where there would be work for an expert like Ethel, as well. It was 1949, a good time to take stock. Martha was now fifty-eight and Ethel sixty-seven. They had given the Children's Bureau a total of fifty years combined. Looking back, they were sure that the gains had outweighed the setbacks along the way, but since the war, they had passed the point of diminishing returns. Ready to make a new start, they promptly resigned from government service, shipped Martha's state-of-the-art oven range and other essentials to Switzerland, and put out the word that "Chez Eliot and Dunham" was about to become the hub of a new and widening circle of friends.[40]

Martha's letters to Abby and Frederick were breathless accounts of "a new world" of learning. Her assignment, overseeing advisory services, involved constant travel, with trips to such cities as Paris, Rome, and Calcutta for on-site visits. Martha's top staff included people from China, Poland, Iran, and Finland, and she was hoping to add at least a New Zealander and a Mexican. Two or three "in the gang" were "neurotics," but they managed well enough, and she was cheered by the peaceful spirit that reigned at the regional meetings. "The Israelis and the Egyptians got along famously together...as if their countries were not at war," she wrote her siblings in mid-October. Despite a brief disagreement over resettlement of the Arabs, their discussions of common problems in public health proceeded "quite amicably." It was "really fun" to be working with an international team, and when Ethel accompanied her as an expert on problems of premature births, the two had a wonderful time comparing notes. But out in the field, these new adventures were sobering. The wretched conditions she saw in Calcutta were so disturbing, she wrote her siblings, that it would take time for the "overwhelming" feelings to settle and clarify. She asked her brother if he would send her some books by Mohandas Gandhi and Albert Schweitzer to help her "sort out her reactions" and find ways to use them productively.[41]

By 1950, the peaceful new world Martha thought she had found when she first came to WHO was looking a lot like the one she had left in Washington. The problems she faced as a woman and maverick had cropped up again overseas, "the same kind of thing" that went on at the FSA and on Capitol Hill. It took only one spoiler, a bureaucrat from the "cut-and-dried" school of administration, to undermine her position in Geneva. He grumbled about her casual way of relating to dignitaries and staff, her failure to treat any policy or procedure as sacrosanct, and her disregard of his "clear-cut lines of how you do this or that." To her mind, this flexibility was essential for innovation. To his, it was unprofessional and slovenly. Martha was sure that her being a female contributed to his discomfort. He had little if any prior experience dealing with women as peers, much less as institutional superiors. She suspected, as well, that these issues of gender affected the denouement. For after he carried his gripes a step higher, the top man, Brock Chisholm, chose not to renew her two-year appointment.[42]

Martha was philosophical. Her years in public service had taught her that any attempt to bring change was "bound to draw opposition." There would be losses as well as gains when playing by different and fluid rules. She remained convinced that on balance her "patterns of operations" were best, and so did Katharine Lenroot, the retiring head of the Children's Bureau. Upon her return from Geneva, Martha was asked to take over as Chief and agreed. Again, living up to her reputation for being too independent, she chafed against the increasingly hostile constraints on the CB's work. When six years later she turned in her resignation to take a professorship at Harvard's School of Public Health, the official to whom she reported in Washington breathed a sigh of relief. "Well, now," he thanked her, "we can get somebody who will play on the team."[43]

——————————————— —— ☙ —— ———————————————

Allies and foes described Martha Eliot's image as part of her weaponry. Her gentle features, framed by graying brown hair teased into a casual bun, and her "self-effacing, humble voice and manner" belied the iron will of the woman who came to be known on the Hill as "Aunt Martha." As far as she was concerned, however, her winning record had much more to do with the tactical methods that she had learned from Grace Abbott, her mentor in government service. She credited Abbott for teaching her the importance of having a plan before rushing into a battle; for showing her how "to confront an opponent" and take a stand, always on the high ground;

and for demonstrating the power of humor to take the sting out of disagreements, diffusing tensions before they could build to an impasse. In short, Abbott modeled the way to fight for a cause "without drawing blood."[44]

Grace Abbott impressed on her people that their vision was at the mercy of words. When she and Martha wrote Title V of the Social Security Act, they had to be scrupulous in their phrasing, presenting its purpose as one of *enabling* states, not in terms of expecting compliance. To underscore its principle of sharing authority, the funded officials were designated "directors" instead of "consultants." They would have to meet Washington's standards but were being empowered to make the decisions. With this clear and accessible speech, there were no "inch-thick" binders among the bills Martha took to the Hill, and no ambiguities.[45]

Martha's inborn suspicion that patience and protocol had their place but were overrated prevented this painstaking work from bogging her down. She made it a rule to trust her own moral antennae and sense of urgency and gave it the credit for some of her proudest moments. On one occasion in 1936 she heard that a colleague who wanted to supplement her MD with a masters in public health had been told that she could take classes at Harvard but could not receive a degree. Not forty-eight hours later, Martha was grilling the dean in his office in Cambridge. Two weeks later, the university's president and corporation voted to change the policy, allowing the School of Public Health to be the entering wedge in what would remain a long struggle for women seeking diplomas from Harvard.[46]

Speed and precision would make the difference again in the 1950s, when Martha was Chief of the bureau, and Red-baiting posses were punishing liberal New Dealers, including some of her staff, by fingering them as subversives. A valued trainer in Martha's juvenile delinquency program was one of these targets. Her husband had been seen at a luncheon where half-a-dozen members of the Communist Party were present, and FBI agents had since been hounding her, showing up at her office and home at all hours until "she couldn't go on." She sent in her letter of resignation, and Martha decided as soon as she read it, she "wasn't going to take this." "And so," she recalled in later years, "I...put on my hat and walked down the street to the fountainhead" and went at once to the Secretary of Health, Education, and Welfare. Insisting on being seen without an appointment, she laid out the situation and told the man what would have to be done. "If I had weaseled," she later explained, "and begun a series of memoranda back and forth...there would have been lots of further openings for trouble." Her trainer agreed to stay on the job and was never bothered again.[47]

Martha believed that the sexes approached their work differently in public life, but not because of intrinsically different natures. As far as she knew, there was no scientific support for this popular wisdom, and experience told her that patterns of conduct were more likely functions of socialization. During World War II, when

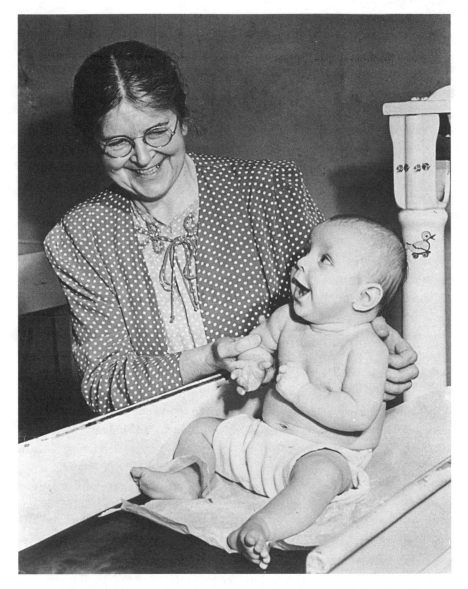

FIGURE 9.3. In 1951, the new chief of the Children's Bureau at a well-baby clinic. Courtesy of the Schlesinger Library, Radcliffe Institute, Harvard University.

infants in war zones were dying because their malnourished mothers did not have the breast milk to feed them, she and a sister physician had hit on the idea of making K rations for babies. Brought up to know "something of cookery" and comfortable putting on aprons at home, they had worked it out in Martha's kitchen without the white lab coats and fancy equipment.[48]

Martha also ascribed her feel for how physical space affected communication to having been raised in a female domain. When she wandered out into the halls at the CB to mingle with lower-tier personnel, or switched from seating her staff in long rows to putting them into small circles, she was conscious of choreographing their interaction as she had been taught when learning to set a table or arrange the parlor for guests. Also trained to be social engineers, the ones who kept peace in households and neighborhoods, women knew how to play give-and-take and win by sharing the credit. They came to Washington knowing that if they could only get a congressman "to believe an idea had started with him," it would have "a chance." Martha was certain that this explained why the Children's Bureau accomplished much more than the organizations where females were banned from higher administration.[49]

Martha had no illusions about the consistency of this pattern. As quick as she was to offer examples of women whose methods improved upon men's, she could cite as many in public life who, as part of a disadvantaged minority, lacked the pride or confidence to identify with their sex. As early as medical school, she had found it was hard to find "really congenial souls." The habits "the hens" developed at Hopkins to prove they could measure up to the men carried over to how they related to one another. Martha was struck by how many "odd sticks" and terrible "scrappers" there were "in the nest," even when they got together for meetings to talk about common concerns. When graduation approached and they had to compete for the few really first-rate positions available to women as interns and residents, the professional pressures and gravitational pull of male power intensified, making sisterly loyalties that much harder. Then came the rift that opened after the services funded by Sheppard-Towner increased the demand for pediatricians. By greatly improving the prospects for women physicians in private practice, this legislation also created a profit motive that pitted their interests against those of Martha's cohort in public health.[50]

If being a female did not guarantee strong support for maternal medicine, such support did not necessarily make a woman an ally, either. Pure-milk crusader Elizabeth Putnam, deeply committed to prenatal care, had championed the work of the Children's Bureau until its mission expanded. When it started assisting the foreign-born population, it collided head-on with Putnam's middle-class bias and staunchly conservative politics. By the time Martha came to Washington, the woman was trying to ambush the CB's enabling bill, the Sheppard-Towner, by casting it as a Bolshevik-driven misuse of public funds. The racial prejudice harbored by white women in the professions was also a factor, as Martha noted unhappily in 1928. To honor her mother, the family had hoped to endow a medical scholarship for "a colored girl," but had yet to find a quality hospital willing to take a black woman to train as a nursing student or resident doctor. Martha feared her black sisters would never get into these medical settings, she told her father, until they were let into white society generally. And heaven only knew when or if that would happen.[51]

Meanwhile, the most ambitious white women played "on the team" with the men, as Martha recalled with unusual bitterness when she thought of Oveta Culp Hobby. In 1953, after making a name for herself as head of the Women's Air Auxiliary Corps during World War II—and receiving a medal for her distinguished service—Mrs. Hobby had reappeared on Washington's radar screen to take command of the FSA and help to engineer its structural upgrade. Watching that screen from where she sat in the Children's Bureau two levels below, Martha knew why the War Department had been so impressed. Even before the agency was converted to a department and its head promoted to Secretary of Health, Education, and Welfare, Mrs. Hobby had sat in on Cabinet meetings and set up the steepest command tower ever in Martha's ten years at the FSA.

This would have been less of a problem had Mrs. Hobby not been so perverse about funding the health needs of children and mothers. The rush of preventive initiatives that came from the Children's Bureau marked "urgent" seemed only to trigger her fear of being upstaged by creative subordinates. She consistently let their proposals pile up on a shelf in the back of her office. This included the plan Martha drafted for mass inoculations of children when the Salk vaccine against polio was deemed safe in 1954. The flood of complaints that millions of youngsters were being exposed to needless risk had no effect on the gatekeeper whatsoever. For all Martha knew, the program—which Mrs. Hobby would wear as a halo in history—would have continued to gather dust if some friends on the Hill had not stepped in.[52]

As to Martha's own record as "a team player," it all depended on whom one asked and what team they were talking about. It was true that she and Ethel were strangers to Washington's social life, preferring to have a small core of friends come over for dinner and drinks. Yet the bureaucrats' charge that Martha was too much a maverick was contradicted by her penchant for working with state-based departments and organizations abroad. Her staff also knew that she was too focused on goals to personalize disagreements, and too efficient to dwell on them or nurse grudges. Associates spoke of her warmth and congeniality. Grace Abbott, for one, as a native Nebraskan, found it remarkable that her medical expert was so unlike the stand-offish, "stodgy," Bostonians she had known. Eliot, Abbott testified, was "extraordinarily successful" in handling difficult people and rough situations.[53]

Another to vouch for Martha's team spirit was fellow Northeasterner Edwards Park, who explained this "Atlas function" as part of her "splendid New England stock." Both were children of Unitarian clergy and understood, as Park often said, that their medical calling continued that humble tradition of parish ministry. From the time they first met as professor and student in medical school, this common background had kept them together as comrades fighting shoulder-to-shoulder for economic, racial, and gender equality.[54]

Park was one of the prominent figures who stepped to the front to defend Martha's cohort, exposing himself to the same abuse, when the Children's Bureau came under attack at the White House Conference in 1930. The Public Health Service Administration's Haven Emerson, the CB's arch rival, was poised to transfer its funds to his own agency while shifting Martha's preventive health business into the private sector. Infuriated by Park's interference, Emerson dashed off a series of letters containing the nastiest insults he knew. Clearly Park had become as "unreasoning and uninformed" as the feminist damsels on whom he was willing to squander his reputation. Was it womanly hormones that made him rush to their side? What else was a real man to make of Park's sympathy with their romantic maternalism, their notion (according to Emerson) that health care for children was just an "emotional or intuitive art"? They seemed to think that being an expert in "variegated and diapered stools" and baby bottles was all they needed to give professional care. For Ned, who shared these letters with Martha and sought her

FIGURE 9.4. Indira Gandhi, Jawaharlal Nehru, and Martha Eliot at the Geneva airport for a UNICEF mission during the 1950s. Photograph by Clarence Moore, UNICEF's chief of coordination. Courtesy of Alexandra O. Eliot.

guidance in answering them, this was just "a very small tempest in a very small teapot" but one that reminded him why he was proud to be on the women's side.[55]

For Martha, too, the experience kept her mindful of where she belonged. This sure-footed sense of place, for which she was known at the Children's Bureau and WHO, kept her on the front lines of maternal and child welfare advocacy after she and Ethel returned to Cambridge in 1957. As the chair of the Massachusetts Commission on Children and Youth, a post she accepted in 1959 and held for a decade, Martha again was "the conscience of the American people toward its children." At a time when the Commonwealth's urban centers were tinderboxes for race and class wars and community leaders were worried the young were becoming collateral damage, Martha knew she was putting her energies and experience in the right place. And so it was again toward the end of the summer of 1963, when Martha joined tens of thousands who gathered in front of Washington's Lincoln Memorial waiting to hear Martin Luther King Jr.'s message of firm, nonviolent reform. Surprised to see her among the throng with her usual lunch bag in hand, an old acquaintance approached her and asked what had brought her so far from Boston. Her answer was simple and characteristic: "I thought I ought to be here."[56]

10

Old Work and New

Never to separate one thing from another.... Woman's work
is always toward wholeness.

    —May Sarton, *Mrs. Stevens Hears the Mermaids*
              Singing (1965)

Abby's destiny—to stay close to home while her siblings hurried to leave—
was an obvious case of birth order trumping endowment. The girl who at
seven could outclimb the others up Owl's Head Mountain came into the
world with as swift and forward a spirit as Martha and Frederick. She knew
she was going to teach little children as soon as she started to kindergarten.
At sixty, she would be recognized as a preschool pioneer, a leader who always
saw "the next step" when the rest were just getting their footing. Abby's
syntax, like Martha's, was integrative and flexible. It called for a language rich
in conjunctions to close the false breaks in conventional thought. Promoting
strong families, good race relations, world peace, and religious growth were
part of the indivisible process that constituted her ministry.[1]

  Whether handing out hymnals, or feeding the hoboes, or teaching
a Sunday school class, Abby's early involvement in church was no less
rewarding for being required. Her duties as the minister's daughter seeded
an interest in social service and planted a lifelong belief in the efficacy of
corporate religion. Not that she ever thought of the church as the place to
have a career. The denomination's bragging about women's equal
opportunities rang hollow after Abby's gifted aunt Anna studied to be
ordained and then was rebuffed by every Unitarian church she approached.

The boasts that females could earn a living wage in the church and be treated as equals were also betrayed by the intimate knowledge the Eliots had of the Tuckerman School, where women were trained to be parish assistants and fill other odd positions. Since this venture was named for the man who had built the consortium of Boston churches that funded the Bulfinch Place ministry, the Eliots had little choice but to show their less-than-heartfelt support for the program. Christopher sat on the board of directors, Mary served on the house committee, and both were on the short list of incorporators. The family and school were also close neighbors, since after its launching in 1907, the operation had moved to a building just up the slope from the Eliots' brownstone. As regular fixtures at graduations and other compulsory functions, the family had no illusions about the school's regressive philosophy. They could barely contain themselves when speakers admonished the new alumnae not to take any "prominent part in the work of public reform" or become involved in the "abstract study of social problems" or be lured away from their sacred domestic calling by malcontents. A discomfiting landmark, Thirty-three West Cedar Street was a daily reminder of the A.U.A.'s double standard and low regard for women's abilities. Abby knew this was not the place for any young woman who wanted "really good training," "high grade companions," and a fulfilling career.[2]

Even if the spirit had been more progressive, the jobs for which women were being prepared would not have lived up to the promises. As difficult as it now was to replace retiring Sunday school teachers and to find volunteers to visit the shut-ins and help with the clerical work, societies were reluctant to hire a stranger to come in and do what the older alliance ladies had done as a matter of conscience. Then, too, as one graduate told the dean, the men who were running the churches had no idea how to treat a professional woman. They gave her the menial tasks of a maid and an office clerk instead of the time to develop the educational programs for which she had trained. Abby felt for these Tuckerman graduates, especially those who ended up floating from parish to parish as field secretaries. Representing the A.U.A.'s interest in keeping in touch with its distant churches, these poorly paid nomads had to endure the frosty handshakes of men like her brother. Frederick, who usually started complaining before they arrived, thought it ludicrous that these amateurs, who had no experience and "never would," were coming to give seasoned clergy like him their advice. They were "nuisances," he snorted. They breezed in, caused "bother and trouble," and left.[3]

Mary, of course, had decided already that Abby would join her sister at Radcliffe, where Harvard professors who genuinely believed in equal education came over and gave the same the lectures they gave to the men "for the sake of the women." With no concentrations to follow, Abby could take whatever seemed relevant, and this meant courses related to economics, ethics, and public welfare. A history of social reform familiarized her with the Marxist critique and with Henry George's final solution to poverty, the Single Tax. A seminar on functionalist philosophy illuminated psychology's practical value in institutional settings. Abby struggled to read the assignments, as yet unaware that she needed glasses, and this took a toll on her grades, which usually ranged from undistinguished to poor. Still, when Abby saw how uninformed her associates were when she took her first job, she was satisfied that she had learned a great deal just by listening closely.[4]

First employed by the Children's Mission to Children, a Unitarian agency where her father was clerk, Abby visited families to judge their fitness for taking in foster children. Frustrated by the slow pace and appalled by the patronizing attitudes, she went over to Boston's Associated Charities, where she supervised cases in one of the most demanding and understaffed districts. Again, the red tape was like quicksand, and the atmosphere was regressive. The Jewish and Catholic charities, which blamed economics and government for their clients' dependency, were willing to use political channels to get more financial relief; but Abby's Protestant agencies, still wearing their Calvinist blinders, saw poverty strictly in terms of personal weaknesses and racial inheritance. As the war in Europe progressed and Americans' feelings against the immigrants hardened, Abby's enlightened position came under heavier fire. In 1920, demoralized after five long years in the trenches, she finally did what her sister had urged for at least the last three and "got out of her rut." Packing in haste, she left for England to study at Oxford, broaden her sights, think about what really mattered in life, and figure out how to achieve it.[5]

The spike in Abby's enthusiasm during the months that followed showed the resilience and optimism for which she had always been known. "Oh, there is so much, such great things to be done!" she glowed, when writing her parents, certain that she would increase her "power for good" by having this year to recharge. The plight of the poor had refined her sympathies with the humble people in Boston. In England, it put a sharper edge on her attitude toward the privileged class, whom she blamed for society's ills both at home and abroad. While she heard the struggling common folk say that the English were brought to their knees by the war, she saw no indication of this among the complacent aristocrats.[6]

As she put these impressions on paper when writing her family, Abby was laying the planks on which she would build her career as an educator. Recommitting herself to the principles of equality and respect, she pounded the "big muck-a-mucks" at Oxford who said they would let women try for degrees but barred them from various lectures because of their sex. She hammered a "pompous" American bishop she heard at Westminster Abbey, a man who "gloated over the vast sums of money" the Church spent on saving lost souls. He made it sound almost as if salvation carried a price, she complained, and worse, that the rich had a right to be proud they were able to foot the bill. Abby later described a day she had spent helping to entertain factory girls at a wealthy estate in a London suburb. "Class division for you as clear as day!" was the caption she put on the picture. The ladies, still wearing their hats but no aprons, fed the girls lunch in one room and then withdrew to another to serve themselves from a separate spread, which was not any different except for being exclusive. Abby's answer to this was to dance with the girls one by one after lunch while they played the Victrola, grinning defiantly at the scandalized volunteers, who gawked from a distance. She was "teaching those girls not to keep their place," she explained in a letter home. To give the hostesses something more to ponder before they left, she put on an apron to butter the bread and pour the afternoon tea.[7]

Along with this jab at upperclass charity, Abby had words for the Church of England's harping on human depravity. She loved the Episcopal services for their beautiful music and sonorous prayers, but "such everlasting repetition of 'Christ have mercy on us'" was at once undeserved and debilitating. What people needed was greater respect for humanity, not more self-loathing. Providing good schools, as the Mays and Eliots always maintained, was the way to save souls, and Abby returned to the States determined to make this her primary mission.[8]

─────────────── ✑ ───────────────

As if reading her mind, Elizabeth Winsor Pearson presently contacted Abby on behalf of the Women's Education Association of Boston. The organization was drafting a plan to open a program where tenement families could bring their small children and where future teachers could train to work with this pre-kindergarten-age group. If Abby were willing to take it on, they would send her back to England to study under the woman who coined the term for it: "nursery school." Margaret McMillan's book by that title had just come out the year before, and Mrs. Pearson lent Abby her copy so she could make an informed decision. McMillan's distinctive focus on the medical mission of schools had emerged from her study of Socialist theory and volunteer work for the labor movement, and from her sister Rachel's work as a sanitation inspector in London.[9]

Having concluded that health was the only capital working-class people possessed, Margaret McMillan had started a clinic and medical home at a school to demonstrate what could be done to ensure the physical strength of poor boys and girls. She used the word *nurture* not only to cover what schools could provide in the way of nourishment, hygiene, safety, and wholesome play, but also to speak about helping the parents do better in meeting these needs at home. The author also envisioned the school as a laboratory where health-care providers, social workers, and teachers could work together, pooling their skills and experience. The tone of her writing suggested that Margaret McMillian would make a wonderful mentor, and Abby was back in London by early June.[10]

The Nursery School in Deptford was, indeed, an immaculate, sunny oasis in one of the city's grimy industrial slums. Miss McMillan greeted her intern and showed her the way to her room in one of the hostels where teachers-in-training were housed. From the window, Abby could see a lush garden where brightly dressed children were running about, and she was struck by how clean and well-nourished they looked, and how well they were supervised. The reason for this emerged as she learned the routine. It began with the student "nurse teachers" bathing the children as they arrived, dressing them in fresh overalls, and, with the girls, even adding a pretty ribbon to keep their hair out of their eyes. Then a simple breakfast was served, followed by guided lessons with modeling clay, building blocks, beads and string, and the like. Next, they might take the children outdoors or let them play musical games inside, and then it was time to get them washed and quieted down for a wholesome dinner. Naps followed, and then there was afternoon tea (with biscuits and milk) and more garden play before they were washed and dressed in their regular clothes and sent home with their parents. Every aspect of these activities, even the bathing and meals, was meant to teach something, be it good manners, regularity, cleanliness, posture, or self-control. Discipline problems were rare. A stern tone of voice was usually all it took to keep the youngsters in line. "It really is well done," was Abby's assessment after her second week.[11]

This said, there were two major areas where the school fell short of what Abby expected. For all Miss McMillan had said in her book about nourishing the young intellect, in practice, her message had not gotten through to the staff. They thought of themselves as health-care providers, not teachers, they told Abby frankly. Their purpose was laying "a road to a healthful people," and if there was any educational benefit, it was incidental. Abby wondered if she was the only apprentice to whom the founder had given her book *Education through the Imagination* as part of the orientation. In addition, this striking disparity between the broad, fluid ideas in her books and the training's narrow rigidity led to a troubling neglect of the youngsters' social backgrounds and family life.[12]

To make up for these disappointments, Abby arranged to get second and third opinions from other nursery school pioneers. While the school in London was closed for the summer, she traveled to Yorkshire to speak with Grace Owen, a more cosmopolitan and approachable woman who had earned a degree from Columbia University's Teachers' College. The English-born Owen's eclectic and generous mind was a trove of ideas that harmonized with the insights Abby had gained as a social worker. A strong proponent of unstructured play that encouraged spontaneous self-expression, she honored the work of Friedrich Froebel, whose prototypical kindergarten, she noted, bore little resemblance to modern-day programs that guided the child's every move. For this corruption of Froebel's idea, Owen faulted Maria Montessori. Her strict protocols, distrust of free play, and indictment of make-believe games had regrettably set the profession way back, Owen feared. Yet unlike Margaret McMillan, who shunned their Italian colleague completely—not even allowing her teachers in Deptford to use the popular apparatus—Grace Owen also acknowledged the virtues of Dr. Montessori's work.[13]

"The greatest joy of all," Abby wrote Mrs. Pearson after her visit with Owen, was feeling her "scientific spirit," her interest in "looking everywhere"—even to novices like herself—for new light" in this endless "experiment." She had felt the force of someone whose mind was "afire with possibilities," so many that it would have taken a Dictaphone to remember them all. But the sum of it, Abby reported, was this: Miss Owen agreed that education should be the nursery school's primary goal, with social services secondary, although, of course, indispensable. A place should be made first for every poor child between the ages of two and five. This was the group that would otherwise be in the streets and at greatest risk of neglect. Yet to make for a realistic and healthy experience in socialization, children of all backgrounds ought to be there. Moreover, the program must strengthen the family, not weaken those ties by replacing them or even seeming to undermine parents, as many now feared it would. In this connection, the school should involve the fathers as well as the mothers. Almost everything Miss Owen said fit so closely with Abby's own thinking and plans that it seemed as if she had been "heaven sent" to keep her "on the right track."[14]

While Grace Owen's practical disagreements with Margaret McMillan were obvious, she had laid them out gently and given her colleague full credit as head of the movement. If anything, she had probably given her "more than her due," Abby thought at the time, and this was before she realized how generous Owen had actually been. When Abby returned to the school in London and gave an accounting of whom she had met, the director's response was so petty and wild, Abby wrote Mrs. Pearson, her pedestal cracked, and she took a hard fall in her visiting student's estimate. Miss McMillan had no respect for Miss Owen, did not get along with her personally, and gave her projects "*no place in the sun.*" Ironically, she was also dismissive of some who considered themselves her disciples. Nor could the woman abide the social workers whom Abby had met and admired. In fact, to hear her diatribes, only the nursery school people were worth anything. Having committed to several more months in Deptford, Abby was heartsick. She would either have to limit her training to flatter this "pig headed" tyrant or risk a permanent rift with the woman everyone held in such high regard. The risk, if carefully executed, seemed worth it. Abby continued to broaden her scope, visiting other nursery schools and saying nothing about how she spent her free time.[15]

Abby returned to the States determined to shift the inflection from *nursery* to *school*. She would put education first without neglecting physical nurture. She would foster closer relationships between the school and the parents, social workers, and other enlightened professionals. Anyone who stopped off at 147 Ruggles Street would see the difference between the old and new concepts of child care immediately. But first, there was hard, hands-on work to be done. Since being acquired by Mrs. Pearson's committee a year before, the building, a dreary clapboard relic of better days in the Roxbury district, had housed a day nursery that served as a holding ground where poor working parents could leave their children and know they were safe and not hungry. The neighborhood had the desired potential for drawing a racially mixed clientele, and the previous occupants had kept the facility spotless and free of hazards. But everything else, from the paint to the policies, needed redoing when Abby arrived on January 2, 1922.[16]

Abby's confidence after her year abroad and her cordial relations with people who worked at the city's Child Hygiene Association enabled the new director to ward off the opposition that came from all sides. With a public health nurse on hand every morning to check the children as they arrived, and a policy of sending those who had symptoms back home immediately, she muzzled the pediatricians who charged that her school was inviting the spread of disease. Likewise, by having her teachers visit the children in their homes and inviting the parents to visit the

FIGURE 10.1. Director Abby Eliot (at left) with a student teacher and some of their charges at the Ruggles Street Nursery School and Training Center in Boston, ca. 1925. Courtesy of Mary C. Eliot.

school, she silenced the skeptical social workers who warned that a program for children so young would weaken the family unit.

As for the kindergarten personnel who accused the nursery school movement of being unwarranted competition, they, too, settled down once it was made clear where the Ruggles Street concept was headed. No longer a daytime depository for children from infancy through fourteen, the range of admissible ages was now restricted to twos, threes, and fours. Using a metaphor popularized by psychologist Arnold Gesell, Abby promoted the nursery school as the downward extension that steadied America's ladder of public education. As it presently stood, it was tall and wide "but did not reach the ground." The Ruggles Street program and others like it were aiming to give it a solid base by nourishing children's growth at the earlier stages of their development.[17]

The prejudices against females in public sectors persisted, however, hampering Abby's attempts to get the education establishment's backing. Those at the higher levels looked down on women who worked with little children, deriding them as small-brained pretenders to credible, grown-up careers. As a partial answer to these detractors, Abby went back to school. A few years before, in 1920, Harvard had taken "the bold move" of starting a graduate school of education. In "a still bolder break with tradition," the founders agreed to accept female candidates for its degrees. With the steady support of one or two faculty, Abby was able to earn both a master's and doctorate in education. But even then, Harvard refused to recognize her achievements as equal to men's. According to one of her faculty allies, who watched from the platform during commencement, the university marshal, having called the candidates to "draw near," would not let the women walk up the steps and cross the stage to receive their diplomas. Reaching up from below to shake hands was as "near" as they got to the honor that they had earned.[18]

Indeed, if these women's advanced degrees in the 1920s had any effect, it was to strengthen the backlash against Abby's cohort. The educators at higher levels derided the nursery school teachers, depicting them as waddling hens who were hurting the image of the profession. The animus was exacerbated by the misogyny and contempt for unmarried females who claimed to know more about children than birth mothers did. The extent to which this resistence deepened over the next twenty years was one of the few discouraging notes when Abby was ready to leave her school and tried to find a home for it in an institution of higher learning. At Boston University (BU), which for a while had reluctantly taken the credits her teachers-in-training had earned and applied them toward BU degrees, professors were now using disincentives to steer future teachers to older age groups. Harvard was even more direct in conveying its lack of interest. "We were not 'academic' enough for them," Abby later recalled, "and they were not really concerned about the education…of very young children." Only at Tufts University was Abby spared the polite condescension and offered a place for her program in the College of Special Studies.[19]

Rather than dwell on the insult of having to stoop to get into the ivory towers, Abby had deftly extended her expertise sideways, taking it into the stagnant Unitarian Sunday schools, where there was an urgent need for progressive change. By 1927, the year her father retired and Ruggles Street School marked its fifth anniversary, Abby's approach to religious education bore no resemblance at all to the standard, didactic curriculum she had used with her Sunday scholars at Bulfinch Place Church around 1910. Those lesson plans had been based on the premise that memorization and drill were the best techniques for imparting traditional values and rooting religion.[20]

Now the head of the Sunday school's lower division at First Parish, Cambridge— an easy walk from the new house her father had built on Francis Avenue—Abby designed the program much as she did at the nursery school during the week except that she added some Unitarian accents and Bible stories. Her Sunday scholars learned circle games and paraded around shaking tambourines while Abby played vigorous marches or hymns on a phonograph or a tune on her fiddle. They put potatoes in jars of water and planted seeds to see what would happen, and, weather permitting, they carried stale bread to the Cambridge Common to feed the birds. There were people at church who never did grasp what this had to do with religious instruction, despite Abby's on-the-spot lectures in cognitive theory. Small children actually learned and *thought* with their whole bodies, not just their brains, she explained, and still the skeptics walked away shaking their heads.[21]

The institutional leaders, however, alarmed by denominational shrinkage, were looking for ways to revive the Sunday school programs and bring in young families with children. To this end, they called on an out-of-town expert, Sophia Lyon Fahs, to oversee the development of a New Beacon Series curriculum. Fahs was known for her radical work in religious education at Riverside Church in New York and the Union Sunday School at Teachers College. Putting behind her the orthodoxy of her Presbyterian parents, she had used the theories of Froebel, William James, John Dewey, and Montessori to build an approach that gave children the freedom to come to their own religious concepts by way of their real and imagined experiences. She believed, as Abby did, that the youngsters' sense of what was religious and what God was like would come through the daily encounters that stirred their minds, awakened their feeling of wonder, and called them into relationships with other people and nature. Once she met the head of the Ruggles Street School and saw how alike their philosophies were, Fahs was convinced that Miss Eliot would be "the most desirable" authority on how the new materials ought to be taught.[22]

The two did not always see eye to eye. As a fugitive from a tradition that was shrouded in Calvinist gloom, Sophia Fahs had a visceral distrust of biblically based instruction. While Abby conceded that Scripture was often misused to diminish the human spirit, she also recalled how the verses her father had read every morning at breakfast had made her feel worthy of God's approval and love. She was certain that Fahs should be introducing these ancient texts right away, rather than putting them off until the sixth grade, as Fahs wanted to do. Fahs maintained that to get something out of it, children had to be old enough to imagine the Bible's historical times and to grasp their different religious and ethical standards. Abby countered that this vast collection of writings had already proven its value in planting such feelings as beauty and truth, and such virtues as kindness and strength, in youngsters too young to realize or care that what they were hearing was history. To avoid using complex words with children before they could grasp their whole meaning, she added, would contradict everything experts had learned about the way language developed.[23]

These disagreements did not keep the women from working collaboratively, however. For fifteen years, Abby critiqued Fahs's manuscripts, pushing for bolder ways of scripting the lessons and raising instructional goals. A series of stories by Verna Hill, named for her characters Martin and Judy, struck Abby as weighed down with ethics and everyday social relationships. These were important matters, no question, but not the stuff wings were made of. The narratives needed more spring, Abby urged, to give the youngsters the bounce for "a little skip or jump off the earth. I want them to soar occasionally!" she persisted. Paradoxically, even as they were keeping "the children's feet dragging along the ground," the authors seemed ill at ease in discussing the physical facts of life. They hurried the youngsters ahead without going into these marvels of God's creation.[24]

A book co-authored by Fahs and Elizabeth Manwell called *Growing Bigger*, and another by Margaret Stanger, *A Brand New Baby*, were glaring examples. If their goal, as the titles suggested, was really to teach young children what families were like, the authors must not underestimate the children's capacity for the truth simply because their own generation was squeamish. Surely parents and Sunday school teachers could "take it" if Beacon's writers just came out and said what it meant, for example, to be "expecting a baby." Was this too much to ask when a book was about a newborn's arrival and growth? Or was it unreasonable to expect that the author mention the father's role in the great collaborative process of procreation? "If that item…is not appropriate for religious education, then none of it is," Abby told the curriculum's editor. How else were youngsters "to feel their way" to the source behind all creation except to be awed by such wonders as the "never-ending production of life?" Indeed, every aspect concerning the family had "spiritual significance."[25]

─────────────────── ❧ ───────────────────

It was not a Bostonian's nature to talk this openly about her own family, but when Abby did lift the curtain a bit for posterity's sake in her later years, one could see that the Eliots served as the model for what she was teaching her teachers.

Her mother's sayings and ways had taught her the value of education, of speaking one's mind, and of turning one's sense of injustice into a positive action. Her father's gentle nobility and support of his wife and daughters had taught her that really strong men were those who were fearless in their respect for strong women. Abby could not think of any particular way her brother had influenced her. She admired his speaking abilities and his institutional leadership but confessed they were never close personally. Now and then, they might find common ground, commiserating, for instance, about the church schools' neglect of the Bible. Yet even then, Frederick's grudging concession that they could agree "on that point anyway" showed that no meeting of minds, however sincere, could bridge their distance.[26]

Martha's attention to Abby's welfare more than balanced out Frederick's detachment. With their similar personalities, Abby recognized Martha's good intentions and trusted her sister to understand if Abby refused to be led on a leash. Abby knew there was not a steadier guide than her sister, or a more generous colleague. Martha had smoothed Abby's way from grade school through college by giving advice, and then pulled her into her network of useful contacts. While the newspapers spotted them working together on public projects from time to time, their personal letters captured two faithful, affectionate correspondents, who traded gossip, discussed their gardens, sent parcels of bulbs and shrubs in season, and synchronized their calendars to allow for good visits at camp.[27]

Having learned that an anchoring love was as vital to life as one's personal freedom, Martha paid special attention to her sister's prospects for finding a partner. She fretted that Abby's "restraining duties" after her graduation from Radcliffe were isolating her socially. Her ever-expanding caseload with the Associated Charities encroached on her evenings and Saturdays, and still she refused to give up her Sunday school class and take the day off. She had no time for meeting "her own kind" of folks, people her age who had similar values and goals. It came as a great relief when the matchmaker learned that her sister was still in touch with a college classmate whom Martha could easily picture as part of the family.[28]

This was Anna Eveleth Holman, the only child of Lydia Newman and Silas Whitcomb Holman. Anna's father, who had belonged to the Mays' Unitarian Church of the Disciples, had been a distinguished physics professor at MIT before succumbing to rheumatoid arthritis at age forty-four. His persistence, despite his constant pain, in moving his research ahead and helping his students and colleagues advance so inspired his friends that after his death, they stepped in to help his widow and child. They found employment for Lydia at MIT, and when Anna was ready for college, they paid whatever expenses her scholarships did not cover at Radcliffe.[29]

Abby's friendship with Anna sprang naturally from their congruent backgrounds, ambitions, and pleasures. The product of homes where progressive, capable mothers served as the dominant parent—one as a matter of inborn traits, the other out of necessity—the girls assumed that their sex's authority, fitness to lead, and obligation to right the world's wrongs were self-evident. As their families had limited means and were sacrificing to put them through school, it was also a given that not a minute of this precious time could be wasted. Their idea of relaxation and play ran to the strenuous occupations that many of their classmates regarded as work. Sharing a love of the out-of-doors, Abby and Anna collected rocks—Anna had a strong scientific bent—went hiking, cleared brush, and dug gardens.

Contrasts in temperament and proficiency also strengthened their bond. Gentle, romantic, and deferential—everything Abby and Martha were not—Anna was dazzled by Abby's energy, braced by her humor, and stirred by her positive attitude despite her marginal grades. When her spirited friend "was having a meltdown," Anna could lower the register. As a talented scribbler—Anna was voted Class Poet by acclamation—she was not only ready to help Abby conquer her writing blocks but was able to put words to feelings that went beyond casual friendship. The relationship captured in Anna's verse was at once transcendent and earthy. When apart, as she wrote, they consummated their nuptials as "soul against soul," renewing their sacred vows in the presence of God. When together, "the air grew warm/ And the blood flowed," and all talking ceased as the "the hands of love" caressed their cheeks as they kissed.[30]

It was Anna, not Martha, who pulled Abby out of the bogs of her casework in Boston by taking a leave from a teaching position and sacrificing a much-needed wage to head up the Radcliffe Unit's war recovery work in 1919. As versatile as she was modest, Anna had handled all the logistics for getting this corps of seven alumnae to France, where they were prepared to drive and maintain a fleet of Model T Fords. When the group was dispatched by *La Croix Rouge* to centers where they were needed most urgently, Anna was sent to Buzy, a small *poste* not far from the Belgium and Luxembourg borders. While it was one of the luckier towns, having come through with half of its houses intact, the destruction was no less haunting. Anna lived in a room with paper windows and holes from a shell in one of the walls. By August 1920, the idea of Anna in uniform driving nurses and doctors to war-ravaged towns, transporting desperately needed goods, and patching up tires to keep it all going inspired Abby to leave her job and book passage across the Atlantic.[31]

If its history and schools made England the logical place to seek renewal, the relative ease of getting to France from there was at least as important for Abby. In December, the three weeks she spent with Anna, riding along as she carried supplies to the villages served by her base, and seeing her confidence and compassion for so many traumatized families, both raised the argument against war and brought to light "very wonderful depths" that Abby had not seen in Anna before.

FIGURE 10.2. The Radcliffe Unit, ca. 1919. Clockwise from left: Mary Burrage (who dropped out of The Club with Martha and Abby in 1913); Julia Collier; Katherine Shortall; and Anna Holman. Courtesy of the Schlesinger Library, Radcliffe Institute, Harvard University.

FIGURE 10.3. Anna Holman on duty in Buzy, France, 1919. Snapshot by Julia Collier. Courtesy of the Schlesinger Library, Radcliffe Institute, Harvard University.

The Eliots began to detect a new longing in Abby's letters, especially after Anna returned to her teaching job near Chicago. Taking this as a promising sign, Martha interpreted it for her parents so they might accommodate Abby's desire to have Anna back in Boston. Abby needed "somebody around" whom she was "interested" in and "responsive" to, and no one fit the bill better.[32]

Mary and Christopher had always enjoyed having Anna at camp and were happy to stand as references when a place opened up at the Winsor School to begin in the fall of 1921. It was only too bad, Martha thought, that her mother was not up to renting two small third-floor rooms to the Holmans, as Abby suggested. But Mary had lost a lot of her stamina since the end of the war. She was barely able to manage the stairs and had all she could do taking care of the linens and meals for one elderly boarder. Martha hinted that it was "perhaps too bad" that the old lodger had to stay on, but with no sign that she would be leaving, she laid out her sister's next step: Abby would have to arrange to spend Sundays with Anna, and during the week, she must have a regular evening for Anna to come by for dinner and spend the night. The arrangements became a lot simpler after both families were living in Cambridge, where the Holmans' apartment at Shady Hill Square was only a brisk five minutes away from the Eliots' house. When Lydia Holman died a few years after

Mary Eliot's death, Christopher renovated two rooms to create an apartment for Anna so she and Abby could finally live together under one roof.[33]

———————————————————— ℮ꝏ ————————————————————

With Anna on board, the family had two professional couples moving full speed down contiguous tracks, powered by blazing work ethics and boundless vitality. Abby and Anna had no end of hobbies and interests. Their tables and bookshelves groaned under volumes on travel, photography, bird life, and history. Titles of poetry favored the work of May Sarton, a scientist's daughter known for her love of nature, women, and solitude. Yet service and work came first for these two, who were always at some level "checking up" with their consciences, reviewing their efforts to better themselves and to do what they could for the world. Anna followed Abby to Harvard for a masters degree in education. Then Abby completed her doctorate, and Anna pursued the interest in science that she had inherited from her father. Granted a leave from teaching in 1932–33, she spent the year at the Cavandish Laboratory in Cambridge, England, watching the work in atomic research give birth to nuclear physics.[34]

While they were as steady and capable in their respective careers as Martha and Ethel, Abby and Anna were also as eager to work collaboratively. The value of teamwork, they always said, exceeded the sum of its parts. For women intent upon making the most of their lives, it was a compelling equation. Abby, who usually took the initiative, called on Anna to teach her trainees how to bring science into the preschool program. Whether informally or as an adjunct instructor, Anna was never too tired to follow when Abby beckoned, not even after becoming the head of the Winsor School's science department, which more than doubled her workload. Anna also joined Abby in teaching and supervising the Sunday schools in the Unitarian churches they attended in Cambridge and Concord. Venturing into new territory where they could discover yet untapped strengths was "pleasure and fun" and rejuvenating.[35]

A sobering trip back to France in the summer of 1927 strengthened the partners' determination to work for a more peaceful world. While the scars in the northern provinces were less grisly now after seven years, they still found the countryside "ragged and broken," with weed-choked rubble where farms and towns had once thrived. Just north of Verdun, where the forts had taken the heaviest tolls, the whole village of Vaux was an unseen grave, "gone forever," with only a cross to mark where its families had lived for hundreds of years. The hardest part, Abby wrote to her father, was feeling the ghosts of the nation's youth, a complete generation cut down and buried before it was able to rise. There were simply "*no* children to speak of between ten and seventeen years of age."[36]

With these scenes of wasted humanity indelibly stamped on their consciences, the women were vexed to be given backseats in the effort to stop the next global slaughter.

As soon as a new branch of war work was formed in the wake of the strike on Pearl Harbor, Anna had rushed to sign up for the WAVES, the Navy's corps of Women Accepted for Volunteer Emergency Service. She had seen herself driving a jeep again, or taking over the radar screens and operating the radios to free the men for combat. But her fiftieth birthday had come along and disqualified her as too old. The only work that females their age were supposed to be good for, she wrote bitterly in her Radcliffe alumnae letter in 1944, was taking care of the elderly and the children, and some people doubted that. The summer job she found teaching crafts at the Somerville playground had been reserved for somebody younger, but luckily, nobody else had applied.[37]

Abby and Anna were grateful that Martha was in a position to mobilize them and draw on their skills as professionals during these years. She enlisted their expertise to set up guidelines for child care centers at factories and other places where mothers were going to work. Martha also deployed them as trainers to teach evacuation procedures, with Abby speaking on children's safety at Boston's Mobilization Center and Anna serving as one of the district air raid wardens in Cambridge. Thankfully, during the school year, teaching the young still allowed her and Abby to feel they were doing their part in protecting the world by instilling such values as peace.[38]

FIGURE 10.4. Abby at her retirement party in 1952, with her cofounder, Elizabeth Pearson, and one of her former teachers-in-training. Courtesy of the Schlesinger Library, Radcliffe Institute, Harvard University.

Ageism intervened again as their sixtieth birthdays approached, and again the women refused to accede to the notion that they were used up. This prejudice was built into the terms of their teaching contracts and gave them no choice but to leave their positions in 1952 and assure their friends that their exits would be retirements only in name. They felt as much in command of their powers at sixty as when they were thirty, and the next school year found them working in California. Abby had been recruited by the Pacific Oaks Friends School in Pasadena to start a training program for preschool teachers. Anna was giving courses in teaching elementary school science through the UCLA Extension Division and L.A. State Teachers College. Nor was it any flagging of energy, only a longing for home, that brought them back to their roots in Massachusetts two years later. Still going full speed, they settled into a house they had bought in Concord and quickly returned to teaching. "Retirement" had no meaning for them and no place in their working vocabulary.[39]

Abby's custodianship of the Eliot infrastructure was ongoing, too. Steeped in tradition, the family's gathering places were deeply beloved by all, but with Frederick and Martha preoccupied and going their separate ways, it had fallen to Abby to keep the moorings secure. If Martha's designation of Abby as always the "homiest" of the three was initially the defensive ploy of a sibling who feared being tied down herself, it became the reality once Mary's health had declined to where they could no longer live in the six-level brownstone on West Cedar Street. Abby's siblings depended on her to create "the real home atmosphere" in the new house in Cambridge. Frederick imagined her digging a garden as soon as the weather got warm and carrying out the old patio chairs so she and their parents could sit and relax. When Mary anointed her younger daughter to take up her mantle after her death, the matter of Abby's role in the family was settled. "When I go, you will take care of your father, won't you?" Abby remembered her asking. And Abby had given her solemn promise she would.[40]

Mary had noticed the constancy of Abby's loyalties during her first year in England after resigning from social work. In London, Abby had looked up her renegade cousin, T. S. Eliot, and made friends with his wife, Vivienne Haigh-Wood, the woman the St. Louis relatives blamed for putting a wedge between them and Tom. The Boston siblings had known "Tom S.," who was just a year older than Frederick, as a lonely, insecure boy who loved books and had a wry sense of humor. The youngest in their uncle Henry and aunt Lotte's brood of six, he had seemed "overwhelmed" by the clinging anxiety and demands of his family. Henry Jr., his only brother and the closest in age, was nine years his senior, and there was a distance of nineteen years between him and Ada, the oldest sibling. Sandwiched in between were his sisters Charlotte, Margaret, and Marian. A fifth sister, Theodora, had died a-year-and-a-half before Tom arrived. Born severely impaired, she had been with the family sixteen months, and during that time, she had "wound herself" around

FIGURE 10.5. Christopher and Mary near Boston Common, ca. 1922. Courtesy of the Schlesinger Library, Radcliffe Institute, Harvard University.

her parents' hearts so securely that their morbid expectation of losing the child was transferred to Tom. Emotionally, he was still being cradled as late as 1905, when, at seventeen, he was sent to the Milton Academy in Massachusetts to ease his transition to Harvard the following year.[41]

Tom's cousins had understood why he felt out of place with his St. Louis family. Their expectations and unemotional Unitarian culture were incompatible with his artistic interests and personality. Uncle Henry, whose advancing deafness had made him that much harder to reach, belittled Tom's love of the theater in college as keeping him "too dramatic bizzy" when he should have been preparing to enter some kind of legitimate work. When Abby remembered, too, how much Tom had enjoyed himself at Maple Hill camp the one time her aunt Lotte let him spend part of a summer away from Eastern Point, she could see why he went overseas and decided to stay, thinking that he would be free of his parents' suffocating concerns. The news that Tom had married a woman he hardly knew in 1915 seemed consistent with this rebellion when Abby heard of it two years after the fact.[42]

When she first started seeing the couple in London early in 1920, Abby had no more idea of Vivienne's mental and physical problems than Tom had before they were married, nor did she have any inkling of what the precipitate vows had cost him since then. In fact, any worries, including the thought that he had severed all ties with his kin, were quickly dispelled by his warmth and his ravenous interest in hearing the news from home. Their relatives' photographs hung on the walls, and she noticed the Eliot ring on his finger. Vivienne's reputation with the family back in the States also gave way to Abby's impression that she was just "the right sort" for Tom. "A nice, gentle, thoughtful, right-minded girl," she was someone who understood the fellow and knew how to give him the "backbone" he lacked. In fact, Abby wrote her parents, Vivienne brought out her cousin's most admirable side, at least to judge from their "very liberal" opinions pertaining to world affairs. Of course, this had put Tom at odds with his family's imperialists, who had cheered when the Germans were starved into signing the Treaty of Versailles.[43]

But Abby was eager to cultivate Vivienne's friendship, and Tom was delighted, thinking this might be a wedge for getting his mother to visit, as well. Vivienne had "always longed to meet an Eliot," he wrote Charlotte, and now that she had, she was "very much taken with her" and looked forward to knowing her better. Lunch dates and trips to the theater had followed whenever Abby could get back to London. She and Vivienne even talked about taking a trip to Berlin in September, a plan that Tom thought unwise and quickly dismantled.[44]

The fact that Abby saw less of Tom than of Vivienne in the ensuing months helps explain why her grasp of their situation was still incomplete when she came back to England to study with Margaret McMillan the following spring. While Vivienne made no secret about Tom's depression—indeed, she harped on it—Abby could tell from the couple's appearance that neither of them was well. Still, Vivienne always described their problems strictly in terms of Tom's rift with his family and the penury in which they were having to live as a consequence. This representation, if incomplete, was certainly credible. Uncle Henry had died the previous year, before Tom was able to mend their break and get him to bless his ambitions; and his father had recently changed his will, limiting Tom's yearly income to the interest on his inheritance. Abby wanted to help, and knowing that Tom had not seen his mother since 1915, made it her mission to get her and Tom's siblings Henry and Marian over to England. "It has seemed so queer to us at a distance," she told her parents, enlisting their aid, "but when you get near, it just develops into a human thing, and after all, the boy is good at heart and has good stuff in him."[45]

In her owlish, dark-rimmed glasses, liberty hat, and homespun suit, Abby looked like an awkward schoolgirl next to Tom's elegant wife. At twenty-eight, Abby impressed him as bright, charming with exquisite manners, and "very young for her age." The wholesome simplicity of her concern for his and Vivienne's welfare was magnified, too, by the sordid realty of their marriage, a secret Tom would hide from most of his kin for another ten years. Yet if Abby was unaware of the worst, she was not as naive as Tom thought. What she had not seen of domestic dysfunction in five

years of charity work in the slums, she had seen in households that bore the afflictions of privilege.[46]

Relatives back in the States misjudged Abby, too. Some were surprised she had
gotten in touch with the fugitive and his wife to begin with, and others that she did
not cut them off when the sordid details began to emerge. Tom's brother Henry and
sister-in-law Theresa had gleaned the seriousness of the problems during the few
days they spent with the couple in Rome in 1926. Tom was drinking too much, and
Vivienne, who by this time had been in and out of sanitariums for a host of ail-
ments, was clearly a woman in crisis. She was painfully thin, and her white face was
blotched by the bromide she took for insomnia. Her erratic behavior caused withering scenes, and a strong smell of ether—prescribed at the time as a tranquilizer
and rubbed on the skin—announced her entries and exits, leaving a trail of gossip
about her addiction.[47]

While Henry was able to keep these problems a secret from most of the family,
there was no preventing his brother from telling the world, in 1928, that he was now
Anglo-Catholic and a "royalist" in his politics, having joined the Church of England
and become a British citizen. Henry's reaction was pained disbelief. Such things
were "impossible" in a rational Unitarian family. He was torn between genuine fear
that Tom had been seized by "religious dementia" and bitter suspicion that he had
half-consciously staged the conversions as "advertising," allowing himself to be used
by the orthodox church to embarrass the liberal cause.[48]

The contrast of Abby's response was at once remarkable and characteristic.
While Henry pulled back in horror as he conjured Tom handing the papists a knife
to thrust in the heart of his family's religion, Abby sought to move closer. Whenever
she got back to London, she made a point of seeing the couple and trying to understand her cousin's motives. She attended some Anglican services to "experience . . . his
belief," and as much as his hardened political views disappointed her early impression of him, she refused to let his fascist affinities poison their feelings as kin. Telling,
too, were the different reactions to Tom's decision to leave his wife. In November
1934, when his siblings learned he had gotten a legal separation from Vivienne, they
were all "very thankful," his sister Ada assured their aunt Rose. They only hoped
Tom would be as successful in repossessing the priceless seal ring that belonged to
their grandfather Eliot. Vivienne had recently used it to seal a letter to Marian, and
they shuddered to think that such a woman had touched it.[49]

When Abby saw Vivienne for the last time in the summer of 1933, her interest
was Vivien's welfare, not the seal ring. As yet unaware that Tom had decided to end
the relationship legally, or that he had slipped away and had a solicitor tell his wife,
Abby was dazed when she went to the flat and found her friend desperate to know
where Tom was. Abby said she would track him down, and when the cousins met at
a restaurant, he swore that Vivienne gave him no choice but to leave and go into

hiding. She clung to him insanely, no longer able to reason or accept the fact of their misery living together. Tom begged Abby not to go back and repeat their conversation to Vivienne, insisting that she would be putting her life in danger. But Abby returned to the flat, as promised, and told her that Tom was gone for good.[50]

Although more at peace with herself for keeping her word to her tormented friend, Abby realized that neither she nor Tom had done nearly enough for her. Vivienne was committed to a mental asylum four years later and died there in 1947, thirteen years before Abby and Anna got back to their old haunts in London. While Abby kept her own counsel regarding her friend's tragic end, neither her fondness for Vivienne nor any disappointment in Tom diminished her welcome of Valerie Fletcher when Tom found the love he had sought all his life and remarried. It was Abby who rounded up five other cousins after his death and led the family delegation to his memorial service at Westminster Abbey in 1965.

———————————————————— ⟋⟍ ————————————————————

Abby also lived up to her pledge to take over her mother's Atlas work as the family steward who held up the roof and kept the crossbeams secure. For nineteen years after Mary was gone, Abby stayed in the Francis Avenue house, keeping "everything going" on top of her many obligations outside. More than her father's "helper and caretaker," she was his "good angel always," Christopher boasted to Dodie and Earl, using the same image he had applied to his mother and then to his wife.[51]

Abby's function as matriarch took on more weight in the early 1930s, when she and Martha arrogated a hefty share of parental authority helping their brother and sister-in-law start a family. Frederick and Elizabeth's failure to lengthen the Eliot line had left an open wound in the tribal psyche. Frederick's aunt Rose lamented the waste of the "physical, mental, and moral qualities" of a superior stock, which now lay fallow. Christopher, whose brother Tom had eighteen grandchildren crowding his branch in Oregon, spoke of the letdown of not being able to pass on the cherished traditions, a disappointment Frederick felt keenly, as well. Both had dreamed of a new generation repeating the rituals of their youth, filing into the front pew at church, taking part in the Sunday school plays, climbing Owl's Head Mountain, and learning to swim and handle a boat at Lake Memphremagog.[52]

Frederick deflected the sorrow by immersing himself in the youth work at church, supervising the Sunday school and teaching all ages from toddlers to teens. He kept his hand in the children's pageants and service projects in town, and he started an interfaith Boy Scout troop, the Little Crows, which he stayed with for years. But while Frederick adjusted by way of a steady, anesthetizing detachment, enjoying the boys as a curious breed of "amusing and interesting animals," no distraction of church or community work had filled the void for Elizabeth. When she finally turned to her sisters-in-law for their expert advice on adoption, Martha took charge of the process of bringing two baby boys into the clan. Richard, or Ricky, the first to arrive, came in 1931, and Christopher, or Kits, joined the tribe two years later. Doing "everything short of carrying them in her womb," as one of the family described it, Martha insisted on checking them out herself in her clinic at Yale before she would hand them over to the new parents. Their aunt Abby also moved in to claim her proprietorial rights, confident that her expertise and the obligations of kinship authorized her to tell the parents how to bring up the children.[53]

Abby's oversight of Abigail Smith, her aunt Rose's only child, raised her standing as family protector of last resort. Cousin Abs had graduated at the top of her class in medical school, but her difficulty in relationships, her breakdowns, and her irrational horrors—including a fear of writing prescriptions for patients—torpedoed her efforts to practice. Rose had named Martha, her medical niece, to keep an eye on Abs after she died, but as one of the family remembered, "Aunt Martha just couldn't stand it and passed her on. Aunt Abby didn't much like it or find it easy, either, but someone had to step in."[54]

Nowhere was Abby's calling more evident than at the camp in Quebec, the meeting ground and "real home" for her scattered and peripatetic clan. For more than fifty years, from the time she took over for Mary, her rule was inviolate. With Anna assisting, she opened and closed the compound, handled the budget and

FIGURE 10.6. Martha and Ricky, 1934. Courtesy of Frederick Lee Eliot.

books, hired locals to check on the place in the winters, and ran the retreat "like a boot camp" during the summers. To get the blood running, aunts Abby and Anna went swimming *au naturel* before grabbing their clothes and sounding a gong to summon the others to breakfast. Accommodations were made for those seeking quiet and solitude, but the tapestry of familiar names that took shape in the log of Camp Maple Hill—a close weave of Eliots, Wilburs, Weils, Mays, and Smiths from all parts of the country—shows Abby's devotion to keeping a family of four generations together.[55]

Abby pulled these threads taut by preserving traditions. She kept up the readings and prayers before breakfast, the hymns after dinner, the lakeside vespers, the pageants on the Fourth of July, and the songfests and races on Labor Day. Every August 11, "Grandfather's Birthday," the campers still met at the "Eliot Elm" to honor the life of the patriarch, William G. Eliot, born in 1811. Once Ricky arrived, his "Half-Birthday" had to be celebrated in August, too. After Kits joined him, "Measuring Day" was observed at a wall where one of the aunts brought a ruler and chalk and announced with great fanfare how much their nephews had grown in the past twelve months.

FIGURE 10.7. The family and three young friends in front of Christopher's cabin in 1942. Standing (l. to r.) are Elizabeth Eliot, Ethel Dunham, Elizabeth's sister Sylvia Lee, Abby Eliot, and behind her, Frederick; seated in the middle row are Anna Holman, Christopher Eliot, and Martha Eliot; and in front on the left, Kits and Ricky Eliot. Courtesy of Frederick Lee Eliot.

As a way of preserving a fading past, these customs assumed greater urgency as civilization encroached. In the summer of 1934, "The Aunties" were "much disgusted" to see a horrible hand-painted sign go up at the old Owl's Head wharf: "Boat Parking. 25 cents." Then the manager of the nearby hotel "objected to parties undressing in the woods for bathing." If they wanted to swim, they could change in his indoor facilities for a fee! While these insults were easy enough to ignore, the more seductive faces of progress began to appear in the aging wood nymphs' own camp. By 1953, there were "sometimes five cars in the camp at one time," and electric lights had been installed in the main cabin, kitchen, and pantry. Next came a rotary telephone, a nice electric stove, and a second-hand refrigerator, conveniences for which, it turned out, Mother Nature was paying on credit. When Anna and Abby climbed to the top of Mount Oxford in 1956, they found a new television transmission tower blocking the view.[56]

In 1979, Kits's teenager, Fred, and a four-month-old kitten were sleeping out in the boathouse with an electric blanket to keep them warm and a stereo, speakers, electric guitar, and motorboat for their pleasure. Alexandra, Fred's mother, who kept the camp journal that summer, marveled that so much technology had not destroyed the restorative beauty and peace of Maple Hill. For all the modern amenities, many things had stayed "just as they were" when the first tents went up on their platforms in 1904. Only the absence of those who had been there belied the illusion of permanence.

Mary, who started the record, was still making entries in 1926, her flowery script noting picnics and teas, a birthday party with cake and games, a church bazaar, and the christening of the family's new inboard motorboat. "She was not quite as well as usual," Christopher later allowed in a footnote, recalling that she had been restless and rather uncomfortable during the nights. Yet she had been "keeping up bravely" when the children began to arrive in August. She had brought her insulin with her and was giving herself injections, and no one had seen any special cause for alarm. Only later had somebody picked up the log and seen that her final entry, the one she had started for Tuesday, the 17th, ' broke off in mid-sentence, leaving the thought hanging ominously on the page. On Friday night, she became gravely ill, and despite the best efforts of Martha and Ethel, Mary died the next morning. The shroud that spread over the compound was still too heavy to lift the next summer, and Maple Hill remained closed for the first time in memory.[57]

The gathering place had ten years to regain its illusion of stability before Rose and Jac Smith, longtime fixtures at camp, passed away in the 1930s. After Christopher's death at age eighty-nine in 1945 and Frederick's massive coronary in 1958, the erosion was striking, and yet the false sense of endurance slowly returned. With Abby looking ahead to another season in 1969, Anna's sudden death from a heart attack in April was inconceivable. She had shoveled the snow all winter and kept up her brisk walks and hikes in the woods, and, with no warning whatsoever, the shock was tremendous. Abby wore a brave face at the Unitarian service in Concord, but her family was not surprised when she said she would not be opening the camp that summer. Maple Hill had already been under a pall for some time. Martha and Ethel had not been seen there since 1963, when Ethel's mind started to fail. Since then, her decline had been steady, and Martha had felt a "strange kind of loneliness" even as they sat at home holding hands and talking quietly. "She was here but moving away from the world," was how Martha described these last years. When Ethel finally died in December 1969, Martha entered the "even deeper loneliness" Abby had lived with since Anna's death.[58]

The sad fact that sisterly love was no guarantee that siblings could live together was forced on Abby and Martha when they tried it after their partners were gone. They had always been close, and never more so than after Abby and Anna had settled in Concord and Martha and Ethel in Cambridge. With Martha's quick hand on the telephone taking the burden off her sister, who worried about making long-distance calls from town to town on her much smaller income, they talked almost every day. But once they tried being housemates, they found they were "too much alike." Both were "aggressive, imaginative, creative, determined," and vocal. Without the insulation of distance, their tempers grew hot and exploded. The experiment ended with Abby returning to Concord and simplifying her life by settling into a room at the Rivercrest-Deaconess Retirement Home, while Martha stayed put and asked her housekeeper back. Then the sisters resumed their relationship over the phone.[59]

But now Abby faced a greater test, for Martha was no longer well. A painful autoimmune disease, dermatomyositis, had forced her once-invincible sister into a wheelchair and sapped her strength. The deafness that she had staved off for years by using an aid had also grown worse, compounding the insult of losing command of her powers. Barely able to follow, much less hold her own in the conversations she liked to direct, Martha grew more impatient and irritable. This was a summons for Abby, who heard the unhappiness in her sister's short temper and answered its cry for help, undeterred by her own advanced age and waning powers. During the last years of Martha's life, when the two were well into their eighties and Abby's bad eyes were fast giving out, there was scarcely a week that she did not ride into Cambridge and spend the day with her sister, trying to ease her isolation and suffering. Supplied with a magnifying glass and a folder of clippings and scraps of paper, Abby spent hours singing and reading into her sister's better ear, invoking the bracing voices of John Greenleaf Whittier, Henry Wadsworth Longfellow, Ralph Waldo Emerson, Eleanor Roosevelt, Martin Luther King Jr., and Norman Cousins. In Martha's last days, Abby turned to the hymns and lullabies their parents had sung, cradling her in their tender words until she drifted away. Martha died on Valentine's Day 1978.[60]

As custodian of her family's legacy, Abby again lived up to her reputation for knowing "the next step" and taking it deliberately at the right time. Paying respect to the struggles of Abigail Eliot Smith and Vivienne Haigh-Wood by trying to strengthen the lifelines for all who were living with mental illness, she put her energy into creating Concord's Community Mental Health Center, using Martha's substantial estate to help keep it running after her death. As guardian of the many causes for which her kin had crusaded, she also used Martha's wealth to continue the work for women's rights, economic and racial justice, public health care and education, religious freedom, and international peace.[61]

The next steps came closer to home when Abby turned over the business end of running the camp to her grandnephew Fred, and, after bringing the log up to date, passed it to Alexandra, his mother. In her nineties, Aunt Abby was still the acknowledged "matriarch of the camp," her niece wrote. As late as the summer of 1985, her last one at Maple Hill, she was able to walk down the hill to the boathouse to swim by supporting herself on two stocks that Anna had brought back from Switzerland decades before. When Abby failed to return the next season, her absence threw off the balance of nature and sent it into convulsions. The clouds turned dark and the gathering winds wailed and moaned as they swept into camp from Judd's Point, barreling past the old cedar cabins and angling in toward the lake. The force uprooted the giant trees that had looked as invincible as the woman who watched them grow up from saplings. Beloved by all, Abby died six years later, ten days after living a century.[62]

11

No Parting Word

Immortal by their deed and word
Like light around them shed,
Still speak the prophets of the Lord,
Still live the sainted dead.
　　　　—Frederick Lucian Hosmer

Consorting with reason and scoffing at hell, the Eliots gave up a lot for the freedom to use their minds with impunity. They were happy to leave the Virgin Birth and Three-person God to the orthodox. They were willing to forfeit the miracles, the loaves and the fishes, the walk on the water. And yet when it came to a life after death, every one of them drew the line. The location and terms were negotiable. Concessions were made to logic and science. Poetry had its bargaining power. But immortality was not for sale. An audacious position for thinking people, it pitted the doctrinal certainty conferred by the minister's office against the nagging, untidy questions inherent in human experience.

For three generations, the Eliot men preached a personal immortality that echoed the language of William Ellery Channing and Henry Ware Jr. From his St. Louis pulpit, William G. Eliot promised a heavenly home where all the loved ones would meet again in eternity. He cautioned that these were figures of speech and not to be taken too literally. The extravagant expectation of finding a mansion above the skies, which Elizabeth Stuart Phelps would exploit in her best-selling book, *The Gates Ajar* (1868), was obviously unworthy of Liberal Christians. There was no way of knowing what spirits and heaven would look like, and there was no need to know, William Eliot said. People of reason and faith would do better improving themselves here and now. Thomas Lamb Eliot also made much of Emerson's mystical vision, where heavenly spirits visited those they left behind on earth. Through intuition and faith, he preached, one could feel their companionship every day as they mingled among the mortals as mentors and guides.[1]

The younger William Eliot refused to relinquish these unseen guests to the mechanistic approaches of a new century. As avenues to an uplifting, usable truth, he warned his congregants, the new ideas in philosophy and psychology were clearly "dead ends"; their secular arrogance served only itself. Appealing instead to a liberal religious sense that was wrapped in historical cloth, he guided his listeners down a road to regeneration that called for a conscious adjustment to the way they had learned to read history. Rather than putting themselves in the place of the figures who lived in the past, let them offer themselves as the texts or hosts for the spirits of the deceased. Even Will's younger cousin Frederick May Eliot, scorned by detractors for courting the humanists, clung to "the great lines of life—the strands of aspiration and influence, memory and expectancy" that kept "the human family connected regardless of time and space."[2]

For the Eliot women, whose quandary was greater for being the ministers' attachés, there was no unequivocal way to translate the pulpits' language of certitude. No matter how often their husbands and sons affirmed the life everlasting, they had to grope for adequate words to offer the women they sought to console. The matriarch's own bereavements had left her heart "tender" to others' grief, but to know "the old story" by heart, as she said, was not to grasp "why it had to be." As a widow, she liked to imagine William surrounded by family and all the old friends and "his gentle voice whispering, 'I am at rest.'" Yet wishful pretending, she told her children, did not make these separations "come easy."[3]

So Abby's surviving daughter learned as she watched her mother's mental decline. Like her brothers, Rose always considered her mother the smartest one in the family. But seeing her in her final months when her mind was "about *all* gone," she could hardly imagine her spirit returning to give her advice or encouragement. Nor could she picture her brother Tom giving the family directions from heaven after her nephew Sam described his condition in 1933. In the few days Sam spent with his father in Portland, the old man had no idea where he was. One minute he thought he was in Chicago, another in Louisville, then in New Orleans. At one point, he thought he was traveling somewhere in Russia. He was now an antique "mosaic" with parts that were "worn or gone," Sam confided to Rose. The outline of the original was still there for them to trace, but to think that someone as badly "misplaced on the map" would find his way back as a spirit required a trust that only the men of Will's vintage possessed nowadays.[4]

The skepticism that Minna had once feared would brand her the family heretic became familiar enough that Dodie's loss of faith at age sixty-one seemed long overdue to the younger siblings. After years of being "a strong believer" who thought she was often stronger than Earl, she had suddenly lost a foundation that proved irreplaceable after Eliot died. On her better days, she assured herself that anybody "with brains" lived with doubt. When it came to religion's big questions, people had only their intuitions to go on. On her bad days, she felt inadequate and betrayed. Earl's success in retaining his faith despite the enormity of their grief only magnified Dodie's spiritual insufficiency. Earl had never believed in telepathy or similar psychic phenomena. The only time he had gone to a séance was when he wanted to prove it a hoax. Yet in the first year-and-a-half after Eliot's death, two remarkable "visitations" convinced him their son, although out of sight, was still with them. He could think of no rational explanation for these unlikely communications, and yet he swore they had flashed through his mind in Eliot's normal voice as distinctly as if he were standing right beside him. The first time this happened, Eliot said he wanted to be remembered with as much happiness "in his larger life" as his parents had felt when they first sent him off to college. They would have "perhaps twenty more years or less of remembering and longing," but then they would all be together again, so there was no need to be sad.[5]

The sequel eighteen months later was much the same. Again as clearly as if he were speaking directly "from heaven" into his ear, Earl heard him say he was fine and wanted his father to forge ahead and be happy. Earl granted that these occurrences might have been nothing more than wishful projections, disguised expressions of what would have been a disabling grief without such an outlet. But whether delusions or "something more real," the thought that came dressed as his son's parting words—"You will do it for my sake, won't you daddy?"—put "new resolution" into Earl's heart. By promising what his son had asked, he was able to live one day at a time, often feeling empty and numb but no less intent upon moving forward.[6]

There were no such mystical visits to reassure Dodie. Her unconscious longing for Eliot only tormented her with its practical jokes. When she dreamed he "had come home from somewhere," her "*inexpressible* joy and relief" lifted "all the dead weight," but then she awoke to the unaltered facts and was crushed. "Perhaps I haven't the right techniques for helping myself," she admitted to Earl, "but one could not dictate these feelings." Still numb after fifteen months, she had ceased to expect there was "*much* more" ahead than this sorry "existence and some kind of work." Rather than be a pretender, she settled for being an honest agnostic and lived with the consequences. What comfort there was came from knowing that other ministers' wives—even the former A.U.A. president Samuel A. Eliot's widow—were in the same boat and not at all sure that they and their loved ones would meet again. "The *Silence*," as Frances Eliot wrote in 1951, prompted by a card of condolence from Earl, was "so impenetrable…as to be overwhelming." One could only go on believing that God was good "and leave it at that."[7]

✄

With the wait for these distant reunions so long and indefinite, memory's highways—the more direct and reliable routes to the dearly departed—were heavily traveled. The Eliot women maintained the road signs and gave the narrative weight and traction by saving historical markers and palpable relics. The Wilburs' cross-country tour of the ancestral shrines in 1930 was as much a pilgrimage as a history lesson. At the church in St. Louis, the family worshipfully stroked "the beautiful tablets for Grandpa and Grandma Eliot," and in Amherst, they paid their respects at the house—now the residence of an Episcopal rector—where Dodie's grandparents had cradled her mother eighty-five years before. In the churchyards

FIGURE 11.1. The family at Riverview Cemetery in Portland after Thomas Lamb Eliot's death in 1936. Standing (l. to r.) Will, Dodie, Grace, Earl, Henrietta, Ellen, Sam, and Thomas Dawes. Etta is seated in front. Courtesy of Warner A. Eliot.

of Hartford and Boston, and in tiny New England hamlets, they made pencil rubbings from gravestones bearing the names of Morse, Greenleaf, Ely, and Cranch.[8]

Yet mortality would have its way with this tangible history, too. The elegant church at Olive and Ninth in St. Louis was razed for a parking garage. The dignified sanctuary and chapel at Yamhill and Seventh in Portland met a similar fate when the building came down and a depot for buses replaced it. The trees that were planted at Camp Maple Hill and Hood River to honor the patriarch vanished, one felled by a storm and the other by land developers. Mementos whose treasured associations expired with the deceased were discarded as trash or left for the children as toys. Young Ricky and Kits "came in for a windfall" the summer after their great-aunt Rose died and her cottage at Spring Bank near Maple Hill was cleaned out. No artifact was too small or mundane to escape the whims of impermanence. A wisp of hair Etta clipped from the small head of Dodie's first baby—a little boy, who lived only three weeks in 1902—was stroked once too often and scattered. In a crueler defeat, Dodie's hope of preserving something of Eliot's spirit by giving his clothes to her nephew was doomed by Peter Scott's own tragic death in a climbing accident several months later.[9]

Visual images—snapshots, studio portraits, and formal paintings—only slowed the erosion of time. Frequently bedridden during the 1950s, Earl could travel the country and 200 years just by turning his eyes to the scenes on the wall a few feet away. There Dodie had hung "the old Amherst house where mother was born, the pictures of 227, outside and in, Shushula and the view down stream from there, and the pictures of father and mother." Yet photographs had both the frailty of other material history and the fraudulent character of their visual culture.[10]

The distortions of posing and touching up, culling and cropping, arranging and framing were not so bad when the subjects in question were buildings and landscapes or notable figures. One had only to see Harvard's president Dr. Charles Eliot in person to understand why his photographers shot him in profile. The "horrible red mark" that covered "the whole of one side of his face—extending over half of his nose," as Kate Stevens Bingham discovered, was needlessly shocking to those who had always admired him from a distance. Yet for Eliot women who hungered for closer connections with distant family, it seemed self-defeating, if not pernicious, to send them these doctored pictures. Etta, for one, grew "so tired of people's artistic attempts to 'look good looking'—striking artistic attitudes, or drooping and draping themselves over chairs, or rolling their eyes, or sweeping their eyelashes," that she took "a sort of vicious delight" in having simple photographs made. Had others' pictures been able to speak, as Etta often wished, she would have asked them impertinent questions: What was left out of the frame, and why? What were the subjects thinking?[11]

The silence of frozen facsimiles, the greatest incumbrance to reaching the dead through their painted and photographed images, heightened the yearning to read

FIGURE 11.2. On 5 August 1933, Elizabeth Lee Eliot, Rose Eliot Smith, Teresa Garrett Eliot, Christopher Rhodes Eliot, and Henry Ware Eliot Jr. gather under Grandfather Eliot's Elm at Camp Maple Hill to mark William Greenleaf Eliot's 122nd birthday. Courtesy of Mary C. Eliot.

their personal writings. Rose, who had grown up surrounded by portraits of her father, admitted that he had only became a three-dimensional man with a history once she was able to go through his notebooks in 1928. There was so much that she, as the last of the fourteen children he sired, had never been told, that reading his entries gave her the strange sense of meeting him for the first time.[12]

The handsome framed portraits and photograph albums were no greater help to the children in Portland who felt they had "never known the real T.L.E." The youngest, Tom Dawes, who regarded himself as the most deprived in this respect, was determined to find any clues he could glean from his father's diaries after he died. "I was number eight," he reminded Earl when enlisting his help, "and he was silent during most of my memory of him, except for occasional sententious gems, prayers, sermons," that sort of thing. "I feel that I would understand myself and my children better if I had some insight into his interaction...within himself" and "with [his] contemporaries." Dodie approached these old writings with the same fervor. Whether or not they contained any "interesting" factual information was incidental to their resonance as an emotional bridge. The "yearnings...longings, reflections" behind the words, "all these indescribable 'feelings'," were "one of the strongest proofs of immortality." In short, the personal writings whose voices connected the past and the present were privileged corridors to the most understandable form of eternity, an all-encompassing unity of experience.[13]

Written records, though, had their own limitations. Paper was as perishable as any fibrous material. The love letters Abby wrote William during their courtship went up smoke when their first house on Olive and Eighth in St. Louis burned down around 1840. The confidences that Sally Smith Flagg, their old friend and helper, had tried to preserve were smothered by layers of heavy, black mold that spread through her diaries during the long humid summers. Every month, moreover, was open season for censors who damaged the records deliberately in the name of filial regard and good taste. If the family journals and correspondence were avenues to the afterlife, whoever got to the sources first was able to guard heaven's gate and decide who got in after checking their baggage.[14]

The bias in favor of public history posed a significant barrier for the women whose lives were preserved in their private writings. Norman Flagg's protective custodianship of his mother's stack of diaries prevented the Eliot progeny from knowing Abby as Sally had. When he finally dusted them off and read them in 1941, what struck him of value was neither his mother's story of orphanhood, grief, and recovery, or her intimate view of the minister's spouse at mid-century. Respect for their privacy kept him from sharing such "VERY personal items" with strangers, he told his old school chum Will Eliot. He doubted the public would find them of interest, anyway. The real gems, he said, were his mother's remarkable summaries of the sermons she heard Will's grandfather give in the late 1840s and 1850s. If one were willing to go through the roughly 250 pertinent entries to cull out these digests and publish them as a record of the minister's preaching, it would certainly "pay big dividends" for historians "now and years hence," Norman thought. The rest of the diaries, which could have been read as a gauge of the sermons' impact, would have to await an uncertain future in silence.[15]

It was logical, if ironic, that women who lived in a false, separate sphere would collude in preserving this artificially narrow version of history. To protect the privacy of the deceased was to safeguard the family reputation, the closest thing females had to a place of their own in the public memory. So it was that Rose Eliot Smith was ready to take drastic steps, if need be, when her father's personal correspondence was passed on to her some forty years after his death. Nan Britton's best seller, *The President's Daughter* (1927), had recently caused a sensation recounting the author's affair in the White House and claiming that Warren G. Harding had fathered her child. Tormented by such examples of how people's private lives could be "cast about," Rose thought about "burning up the whole lot" before she came up with a compromise. She sent the letters to Portland and asked Will to settle their fate and torch whatever he thought his grandfather would not have wanted outsiders to read. Whatever he did, the Portland siblings were grateful their aunt had not asked Henrietta. Knowing how quick she was to reach for the matches, the youngest, Tom Dawes, was desperate to get his hands on his father's notebooks before his sister destroyed them "in a fit of mythic sentiment."[16]

That the Eliot women could be just as ruthless in hiding their own sex's narratives was apparent when Charlotte, eager to make a small place for herself as a delivered author, bowed to convention in writing a book about William G. Eliot after he died. Desperate to salvage a scholarly bent that had languished for thirty years, Charlotte had disregarded her subject's well-known instructions that nothing be written and published the life of her father-in-law with Riverside Press in 1904. The family applauded, and James Freeman Clarke absolved her of going against his friend's wishes, insisting that it was "as idle" for someone like William "to try to conceal his manliness" as for a scoundrel to try "to conceal his faults." If this was so, it was also as idle for women to think they could publish a book without perpetuating the methods that banished their sex from the record. Charlotte's only concession to Abby's part in William's fifty-year ministry was to cite her account of their trip to St. Louis in 1837 and to mention Mrs. Eliot twice in passing. Charlotte had earlier gone through William's personal journals, expunging whatever she found incompatible with the public image she wanted preserved.[17]

Not so strangely, the book's publication did not resolve Charlotte's bitterness. A letter to T. S. Eliot while he was a student at Harvard showed her several years later still nursing her thwarted dream of going to college and proving herself in the larger world of letters. Not being a boy, she told her son, the best she could get was the preparation to teach in the lower grades, and although she had graduated from normal school with the highest distinction, impressing her teachers with her "unusual brilliancy as a scholar," her intellectual talents "counted for nought" in her assigned niche. She still had that old testimonial with her diploma as a reminder of what she might have made of herself had she been a man instead.[18]

Never having aspired to authorship, Henrietta had a much easier time accepting history's gender gaps and unfair slights to her sex. While reading a book on John Fiske, the historian and philosopher who had popularized Darwin's work and had once been a guest at "227" in Portland, she made a mental note of his failure to give her mother "even a mention" when he recounted his pleasant visit with Dr. Eliot's family. But these were gaffes Henrietta dismissed as harmless blind spots congenital to the male species. She learned to accept the glass as half-full when women were mentioned at all.[19]

Henrietta's notorious policy of "the less told the better" was consonant with the role she carved out as her aging parents' protector. It was also a bracing vote of confidence for her brother-in-law Earl Wilbur while he was writing *The Life of Thomas Lamb Eliot* at the children's behest. Earl's account, begun after their father's death in 1936, was deferential and formal, and it drew mixed reviews when it circulated prior to final revisions. The younger brothers especially yearned to see more of their father's human side, for which there was no better mirror than his relationship with their mother. "The despotic aspects of Father's home rule," which were never suggested at all, could have been noted gently along with his kind heart, courage, and generosity. Henrietta, however, was adamant that their brother-in-law had made the right choice in avoiding details that were sometimes "awfully funny but unrepeatable outside the…family" circle. She lauded Earl for defending his methods as those of any respectable scholar. His purpose had been to capture his subject's moral power and public acts by using broad strokes and primary colors, and, surely, he had succeeded in this. As he said, these significant contours emerged without "the light and shade" of "familiar and trivial incidents," and those who thought it essential to fill in the shadows would have to imagine them. So it was, that with Henrietta's approval, her mother—the indispensable woman who got her father through college, helped write his sermons, and roused the women who raised the money to keep the church solvent—came in for fewer than 500 words in the published account of her husband's vocation.[20]

⟶ ∽ ⟵

It took the mavericks like Martha and Abby, who scripted unorthodox lives for themselves, to author the open-door narratives that were destined for immortality. Neither had rushed to write herself or her foremothers into the record. Their days had always been much too full, and the Eliot modesty too firmly set. But their personal and professional papers were waiting in a safe place when the surging feminist consciousness came in the later 1960s, creating an audience clamoring to hear women's side of the story. For the Eliot sisters, who had for years been redacting their personal letters for fear of their being profaned by alien eyes, it took a great deal of courage and trust to place their papers in Radcliffe's archives. But they were ready to take this step, and in turning this page, left a legacy that defied convention and closure.[21]

Martha was eighty-two in the spring of 1973 when she was asked to work on a taped retrospective to put with her papers. Dependent on glasses and two hearing aids, and confined to a wheelchair, she welcomed this chance to take charge of her life again by telling her story. The taping took place in her living room, where her files, on small tables, were easy to reach, and the twenty sessions between late October 1973 and mid-September the following year gave her plenty of time to get everything said. The result was a copious history, 450 pages transcribed, that traveled along a methodical track of carefully verified facts and context, stopping as needed to pick up her fellow travelers.[22]

Among the party were Martha's elders, honored for planting a faith in salvation through character, and her brother, sister, and Ethel Dunham, all recognized for their worthy public accomplishments. Frances Perkins, Grace Abbott, and Edwards Park, whom she had so often acknowledged in public, were summoned as wonderful mentors and colleagues of great and rare integrity. And here, for the first time, she also named her antagonists and described their offenses: the bullies and self-serving operatives at the Public Health Service and Labor Department who sacrificed the poor at the altar of medicine's private sector; Oveta Culp Hobby, whose treacherous mimicry of the egotistical males had killed or delayed such vital work as protecting the public from polio; the shameful treatment of Japanese American citizens after Pearl Harbor, and the Red-baiters' persecution of New Deal liberals. The only stain worse than these "horrible things that our government has done," Martha said, was the silence that let them happen. "That's why I've been wanting to speak about this," Martha trumpeted at the end. She had relished this opportunity to rescue facts that had almost been lost, and now, she said as her final thought, "I hope it won't be buried."[23]

Abby's memoir, *A Heart of Grateful Trust*, was a much leaner ninety pages, and that was counting the photographs, index, and notes that her editor, Marjorie Manning, a training school colleague, inserted. By the time Abby finally got around to recording her memories on tape, she had lost too much of her sight to make use of her files, as Martha had done. But the length of the book, which was privately printed in 1982, was deceptive. Its content was drawn to the scale of a ninety-year-old who, according to Manning, while "far from being conceited," was yet "completely aware" that her many achievements had been "considerable."[24]

Abby's textured life required she speak of her interest in music, religion, and gardening, as well as her all-encompassing service in the public domain. Her life, she explained, had covered not one, but "three careers," which in tandem addressed every stage of human development. The first was the nursery school for small children. The second was starting a mental health center for youngsters and their parents. The last was providing quality housing for elderly people, the group to which Abby belonged when she took up this cause for those who were not as well off. Like Martha's, her vast work was framed by the larger history that moved from her distant ancestors up to the youngsters who now kept the old May and Eliot spirit alive. Boundless, too, in its open affection for Anna, Abby's memoirs celebrated the "calm, loving personality," whose "deep understanding of people" and gifts as a painter, poet, and naturalist had enriched Abby's life beyond measure.[25]

While these stories captured the multitude who had shaped and enlarged the sisters' lives, to feel their collective authorship on a personal level, the next generations would have to read such intimate writings as Ned Park's letters to Martha. Ned had continued to relish their common endowment as children of liberal clergy and never let Martha forget that legacy's power. When buried in work and outstanding bills and unable to visit with her and Ethel, he sent his regrets with a playful reminder that "Abigail Adams, the Reverend May and…Apostles Eliot"—all of them "chained" by the same "Puritanical egotism and…penury" as his forebears— would have been understanding and granted a rain check. As Martha's influence spread in the halls of Congress, Ned ascribed her success to the "unabated Atlas function" of her New England stock. And when T. S. Eliot garnered the Nobel Prize in Literature, he put Martha's "superb accomplishments" on a par with the honoree's. Of "the statesman-like-kind," her contributions, like her cousin's, were traceable to the famous Adamses' "selfless feeling of social responsibility."[26]

In their autumn of life, when their closest companions were "barely clinging" and "dropping fast," Ned's letters addressed Martha's growing unease about her apostasy as the skeptical child of a Liberal Christian pastor. Like Martha, who was circling seventy, Ned, who was now in his eighties, had stopped believing the story of Christ before he was finished with grade school, but he had managed to put any hectoring doubts behind him for good. He had long since decided that skepticism put people like them on a safer footing than if they had clung to impossible hopes. Ned had seen this when Agnes, his wife, lost her orthodox anchorage after a near-fatal stroke and suddenly realized the future was not a sure thing. When she called on her faith and it mutinied, she changed from a jovial, even-keeled spouse to a panicky, chronic complainer. At least he and Martha had known where they stood all along. As for a final judgment, the prospects of physical suffering and becoming a burden to others were chastening enough without inventing irrational punishments waiting for them in the grave.[27]

Ned empathized fully with Martha as Ethel's long illness ravaged her memory, leaving her partner bereft in "a strange kind of loneliness" for five years. If there was

FIGURE 11.3. Child being walked to the Nursery Training School, 1935. Courtesy of Tufts Digital Library, Boston, Mass.

a hell, he was sure it was living without those to whom they felt closest. Ned trembled to think what it would be like to have his sister Marion die. "It would mean that all the past which is concentrated in her would be gone." Yet, Ned insisted, if anyone had the ability to stand by Ethel and see her into a larger life, it was Martha. She was born to a larger tradition of ministry, one she had reconfigured but never deserted. That she had repudiated medicine's culture of profit, Ned noted, was proof that she

FIGURE 11.4. The Martha Eliot Health Center, ca. 1970. Courtesy of Children's Hospital Archives, Boston, Mass.

FIGURE 11.5. The Martha Eliot Health Center of the twenty-first century. Courtesy of Children's Hospital Archives, Boston, Mass.

had consecrated herself to the healing arts, driven by the same pastoral impulse that animated her parents' work. This explained why her doubts as a scientist had not diminished her love of the uplifting language and psychological resonance of the Christian canon.[28]

As he saw it, agnostics were just Unitarians "one further stage along." Their "broad understanding" let them abandon the literal heaven and Christian God without capitulating to death's finality or spurning their families' texts as incompatible with their secular faith. The parables, which Martha's father had called "earthly stories with heavenly meanings," were as relevant to the humanist odyssey as to the Christian pilgrimage. If Martha would think of herself as the servant in John's Bunyan's allegory, Ned coached, she would find "the satisfaction of Great Heart in *Pilgrim's Progress*, who selflessly piloted Christian and [the] children to the Celestial City." Without pretending to be a believer, Ned liked "to think in that way" and he urged his friend to do so as Ethel gradually left for the City of Zion.[29]

If Martha found solace in this at the time, neither she nor the more poetic Abby let it distract them from ministering to the needs of their visible world. They continued to work for a healthier planet by organizing "more planning and talk." And while Martha now told a colleague, "That's all I am good for now," nobody minimized what the Eliot sisters' words could accomplish. So it was, that in breaking away from the pattern to which their foremothers tried to adapt, Martha and Abby also escaped the earthly closure that ended with death and a heaven that they had outgrown. They wanted cremations and asked that their ashes be scattered after they died. They were satisfied to think of their atoms being returned to the universe, there to combine with others and take on an infinite number of new forms and missions. In the meantime, they would continue to live by the same cosmic principle as before, mindful that individuals were particles of humanity who were meant to unite and work together creatively.[30]

Not waiting to rise above the clouds to look down at history running its course, and not standing quietly off to the side when civilization was spinning its wheels, these Eliot sisters claimed their portion of immortality in the present. The only relevant City of God for these daughters of Unitarians was the planet they lived on, the same one their ancestors tried to infuse with justice and love, only newly arranged to fit a modern apostasy. Now the neediest families, the immigrants and native-born people of color—who might have been blocked at Channing's gate had Americans taken a vote—were given a rightful salvation on earth through education and medical care. Incapable of walking the earth in silent witness and counting the days, these Eliot women had no parting word for this life. They had already joined the immortals.

The Family Roster

Abigail [Smith] Adams (1744–1818), the great-aunt of Abigail Adams Cranch Eliot, was at once a wife, mother, manager of the family farm, advisor to one of the Founding Fathers, and First Lady during John Adams's tenure as President of the United States. Unable to fathom a three-person God, she considered herself "unitarian."

Anna "Nancy" [Greenleaf] Cranch (1772–1843) was the wife of Judge William Cranch and the mother of Abigail Adams Cranch Eliot. Her example in bracing her spouse helped her daughter prepare for her marriage to the Rev. William Greenleaf Eliot.

Judge William Cranch (1769–1855),the husband of Nancy Greenleaf Cranch and father of Abigail Adams Cranch Eliot, was so inept at managing money, he had to be rescued from debtors' prison by his mother's sister Abigail Adams. Thanks to his aunt's intervention, his uncle, the President, named him to sit on the Circuit Court of the District of Columbia.

Ethel Collins Dunham, MD. (1883–1969), was for fifty-five years the life partner and public health colleague of Martha May Eliot. A pioneer in the care of premature babies and newborns, she became the first woman to be awarded the John Howland Medal, the American Pediatrics Association's highest honor.

Abby Adams Eliot, EdD (1892–1992), was the younger daughter of Mary Jackson May Eliot and the Rev. Christopher Rhodes Eliot, the life partner of Anna Holman for more than fifty years, and a pioneer in America's nursery school movement. Faithful to the legacy left by the grandmother for whom she was named, she became the matriarch of the family, keeping the tribe together in spirit as steward of Camp Maple Hill.

Abigail Adams [Cranch] Eliot (1817–1908), who was named for her maternal great-aunt, was the wife of the Rev. William Greenleaf Eliot and for seventy years the matriarch of the Eliots' St. Louis branch.

Charlotte Champ [Stearns] Eliot (1843–1929), Abigail's daughter-in-law and Henry Ware Eliot's wife, salvaged her thwarted ambition of making a name for herself in the world of letters by writing a published biography of her father-in-law. After losing a baby who lived for over a year with serious birth defects, Charlotte transferred her morbid and clinging concern to her youngest child, Thomas Stearns (T.S.) Eliot, paving the way for his early escape to England.

The Rev. Christopher Rhodes Eliot (1856–1945), the third surviving son of Abigail Adams Cranch Eliot and the Rev. William Greenleaf Eliot, was the husband of Mary Jackson May Eliot and the father of Frederick, Martha, and Abby. As pastor of Bulfinch Place Church in Boston's West End, he based his community ministry on a program of hands-on social work, providing a model his children adapted to their professional goals.

Elizabeth Berkeley [Lee] Eliot (1888–1967), a graduate of Radcliffe College, Class of 1910, was a promising student at the School of the Museum of Fine Arts in Boston when she gave up all other ambitions and surrendered her identity to become the wife of the Rev. Frederick May Eliot.

The Rev. Frederick May Eliot (1889–1958) was the oldest child of Mary Jackson May Eliot and the Rev. Christopher Rhodes Eliot, the brother of Martha and Abby, and the husband of Elizabeth Lee. His twenty-year tenure as minister of Unity (Unitarian) Church in St. Paul, Minnesota, prepared him to serve another two decades as President of the American Unitarian Association.

Henrietta "Etta" Robins [Mack] Eliot (1845–1940) had a rare gift for language that would have taken her into the pulpit had she been a male. As it was, she married the Rev. Thomas Lamb Eliot and helped him compose his sermons, counseled his troubled parishioners, ministered to herself and others by publishing verse and short stories, and reared seven children, including one minister and two ministers' wives.

Henrietta Mack Eliot (1879–1978), the youngest surviving daughter of Henrietta Robins Mack Eliot and the Rev. Thomas Lamb Eliot, served as her parents' personal aide and custodian of their papers.

Henry "Hal" Ware Eliot (1843–1919), was the second surviving son of Abigail Adams Cranch Eliot and the Rev. William Greenleaf Eliot, The first to reject his father's plan for his sons to enter the ministry, Hal found his niche after several false starts as a partner in the Hydraulic-Press Brick Company in St. Louis. When his artistic son, T. S. Eliot, failed to enter a business or "manly" profession, Hal's disappointment was just as profound as his own rebellion had been for his father.

Margaret Greenleaf [Dawes] Eliot (1789–1879) was the wife of William Greenleaf Eliot Sr., and the mother of his namesake, whom Abigail Adams Cranch married

Martha May Eliot, MD (1891–1978) was the older daughter of Mary Jackson May Eliot and the Rev. Christopher Rhodes Eliot, sister of Frederick and Abby, devoted life partner of Ethel C. Dunham, and powerhouse at the U.S. Children's Bureau, eventually serving as Chief. Her international work on behalf of the world's needy families included a stint as the World Health Organization's Assistant Director-General and several tours as medical consultant to UNICEF's work overseas.

Mary Jackson [May] Eliot (1859–1926), daughter of one of New England's most fiercely reform-minded Unitarian families, injected a newly radical spirit into the Eliot line as the wife of the Rev. Christopher Rhodes Eliot and the mother of Frederick, Martha, and Abby. Unable to go to college herself, she vowed that her daughters, as well as her son, would have that advantage. In doing so, she planted a value on education that blossomed in both of her daughters' careers. The feminist impulse that helped them succeed was also a part of her legacy.

Mary Rhodes Eliot (1838–1855) was the first child to be born to Abigail Adams Cranch Eliot and the Rev. William Greenleaf Eliot in St. Louis. After her death at the age of sixteen, a staggering blow to her parents and friends, her father named Washington University's Mary Institute in her memory.

Minna Charlotte Sessinghaus Eliot (1868–1944) was a summa cum laude graduate of Washington University, who gave up her plan of becoming a scholar and college professor to marry the Rev. William Greenleaf Eliot Jr. Physically over-worked while intellectually "underemployed," and finding her job as a minister's wife to be thankless, Minna suffered a series of breakdowns that eventually left her an invalid.

Ruth Kayser Eliot [Prentiss](1899–1994), the younger daughter of Minna Sessinghaus Eliot and the Rev. William Greenleaf Eliot Jr., had her family to thank for her rescue from a bad marriage and her new lease on life as a single mother of William Eliot Prentiss.

The Rev. Samuel Atkins Eliot (1862–1950), son of Harvard's progressive president Charles William Eliot, was for thirty years the American Unitarian Association's chief executive officer. While he was only a distant relation to the Eliot clan in St. Louis, his micromanagement of their increasingly small denomination affected them no less personally.

Samuel Eli Eliot (1882–1976) was Henrietta Mack Eliot and the Rev. Thomas Lamb Eliot's seventh child and second son. His experience after the turn of the century as a Rhodes Scholar at Oxford University caused him to question his fitness to enter the ministry and firmed his decision to go into social settlement work instead.

Theodore Sessinghaus Eliot (1900–1996), the youngest child of Minna Sessinghaus Eliot and the Rev. William Greenleaf Eliot Jr., went on to become a professor of anatomy at the University of Tennessee Medical School in Memphis and the University of Colorado School of Medicine in Denver.

Thomas Dawes Eliot (1889–1973) was the youngest child of Henrietta Mack Eliot and the Rev. Thomas Lamb Eliot. Sharing his brother Samuel Ely Eliot's disinclination to enter the ministry, he became a professor of sociology at Northwestern University.

The Rev. Thomas Lamb Eliot (1841–1936), the oldest surviving son of Abigail Adams Cranch Eliot and the Rev. William Greenleaf Eliot, moved west with his wife, Henrietta, and toddler William Greenleaf Eliot Jr. to shepherd a new Unitarian church in Portland, Oregon. His work for the larger community's uplift produced a system of good public schools, a library, art museum, public parks, and Reed College.

Thomas Stearns "T. S." Eliot (1888–1965), the youngest son of Charlotte Champ Stearns Eliot and Henry Ware Eliot, would bring his family an equal measure of disappointment and pride—on one hand, leaving its faith and homeland to live in England and join its church, on the other hand, garnering accolades for his influence in the world of letters.

The Rev. William Greenleaf Eliot (1811–1887), the second son of William Greenleaf Eliot Sr., was the founding pastor of the first Unitarian Congregational church in St. Louis. In the course of his marriage to Abigail Adams Cranch Eliot, he fathered five children who lived to adulthood, two of them ordained clergy who carried his legacy to both coasts. This second William Greenleaf Eliot chose not to use "Jr." after his name, saving it for his first grandson.

The Rev. William Greenleaf Eliot Jr. (1866–1956), the oldest child of Henrietta Robins Mack Eliot and the Rev. Thomas Lamb Eliot, succeeded his father in Portland's Unitarian pulpit in 1906. A devoted husband to Minna Sessinghaus Eliot, he took on the role of a live-in nurse as his wife's emotional health declined, as well as the care of their grandson Billy after their daughter Ruth's divorce.

William Greenleaf Eliot Sr. (1781–1858), the Rev. William Greenleaf Eliot's father, had been a merchant and shipowner before the embargo imposed by the War of 1812 ruined his business. Moving his family south to the young nation's capital city, he went to work in the U.S. Postal Service's Dead Letter Office and stayed there for thirty-five years. With Judge William Cranch, John Quincy Adams, and others, he was instrumental in organizing the first Unitarian society in Washington, D.C.

William Greenleaf Eliot III (1897–1990), the oldest son of Minna Sessinghaus Eliot and the Rev. William Greenleaf. Eliot Jr., outgrew the boyish mischief that made him a cross to his mother at church as he and his siblings learned from their father the need to protect her from undue stress. He went on to become an economist and highway engineer with the U.S. Bureau of Public Roads in Washington, D.C.

There he also served on the board of trustees of All Souls Unitarian Church, the society his great-grandfather helped to establish in the capital city.

Anna Eveleth Holman, MA (1892–1969), poet, photographer, naturalist, and devoted companion, met Abby Adams Eliot when they were students at Radcliffe College and became her life partner. Anna's interest in science, a legacy from her father, MIT physics professor Silas W. Holman, was manifest in her long career at the Winsor School in Boston, where she taught science and served as the chair of her department.

Rebecca [Robins] Mack (1814–90) was the mother of Henrietta Robins Mack Eliot. Her oppressive orthodox faith was at once a hindrance and prod to her daughters' defections to Unitarian Christianity.

Abigail Williams May (1829–88). Mary Jackson May Eliot's aunt, inspired her nieces by scorning convention to fight for such causes as abolition, education reform, and the full raft of women's rights.

Frederick Warren Goddard May (1821–1904), Mary Jackson May Eliot's father, was a businessman and active supporter of abolition, prison reform, care of the mentally ill, and women's suffrage.

The Rev. Samuel May (1810–1899), the uncle of Mary Jackson May Eliot, served as minister of the Leicester, Massachusetts, Unitarian church before leaving to put all his energy into the state's Anti-Suffrage Society.

The Rev. Samuel Joseph May (1797–1871), great-uncle of Mary Jackson May Eliot, was known for his fierce opposition to slavery and work for temperance and women's equality. During the Civil Rights struggle nearly a century after his death, the society he had served for twenty-five years in Syracuse, New York, adopted the name, May Memorial Unitarian Universalist Church.

Elizabeth Fuller [Wilbur] Nelson (1907–1987) was Dorothea Eliot Wilbur and the Rev. Earl Morse Wilbur's "miracle" baby, the first to survive the trauma of birth and fulfill their long thwarted hopes of starting a family. Determined that she would support herself, Elizabeth trained to teach nursery school and kindergarten and worked in that field for more than a decade before becoming a wife and stay-at-home mother.

Anna [May] Peabody (1865–1939), Mary May Eliot's younger sister, hoped to become a minister but could not find a church to ordain her. Her feminist outrage was also fueled by her marriage to Frederick Peabody, a predatory attorney who stole her inheritance.

Clara [Eliot] Raup, PhD (1896–1976), the oldest child of Minna Sessinghaus Eliot and the Rev. William Greenleaf Eliot Jr., earned a doctorate degree and taught economics for many years at Columbia University's Barnard College. For her mother, Clara's attainments were at once gratifying and bitter reminders of what Minna Eliot sacrificed by choosing to marry a minister.

Elizabeth Robins (1865–1952), Henrietta Robins Mack Eliot's "cousin Bessie," achieved fame and wealth as an actress, writer, and ardent champion of women's rights. Living comfortably and on her own terms in England, she acknowledged her limits in trying to grasp the plight of less fortunate women, and in doing so, helped Etta Eliot keep her own shortcomings in perspective.

Grace Cranch [Eliot] Scott (1875–1973), was the fifth daughter born to Henrietta Mack Eliot and the Rev. Thomas Lamb Eliot, and the fourth to reach adulthood. Her humor and optimistic spirit helped her move past a painful divorce and the loss of her youngest son, Peter, the following year.

Abigail "Abs" Eliot Smith, MD (1900–1984), was the only child of Rose Eliot Smith and Holmes "Jac" Smith. Unstable emotionally, she excelled in medical school but was never able to hold down a practice. After her parents died, her cousin Abby Adams Eliot looked after her.

Rose Greenleaf [Eliot] Smith (1862–1936), the youngest surviving child of Abigail Cranch Eliot and the Rev. William Greenleaf Eliot, married Holmes "Jac" Smith (1863–1937), an art professor at Washington University. She had a great love of music and a lovely singing voice, and the loss of her hearing in middle age was a great trial to her and her family.

Sarah [May] Stowell, MD (1867–1961), Mary Jackson May Eliot's youngest sister, married and shared a practice with pediatrician Edmund Channing Stowell. Her example encouraged her niece Martha May Eliot to become a physician.

Ellen Smith [Eliot] Weil (1873–1971), the fourth child born to Henrietta Mack Eliot and the Rev. Thomas Lamb Eliot, was the second daughter, after her sister Dorothea, to marry a minister. She and her future husband, the Rev. Fred Alban Weil, met in Meadville, Pennsylvania, while he was attending the Unitarian theological school. Her brother-in-law Earl Morse Wilbur was minister of the town's liberal Congregational church at the time.

Alice [Heustis] Wilbur (1871–1952) was the sister-in-law of Dorothea Dix Eliot Wilbur and the Rev. Earl Morse Wilbur. A native of privileged Boston and a Radcliffe College alumna, she married Earl's brother Ralph and joined him in Portland, Oregon. A staunch conservative in and beyond the Unitarian church, she headed the state's anti-suffrage campaign and ridiculed women ministers.

Dorothea "Dodie" Dix [Eliot] Wilbur (1871–1957), the second daughter born to Henrietta Mack Eliot and the Rev. Thomas Lamb Eliot, was the first girl to live to adulthood. Her marriage to Earl Morse Wilbur, her father's associate pastor in Portland, was marked by constant financial distress, difficulties in starting a family, and the challenges of rearing two children as well as a theological school.

The Rev. Earl Morse Wilbur (1866–1956) was Thomas Lamb Eliot's junior colleague in Portland's Unitarian church when he met and married the Eliots' daughter Dorothea. After serving four years with the liberal church in Meadville, Pennsylvania, he was tapped to create the Pacific Unitarian School for the Ministry, which he struggled—first in Oakland and then in Berkeley—to keep alive. Retiring after three decades, he devoted himself to research and writing, eventually completing a two-volume *History of Unitarianism.*

Ralph W. Wilbur (1869–1952) was the Rev. Earl Morse Wilbur's younger brother, a pillar of Portland's Unitarian church, and a prosperous Portland attorney.

Thomas Lamb Eliot "Eliot" Wilbur (1912–1931), the only son of Dorothea Dix Eliot Wilbur and the Rev. Earl Morse Wilbur, had been a difficult child but was finally making his parents proud when, three weeks before his twentieth birthday, he died in the campus infirmary at Pomona College in Claremont, California.

MAJOR EVENTS

	Family	Unitarian	Women	Other
1811	William Greenleaf Eliot Jr. born in Bedford, MA. ("Jr." is dropped, later used by his grandson)			
1817	Abigail Adams Cranch born in Alexandria, VA			
1819		W.E. Channing delivers "Unitarian Christianity"		
1821	Eliots and Cranches help organize first Unitarian church in nation's capital			
1825		Liberal Congregational clergy create American Unitarian Association (A.U.A.)		
1831			Lydia Maria Child's *Appeal in Favor of that Class of Americans called Africans*	
1834	WGE to St. Louis			
1835		First Unitarian Congregational Society organized in St. Louis		
1837	Abigail Cranch and WGE marry		National Female Anti-Slavery Society organized in NYC	
1838	Mary Ely Eliot first of twelve babies born in St. Louis parsonage	R.W.Emerson delivers Divinity School Address		Trail of Tears: removal of Cherokee Nation to "Indian" Territory
1841	Thomas Lamb Eliot born; brother William dies eleven days later	T. Parker, "The Transient and the Permanent in Christianity"		Dorothea Dix begins crusade for the mentally ill and incarcerated

(continued)

MAJOR EVENTS

	Family	Unitarian	Women	Other
1843				H. Bushnell's *Christian Nurture* sets domestic religion in stone
1844		Meadville Theological School founded in northwest PA		
1845	Henrietta Robins Mack born in Amherst, MA		Margaret Fuller's *Women in the 19th Century*	
1848			1st women's rights convention in Seneca Falls, NY	
1849	WGE tends cholera victims; pregnant AACE afraid of becoming a widowed mother		E. Blackwell becomes first female to earn M.D.; H.Tubman escapes from slavery, starts Underground Railroad	
1852		WGE organizes Western Unitarian Conference		
1855	Mary Eliot dies			
1856	Christopher Rhodes Eliot born in St. Louis			
1857	WGE oversees inauguration of Washington University			Vulcanization of rubber provides reliable condoms
1859	Mary Jackson May born in Dorchester, MA			
1860	Ocean voyage fails to cure TLE's painful eyes		Olympia Brown rejected by Meadville, accepted by Canton Theological School	
1861	HRM and TLE meet in St. Louis		Dorothea Dix to St.Louis, helps WGE recruit nurses for Western Sanitary Commission	Civil War begins

(continued)

Year				
1862	Rose Greenleaf Eliot born, AACE's last baby; TLE enlists in Hallack Guard			Emancipation Proclamation does not apply to Missouri
1863	Eliots rescue Archer Alexander, fugitive slave		Olympia Brown ordained by St. Lawrence Ass'n, of Universalists; first clergywoman so recognized	
1865	Henrietta Mack, Thomas L. Eliot marry	First meeting, Nat'l. Conf. of Unit. Churches		Civil War ends; Lincoln assasinated
1866	William G. Eliot Jr. born to HRME and TLE in Portland; Earl Wilbur born in Jerico, VT			
1867	HRME, TLE, WGE Jr., to Oregon via Isthmus of Panama	Radicals' Free Religious Ass'n. created with O.B.Frothingham president		E. S. Phelps's best-seller *The Gates Ajar* gives detailed description of heaven
1868	TLE becomes pastor in Portland; Minna Sessinghaus born in St. Louis	Second Liberal society, Church of the Unity, formed in St. Louis		
1869	AACE, WGE, daughter Rose visit Portland			Transcontinental railroad completed
1871	Dorothea Dix Eliot born to HRME, TLE in Portland		Portland's Ladies' Relief Society incorporates "The Home"	
1873	HRME's "Appeal to Conscience" in *Christian Union and Christian Register*			Comstock Law makes sale of condoms illegel
1875			Julia Ward Howe convenes first Women Ministers Conference; Mary Baker Eddy publishes *Science and Health*	
1876	TLE granted year's sick leave; drops family off in St. Louis, travels abroad		Women's Christian Temperance Union founded	

MAJOR EVENTS

	Family	Unitarian	Women	Other
1878	Nine-year-old "Mamie" Eliot dies in Portland			Formal end of Reconsuuction
1879			Opening of Radcliffe Annex	
1882	Christopher Eliot accepts call to Dorchester, MA; meets Mary Jackson May			
1884		American Unitarian Ass'n. formed as representative body for congregations; eventually absorbs Nat'l. Conf.		
1886		Jabez T. Sunderland publishes *The Issue in the West*		
1887	WGE dies	W.C. Gannett's *The Things Most Commonly Believed Among Us* adopted by W.U.C.		
1888	Mary May and Christopher Eliot marry; T.S. Eliot born to Charlotte Stearns, Henry Eliot in St. Louis			
1889	Frederick May Eliot born to MJME, CRE in Dorchester			
1890	Earl Morse Wilbur called to be TLE's assistant in Portland		National Alliance of Unitarian Women founded in Boston	
1891	Martha May Eliot born to MJME, CRE in Dorchester, MA			
1892	Abby Adams Eliot born to MJME, CRE; Anna Evelyth Holman born in Newton, MA			
1893		Jenkin Lloyd Jones organizes World Parliament of Churches in Chicago		

260

(*continued*)

1894	Minna and WGE Jr. marry; Dorchester Eliots to Beacon Hill	Boston's Bulfinch Place Church calls CRE	
1895	HRME collaborates with Susan Blow, translates Mottos for *Mother Play*		
1898	Marriage of Dorothea Dix Eliot, Earl Morse Wilbur		
1896		First Unitarian Church of Milwaukee calls WGE, Jr.	
1899		First joint discussion of merger with Universalists	
1900	DDEW and EMW in Meadville, PA	Samuel Atkins Eliot named President of A.U.A.	
1902		A.U.A. publishes eugenicist David Starr Jordan's *The Blood of a Nation*	
1903	Minna has nervous breakdown		
1904	MJME and CRE open Camp Maple Hill; Wilburs become dean and "deanness"	Pacific Unitarian School for the Ministry opens in Oakland, CA	
1906	WGE, Jr. installed as pastor in Portland		
1907	Elizabeth Wilbur born in Portland	Tuckerman School for Parish Assistants opens in Boston	
1909			N.A.A.C.P founded
1912	Eliot Wilbur born in Berkeley, CA		Pres. W.H. Taft signs law, creates Children's Bureau
1914	MME, ECD to medical school; AAE into social work	Rev. Arthur M. Smith lobbies to close PUSM	Start of World War I
1915	Elizabeth Lee and Frederick Eliot marry	Exposure of Smith's sordid life saves PUSM but hurts A.U.A.'s reputation in Wilburs' district	

MAJOR EVENTS

	Family	Unitarian	Women	Other
1916			Margaret Sanger opens first U.S. birth control clinic	
1917	FME called to church in St. Paul	Pres. S. A. Eliot pressures pulpits to back the war		
1918	MME, ECD finish medical school			World War I ends
1919	Anna Holman to France with Radcliffe Unit; AAE to Oxford	Unitarian Laymen's League founded		
1920	MME "comes out" to parents: Ethel "central to everything"		19th Amendment, women gain right to vote	
1921	AAE studies with M.McMillan in London; MME to Yale; Ruth Eliot, Edward Prentiss marry in Portland	Humanism debated by J.H. Dietrich, W. L. Sullivan at Nat'l. Conf,	Sheppard-Towner Act passed, protects welfare of mothers and infants	
1922	AAE opens Ruggles St. Nursery School; "Billy" Prentiss born; Ruth files for divorce	Church in Portland harassed by Klansmen		
1923	MME gets name in textbooks with study of rickets and vit. D			
1924	MME joins CB	Publication of EMW's *Our Unitarian Heritage*		
1926	MJME dies at Maple Hill			

Year			
1929	Minna and Will to Europe, their Second honeymoon		Stock Market crashes
1931	EMW retires from PUSM; Cutler scandal brings Wilburs from Europe; ELE, FME adopt "Ricky"	Secound A.U.A. commission considers consolidation with Universalists	
1932	Eliot Wilbur dies in Claremont, CA		
1933	ELE and FME adopt "Kits"		
1934	WGE, Jr. made pastor emeritus		
1935	DDEW rents out rooms, supporting EMW's full-time work on his history		MME, K. Lenroot draft Title V of S.S. Act, create grants for mothers' and children's welfare
1936	TLE dies in Portland		
1937	Children of HRME publish book of her poems	FME elected A.U.A. President; recruits S. Fahs to modernize S.S. curricula	
1939		Service Committee created	WWII begins
1940	HRME dies		
1941			Pearl Harbor attacked, U.S. enters World War II
1944	Minna dies	A.U.A. elects first female Moderator, Aurelia Reinhardt	MME inspects, is outraged by camps holding Japanese-American families

(continued)

MAJOR EVENTS

	Family	Unitarian	Women	Other
1945	CRE dies	EMW's *History of Unitarianism, vol. I* published		World War II ends; House Committee on Un-American Activities
1946				UNICEF created by MME's cohort
1949	MME, ECD to Geneva		MME Ass't.Director-General of World Health Organization	
1950	AAE, AEH to Concord, MA; AAE begins "second career" in mental health			
1951	MME returns to CB as Chief			
1952		EMW's *History of Unitarianism, vol. II*		
1954			MME gets funding for mass polio immunization for children	*Brown vs. Board of Education* makes school segregation illegal
1956	EMW dies; WGE Jr. dies			
1957	DDEW dies			
1958	FME dies			
1961		AUA and UCA consolidate as Unitarian Universalist Ass'n.		
1963	MME travels from Cambridge to show support for March on Washington		B. Friedan's *Feminine Mystique* starts second wave of Feminist Movement	

264

Year		
1964	UUA challenges congregations to seek candidates of both sexes when hiring ministers	
1965	More than two hundred UU clergy and laypeople join march on Selma; Rev. James Reeb, Violet Liuzzo among those killed	
1969	Anna Holman, Ethel Dunham die	Stonewall Revolt, start of modern gay civil rights movement
1973	MME starts taping oral history	
1978	MME dies	
1984	Women now 15% of UU clergy in Fellowship	Twenty-nine UU women ministers in Final Fellowship
1982	AAE tapes memoirs for *A Heart of Grateful Trust*	
1992	AAE dies	

Abbreviations

Persons

AACE	Abigail Adams Cranch Eliot
AAE	Abby Adams Eliot
AEH	Anna Eveleth Holman
AES	Abigail Eliot Smith
AHW	Alice Heustis Wilbur
CCSE	Charlotte Champs Stearns
CER	Clara Eliot Raup
CRE	Christopher Rhodes Eliot
DDEW	Dorothea "Dodie" Dix Eliot Wilbur
DLD	Dorothea Lynde Dix
EMW	Earl Morse Wilbur
EWN	Elizabeth Wilbur Nelson
FME	Frederick May Eliot
GES	Grace Cranch Eliot Scott
HME	Henrietta Mack Eliot
HRME	Henrietta "Etta" Robins Mack Eliot
HWE	Henry Ware Eliot
KSBB	Kate Stevens Bingham Bates
MCE	Mary Caroline Eliot
MJME	Mary Jackson May Eliot
MME	Martha May Eliot

MSE   Minna Sessinghaus Eliot
RES   Rose Eliot Smith
RWW   Ralph W. Wilbur
RRM   Rebecca Robins Mack
SAE   Samuel Atkins Eliot
SEE   Samuel Ely Eliot
SLG   Sarah Lane Glasgow
SSF   Sarah "Sally" Smith Flagg
TDE   Thomas Dawes Eliot
TLE   Thomas Lamb Eliot
TLEW   Thomas Lamb Eliot "Eliot" Wilbur
WGE   William Greenleaf Eliot
WGE2   William Greenleaf Eliot Jr.

Sources

AOE   Family Papers of Alexandra Osti Eliot
EGM   Oral history and family papers of Eleanor Goddard May II
GHS   Georgesville Historical Society, Quebec
GTU   Hewlett Library, Graduate Theological Union, Berkeley, Calif.
HDS   Andover-Harvard Library, Harvard Divinity School
HL   Houghton Library, Harvard University
MCE   Family Papers of Mary Caroline Eliot
MHS   Massachusetts Historical Society, Boston
MLTS   Meadville Lombard Theological School, Chicago
MOHS   Missouri Historical Society, St. Louis
OHS   Oregon Historical Society, Portland
PFUU   Archives of First Unitarian Church, Portland, Ore.
Reed   Hauser Memorial Library Archives, Reed College, Portland, Ore.
SL   Schlesinger Library, Radcliffe Institute, Harvard University
UO   Knight Library, Special Collections, University of Oregon, Eugene
USIE   Lovejoy Library Archives, University of Southern Illinois, Edwardsville
WAE   Family Papers of Warner Ayers Eliot
WUSL   Olin Library, Washington University, St. Louis, Mo.

Notes

CHAPTER 1

1. For an overview of the now-merged traditions, their common ground, and evolving relationship, see David Robinson, *The Unitarians and the Universalists* (Westport, Conn.: Greenwood, 1985). Charles H. Lyttle illuminates the tensions between the Christian theists and the radical advocates of a more inclusive religious tradition in *Freedom Moves West: A History of the Western Unitarian Conference, 1852–1952* (Boston: Beacon, 1952). Also see Arnold Crompton's *Unitarianism on the Pacific Coast: The First Sixty Years* (Boston: Beacon, 1957) for the challenges to liberal religious expansion in the Far West.

2. See Lawrence Buell, "Joseph Stevens Buckminster: The Making of a New England Saint," *Canadian Journal of American Studies* 10 (1979): 1–29.

3. In 1831, the Unitarian and Universalist bodies were considered too small to count, and neither group appeared in *The American Almanac and Repository of Useful Knowledge* (Boston: Gray and Bowen). In 1849, when both were included, the Unitarians were numbered at thirty thousand. This was half as many as the Universalists, who ranked seventeenth in a fairly small field of denominations. By 1887, both groups had reported a shrinkage of 50 percent.

4. For the history of Frederick May Eliot's years at the helm, see Conrad Wright, "It Was Noontime Here..." in *A Stream of Light: A Short History of American Unitarianism* (Boston: The Unitarian Universalist Association, 1975), 125–55.

5. Exacerbating the problem was the propensity of Harvard-trained clergy to speak of parishioners as a family and of the church as a home where communicants gathered before a "domestic altar." Daniel W. Howe notes this

tendency in *The Unitarian Conscience: Harvard Moral Philosophy, 1804–1861* (Cambridge, Mass.: Harvard University Press, 1979), 128–29.

6. "The Education of Women," *Westminster Review* 29 (1831); Horace Bushnell, *Christian Nurture* (New York: Charles Scribner's Sons, 1890), 19ff.

7. William G. Eliot's notebooks show that he shared this concern. To ensure that the unfit would not gain control and wreak havoc by casting their ballots, he endorsed women's suffrage "almost against [his] will," convinced that property ownership and education, rather than gender, would be the safest basis for determining who could vote (Notebook 8, 16 February 1875. William Greenleaf Eliot Papers, Washington University Archives, St. Louis).

8. William Greenleaf Eliot, "Notes on a Talk to Be Given before the Missouri State Teachers' Association in Sedalia, 28 December 1870," in Notebook 7, 104ff., WUSL.

9. I have reconstructed this history in *Prophetic Sisterhood: Liberal Women Ministers of the Frontier, 1880–1930* (Boston: Beacon, 1990); and more broadly in "Women in the Unitarian Universalist Ministry" in *Religious Institutions and Women's Leadership*, ed. Catherine Wessinger, 79–100 (Columbia: University of South Carolina Press, 1996).

10. Ann Douglas explores this phenomenon in *The Feminization of American Culture* (New York: Knopf, 1977).

11. Samuel Atkins Eliot to Mary Augusta Safford, 5 November 1896, 5 December 1898. American Unitarian Association, Presidential Papers, Andover Harvard Library, Cambridge, Mass.

12. An excerpt from a sermon by Portland, Oregon's Rev. Earl Morse Wilbur describing the church as a place where men could develop their social and physical sides as well as the spiritual appeared in *The Guidon*, March 1892. For an interesting comparative study, see L. Dean Allen, *"The Men and Religion Forward Movement" and the "Promise Keepers* (Macon, Ga.: Mercer University Press, 2002).

13. Ellen Tucker Emerson to Lidian Emerson, 8 January 1854, and to Clara Dabney, 28 July 1881, in *The Letters of Ellen Tucker Emerson*, 2 vols., ed. Edith E. W. Gregg (Kent, Ohio, 1982); William Greenleaf Eliot to Thomas Lamb Eliot, 22 September 1864, WUSL.

14. Diary of Ruth Irish Preston, 14 May 1933, 3 March 1935. Archives of the Unitarian Church, Davenport, Iowa.

15. Sally Smith [Flagg], diary, 21 January 1849, 28 December 1849, 28 December 1848. Norman G. Flagg Papers, University of Southern Illinois, Edwardsville.

16. Karin E. Gedge looks at the clergy wives' pastoral role in the context of their husbands' interaction with female parishioners in *Without Benefit of Clergy: Women and the Pastoral Relationship in Nineteenth-Century American Culture* (New York: Oxford University Press, 2003), 133–35, and *passim*.

17. Far from unique, the trials that tested the Eliot women were also burdens for clergy wives as different as Sarah Ripley (1793–1867) and Mary Ware (1798–1849). All had moments, if not years, in which they despaired as Sarah did when she married George Ripley and saw what his country parish was like in Waltham, Massachusetts. Like Sarah, they worried about being up to the task when they first got engaged but never imagined their husbands would take them to cultural deserts and bridle their minds. Subdued by a "husband's foreboding voice" admonishing each not to show off her learning, the Eliot spouses shared Sarah's "fatigue of affected sympathy" with earnest people who, frankly, bored them to death. There would be many times when they prayed, as she had, for "any

hole" by which to escape "this most servile of all situations." They would find, too, as Mary Ware did when she married the widowed pastor of Second Church, Boston, that parsonage wives could not expect to be ministered to by the ministers. After conquering first her religious doubts and then her "self-governed being," Mary was ready to "look to another for guidance and happiness" when she married. But Henry Ware Jr., the father of two and on the verge of a breakdown, was the delicate one who needed the cheering up and a shoulder to lean on. See Sarah Ripley to Mary Moody Emerson, 12 June 1817, cited by Joan W. Goodwin in *The Remarkable Mrs. Ripley: The Life of Sarah Alden Bradford Ripley* (Boston: Northeastern University Press, 1998), 66, 100, 96; and Edwards Brooks Hall, *Memoir of Mary L. Ware, Wife of Henry Ware, Jr.* (Boston: Crosby, Nichols, 1853), 184. In her essay, "In the Parsonage, In the Parish: Experiences of Nineteenth-Century Unitarian Ministers' Wives" (Unitarian Universalist Heritage Society, Occasional Paper Series, February 2002), Emily Mace compares Mary L. Ware, Anna Tilden Gannett, and Sarah Ripley.

18. In one of her few references to her mother-in-law, Charlotte C. Eliot cites Abby's recollection of what she expected as a young bride in *William Greenleaf Eliot* (Boston: Houghton Mifflin, 1904), 36–37.

19. Margaret Fuller (1810–50), the first female book editor of the *New York Tribune*, was in fact a prodigious, unladylike critic not only of literature but also of social systems and politics. Her feminist treatise, *Woman in the Nineteenth Century* (1845), was enormously influential as part of the feminist canon. Yet the liberties taken by Ralph Waldo Emerson, William Henry Channing, and James Freeman Clarke in editing Fuller's *Memoirs* ensured that the Fuller known to posterity would be a woman whose oversized ego was ludicrous given that she had "willingly" stayed "in the usual circles...of female talent" (*Memoirs of Margaret Fuller Osoli* [1852], 1:322). Julia Ward Howe, known today almost solely for writing the words of "The Battle Hymn of the Republic," was both a prolific author and a speaker of wide repute in her time. She was also an unhappy wife whose published volume of transparent poetry infuriated not only her husband, Samuel Gridley Howe, but also outraged such scandalized critics as Nathaniel Hawthorne. By the time Samuel died in 1876, his widow, now more concerned about perfecting her public image, produced a memoir that painted over the sordid reality of their relationship. Howe's daughters colluded, determined that she would live on as a model of womanly dignity. In her later years and after she died, they invented their own reality, suppressing the onerous facts in writing their mother's biography. Their two-volume work on Julia Ward Howe won a Pulitzer Prize in 1916. See Valarie H. Ziegler, *Diva Julia: The Public Romance and Private Agony of Julia Ward Howe* (Harrisburg, Pa.: Trinity Press International, 2003).

CHAPTER 2

1. WGE2, "Memories of '70s and '80s," typescript, Missouri Historical Society; WGE2, diary, 1887, 26–27, Reed; Christopher Rhodes Eliot, journal, 24 February 1887, MOHS.

2. Quoted by Paul C. Nagel, *The Adams Women* (New York: Oxford University Press, 1987), 29.

3. Ibid., 130–34. A handwritten note by granddaughter Dorothea Dix Eliot Wilbur, lent by Warner A. Eliot, mentions this formality of address in the Cranches' home.

4. AACE to Margaret Cranch (sister), 11 December 1835, transcribed by Rose Eliot Smith, ca. 1930, Mary C. Eliot.

5. AACE to Dear Friend, n.d. [ca. 1895], typescript intended for presentation at Wednesday Club in St. Louis, MOHS.

6. Ibid.

7. Charlotte C. Eliot, *William Greenleaf Eliot: Minister, Educator, Philanthropist* (Boston: Houghton Mifflin, 1904), 4.

8. Ibid., 1–7. Margaret's own ample gifts were denied any public life. Hymns she composed for the Eliots' daily devotions at home would have made their way into a book of readings that Dorothea Dix was compiling had Abby's father not objected. AACE to Margaret Cranch, 11 December 1835, transcribed by RES ca. 1930, MCE.

9. Ibid., 7.

10. Ibid., 7–8; Walter Samuel Swisher, *A History of the Church of the Messiah, St. Louis, 1839–1934* (St. Louis: Church of the Messiah, 1934), 12, 16–20.

11. Swisher, 24–25.

12. Henry Ware Eliot Jr., *A Short History of the Church of the Messiah* (St. Louis: Eliot Alliance, 1916), MOHS; Jacob N. Taylor, *Sketch Book of St. Louis* (St. Louis: George Knapp, 1858).

13. Henry Clay Lackland to Norma Lackland, n.d. [1848], MOHS; Anne Lane to Sarah Glasgow, 19 January 1852, MOHS. On the writing of sermons from memory, a carry-over from New England Congregational training, see Sarah Wilder, "'Most Glorious Sermons': Anna Tilden's Sermon Notes, 1824–1831," in *Studies in the American Renaissance*, ed. Joel Myerson, 1–93 (Charlottesville: University of Virginia Press, 1989).

14. AACE to TLE, 13 October 1889, Reed; AACE to SSF, 31 March 1878, Reed.

15. SSF, diary, 13 February 1848, 14 January 1849, 26 November 1848, 16 December 1849, 5 December 1855.

16. *William Greenleaf Eliot*, 26–27; SSF, diary, 1 September 1852, 5 January 1853; AACE to TLE, 21 March [1875]. According to the *Presbyterian* 31 (18 July 1861), the average minister's salary was something under $500 in 1860.

17. Sarah Lane Glasgow to William Glasgow Jr., 17 March 1847, MOHS; AACE to SLG, 22 March 1848, MOHS.

18. Ibid. See Judith Walzer Leavitt, "Under the Shadow of Maternity," in *Women's America*, ed. Linda K. Kerber and Jane Sherron DeHart, 184–91 (New York and Oxford: Oxford University Press, 1995).

19. *William Greenleaf Eliot*, 50–52.

20. SSF, diary, 6 January 1855.

21. TLE, journal, 6 January 1855, Reed; SSF, diary, 9 January 1855.

22. SSF, diary, 6–28 January 1855; TLE, journal, 7 January 1855, Reed; Anne E. Lane to Sarah L. Glasgow, 26 May 1860, MOHS. William G. Eliot's collection of sermons, *The Discipline of Sorrow*, which was edited later that year, made no direct reference to his personal motive for writing them.

23. WGE explained his position in drafting a letter to the *Christian Register*: It was "better to do too little than to do what must be undone," but also unhelpful to have the "interference of societies and individuals who [were] too far distant from the scene to know what ought to be done." Notebook 4, 15 November 1853.

24. Chapter 8: "Emancipation as a War Measure," *William Greenleaf Eliot*, 182–211; SSF, diary, 15 November 1853, USIE; John F. Scheck, "Transplanting a Tradition: Thomas Lamb Eliot and the Unitarian Conscience in the Pacific Northwest, 1865–1905" (PhD, diss., University of Oregon, 1969), 20–24.

25. Henry Ware Eliot, "The Reminiscences of a Simpleton" (1910), typescript, WUSL, 30.

26. William G. Eliot, *The Story of Archer Alexander: From Slavery to Freedom* (Boston: Cupples, Upham, 1885), 54; WGE to SLG, 11 February 1859, WUSL.

27. Henry Ware Eliot, "Reminiscences," 58.

28. TLE to AACE, 27 July 1862, WUSL; on TLE and the Halleck Guard, see Earl Morse Wilbur, *Thomas Lamb Eliot, 1841–1936* (Portland, Ore.: Privately printed [G. M. Allen and Son], 1937), 14, 122n16.

29. Henry Ware Eliot, "Reminiscences," 52.

30. *William Greenleaf Eliot*, 207–9.

31. See E. Anthony Rotundo, *American Manhood: Transformations in Masculinity from the Revolution to the Modern Era* (New York: Basic, 1993), 177–78.

32. The commission that Bellows headed, anchored in Washington, seemed to Eliot too far away to appreciate and address the problems of distribution in states like Missouri. In St. Louis, he tried to explain to Bellows, who took affront at his action, fewer than one out of every four citizens was a Union supporter, and half of the canons defending the city might just as well have been aiming at it, so great was the animosity toward its Yankee residents. The suspicion toward anyone who got involved in the war work, even the hygiene and health side, was so intense that initially, Eliot said, it had to proceed under cover (*William Greenleaf Eliot*, 221–22 and *passim*).

33. DLD to WGE, 8 July (1874) SL; Christopher Rhodes Eliot, memorial sermon for Dorothea Lynde Dix, 24 July 1887, SL; David L. Gollaher, *Voice for the Mad: The Life of Dorothea Dix* (New York: Free, 1995), 49–51, 409, 410, n23.

34. WGE, notebook 10, 6 January 1877; AACE to DLD, 3 August 1878, 1 March 1880, The Schlesinger Library.

35. TLE, diary, 10 February 1855, Reed; WGE to TLE, 6 October 1864, WUSL; S. W. Hosmer to WGE, 19 July 1865, Reed.

36. WGE to TLE, 12 August 1865, WUSL.

37. WGE to TLE, n.d. [June 1865] WUSL; TLE to WGE, 22 June 1866, Reed.

38. WGE, notebook 10, 51, WGE to TLE, 21 November 1878, 16 November 1867, WUSL.

39. AACE to HRME, 23 February 1868, 21 May 1868, 6 September 1868, Reed.

40. AACE to TLE, 5 March [1874], Reed; AACE to DLD, 9 January [1882], SL; AACE to TLE and HRME, 6 September 1868, Reed.

41. Maria Wicker to Cyrus French, 19 June 1871, MOHS.

42. AACE to TLE, 4 October 1886, Reed.

43. WGE to TLE, 21 December 1872, WUSL; WGE, notebook 9, 25 June 1876, 129, WUSL; WGE to TLE, 10 November 1869, Reed.

44. AACE to TLE, September 1886.

45. WGE to TLE, December 1864, WUSL; AACE to TLE, 8 January 1865, MCE; AACE to HRME, 8 November 1898; AACE to TLE, February 1868; AACE to HRME, 9 August 1868, Reed.

46. AACE to Edward Cranch Eliot, 24 July 1883; AACE to HRME and TLE, 29 March 1887; AACE to HRME and TLE, [1887]; AACE to HRME and TLE, 7 April 1895; AACE to TLE, 28 August 1897, Reed.

47. Henry Ware Eliot, "Reminiscences," 46.

48. Clarke's position is cited by James M. McPherson in "A Brief for Equality: The Abolitionist Reply to the Racist Myth, 1860–1865," *The New England Quarterly* 45 (1972): 408–16.

49. WGE, *Archer Alexander*, 58; Henry Ware Eliot, "Reminiscences," 11–12.

50. Henry Ware Eliot, "Reminiscences," 2.

51. AACE to Edward Cranch Eliot, 24 July 1883, Reed. When Ralph Waldo Emerson learned that the Jackson administration had brokered a treaty to take the Cherokees' territory and send them to what would become Oklahoma, he castigated the government for dealing with bogus agents who signed a contract to herd an "active nation" into the wilderness after packing them into carts and boats, and dragging them over the mountains and rivers. They needed the chance "to redeem their race from the doom of eternal inferiority" by adopting Caucasians' "arts and customs." It was possible, Emerson granted, that they would never be able to free themselves of their aboriginal ways and learn to be Christian citizens. Citing the Rev. John Eliot's failure to Christianize the tribes of colonial Massachusetts, Emerson insinuated that it was not only because of white people's prejudice. Their seemingly "dwindled souls" had kept the indigenous people from "being elevated to equality with their civilized brother," he wrote Martin van Buren on 23 April 1838. *The [Washington] Daily National Intelligencer* reprinted the letter on 14 May 1838.

52. WGE to Mayor J. H. Britton, 13 October 1875; newspaper clipping of Eliot to Mayor Henry Overstole, 13 November 1877; WGE notebooks 9, 10, and 43, WUSL.

53. AACE to HRME, 8 August 1877; AACE to HRME, 25 [May] 1885; AACE to TLE, 20 January 1892; AACR to HRME, 3 August 1892, Reed.

54. AACE to HRME, 9 October 1887; AACE to HRME, 1889, Reed.

55. AACE to HRME and TLE, 4 December 1888; AACE to HRME and TLE, 8 February 1889, Reed.

56. WGE to TLE, 6 October 1864, WUSL; WGE2 to EMW, 30 November 1896, Lamson Library, Graduate Theological Union, Berkeley.

57. Unidentified member of the National Women's Alliance to Mrs. Richardson, 2 January 1889, Meadville Lombard Theological School; "The History of the Western Women's Unitarian Conference," 13ff., MLTS.

58. AACE to TLE, 22 December 1893, Reed.

59. Much as Eliot hated to stir up dissent, he feared a worse outcome if he continued "to continence skepticism and infidelity." The enemy here was actually worse than the radical camp, he said. It posed the danger of shallowness being passed off as substantial religion. Allowing one generation to grow up under such superficial instruction would surely give birth to another of far lower grade, he said. While he never attacked Snyder openly, the pastor emeritus had never trusted him fully and would have been happy to see Snyder go had there been any better candidates (WGE to DLD, 23 April 1876, SL).

60. AACE to TLE, 30 June 1889, Reed.

61. Notes by Henry Scott on Cranch lineage, loaned by Warner A. Eliot; phone conversations with Robbie L. Cranch, 2004–5.

62. SLG to William Glasgow, 18 October 1882, MOHS; AACE to HRME and TLE, 5 December 1886, Reed.

63. AACE to HRME and TLE, 8 March 1887, Reed.

64. AACE to TLE, 13 September 1889; AACE to TLE, [1889], Reed; AACE to DLD, [1878], SL; AACE to TLE, 4 December 1888; AACE to TLE, 25 April 1897, Reed.

65. TLE to HRME, n.d. [October 1908], Reed. HWE wrote this in pencil on the last page of his "Reminiscences."

CHAPTER 3

1. Adams Family Papers, Massachusetts Historical Society.

2. According to Emily Dickinson, who was fifteen years old and living with her family next door to the Macks when Etta was born, the baby girl was reputed to be "an ornament to society" and "an embryo of future usefulness." Emily Dickinson to Mrs. A. E. Strong, n.d. [4 August 1845], in *Letters of Emily Dickinson*, 2 vols., ed. Mabel Loomis Todd (Boston: Roberts Brothers, 1894), 10. Etta remembered another neighbor, Emily Webster Fowler, more clearly, for she had made a ritual out of feeding her love for language. When she and Rebecca visited, Mrs. Fowler would hoist her onto a chair and repeat the story of how her grandfather, Noah Webster, had sat in that seat while compiling his book of words. Then producing his famous dictionary, she opened it to a page where he had included a picture of the chair in which Etta was sitting. See DDEW, handwritten notes, courtesy of Warner A. Eliot. Rebecca Amelia Robins Mack to Samuel Ely Mack, 9 July 1848, Reed; Ruth Eliot Johnson oral history, 23 February 1984.

3. On Beecher's "mental and moral philosophy," see Kathryn Kish Sklar, *Catherine Beecher: A Study in American Domesticity* (New Haven, Conn.: Yale University Press, 1973), 78ff.

4. Samuel E. Mack to My dear little Etta, 14 June 1855; 5 January 1860, WAE.

5. HRME to TLE, 30 July 1865, Reed.

6. HRME to Rebecca Robins Mack, n.d. [late 1860s], GTU; the Rev. Octavius Brooks Frothingham was a leader of the Unitarians' radical wing, whose Free Religious Association held its first meeting in 1867; Henry Eliot Scott, notes on TLE's feelings about his mother-in-law, WAE.

7. HRME to TLE, 11 October 1863, 1 September 1863, Reed.

8. TLE, "Journal of Incidents in a Voyage from New York to San Francisco" [1860–61], 54, 89–94, 128, Reed.

9. WGE to "Dear Count," 6 April 1862, WUSL; AACE to TLE, 7 December 1864, MCE; Elizabeth Robins to HRME, 3 April 1910, GTU.

10. Etta and Tom's expectations were strongly influenced by Samuel Bowles's popular travel book *Across the Continent: A Summer's Journey to the Rocky Mountains...and the Pacific States* (Springfield, Mass.: S. Bowles, 1865), 182–83, 197.

11. Matthew P. Deady, "Portland-on-Willamet," *Overland Monthly* 1 (July 1868): 34–43; HRME to Rebecca Robins Mack, 4 December 1868, GTU.

12. HRME to Mary Mack, 25 January 1868, GTU.

13. HRME to AACE, 4 December 1868, GTU.

14. From mid-January through February 1869, the *Pacific Christian Advocate* furnished the stage for the clergy's response to the Oro Fino lectures. The accusations cited here appeared in an editorial signed "W" in the 6 February issue.

15. The history of the Ladies' Relief Society and The Home was told in *The Oregonian*, 19 March 1967, and again with special attention to the legal machinations by E. Kimbark MacColl in "The Women to the Rescue," an address at the annual meeting of the Parry Center (Portland, 23 September 1980), PFUU; HRME to Mary Mack, 25 January 1868, GTU.

16. HRME to Rebecca Robins Mack, 1871, GTU; HRME to TLE, 17 August 1874, 18 August 1874, Reed.

17. TLE, journal, 14 and 16 February 1864; HRME to TLE, n.d. [1874], Reed; on the YMCA's rebuttal, see Evadne Hilands, *A Time to Build: The First Unitarian Society of Portland, Oregon, 1866–1966* (Portland: First Unitarian Society, 1966), 140.

18. HRME to TLE, 11 May 1872, Reed.

19. HRME to TLE, 21 February 1893, Reed.

20. HRME to TLE, 7 March 1893, Reed; Earl Morse Wilbur describes the strict regimentation Etta had to maintain at home for Tom's sake in *Thomas Lamb Eliot, 1841–1936* (Portland, Ore.: Privately printed [G. M. Allen and Son], 1937), 101–8.

21. AACE to HRME, 9 August 1868, Reed; WGE to HRME, 6 March 1872, Reed; HRME to AACR, 2 June 1871, GTU; HRME to Rebecca Robins Mack, 1871, GTU.

22. HRME to TLE, 30 September 1874, Reed.

23. DLD to HRME, 2 June 1870, transcribed from original by TLE, Reed.

24. HRME to TLE, 13 May 1872, 20 May 1872, Reed.

25. HRME to TLE, 18 June 1866, Reed.

26. Wilbur, *Thomas Lamb Eliot*, 106; HRME to Mary Mack, 25 January 1868, GTU; HRME to Rebecca Robins Mack, n.d. [1871], GTU.

27. HRME to TLE, 6 May 1872, 11 May 1872, Reed.

28. *Christian Register* 52, no. 52 (27 December 1873), 1.

29. WGE to TLE, 4 January 1874, WUSL; HRME to TLE, 10 September 1893, Reed; HRME to TLE, 18 August 1895, Reed; "Out of the Silence," *The Unwelcome Guest and Other Verses* (Portland, Ore.: Privately printed, 1937), 27.

30. HRME to TLE, n.d. [January 1877], Reed; Etta's story was called "The Adopted Chicken," her poem "Unawares."

31. TLE to R. Glison denying the rumors, 17 October 1877; TLE, journal, Reed. Etta would also credit her writing with helping her through another miscarriage in 1885, the loss of a stillborn two years later, and similar disappointments her daughter Dodie went through before she gave birth to a healthy baby who lived to adulthood. AACE to TLE, 1 June 1885, Reed; DDEW to EMW, 2 July 1897, GTU.

32. Harvey Scott, ed. *History of Portland, Oregon* (Syracuse, NY: D. Mason, 1890), chapter 12, gives a good overview of the churches and benevolent organizations, including the Seamen's Friend Society of which Stubbs was chaplain; TLE, journal, 25 April 1878, Reed.

33. HRME to WGE2, 29 September 1901; HRME to TLE, n.d. [May 1878], Reed.

34. In 1882, Galvin left the active Unitarian ministry to become superintendent of the Chicago Athenaeum, a position he held until 1894.

35. AACE to TLE, 10 April 1887, Reed; "The Unwelcome Guest," *The Unwelcome Guest*, 13. In his final years when almost all of his memory was gone, Tom repeatedly spoke of Etta's consuming grief after Mamie's death. This was told to Rose Eliot Smith by her nephew Samuel Ely Eliot in a letter, 11 September 1933, Reed.

36. DDEW to EMW, 26 July 1897, GTU.

37. While making a place for the colorful balls, blocks, nested cubes, pebbles, and sticks, which were used to help build the powers of observation and classification, Blow contended that teachers stunted creative growth by being too regimented and strict about how the objects were handled. More problematic, Blow argued, the Gifts had given rise to a culture of fetish-worship, which undercut the premise of education. She complained that many teachers attributed almost magical powers to these material objects, crediting them with accomplishing what any genuine educator would ascribe to the children's natural faculties. See Dorothy W. Hewes, *W. N. Hallmann: Defender of Froebel* (Grand Rapids, Mich., 2001), 91–92. The collaboration between Susan Blow and Henrietta R. Eliot was published as *The Mottoes and Commentaries of Friedrich Froebel's "Mother Play"* (New York: Appleton, 1895).

38. William Eliot was typical of the community leaders, who hailed Blow's supervised classrooms as salutary alternatives to the street life where poor neglected youngsters ran loose and were being corrupted. Similarly, while kindergartens were not meant to serve as vocational schools, Eliot also saw the practical benefits of the "Gifts" to teach manual skills and basic concepts of measurement and geometry, which impoverished children could use to support themselves later. Blow's successes also drew fierce opposition from Catholics who deeply resented their tax money paying for programs from which their children, who went to parochial schools, drew no benefit. See Selwyn K. Troen, *The Public and the Schools: Shaping the St. Louis System, 1838–1920* (Columbia, Mo., 1975), 99–115 and *passim*. As both women were raised in orthodox faith traditions that they had outgrown, Etta was able to sympathize and reassure Susan when she was trying to muster the courage to cut her Presbyterian roots and transplant herself among the Episcopalians. The rapport that developed during this time is evident in their collaborative work, to which they brought a similar spirituality and religious hope and a passion to make themselves understood. Agnes Snyder, "Susan E. Blow" in *Dauntless Women in Childhood Education, 1856–1931* (Washington, D.C.: Association for Childhood Education International, 1972), 59–85.

39. Etta's other publication outlets—acknowledged when a collection of Etta's poetry was published by the family in 1937 as *The Unwelcome Guest and Other Verses*—were *Open Court, Springfield Republican, Christian Register, Westminster Gazette, Leslie's Weekly, Overland Monthly, Youth's Companion, Pacific Unitarian, Wide Awake,* and *Everybody's*. See "Poetry in Human Life," undated clipping in WGE2 scrapbook, PFUU, HRME to WGE2, 8 March 1902, Reed.

40. Notebook, July 1870–June 1871, 104ff.; "Address to Missouri State Teachers Assn," *St. Louis Democrat,* 5 January 1871.

41. AACE to HRME and TLE, 8 March 1887, Reed. William Eliot's notebook confirmed that he suffered "prostration of mind, depression of spirits, an utter failing of the heart, contempt of self, together with nervousness of body" "in the few hours after each preaching." Notebook, November 1847–October 1848, 10; Ruth Eliot Johnson, interview by Lorraine McConnell and Ruth P. Nelson, 23 February 1984, Portland, Oregon, audiocassette,

PFUU. Earl Morse Wilbur, Dodie Eliot's husband, and her father's biographer, dismissed the idea of Etta writing Tom's sermons as a "legend" and traced it to a "natural misunderstanding" (*Thomas Lamb Eliot*, 123n27). HRME to TLE, 8 March 1887, Reed; *Pacific Unitarian* 3 (August 1895): 305. For the broader picture of church development, see Arnold Crompton, *Unitarianism on the Pacific Coast: The First Sixty Years* (Boston: Beacon, 1957), 126 and *passim*.

42. HRME to TLE, 20 May 1895, Reed.

43. HRME to WGE2, 29 September 1901, 21 October 1901, Reed; HRME to MSE, n.d. [October 1901], Reed.

44. In addition to teaching her Bible class, Etta continued delivering papers under the auspices of the Women's Alliance. In August 1913, *The Pacific Unitarian* (21, no. 10, 301) announced the conclusion of "instructive lectures on 'The History of Unitarianism and Its Scriptural Justification' by Mrs. T. L. Eliot"; HRME to Rose Eliot Smith, 18 January 1933, MCE; HRME to EMW, 22 December 1928, GTU; Alice Heustis Wilbur to DDEW, n.d. [January 1929], GTU.

CHAPTER 4

1. *Writing a Woman's Life* (New York: Norton, 1988), 47.

2. Hazard Stevens, *The Life of Isaac Ingalls Stevens* (Boston: Houghton Mifflin, 1900).

3. Diary of Kate Stevens Bingham, 1880–81, 23; 10 September 1893, 16 September 1888. Housed at the University of Oregon in Eugene, and called diaries by their author, these private writings of Kate Stevens Bingham [Bates] were neither daily nor uniform in their dating. The citations hereafter reflect these inconsistencies.

4. Diaries, early summer 1885, 12 and 13 September 1885, summer 1885.

5. Diaries, 10 and 13 December 1885, 12 December 1885, January 1886.

6. Diaries, 13 December 1885, August 1889.

7. Diaries, 13 June 1888, 1 February 1891.

8. Diaries, July 1889, ca. April 1893, February 1894.

9. AACE to TLE, 20 January 1992, Reed. See John F. Scheck, "Transplanting a Tradition: Thomas Lamb Eliot and the Unitarian Conscience in the Pacific Northwest, 1865–1905" on the Eliots and temperance, 288–312; diaries, 12 September 1894, ca. March 1890.

10. EMW to parents, 23 August 1891, 6 March 1895, 4 September 1893, GTU; TLE to HRME, 24 February 1896, Reed. Dr. Leslie E. Keeley's treatment relied largely on injecting addicts with "bichloride" of gold. After his first facility was opened in 1879, his centers proliferated. The "gold cure" was largely discredited by 1900.

11. KSBB to TLE, 3 February 1919, Reed; diaries, 25 October 1896.

12. Scheck, 289–92; HRME to AACE, 4 April 1874, Reed.

13. "Death of E. W. Bingham," *The Morning Oregonian*, 2 January 1904; "The Late E. W. Bingham, An Appreciative Sketch," *The Sunday Oregonian*, 10 January 1904; Edward W. Bingham to KSBB, 16 December 1901, 20 February 1902, UO; diaries, 23 February 1898, 22 January 1899.

14. The collaborative effort paid off with the passage in 1891 of the "Australian Ballot" and the "Consolidation" measures, significant pieces of legislation that paved the way for

others: the "Registration" bill in 1899 and the 1904 Direct Primary measure. See Scheck, 322–28; TLE to HRME, 24 February 1896, Reed.

15. Diaries, 25 September 1892, July 1889, 7 July 1892.

16. Diaries, 28 July 1891.

17. Diaries, 28 July 1891, 29 May 1892, 31 May 1896, 7 May 1899.

18. Diaries, 14 February 1892, 3 February 1900.

19. Diaries, 30 September 1894.

20. Diaries, 25 December 1894, 25 December 1896, 12 March 1899.

21. HRME to TLE, 29 October 1887, Reed; DLD to TLE, 17 January 1872, 26 January 1872, 14 January 1872, Reed. Thirty years before, Abby Eliot's friend Sarah Glasgow had voiced the same concern about William Eliot giving away his wife's household funds. SLG to William Glasgow Jr., 17 March 1847, MOHS.

22. WGE to HRME, 28 March 1879, WUSL; HRME to TLE, 14 June 1880, Reed; Theodore R. E. Wyant to TLE, 25 December 1882, Reed; C. W. Burrage to TLE, 14 November 1882, Reed; R. J. Reeves to TLE, 7 January 1888, Reed; Elizabeth Wilbur Nelson to TLE, 11 October 1931, GTU.

23. HRME to TLE, 15 March 1892, Reed.

24. HRME to TLE, 2 July 1903, 17 June 1901, Reed.

25. See Joanne E. Gates, *Elizabeth Robins, 1862–1952: Actress, Novelist, Feminist* (Tuscaloosa: University of Alabama Press, 1994).

26. ER to HRME, 10 December 1909, GTU.

27. Diaries, ca. March 1890; Women's Alliance Scrapbooks and Records, PFUU. For a broader view of the role clubs played in fostering women's appreciation for one another, see Karen Blair, *The Clubwoman as Feminist: True Womanhood Redefined, 1868–1914* (New York: Holmes and Meier, 1980); and Theodora Penny Martin's history of women's study groups, from 1860 to 1910, *The Sound of Our Own Voices: Women's Study Clubs, 1860–1910* (Boston: Beacon, 1987).

28. The fund-raisers' clout was more than a myth. In 1900, the church almost folded when, vexed by the trustees' disorganization, the women refused to solicit subscriptions. Before they would budge, the treasurer grumbled, the Finance and Ways and Means Committee had to give them their way "in every particular." Without their consent, the treasurer complained, he could not even hire a janitor or use the spare desk in the secretary's office to work on the church's accounts. By the following May, the men had apparently made amends, for Etta wrote Tom that the rummage sale was "exceeding [all] expectations." She thought it would get them out of debt and keep them there if they did their job. "I am planning a little speech to that effect before the [Alliance]," she wrote on May 5. Ralph Wilbur to EMW, 28 June 1900, GTU. Also see Evadne Hilands, *A Time to Build: The First Unitarian Society of Portland, Oregon, 1866–1966* (Portland: First Unitarian Society, 1966), 109.

29. Diaries, 8 October 1899, January 1893, 30 October 1898, 22 March 1895, 26 March 1899, 12 March 1899, 21 July 1900.

30. Diaries, 20 March 1892, 8 May 1892, May 1892.

31. Diaries, 27 June 1894, 16 June 1899, 3 September 1899, February 1891, 9 March 1899.

32. *Programme of the William G. Eliot Fraternity, 1893–1894*, PFUU. The alliance's membership shot up by almost a fourth during Kate's first year as recording secretary,

bringing the rolls to seventy-three by the time she was reelected in 1893. See diaries, January 1893, 1 January 1896, 24 January 1897.

33. "The Anniversary Meetings of the A.U.A., typescript, 8 pp., n.d.; Mrs. C. W. Burrage to KSBB June 1914, UO.

34. EWB to KSBB, 12 December 1901, 14 December 1901, UO.

35. HRME to TLE, 6 January 1903, Reed.

CHAPTER 5

1. AACE to HRME and TLE, 2 February 1871, Reed; DDEW to TLE, 30 December 1887, GTU; DDEW to EMW, 23 September 1899, GTU.

2. DDEW to EMW, 22 July 1897, GTU; DDEW to EMW, 7 July 1900, GTU; HRME to TLE, October 1902, Reed; Edward H. Clarke, *Sex in Education; Or, A Fair Chance for the Girls* (Boston: Osgood and Company, 1874); HRME to TLE, n.d. [ca. 1895], Reed; DDEW to EWN, 24 July 1935, GTU.

3. Fragment of letter from HRME to RRM, n.d. [early 1890s], GTU; DDEW to MSE, 28 August 1893, WAE; HRME to RRM, [Winter 1888–89], GTU.

4. HRME to RRM, 27 July 1890, GTU; Elizabeth Wilbur Nelson, "Earl Morse Wilbur," typescript, n.d., WAE; Earl Morse Wilbur, "A Father's Reminiscences," 69, GTU.

5. Nelson, "Earl Morse Wilbur"; Wilbur, "A Father's Reminiscences," 77–78.

6. Wilbur, "A Father's Reminiscences," 83–84; Mrs. D. P. Thompson to TLE, 10 February 1893. Reed; Nelson, "Earl Morse Wilbur"; EMW to Mercy Jane Morse Wilbur, 16 November 1891, GTU; TLE to HRME, 14 June 1891, Reed.

7. HRME to EMW, 27 January 1891, GTU; EMW to Mercy Jane Morse Wilbur, 25 October 1894, GTU.

8. EMW to LaFayette and Mercy Jane Morse Wilbur, 28 January 1895, GTU.

9. HRME to TLE, 18 April 1894, Reed; EMW to LaFayette and Mercy Jane Morse Wilbur, 31 August 1893, GTU.

10. Wilbur, "A Father's Reminiscences," 82–83, 90; EMW to LaFayette and Mercy Jane Morse Wilbur, 12 December 1893, GTU; DDEW to EMW, 14 February 1895, GTU; DDEW to EMW, 6 August 1895, GTU.

11. DDEW to EMW, 8 September 1897, GTU; HRME to RRM, 23 August 1898, GTU; Wilbur, "A Father's Reminiscences," 89–93, 94, 97.

12. Alice Heustis Wilbur to EMW and DDEW, 9 December 1898, GTU; AHW to EMW and DDEW, 28 December 1898, GTU.

13. Ralph W. Wilbur to EMW, 22 February 1899, GTU; DDEW to TLE, 21 April 1899, GTU.

14. KSBB, diary, 9 April 1899; DDEW to TLE, 21 April 1899, GTU; Evadne Hilands, *A Time to Build: The First Unitarian Society of Portland, Oregon, 1866–1966.* (Portland: First Unitarian Society, 1966), 51–52; AHW to DDEW and EMW, 16 June 1899, GTU.

15. Nelson, "Earl Morse Wilbur"; DDEW to EMW, 13 September, GTU; DDEW to EMW, 19 September 1899, GTU. Also see Earl Morse Wilbur, *Historical Sketch of Independent Congregational Church of Meadville, Pennsylvania* (Meadville, Pa., 1902).

16. EMW to TLE, 10 April 1900, GTU; EMW to TLE, 15 January 1900, GTU; EMW to TLE, 29 January 1900, GTU.

17. EMW to DDEW, 9 June 1900, GTU.

18. DDEW to EMW, 18 August 1902, GTU.

19. EMW to TLE, 10 October 1900, GTU; DDEW to WGE2, n.d. [1901], GTU; DDEW to EMW, 13 June 1900, GTU; EMW to WGE2, 26 January 1901, Reed; DDEW to EMW, 17 May 1901, GTU.

20. DDEW to EMW, 25 June 1900, GTU; EMW to LaFayette and Mercy Jane Morse Wilbur, 27 September 1893, GTU; H. D'Arcy Power to EMW, 26 September 1893, GTU; EMW to TLE, 9 October 1893, GTU.

21. HRME to TLE, November 1902, Reed; DDEW to EMW, 15 May 1903, GTU.

22. DDEW to EMW, 5 July 1900, GTU.

23. DDEW to EMW, 11 June 1900, GTU; DDEW to EMW, 15 May 1903, GTU; EMW to DDEW, 19 June 1900, GTU; HRME to WGE2, 19 June 1893, loaned by WAE; DDEW to EMW, 9 September 1899, GTU; EMW to TLE, 13 June 1900, GTU; DDEW to EMW, 22 September 1899, GTU; EMW to LaFayette and Mercy Jane Morse Wilbur, 4 January 1895, GTU.

24. DDEW to EMW, 5 July 1900, GTU; DDEW to EMW, 5 July 1900, GTU; EMW to TLE, 10 April 1900, GTU.

25. Wilbur, "A Father's Reminiscences." Typescript, 1953. Courtesy of WAE; *Christian Register* 83 (12 May 1904): 506.

26. See Earl Morse Wilbur, *Pacific Unitarian School for the Ministry: The History of Its First Twenty-five Years, 1904–1929* (Berkeley: Pacific Unitarian School for the Ministry, 1930). For the larger context of West Coast development, see Arnold Crompton, *Unitarianism on the Pacific Coast: The First Sixty Years* (Boston: Beacon, 1957). For the school's larger history, see Arliss Ungar, *With Vision and Courage: Starr King School for the Ministry, the History of Its First Hundred Years, 1904–2004* (Lincoln, Neb.: iUniverse, 2006).

27. EMW to DDEW, 13 August 1904, GTU; EMW to DDEW, 19 August 1904, GTU; Wilbur, *Pacific Unitarian School*, 46–47.

28. DDEW to EMW, n.d. [May 1909], GTU; DDEW to EMW, n.d. [June 1908], GTU.

29. DDEW to EMW, June 1908, GTU; DDEW to EWN, 6 January 1939, GTU.

30. RWW to EMW, 25 January 1910, GTU; TDE to EMW, 2 January 1919, GTU.

31. DDEW to EMW, 24 May 1910, GTU.

32. EMW to WGE2 27 October 1910, GTU; EMW to WGE2, 14 August 1910, GTU.

33. DDEW to EMW, 17 September 1899, GTU.

34. In an undated letter he drafted but never sent to friends of the school, Wilbur gave these details as well as his argument in defense of the record. For the actual enrollment figures, see his *Pacific Unitarian School*.

35. The scandal, which broke on January 22, 1915, was picked up by the International News Service, while the San Francisco *Examiner* and the *New York Tribune* covered the story directly. EMW to DDEW, 14 December 1914 and notes on back of envelope; TLE to EMW, 11 January 1915, GTU; TLE to EMW, 27 January 1915, GTU; Benjamin A. Goodridge to EMW, 19 January 1915, GTU.

36. Frances Power Cobbe, *The Duties of Women: A Course of Lectures* (London: Williams and Norgate, 1881), 190.

37. DDEW to MSE, 15 June 1900, GTU; DDEW to MSE, 26 July 1897, GTU.

38. EMW to TLE, 19 April 1900, GTU.

39. DDEW to EMW, 15 June 1900, GTU; DDEW to EMW, 22 July 1900; EMW to TLE, 13 June 1900, GTU; DDEW to EMW, 11 June 1900, GTU.

40. AHW to DDEW and EMW [late March 1900], GTU; ASCE to HRME and TLE, 10 April 1900, Reed. As Margaret Marsh and Wanda Ronner point out in *The Empty Cradle: Infertility in America from Colonial Times to the Present* (Baltimore: Johns Hopkins University Press, 1996), 3–5, the rate had neither changed nor would change significantly. For the pressures on childless couples, see also Elaine Tyler May, *Barren in the Promised Land: Childless Americans and the Pursuit of Happiness* (Cambridge, Mass.: Harvard University Press, 1997).

41. DDEW to EMW, 11 June 1900, GTU.

42. DDEW to EMW, 23 June 1903, GTU; DDEW to EMW, 15 June 1900, GTU; DDEW to EMW, 11 June 1903, GTU.

43. DDEW to EMW, 13 September 1907, GTU; DDEW to EMW, 20 September 1907, GTU.

44. DDEW to EMW, 19 September 1907, GTU; DDEW to EMW, 4 October 1907, GTU.

45. DDEW to EMW, July 1907, GTU.

46. Even more moderate Unitarian voices decried the failure of old Yankee families to reproduce at a vigorous rate. The A.U.A.'s chief officer, Samuel A. Eliot, repudiated the xenophobic dimension of Jordan's work and the Teutonist doctrine that Anglo Saxons monopolized all the virtues. Yet he believed as strongly as any eugenicist in the importance of protecting the racial purity of the best lines. *The Human Harvest*—first printed by the A.U.A. as a tract, "The Blood of the Nation" (Boston: American Unitarian Association, 1907), 39; SAE to Mr. Smith, 10 January 1898, HDS. Convinced that the nation's democracy would refine all its people's best traits, the A.U.A. opposed immigration restrictions. Nonetheless, *The Human Harvest* and other alarmist writings by Jordan would not have carried the A.U.A. imprint without its top officer's blessing.

47. *Empty Cradle*, 113; DDEW to EMW, 1 August 1902, GTU.

48. Wilbur, "A Father's Reminiscences," 2.

49. Ibid., 6, 8; DDEW to EMW, fragment [ca. 1921], GTU.

50. DDEW to HRME, 14 February 1929, GTU; DDEW to TLE, 9 October 1928, GTU.

51. DDEW to EMW, 15 July 1923, GTU.

52. EMW to EWN, 3 June 1933, GTU; DDEW to EMW, 31 October 1933, GTU; DDEW to EMW, 2 November 1933; DDEW to EWN, 6 January [1934], GTU.

53. EMW to TLEW, 9 September 1930, GTU; DDEW to EMW, 9 October 1930, GTU.

54. Ungar, *With Vision and Courage*, 44, and *passim*.

55. Eager to stake his claim, Earl Wilbur had managed in 1925 to have Beacon Press publish *Our Unitarian Heritage*, a reworking of lectures that he had been giving his students for twenty years.

56. DDEW to TLE, 22 April 1931, GTU; DDEW to TLE, 2 May 1931, GTU.

57. DDEW to HRME and TLE, 22 August 1931, GTU.

58. DDEW to TLE, August 1931, GTU.

59. DDEW to EMW, 29 July 1902, GTU; DDEW to HRME and TLE, 20 September 1931, GTU; EMW to DDEW, 26 February 1934, GTU.

60. DDEW to EMW, 3 December 1934, GTU; EMW to WGE2, 18 February 1934, GTU.

61. DDEW to EMW, 25 April 1932, GTU.

62. WGE2, sermon file, Reed; DDEW to HRME, 7 June 1933, GTU.

63. AHW to DDEW and EMW, 13 March 1933, GTU; EMW to TLE, 8 April 1933, GTU.

64. Lillian Burt to DDEW and EMW, 13 March 1933, GTU; Lillian Burt to EMW, 21 March 1933, GTU; Lillian Burt to EMW, 25 April 1933, GTU; DDEW to HRME, 7 June 1933; Lillian Burt to EMW, 21 March 1933, GTU.

65. EMW to DDEW, 24 October 1933; EMW to EWN, 18 November 1933, GTU.

66. DDEW to EMW, 8 January 1934, GTU.

67. DDEW to WGE2, 21 December 1923, GTU.

68. SEE to RES, 11 September 1933, Reed; DDEW to EMW, 25 February 1934, GTU.

69. DDEW to EMW, 18 February 1934, GTU; EMW to DDEW, 2 March 1934, GTU.

70. EMW to EWN, 13 November 1938, GTU; DDEW to WGE2, [February 1938], GTU.

71. DDEW to WGE2, 10 February 1949, GTU.

72. EMW to WGE2, 23 November 1952, GTU.

73. EMW to WGE2, 24 November 1944, GTU; EMW to WGE2, 4 November 1954, GTU; Earl Morse Wilbur's translation of *Socinianism in Poland by Stanislas Kot* was published posthumously by Starr King School for the Ministry in 1957.

74. DDEW to WGE2, 14 January 1951, GTU; EMW to WGE2, 4 November 1954, GTU.

75. EWN to DDEW and EMW, 14 February 1939, GTU; DDEW to EWN, 10 July 1935, GTU; SEE to WGE2, 30 August 1945, Reed.

CHAPTER 6

1. MSE to WGE2, 14 August 1893, WAE; WGE2 to MSE, 8 August 1893, WAE; WGE2 to MSE, 14 August 1893, WAE.

2. MSE to WGE2, 12 November 1893, WAE; DDEW to MSE, 15 July 1893, Reed.

3. MSE to WGE2, 3 June 1894, WAE.

4. MSE to WGE2, 26 January 1894, WAE. Norman and Will had been best of friends since their Smith Academy days, but Will had not told him about his plan to come home and propose to the woman he loved, no doubt because Norman was also smitten by Minna.

5. Ibid.

6. Carroll Smith-Rosenberg, "The Hysterical Woman: Sex Roles and Role Conflict in Nineteenth-Century America," *Social Research* 39 (Winter 1972): 652–78.

7. MSE to WGE2, 7 August 1893, WAE; MSE to WGE2, 10 July 1893, WAE; MSE to WGE2, 13 September 1893, WAE.

8. MSE to WGE2, 28 August 1893, WAE; 13 November 1893, WAE; MSE to WGE2, 8 August 1893, WAE.

9. MSE to WGE2, 14 January 1894, WAE.

10. MSE to May Patterson, 25–26 December 1888, enclosed with MSE to WGE2, 13 July 1893, WAE.

11. MSE to WGE2, 10 September 1893, WAE.

12. MSE to WGE2, 19 November 1893, WAE; MSE to WGE2, 4 February 1894, WAE; MSE to WGE2, 2 January 1894, WAE; MSE to WGE2, 18 March 1894, WAE.

13. MSE to WGE2, 10 September 1893, WAE; MSE to WGE2, 17 November 1893, WAE; MSE to WGE2, 19 January 1894, WAE.

14. MSE to WGE2, 19 June 1894, WAE; MSE to WGE2, 21 August 1893, WAE.

15. MSE to WGE2, 16 May 1894, WAE.

16. MSE to WGE2, 10 July 1993. Mary Patterson to MSE, 25 June 1907, Reed; MSE to WGE2, 16 May 1894, WAE. For a study of the Martineau siblings' relationship, see Valerie Sanders, "James and Harriet: Brother and Sister," *Transactions of the Unitarian Universalist Historical Society* 22 (April 2002): 322–38.

17. MSE to WGE2, 17 May 1894, WAE.

18. Margery Howarth Eliot, the second wife of Minna and Will's son William Greenleaf Eliot III, explained—in a telephone interview with the author on 16 May 1996—that Minna's children attributed her unhappiness to her constant feeling of being "underutilized." See also WGE2 to EMW, 1 January 1896, GTU; WGE2 to EMW, 1 December 1897, GTU.

19. George W. Stone to TLE, 31 December 1900, PFUU. Arnold Crompton, *Unitarianism on the Pacific Coast: The First Sixty Years* (Boston: Beacon, 1957), 152–53, 157, 168. A.U.A. headquarters, citing its own insufficiency, had cut back on the loans that had kept many churches alive during the ten years Charles W. Wendte served as the West Coast's superintendent. Others were left to die of neglect after Wendte resigned and moved back east. The A.U.A. waited four years to refill the position.

20. MSE to WGE2, 22 April 1902, Reed; MSE to WGE2, 20 April 1902, Reed.

21. MSE to WGE2, 22 April 1902, Reed.

22. TLE to HRME, 2 October 1902, Reed.

23. HRME to MSE, 28 July 1902, Reed.

24. Mary Jackson May Eliot to MSE, 15 August 1893, WAE.

25. HRME to WGE2, 29 September 1901, Reed; HRME to WGE2, 21 October 1901, Reed.

26. WGE2, diary, 3 October 1885–31 October 1885, Reed.

27. Ruth Eliot Johnson, interview by Lorraine McConnell and Ruth P. Nelson, 23 February 1984, Portland, Oregon, Portland First Unitarian Church, audiocassette, PFUU.

28. William Greenleaf Eliot Jr., "Beginning and Influence of the Portland Church," *Christian Register* 101 (13 July 1922): 664.

29. A.U.A. Papers, SAE to [E. H.] Gammons, [Fall 1898], HDS.

30. Lord was one of the clergy who organized the Anti-Imperialist League in Boston in 1898, when Congress was moving to annex Hawaii, Puerto Rico, and the Philippines. The conservative bent in Portland only strengthened Lord's stand for self-rule, provoking his denunciation of President William McKinley for violating a principle on which the nation was founded. While Lord was opposing McKinley's bid for a second term in the White House, Will Eliot, without calling himself an "expansionist," was supporting the commander-in-chief and arguing that America would be derelict in her moral duty if she did not take the Philippines under her wing (AHW to DDEW, [November 1900], GTU; WGE2 to EMW, 5 October 1898, GTU; WGE2 to EMW, 14 March 1899, GTU; 5 November 1900, GTU).

31. GES to WGE2, 16 June 1901, Reed; GES to WGE2, 28 May 1902, Reed; SAE to WGE2, 9 November 1904, HDS.

32. AHW to EMW, 8 September 1901, GTU; AHW to EMW, [May 1902], GTU; AHW to EWM and DDEW, 10 June 1904, GTU.

33. AHW to EMW, 10 June 1904, GTU. Known for rushing to church from a sickroom or prison without any message in hand, Will was also forgiven for losing his focus and taking forever to get to a point. He saw no great need to apologize, either, contending that active worship, not passive consumption of sermons, should be the main reason for coming to church. His people agreed that the way their minister lived could say more than the best-framed orations. TLE to HRME, 26 April 1908, Reed; TLE to HRME, 27 July 1908, Reed; TLE to HRME, 25 October 1908, Reed; WGE2, "A Liturgical Service: Its Use and Abuse," 4 May 1924, Reed; Ruth Eliot Johnson, interview by Lorraine McConnell and Ruth P. Nelson, PFUU.

34. Earl Morse Wilbur, *Thomas Lamb Eliot, 1841–1936* (Portland, Ore.: Privately printed [G. M. Allen and Son], 1937), 90–92; Roy E. Roos, *History and Development of Portland's Irvington Neighborhood* (Portland: R. E. Roos, 1997).

35. MSE to WGE2, [1903], Reed.

36. Ibid.

37. WGE2, Annual Report to the Church of Our Father, First Unitarian Church, Portland, Ore., 1907, Reed; WGE2 to N.A. Baker, 25 March 1908, Reed.

38. MSE to WGE2, 23 June 1907, Reed; WGE2 diary, entries for July and August, Reed.

39. Wilbur, *Thomas Lamb Eliot*, 93.

40. Ruth Eliot Johnson, interview by Lorraine McConnell and Ruth P. Nelson.

41. Ibid.; Margery Howarth Eliot, telephone conversation with Cynthia Grant Tucker, 4 May 1994.

42. Clipping from *The Sunday Oregonian*, 26 June 1910, n.p., WAE.

43. WGE2 to MSE, 5 September 1916, Reed; Mary Belsora Knowles to WGE2 and MSE, 16 July 1919, Reed.

44. MSE to Clara Eliot Raup, 18 September 1919, Reed.

45. WGE2 to MSE, 13 August 1917. *The Farmer's Campaign for Credit*, by Clara Eliot Raup, would be published by Appleton in 1927.

46. MSE to CER, 27 December 1919, Reed.

47. MSE to CER, 20 March 1920, Reed.

48. MSE to CER, 13 January 1920, Reed.

49. RES to TLE, 12 June 1922, Reed.

50. WGE2's diary entries from 4 February through 5 October 1922 trace the marriage's breakdown, with the last entry mentioning Ruth's telling Minna that she had considered suicide.

51. WGE2 to Clara Sessinghaus Vickroy, 5 June 1934, Reed; WGE2 to Clara Sessinghaus Vickroy, 18 April 1922, Reed.

52. On the Klan's presence in the Northwest, see David A. Horowitz, "Social Morality and Personal Revitalization: Oregon's Ku Klux Klan in the 1920s," *Oregon Historical Quarterly* 90 (1989): 365–84.

53. WGE2, diary, 7 May 1922, Reed.

54. WGE2, diary, 12 July 1934, Reed. Bill Prentiss would later recall—in a letter to Cynthia Grant Tucker, 11 July 1994—that Will was his "Dad": "He did more than many a Grandfather would have done in replacing a Father I did not have. He played ball with me, took me trout (stream) fishing, horseback riding....I have nothing but fond memories."

55. Hilands, Evadne. *A Time to Build: The First Unitarian Society of Portland, Oregon, 1866–1966*. Portland: First Unitarian Society, 1966.

56. WGE2, diary, 1934, *passim*.

57. MSE to WGE2, 4 March 1894, WAE.

58. HRME to TLE, 17 May 1920, Reed; DDEW to EMW, 25 February 1934, GTU; WGE2 to Clara Sessinghaus Vickroy, 5 June 1934, Reed; WGE2, "Set Your House in Order," [1920s], Reed; TDE to EMW, 2 January 1920, GTU; TDE to EMW, 19 September 1920, GTU. Will's younger brother Tom Dawes was the exception in pushing Freud. Tom, who was more than twenty years younger, had verged on a breakdown after losing his three-year-old son in 1919. He credited psychotherapy for getting him past the trauma without the symptoms that might have developed if his unconscious had not been explored. On hearing from Will that Earl Wilbur was still having problems with neurasthenics, Tom urged Earl to look at some Freudian texts, confident that they would help. Earl's awkward reply—that he was too old and would have to assume that the pressures at work and at home were the source of the problem—cured Tom of trying to proselytize Will's generation (Margery Howarth Eliot, telephone conversation with Cynthia Grant Tucker, 4 May 1994); Ruth Eliot Johnson, interview by Lorraine McConnell and Ruth P. Nelson; Letter from William Eliot Prentiss to Cynthia Grant Tucker, 11 July 1994.

59. WGE2 to Clara Sessinghaus Vickroy, 5 June 1934, Reed.

60. HRME to TLE, 26 May 1921, Reed; RES to WGE2, 10 October 1933, Reed; WGE to Clara Sessinghaus Vickroy, 5 June 1934; WGE2, diary, 19 April 1934, Reed.

61. Maud Rittenhouse, *Maud: Her Own Journal*, ed. Richard Lee Strout (New York: Macmillan, 1939). "They are a little afraid she may get where she can't speak anymore," Dodie wrote Earl on 11 March 1940. "She only about whispers now."

CHAPTER 7

1. Letters to WGE2, 31 March 1924, 11 February 1924, 28 October 1923, Reed.

2. Among the sprinkling of females who were gathering congregations and speaking on the West Coast in the 1890s were the Rev. Sarah Pratt Carr, who served in Lemoore and Hanford; Mrs. Laura Chant, who preached at First Unitarian Church in San Francisco; and the Rev. Eliza Tupper Wilkes, who now and then filled the pulpit in Oakland. Notes submitted by A.U.A. Field Secretary Charles W. Wendte, *The Pacific Unitarian* (October 1893): 151–52; (March 1895): 140–41; (January 1893): 59.

3. Jay William Hudson to WGE2, 1 June 1902, Reed. "Set Your House in Order," n.d., WGE2 sermon file, Reed. In 1925, with the country's economy booming, Bruce Barton's best-selling book, *The Man Nobody Knows*, represented Jesus as a consummate salesman and CEO, delighting a public who yearned for permission to make and spend money without feeling guilty. The following year, Will Eliot was presented with a stylish sedan as a gift from the church so he would no longer embarrass the parish by driving his old jalopy (AHW to EMW, 23 February 1926, GTU).

4. "Where Are the Men?" undated clipping from *The Portland Spectator*, WGE2 scrapbook, PFUU.

5. For a useful if not impartial overview of the spread of Christian Science on the Pacific Coast from 1880 to 1915, see Rolf Swensen's "Pilgrims at the Golden Gate: Christian Scientists on the Pacific Coast, 1880–1915," *Pacific Historical Review* 72 (May 2003): 229–63.

6. Thomas Van Ness, *The Religion of New England* (Boston: Beacon, 1926), 166–71. The Rev Caroline Bartlett Crane captured the liberals' complaint in a column on "Christian Science" in *Unity* 47 (1901): 53. In it, she said that for all its pretensions, the Eddy movement was neither Christian nor scientific. On the first count, its self-centered, systematic denial precluded compassion and acts of benevolence, and on the second, its effort to banish the factual world was the stuff of magic, not science. If anything, its practices were misguided and selfish impediments to the advances legitimate science was making in public health and preventive medicine.

7. Had Anthony's brief flirtation become something more, she would have learned that the structure, if not androcentric, was close to it: a hierarchy with a single imperious woman on top, and around her a small band of men who controlled her followers' lives in every detail. See Cynthia Grant Tucker, *A Woman's Ministry* (Philadelphia: Temple University Press, 1984) [reissued as *Healer in Harm's Way: Mary Collson, A Clergywoman in Christian Science* (Knoxville: University of Tennessee Press, 1994)], esp. 80–86; and Susan Hill Lindley, "The Ambiguous Feminism of Mary Baker Eddy," *The Journal of Religion* 64 (1984): 318–31.

8. Mary Baker Eddy to Clara Choate, cited by Robert Peel, *Mary Baker Eddy: The Years of Trial* (New York: Holt, Rinehart and Winston, 1971), 109.

9. EMW to LaFayette and Mercy Jane Morse Wilbur, 25 September 1891, GTU.

10. John A. Lee, "Social Change and Marginal Therapeutic Systems," in *Marginal Medicine*, ed. Roy Willis and Peter Morley (New York: Free, 1976), 23–41. Also see Ann Braude on "Medical Mediums" in *Radical Spirits* (Beacon, 1989), 145–51; EMW to LaFayette and Mercy Jane Morse Wilbur, 15 July 1894, GTU; Laura E. Walker to EMW, 28 July 1894, GTU; Walter E. Putnam to TLE, 12 August 1895, Reed. Will Eliot, still having to answer this argument ten years later, conceded that liberal preaching's neglect of people's practical needs had to bear some responsibility for the rise and spread of the healing cults. He also acknowledged the merit of treating diseases holistically when explaining his reservations about the nascent Emmanuel Movement. His complaint was that the appeal of these movements was in their physical cures and material benefits, not in their moral uplift. WGE2, "The Emmanuel Movement: Its Limitations, Perils, and Positive Values" and "The Emanuel Movement in Portland," clippings from *The Oregonian* [Spring 1907, 25 October 1908], WGE2 scrapbook, PFUU. See also, "The Immorals of Mrs. Eddy's Theology," notes for discussion, 18 January 1910, Reed.

11. Jennie Viele to EMW, 2 June 1893, Reed; Jennie Viele to TLE, 6 September 1895, Reed; Jennie Viele to EMW, 18 March 1897, Reed.

12. "The Story of the Post Office Mission," undated handwritten manuscript [ca. 1886], 17, MLTS; *The Post-Office Mission* (Boston: The Alliance of Unitarian and Other Liberal Christian Women, 1915), MLTS.

13. William R. Alger, "Women and Religion," *Pacific Unitarian* (August 1897): 352; William R. Alger, "Work for All," *Unitarian* 5 (August 1910): 288.

14. AHW to EMW, 28 October 1894, GTU.

15. Joseph Tuckerman (1778–1840) had organized Boston's Benevolent Fraternity, a ministry-at-large maintained by the Unitarian churches. The A.U.A.'s published intention was to honor the man as well as the "the noble band of women" whose labors had kept, and would keep, Joseph Tuckerman's vision alive. *New Unitarian* (June 1906): 201–2; SAE to

Mrs. W. Scott Fitts, 15 June 1906, Tuckerman School Papers, HDS; L. P. Jacks, address to the students and faculty, 28 January 1912, Tuckerman School Papers. For more on the Tuckerman School, see Jeanne Lloyd, *The Minister's Double: The Life of Frances Wayland Wood* (Simsbury, Conn.: netLibrary ebook, 1998).

16. Mary A. Safford, *The Christian Register* 87 (28 February 1908): 6–7; 86 (21 March 1907): 6.

17. WGE2 to EMW, 25 May 1926, GTU.

18. UUA Dead Ministers File, HDS.

19. Egbert W. Mersereau to Carrie Aitken, 25 February 1927, Reed.

20. WGE2 to Charles W. Wendte, 27 May 1927, PFUU; AHW to EMW, [1927], GTU.

21. John F. Scheck, "Transplanting a Tradition: Thomas Lamb Eliot and the Unitarian Conscience in the Pacific Northwest, 1865–1905" (PhD diss., University of Oregon, 1969), 312–20, describes the older William Eliot's suffrage position and explains its influence on Thomas Lamb Eliot's. Also see Ruth Barnes Moynihan, *Rebel for Rights: Abigail Scott Duniway* (New Haven, Conn.: Yale University Press, 1985); and for Mrs. Duniway's version of her part in Oregon's suffrage movement, see Abigail Scott Duniway, *Path Breaking: An Autobiographical History of the Equal Suffrage Movement in Pacific Coast States* (Portland, Ore.: James, Kerns and Abbott, 1914).

22. KSB, diaries, January 1896, UO.

23. EMW to TLE, 13 June 1900, GTU; AHW to DDEW, 12 November 1899, GTU; DDEW to EMW, 10 March 1900, GTU; DDEW to EMW, 3 July 1900, 28 July 1900, GTU. Earl Wilbur's position was summarized under the headline, "Talks on Equal Suffrage," in Portland's *Evening Telegram*, 11 August 1894.

24. DDEW to EMW, [1908], GTU; WGE2 to MSE, 15 July 1917, Reed.

25. DLD to HRME, 6 April 1870, Reed; DLD to HRME, 20 June 1874, Reed; DLD to HRME and TLE, undated fragment [ca. 1872], Reed; Elizabeth Robins to HRME, 10 December 1909, GTU.

26. C. Louise B. Lee to WGE2, [Winter 1923–24], Reed.

27. E. Kimbark MacColl reconstructs this chapter of Portland history in "The Women to the Rescue," first delivered at the Parry Center for Children (previously The Home) on 23 September 1980, and reprinted by the Center later that year, PFUU.

28. WGE to TLE, 24 December 1871, WUSL.

29. TDE to EMW, 2 January 1920, GTU; HME to DDEW and EMW, 20 May 1922, GTU; HRME to TLE, 26 January 1903, Reed.

30. HRME to TLE, 26 May 1921, Reed. In E. B. MacNaughton, Portland's liberals still had an iconic figure to validate the myth of Christian manhood. MacNaughton was one of the most respected men in the Unitarian pews long before he officially joined the fold in the early 1940s. In 1923, while holding a seat on the city's Planning Commission and building a personal fortune in real estate, he worked out a deal that enabled the church to erect a larger building downtown. He bought its original land for ten times the $2,000 the founders had paid in 1867 and made a killing, himself, by reselling the parcel for six times his cost. This so inflated the property values that all but the rich were squeezed out of the district, but this did not take the sheen off his reputation. Long hailed as a capitalist who urged his fellow businessmen to get "their noses out of . . . account books and take a long look at human values," MacNaughton went on to serve his denomination

as moderator, occupying the highest lay office there was. See the *Oregon Journal*, 23 August 1960.

31. HRE to EMW, 3 November 1930, GTU; Parry Center (Children's Home) Papers, OHS.

32. TLE to William Ladd, 22 February 1923, 10 March 1923, Reed; William Ladd to TLE, 20 February 1923, 5 March 1923, Reed.

CHAPTER 8

1. Abigail Adams Eliot, *A Heart of Grateful Trust*, ed. Marjorie Gott Manning (Concord, Mass.: Privately printed, 1982), 7.

2. See *Descendants of John May of Roxbury, Mass., 1640*, 2nd ed., revised, supplemented, and indexed by John Franklin May (Baltimore: Gateway, 1978).

3. Alcott's sequels to *Little Women* reiterated these principles. *An Old Fashioned Girl* (1870) promoted a world where "love and liberty prevailed," and talent and character "took the first rank," not money, fashion, or social position. In *Rose in Bloom* (1876), the protagonist's heroes came straight from the May hall of fame: social reformers and abolitionists Frank Lloyd Garrison, Samuel Gridley Howe, and Charles Sumner. See Madeleine B. Stern, *Louisa May Alcott: A Biography*, rev. ed. (Boston: Northeastern University Press, 1999); and "Louisa Alcott's Feminist Letters," *Studies in the American Renaissance*, ed. Joel Myerson (Boston: Twayne, 1978), 429–52.

4. For a fuller sketch, see Shirley Phillips Ingebritsen, "Abigail Williams May," in *Notable American Women, 1607–1950* (Cambridge, Mass.: Harvard University Press, 1971).

5. "Selected Excerpts from the Journals of Abby W. May, 1853–1874, Describing the First Twenty-One Years of the Life of Eleanor Goddard May." Typescript 1994. Courtesy of Eleanor Goddard May II. The entries for June 1862 speak both of Abby May's fractured days and nine-year-old Nellie's praise of her guardian's passion for service.

6. In a letter to Will dated 27 June 1893, Minna wrote of having met Anna while visiting his uncle Christopher's family in Boston. Anna, said Minna, was studying independently for the ministry in hopes of eventually being ordained by a church. In 1943, Anna's daughter Mary (Mrs. J. Leslie Hotson) would mention her mother's thwarted ambition in "Mrs. Frederick W. Peabody (Anna Greenough May), Non-graduate Student 1893–94," an essay written for Radcliffe's alumnae files.

7. Frances E. Willard, *Minutes of the National WCTU at Its 11th Meeting* (Chicago: Woman's Temperance Publishing Association, 1884), 51–52. Livermore's remarks were reported in "Band of Women Ministers: Conference of their Union at the Church of the Disciples," the *Boston Herald*, 31 May 1890. On the ideology of domestic reform, see Seth Konen and Sonya Michel, eds., "Introduction: 'Mother Worlds,'" *Mothers of a New World: Maternalistic Politics and the Origins of Welfare States* (New York: Routledge, 1993), 10–11; and Paula Baker, "The Domestication of Politics: Women and American Political Society, 1780–1920," *American Historical Review* 89 (1984): 620–47.

8. AACE to TLE, 12 May 1888, Reed.

9. Christopher Rhodes Eliot, "Our Record Is on High," MHS, passim.

10. CRE, "Boston Letter," *Christian Register* 24 (5 April 1906): 387.

11. Ibid.

12. Ibid.

13. Ibid.; Charles W. Wendte to CRE, 10 July 1924, HDS.

14. MJME and WGE2, 24 May 1896, Reed.

15. "Mary May Eliot," *Our Work* [Bulfinch Place Church parish bulletin] 22 (October 1926): 1.

16. Abigail Adams Eliot, *A Heart of Grateful Trust*, 53.

17. Ibid., 16; FME to MJME, 26 May 1912, HDS; MME to MJME, 30 May 1922, SL; MME to MJME and CRE, 12 February 1915, SL.

18. For this history of the Barrowses' and Eliots' summer retreats, the author has drawn extensively on historian John Scott's prodigious research into the families and camps at Lake Memphremagog. See also Abigail Adams Eliot, *A Heart of Grateful Trust*, 17–20.

19. Samuel June Barrows described the first trip to the lake in "Unitarian Raid on Canada, Lord's Island, Lake Memphremagog, August 1878," in the *Christian Register*, and later more extensively in *The Shaybacks in Camp: Ten Summers under Canvas* (Boston: Houghton Mifflin, 1887), which he and Isabel coauthored. The unpublished manuscript of Isabel's partial autobiography, "Chopped Straw," is housed at the Georgesville Historical Society in Quebec.

20. Leslie. H. Fishel, "Barrows, Samuel June," *American National Biography Online* (February 2000). Also see Paul U. Kellogg, "Samuel June Barrows: A Circuit Rider in the Humanities," *The Survey* (May 29, 1909): 307–13.

21. Obituary and reminiscence of Isabel Barrows by lakeshore friend and neighbor Theodore Clark Smith, excerpts copied from typescript at GHS and loaned by John Scott.

22. Alice Stone Blackwell, "Women in Camp," *Woman's Journal* 30 (July 1890): 1; Isabel Chapin Barrows to Samuel June Barrows, 6 July 1900, HL.

23. Blackwell, "Women in Camp"; Isabel Chapin Barrows to Samuel June Barrows, 13 July 1900, 14 July 1900, 16 July 1900, HL.

24. Florence Buck to Isabel Barrows, 23 July 1990, HL.

25. MJME to WGE2, 10 July 1903, Reed.

26. Alice Stone Blackwell, "A Sunday in Camp," *Woman's Journal* 42 (6 September 1902): 281.

27. Alice Stone Blackwell, "A Wedding at Camp," *Boston Transcript* (6 July 1905); Isabel Barrows, "A Cabin Colloquy," *The Survey* (7 May 1910): 251–55.

28. Abigail Adams Eliot, *A Heart of Grateful Trust*, 20.

29. Ibid., 20; Camp Maple Hill Journal, courtesy of Frederick Lee Eliot; DDEW to EMW, 29 February 1902, GTU.

30. Frederick Peabody earned much of his reputation from representing Mary Baker Eddy's sons in a suit against their mother's estate and from publishing searing invectives against her Christian Science organization. Gillian Gill documents his messy divorce in *Mary Baker Eddy* (Reading, Mass.: Perseus, 1998), 435–39. In an e-mail to the author, sent on 1 April 2004, Eleanor Goddard May II provides further insight into the family dynamic. EGM recalls that her great-aunt Sarah's husband, Edmund Channing Stowell, "quit working when in his forties" after being "passed over for a promotion at Tufts Medical School." This led to "a real hiatus in the family," with one of the Stowell sons following his mother's profession and "the others resenting their brother for kowtowing to her all his life."

31. Martha May Eliot, interview by Jeannette B. Cheek, Cambridge, Mass., November 1973–May 1974. Schlesinger-Radcliffe Oral History Project, tapes and transcript, 18; Abigail Adams Eliot, *A Heart of Grateful Trust*, 11–12.

32. MME, oral history, 10–11; Abigail Adams Eliot, *A Heart of Grateful Trust*, 12. On the origins of Radcliffe, see Sally Schwager, "Taking Up the Challenge," in *Yards and Gates: Gender in Harvard and Radcliffe History*, ed. Laurel Thatcher Ulrich (New York: Macmillan, 2004), 87–115.

33. Abigail Adams Eliot, *A Heart of Grateful Trust*, 23–25; MME, oral history, 20–22.

34. Elizabeth M. Doherty, "Old Girls Club: The Life and Death of Radcliffe's First and Only Secret Society," *Harvard Crimson* (9 November 2005); http://www.thecrimson.com/article/2005/11/9/old-girls-club-span-stylefont-style-italicwethe

35. Log books, Club Records, SL.

36. Ibid.

37. MME to MJME, 17 April 1915, SL.

CHAPTER 9

1. This unidentified witness to Martha's prowess on Capitol Hill was quoted by Dorothy Barclay in "Godmother to the Nation's Youngsters," *The New York Times Magazine* (6 April 1952): 52.

2. See David M. Robinson's overview of Frederick May Eliot's tenure at the denominational helm in *The Unitarians and the Universalists* (Westport, Conn., Greenwood, 1985), 159–68.

3. FME's baby book, HDS; CRE, "Our Record Is on High," typescript, MHS; MJME to MSE and WGE2, 11 December 1892, Reed.

4. AAE, *A Heart of Grateful Trust*, ed. Marjorie Gott Manning (Concord, Mass.: Privately printed), 7; FME to MJME, 7 September 1900, 15 July 1904, HDS.

5. AACE to HRME, 8 April 1891, Reed; MJME to MSE and WGE2, 11 December 1892, Reed; MME, interview by Jeannette B. Cheek with Martha M. Eliot, November 1973–May 1974, 11ff.; CRE, "Our Record Is on High," MHS; AAE, *A Heart of Grateful Trust*, 55–56.

6. FME to MME, 9 July 1900, SL.

7. CRE to TLE, 4 November 1907, Reed.

8. FME to MJME, 12 November 1911, 26 August 1911, SL.

9. See D. Roy Freeman responding to a survey in the *Unitarian* 2 (July 1907): 248–49.

10. MME, interview by Jeannette B. Cheek, 442–43; FME to CRE, 8 March 1920, HDS; FME to Charles Lesley Ames, 15 January 1949, HDS.

11. FME to MJME, 18 November 1922, SL; FME to CRE, 22 May 1927; Alexandra Osti Eliot and John Marshall, interview by Cynthia Grant Tucker, 27 April 2003, Belmont, Mass.

12. MME, interview by Jeannette B. Cheek, 24, 27; FME to MJME, 14 March 1918, SL.

13. MME, interviews by Jeannette B. Cheek, 379, 24. Bryn Mawr president M. Carey Thomas and her longtime friend Mary Garrett persuaded Johns Hopkins to open its medical school on a coeducational basis by raising the needed endowment and presenting it to the trustees on condition that this be the policy from the outset.

14. A scrap of paper that surfaced after her grandfather's death confirmed the story of William Eliot's effort in women's behalf. This "aide memoire," a note he had written himself

in 1871 just before sitting down with his board of trustees at Washington University, prompted him to push for a medical school to which "*women must be admitted*" (MME, interview by Jeannette B. Cheek, 4, 12). Writing to Tom and Etta around the time he was meeting with his trustees, WGE described the opposition to women's admission to medical school as "old prejudices" and the kind of "absurd fancies" conjured up in the minds "of unclean men" (26 April 1871,WUSL).

15. MME to MJME, 14 March 1920, SL; "Martha May Eliot, Twenty-two interviews,"30–31.

16. Jessie M. Bierman, "Martha May Eliot, M.D.: An Introduction," *Clinical Pediatrics* 5 (September 1966): 571; Barclay, "Godmother to the Nation's Youngsters," 52.

17. On the development of public health, see Ellen S. More, *Restoring the Balance: Women Physicians and the Profession of Medicine, 1850–1995* (Cambridge, Mass.: Harvard University Press, 1999), 4, 81.

18. Ida M. Cannon, *On the Social Frontier of Medicine: Pioneering in Medical Social Service* (Cambridge, Mass.: Harvard University Press, 1952) gives an excellent account of the background and methods of her work at the Massachusetts General Hospital.

19. MME, interview by Jeannette B. Cheek, 30–31.

20. MME to MJME, 15 April 1916, 23 January 1915, SL.

21. MME to MJME, 11 June 1914, SL; MME to MJME and CRE, 12 February 1915, SL.

22. MME, interview by Jeannette B. Cheek, 40.

23. Ibid., 39; Bierman, "Martha May Eliot, M.D.," 571.

24. "Martha May Eliot, Twenty-two interviews," 46–51. Richard A. Meckel, *Save the Babies: American Public Health Reform and the Prevention of Infant Mortality, 1850–1929* (Baltimore: Johns Hopkins University Press, 1990), 142.

25. Marion Hunt, "Ethel Collins Dunham," *American National Biography* 7 (New York: Oxford University Press, 1999), 84–86.

26. MME to MJME, 24 November 1917, 28 April 1918, SL.

27. MME to MJME, 24 March 1915, 4 December 1915, 26 February 1916, SL.

28. MME to MJME, 14 May 1916, SL. For the evolving discussion of women's intimate friendships and the historiography of lesbian representation, see Carroll Smith-Rosenberg, "The Female World of Love and Ritual," *Signs* 1 (1979): 1–29; Judith Schwarz, "Questionnaire in Lesbian History," *Frontiers* 4 (1979): 4–5; Lillian Faderman, *Surpassing the Love of Men* (New York: William Morrow, 1981); and Lillian Faderman, "Introduction," *To Believe in Women* (New York: Houghton Mifflin, 1999), 1–12.

29. Alexandra Osti Eliot, e-mail message to Cynthia Grant Tucker, 7 May 2004.

30. MME to MJME, 4 July 1920, October 1920, SL.

31. MME to MJME, 28 April 1918, [March 1923], SL.

32. In *Children and Youth in America: A Documentary History, Volume 2: 1866–1932* (Cambridge, Mass., Harvard University Press, 1971), 1013, 1014, Robert H. Bremner discusses the taunts to which the unmarried women were subject. Bremner's documentation includes Reed's remarks during debate of the Sheppard-Towner Act, as preserved in the *Congressional Record, 67th Congress, 1st Session* (1921), LXI: 8759–60, 8864–65, 8767.

33. More, "The Eclipse of Maternalist Medicine," *Restoring the Balance*, 148–81; 152, 153.

34. Ibid., 159–60; MME, interview by Jeannette B. Cheek, 61–67.

35. After Martha moved into Lenroot's position in 1935, Ethel took Martha's place as director of research in child development and used the newly available funds to produce a model for integrating pediatric, nursing, and social work services in a community setting. Ethel also had the resources to pioneer a study that led to the first textbook—Premature Infants: A Manual for Physicians (Washington, D.C.: Children's Bureau Publication No. 325, 1948)—establishing uniform standards for neonatal care. See "Martha May Eliot, Twenty-two interviews," 69–77.

36. MME, interview by Jeannette B. Cheek, 158–65.

37. MME, interview by Jeannette B. Cheek, 444–47.

38. MME to MJME, 14 March 1920, SL.

39. Julius B. Richmond, "From Minority to Majority," *The Journal of Public Health* 61 (April 1971): 680; William M. Schmidt, address at the Harvard University Memorial Church, 21 March 1978, "Martha May Eliot: Social Pediatrician, Children's Bureau Chief," SL.

40. As early as 1935, Martha attended a League of Nations conference on child welfare issues. The following year, a conference on family nutrition became the centerpiece of a tour that took her through seven countries in Europe to study the strengths and weaknesses in their governments' child and maternal health care (MME to AAE, 27 September 1949, SL).

41. MME to AAE, 16 October 1949; MME to FME, 15 October 1949, SL.

42. "Martha May Eliot, Twenty-two interviews," 263–65.

43. MME, interview by Jeannette B. Cheek, 289, 378.

44. Wendall Weld, "Woman with a Mission," *Modern Medicine* (1 April 1958): 183; MME, oral history, 332–36.

45. MME, interview by Jeannette B. Cheek, 289, 333–36.

46. Ibid., 443, 82–83, 328–29, 396–97.

47. Ibid., 442–43, 406–7. For a telling contrast, see Conrad Wright, *A Stream of Light* (Boston: The Unitarian Universalist Association, 1975), 142–44, on how Martha's brother Frederick responded to similar pressures from the House Un-American Activities Committee.

48. MME, interview by Jeannette B. Cheek, 175–77.

49. Ibid., 409, 268, 300ff.; Jean Dietz, "Woman Doctor, 79, Fights On to Aid Children," *Boston Sunday Globe* (3 May 1970): 53.

50. MME to MJME, 12 February 1916, SL; Sydney Halpern, *American Pediatrics: The Social Dynamics of Professionalism* (Berkeley and Los Angeles: University of California Press, 1988), 90–95. As More notes in *Restoring the Balance*, 158–59, the prosperity of the 1920s also diminished middle-class women's interest and active support of the public health services. This led organizations such as the General Federation of Women's Clubs to retreat from the political agenda—including the Sheppard-Towner Act—which they had supported earlier.

51. See Sonya Michel and Robyn L. Rosen's account of Putnam's reform career in "The Paradox of Maternalism," *Gender and History* (Autumn 1992): 364–86. See also MME to CRE, 27 February 1928, SL.

52. MME to MJME, 14 March 1920, SL; MME, interview by Jeannette B. Cheek, 278–79, 284–85, 453, 354–58. Ironically, having garnered the credit for the mass vaccinations, Mrs. Hobby bore the brunt of the panic and condemnation caused by an

outbreak of post-inoculation polio cases ascribed to two tainted batches of vaccine produced by the Cutter laboratory. For the full story, see Paul A. Offit, *The Cutter Incident: How America's First Polio Vaccine Led to the Growing Vaccine Crisis* (New Haven, Conn.: Yale University Press, 2005).

53. MME, interview by Jeannette B. Cheek, 378, 5, 334–36. On Martha's relationship with Grace Abbott, see Lela B. Costin, *Two Sisters for Social Justice: A Biography of Grace and Edith Abbott* (Urbana: University of Illinois Press, 2003), 217 and notes 35, 37.

54. Edwards Park to MME, 20 December 1934, March 1965, SL.

55. Edwards A. Park to Haven Emerson, 1 December 1930, SL; Emerson to Park, 1 December 1930, SL; Emerson to Park, 4 December 1930, SL; MME to Park, 8 December 1930, SL; Park to MME, 20 December 1934, SL.

56. Julius B. Richmond, "From a Minority to a Majority," *The Journal of Public Health* 61 (April 1971): 683.

CHAPTER 10

1. MME, oral history, 12–13; Abigail Adams Eliot, *A Heartful of Grateful Trust*, edited by Marjorie Gott Manning (Concord, Mass.: Privately printed, 1982), 24; Mabel Barrows to Samuel June Barrows, 28 July 1900, Barrows papers, HL; Mary C. Shute, "An Old Friend Speaks," *The New England Association of Nursery Education: A Tribute to Abigail Adams Eliot* (Spring 1952): 24.

2. Tuckerman School Records, HDS; AAE to MJME, 29 February 1920, SL.

3. FME to MJME, 18 February 1929, HDS.

4. Alumnae Records, Radcliffe College, Harvard University, Cambridge, Mass.; *A Heart of Grateful Trust*, 23–24.

5. Susan Traverso describes these attitudes in Protestant charity work in *Welfare Politics in Boston,* 1910–1940 (Amherst: University of Massachusetts Press, 2003); MME to MJME, 17 August 1919, SL.

6. AAE to MJME, 11 August 1920, SL.

7. AAE to CRE, 22 February 1920; AAE to MJME, 11 July 1920; AAE to MJME, 11 July 1920; AAE to MJME, 24 July 1920, SL.

8. AAE to MJME, 19 July 1920, SL.

9. Elizabeth Winsor Pearson, "Early Memories," *The New England Association of Nursery Education: A Tribute to Abigail Adams Eliot* (Spring 1952): 3–11; *A Heart of Grateful Trust,* 28.

10. For an overview of Margaret and Rachel McMillan's contributions, see V. Celia Lascarides and Blythe F. Hinitz, *History of Early Childhood Education* (New York: Falmer, 2000), 119–24.

11. AAE to Elizabeth Winsor Pearson, 21 June 1921, SL.

12. Ibid., 14 June 1921, SL.

13. See Lascarides and Hinitz, *History of Early Childhood Education*, on Friedrich Froebel (85–115), Grace Owen (117–19), Montessori (143–67), and Abigail Adams Eliot (332–39). AAE to Elizabeth Winsor Pearson, 20 July 1921, 21 August 1921, SL. Owen noted that Montessori's construct of the "absorbent mind" had thrown important new light on the value of sensory training such as gardening and music in the children's powers of

memory, reason, and comprehension. Notable, too, in this decade before her *Peace and Education* was published, was Montessori's implicit vision of educators as agents of peace who, in teaching cooperation, self-control, and respect for one's neighbors, were sowing the seeds of a less violent world for tomorrow. Their colleague in Italy, Owen said, was bringing the peaceable kingdom on earth that much closer.

14. AAE to Elizabeth Winsor Pearson, 21 August 1921, SL.

15. Ibid., 26 August 1921, 28 August 1921, SL.

16. *A Heart of Grateful Trust*, 31–37.

17. Ibid., 31–33; Mary C. Shute, "An Old Friend Speaks," *A Tribute to Abigail Adams Eliot*, 24.

18. Henry W. Holmes, professor of education emeritus, Harvard Graduate School of Education, "Traditions Broken," *A Tribute to Abigail Adams Eliot*, 16–18.

19. *A Heart of Grateful Trust*, 44.

20. The Rev Lynn P. Smith-Roberts, "A Carefully Loaded Ship: Our Tradition of Religious Education" (paper presented to the Ohio River Group at the Shrine Center for Renewal, Columbus, Ohio, 30 September 1997.) Loaned by the author.

21. *A Heart of Grateful Trust*, 77–78.

22. As Kaye McSpadden explains in "The Sunday School Revolution"—a paper presented at the Unitarian Universalist Church, Lafayette, Indiana, in January 1997, and loaned by its author—as early as 1912, the denomination had launched a Beacon Course of lesson plans giving teachers the chance to use the secular educational theory and modern religious psychology Abby was then absorbing at Radcliffe. The teachers' guides for the youngest children also began to replace the old catechisms with stories and guided discussion, supplemented by pageants and crafts. There was also some effort to broaden the children's worldview—on which rested such concepts as love of country and religious citizenship—through the introduction of folktales and narratives sacred to cultures outside Christianity.

23. *A Heart of Grateful Trust*, 73–75; AAE to Sophia Lyon Fahs, 7 September 1953, SL.

24. Sophia Lyon Fahs to AAE, 16 June 1937, SL. The sweeping view of religion was quintessentially Unitarian, and the concept of God "magnificent," Abby congratulated Fahs in 1953 after reading *Today's Children and Yesterday's Heritage*. Here Fahs had laid out her philosophy of "creative religious development."

25. AAE to Sophia Lyon Fahs, 26 December 1941, 14 July 1942, 7 September 1953, SL.

26. *A Heart of Grateful Trust*, 22, 53.

27. *Christian Register*, 19 October 1941.

28. *A Heart of Grateful Trust*, 56; MME to MJME, 17 August 1919, SL; AAE to MJME, 26 October 1919, SL.

29. John R. Freeman, "Silas W. Holman," *Technology Review* 3 (Boston: George H. Ellis 1901): 6–9.

30. Anna Holman's original drafts of poetry, loaned by Alexandra O. Eliot, *A Heart of Grateful Trust*, 63. In *A Heart of Grateful Trust*, 34–35, Abby speaks of touch as the most vital language in life, from infancy on.

31. On the women's college units, see Dorothy Schneider and Carl J. Schneider, *Into the Breach: American Women Overseas in World War I* (New York: Viking, 1991). In her 1963 response to the Radcliffe Class of 1914 questionnaire, Anna describes her arrival and initial

contacts with families as they returned from exile in Belgium. Two volumes titled *Radcliffe College in France*, which AEH donated to the Radcliffe College Archives, contain letters from her to Christina Hopkinson Baker, chairman of the Radcliffe Alumnae Association War Work Committee, and other historical documentation of the Unit's formation and mission.

32. AAE to MJME, 14 December 1919; AAE to CRE, 6 January 1920, SL; Martha to MJME, 27 July 1921, SL.

33. AAE to MJME, 7 September 1921, SL; MME to MJME, 27 July 1921, SL; DDEW to EMW, 31 October 1933, GTU, describes the "beautiful suite" that was made for Anna in the Francis Avenue house by combining Mary's old sewing and guest rooms.

34. AEH, "Radcliffe Class of 1914 Alumnae Questionnaire," May 1963. Radcliffe College Archives.

35. Although Anna listed herself as Episcopalian as late as 1914, this appears to have been more in deference to her mother than a statement of faith. Her perception of Creation as a unity—as summarized in her essay, "Matter," *Radcliffe Quarterly* (October 1934): 223–34—and the consistent integration of spirit and flesh in her poetry echo her father's humanistic Unitarianism rather than the creeds and temperament of the Episcopal Church.

36. AAE to CRE, 24 July 1927, SL.

37. Notes from the field, *Christian Register* (19 October 1941); AEH to "Robins," [the Radcliffe alumnae who circulated round-robin letters at the end of each year], 26 December 1944, Radcliffe College Archives.

38. AEH to "Robins" 26 December 1944, Radcliffe College Archives.

39. Abby taught nursery school, kindergarten, and early elementary grades at the nonsectarian private Brooks School in Concord while working part-time with her former staff at the training center, now housed at Tufts. Anna resumed her full-time teaching and headed the science department at the Dana Hall School in the nearby town of Wellesley. See *A Heart of Grateful Trust*, 45–47.

40. MME to MJME, 11 October 1919, SL; FME to MJME, 21 February 1929, HDS; *A Heart of Grateful Trust*, 22.

41. AACE to TLE and HRME, 5 December 1886, Reed. According to Abby Cranch Eliot, who gave "water on the brain" as the cause of Theodora's death, the child had been slow in getting her teeth "and in developing every way," and "was born with one pair of limbs and no strength in the legs." When it was discovered that Tom had been born with a double-hernia, its gravity was exaggerated, exacerbating the clutching parental anxiety. Abby Adams Eliot speaks of her cousin in an interview by Steven Cross, *The Mysterious Mr. Eliot*, BBC, 3 January 1971.

42. *A Heart of Grateful Trust*, 60; HWE to TLE, 25 March 1910, Reed; MME to MJME, 3 February 1917, SL.

43. AAE to MJME, 4 January 1920, 18 January 1920, SL; AAE to CRE, 27 January 1920, SL; MME to MJME, 11 April 1920, SL; *A Heart of Grateful Trust*, 60–61.

44. AAE to MJME, 28 August 1920, 5 September 1920, SL; TLE to Charlotte C. Eliot, 6 January 1920, HL.

45. AAE to CRE, 27 January 1920, SL; AAE to MJME, 11 April 1920, SL.

46. AAE to MJME, 26 October 1919, SL; TSE to CCSE, 9 August 1920, HL.

47. Peter Ackroyd, *T.S. Eliot: A Life* (New York: Simon and Schuster, 1984), 158–59.

48. The West Coast branch had clearly heard nothing of Vivienne's mental illness or any addiction. Minna and Will, who called on the couple in London during their second honeymoon in the summer of 1929, saw nothing untoward. Nor had Dodie and Earl when they visited Tom and Vivienne in their flat three years later. Relieved by how cordial her cousin Tom had been, Dodie ascribed his wife's odd behavior to vanity. The woman had a way of trying to smile without moving her lips, no doubt "for fear of showing bad upper teeth." As for the odd contributions Vivienne made to the conversation, apparently "she was a little deaf and wouldn't speak of it" (DDEW to family, 19 September 1931, GTU; HWE Jr. to Thomas Dawes Eliot, 25 February 1934 [copy of original], WAE). T. S. Eliot announced his conversion to the Anglican Church and his British citizenship in a preface to his collection of essays *For Lancelot Andrews.*

49. *A Heart of Grateful Trust*, 60. Ada Eliot Sheffield to Rose Eliot Smith, 13 November 1934, MCE; CCSE to TLE, 7 March 1923, quoted by John Soldo in his Harvard dissertation (1972), published as *The Tempering of T.S. Eliot, 1888–1915* (Ann Arbor: University of Michigan Research, 1984).

50. Indicative of their relationship's warmth is a visit to London in 1960—which Abby recalls in *A Heart of Grateful Trust*, 61—during which she and Anna saw a production of Tom's play *The Cocktail Party* and several days later accepted an invitation to lunch with him. A letter from Abby to Martha (27 July 1960) mentions their having joined him and Valerie Fletcher later "for 'drinks.'" The hosts had made an exception for them. Tom, who was suffering from bronchial asthma, had just gotten out of a nursing home, and they were jealously guarding his strength before going to Leeds for a holiday. In addition to Abby, the delegation to Tom's memorial service included Martha and Abigail Eliot Smith. Tom's siblings had all preceded him in death.

51. AAE to MJME, 9 July 1921, SL; CRE to WGE2, MSE, and Ruth Eliot, Reed; CRE to EMW and DDEW, 24 January 1944, MCE.

52. RES to WGE2, 26 February 1924, Reed; CRE to TLE, 18 December 1919, Reed.

53. If Frederick followed the guidelines he gave the couples he married, one has to assume that Elizabeth decided that they should adopt. While the husband, Frederick would tell the groom, should make all "the major decisions, those that affect the nation and world," he must let his wife make "those concerning their home life and children." Eleanor G. May, e-mail message to Cynthia Grant Tucker, 8 August 2004, on Frederick's counsel to her brother David and sister-in-law at their wedding rehearsal. See also Camp Maple Hill Journal, 10 July 1931; Alexandra O. Eliot and John Marshall, interview by Cynthia Grant Tucker, 27 April 2003.

54. Alexandra Osti Eliot, e-mail messages to Cynthia Grant Tucker, 27 February 2004, 9 February 2006.

55. According to Alexandra Osti Eliot—in an e-mail to Cynthia Grant Tucker, 17 March 2004—Abby was "fit to be tied" when she read the will in which Christopher left the acreage at camp to Frederick and Elizabeth. It apparently seemed only fair as he had left the house in Cambridge to his daughters. In an e-mail sent 25 April 2004, Eleanor G. May testifies to Abby's respect for the campers' privacy.

56. Spring Hill Journal, 17 August 1934, MCE; Camp Maple Hill Journal, *passim*, loaned by Frederick Lee Eliot. The telephone's installation was also a boon for the neighbors, who were on the Eliots' party line. Whenever they got a message that Martha

was going to talk to President Truman, one of them always alerted the others so they could all listen in. Alexandra Osti Eliot to Cynthia Grant Tucker, typed notes ca. 2005.

57. CRE, undated notation in Camp Maple Hill Journal, 1926.

58. Alexandra Osti Eliot e-mail message to Cynthia Grant Tucker, 17 March 2004; MME to William M. Schmidt, 7 May 1974, SL.

59. *A Heart of Grateful Trust*, 58–59, 60.

60. Typical of the material Abby selected were excerpts from Norman Cousins, *The Celebration of Life* (New York: Harper and Row, 1974); and *Anatomy of an Illness* (New York: Norton, 1979), where the author described his recovery from a serious disease by harnessing the powers of humor and optimism. Clippings loaned by Alexandra Osti Eliot. See also *A Heart of Grateful Trust*, 59.

61. Mary C. Shute, "An Old Friend Speaks," *A Tribute to Abigail Adams Eliot*, 24–25; *A Heart of Grateful Trust*, 67–68.

62. Camp Maple Hill Journal.

CHAPTER 11

1. For Emerson's derision of these literal readings of Channing and Ware, see his essay "Immortality," *The Complete Works of Ralph Waldo Emerson*, vol. 8, *Letters and Social Aims (1876)* (Boston and New York: Houghton Mifflin, 1904); Sally Smith Flagg diary, 8 April 1849, Norman G. Flagg Papers, University of Southern Illinois, Edwardsville.; TLE, "Except a Man Be Born Again," Reed.

2. WGE2, "Face to Face: An Easter Sermon," [n.d.], and "How We Are Helped in Our Pilgrimage by Invisible Companions (1932), Reed; FME, "Humanism and the Inner Life," *Humanist Sermons*, ed. Curtis W. Reese (Chicago: Open Court, 1927), 185–93; TLE, "Except a Man Be Born Again," Reed.

3. AACE to SSF, 31 March 1878, Reed; AACE to HRME, 10 April 1887, Reed; AACE to HRME and TLE, [1887], Reed; AACE to TLE, [1887], Reed.

4. SEE to RES, 11 September 1933, Reed; WGE2, "Face to Face: An Easter Sermon," PFUU.

5. DDEW to Elizabeth Wilbur, 5 November 1934, GTU; EMW to DDEW, 14 May 1923, 8 December 1932, 23 January 1934, GTU; EMW, "Memories of Eliot Wilbur 1911–32, by His Father," typescript, [1935], 56–57, WAE.

6. Earl Morse Wilbur, "Memories of Eliot Wilbur," 56–57.

7. DDEW to EMW, 18 February 1934, 25 February 1934, GTU; DDEW to EWN, 3 November 1934, GTU; Frances H. Eliot to EMW, 7 May [1951], GTU.

8. DDEW to HRME, 28 June 1930, GTU.

9. HRME to WGE2, 3 September 1924, GTU; HRME to DEW, n.d., Reed; DEW to EMW, 18 February 1934, GTU; WGE2 to KSBB, 20 July 1923, UO; Abigail Eliot Smith, "Internal History," journal, vol. 3, 1936, MCE.

10. EMW to WGE2, 4 November 1954, GTU.

11. Kate Bingham described the birthmark in "Some of the Unitarian Churches in Boston and New York," UO; HRME to TLE, 21 February 1893, Reed.

12. RSE to HRME, 20 April 1928, MCE.

13. Thomas Dawes Eliot to EMW, [1936], GTU; DEW to EMW, 3 July 1900, GTU.

14. MSE to WGE2, 11 December 1893, WAE; Thomas Dawes Eliot to EMW, [1936], GTU.

15. Norman G. Flagg to WGE2, 6 February 1941, 7 June 1941, 23 April 1946, WUSL.

16. Now housed at Washington University, Charlotte's scrapbook of newspaper clippings of WGE's published letters and articles went back as far as her marriage to Henry in 1868. The materials left to Rose included TLE's diaries from 1865–1933. Gravely ill in the 1950s, Henrietta, for her part, burned more than fifty years' worth of her own pocket date books to keep them from prying eyes. Her recovery gave her twenty years to regret this peremptory act whenever a younger relative, eager to know the ancestors' history, turned to her to confirm names, places, and dates. See RES to TLE, 3 November 1928, Reed.

17. April 1910, HL. William Eliot's children all knew that he loathed biographies as narcissistic and totally "inconsistent" with Christian service. He had even added a codicil to his will forbidding such "book body-snatching" when his became available. He wanted "no funeral sermon, and no biography, —no use of Mss." "Like the scissors Grinder," he told his family, "I have no story to tell" (WGE to TLE, March 1875, WUSL).

18. Charlotte C. Eliot to TSE, April 1910, HL.

19. HMF to EMW, 21 April 1918, GTU; John Spencer Clark, *The Life and Letters of John Fiske* (Boston and New York: Kessinger, 1917).

20. EMW to "My dear brothers and sisters," [1936], GTU.

21. "For quite some time after Anna's death," Abby's intensely protective feelings about their private life were still strong and rather surprising to the much younger Eleanor Goddard May II. Abby was not at all pleased that a favorite poet of theirs, May Sarton, was using her prose to write about her lesbian relationships. E-mail from EGM to Cynthia Grant Tucker, 15 March 2006.

22. MME oral history, 22, 445–54, and *passim*. On the taping of Martha Eliot's oral history, see Jeannette B. Cheek, "I Don't Know What You Mean by Retirement," *Radcliffe Quarterly* (March 1975): 4–6.

23. MME, interview by Jeannette B. Cheek with Martha M. Eliot, 447, 454.

24. *A Heart of Grateful Trust*, 63.

25. Ibid.

26. Edwards A. Park to MME, 26 October 1930, 20 December 1934, 9 January 1965, SL.

27. Edwards A. Park to MME, 9 January 1965, 7 December 1958, 21 March 1958, SL.

28. Edwards A. Park to MME, 6 April 1968, SL.

29. Ned, himself, tried to hold onto Ethel by writing her simple letters and savoring her charming replies, with their "bits of her old self" still there. When Martha finally wrote that Ethel could no longer recognize words or write back, the news, he told Martha, could not have been "sadder" if it had "announced her death" (Edwards A. Park to MME, 1 May 1967, 12 June 1968, 26 August 1967, SL; *A Heart of Grateful Trust*, 75).

30. MME to William M. Schmidt, 7 May 1974, SL; Edwards A. Park to MME, [March 1965], SL.

Selected Bibliography

MANUSCRIPT COLLECTIONS

Alumnae Records, Radcliffe College, Harvard University, Cambridge, Mass.

Barrows Family Papers, Houghton Library, Harvard University, Cambridge, Mass.

Bates, Kate Stevens Bingham. Papers. Knight Library, University of Oregon, Eugene.

Bulfinch Place Church. Records. Andover-Harvard Library, Harvard Divinity School, Cambridge, Mass.

Church of Our Father [First Unitarian Church of Portland, Ore.]. Records. First Unitarian Church, Portland, Ore.

Church of the Messiah [First Unitarian Church of St. Louis]. Records. First Unitarian Church, St. Louis, Mo.

Dunham, Ethel Collins. Papers, 1952–1965. Harvard Medical Library in the Francis A. Countway Library of Medicine, Center for the History of Medicine, Harvard University, Cambridge, Mass.

Eliot, Abigail Adams. Papers. Schlesinger Library, Radcliffe Institute, Harvard University, Cambridge, Mass.

Eliot, Christopher Rhodes. Papers. Andover-Harvard Library, Harvard Divinity School, Cambridge, Mass.

Eliot Family Photographs. Privately owned. Courtesy of Christopher Rhodes Eliot III.

Eliot Family Papers. Privately owned. Courtesy of Mary C. Eliot.

Eliot Family Papers. Privately owned. Courtesy of Warner A. Eliot.

Eliot, Frederick May. Papers. Andover-Harvard Library, Harvard Divinity School, Cambridge, Mass.

Eliot, Martha May. Papers. Schlesinger Library, Radcliffe Institute, Harvard University, Cambridge, Mass.

Eliot, Thomas Lamb. Papers. Hauser Memorial Library Archives, Reed College, Portland, Ore.

Eliot, William Greenleaf. Papers. Missouri Historical Society, St. Louis, Mo.

Eliot, William Greenleaf. Papers. University Library, Washington University, St. Louis, Mo.

First Parish of Dorchester. Papers. Massachusetts Historical Society, Boston, Mass.

Flagg Family Papers, Lovejoy Library, University of Southern IllinoisEdwardsville.

Flagg Family Papers, University Library, University of Illinois at Urbana-Champaign, Urbana.

Holman, Anna Eveleth. Papers. Schlesinger Library, Radcliffe Institute, Harvard University, Cambridge, Mass.

Holman, Silas W. Papers. Institute Archives, Massachusetts Institute of Technology, Cambridge, Mass.

Jones, Jenkin Lloyd. Papers. Meadville/Lombard Theological School, Chicago, Ill.

May-Goddard Papers. Schlesinger Library, Radcliffe Institute, Harvard University, Cambridge, Mass.

Pacific Unitarian School for the Ministry Records. Archives. Starr King School for the Ministry, Berkeley, Calif.

Ruggles Street Nursery School and Training Center Records. Eliot-Pearson Department of Child Development, Tufts University, Medford, Mass.

Tuckerman School Records. Andover-Harvard Library, Harvard Divinity School, Cambridge, Mass.

Wilbur, Earl Morse. Papers. Hewlett Library, Graduate Theological Union, Berkeley, Calif.

UNPUBLISHED SOURCES

Camp Maple Hill Journals. Privately owned. Courtesy of Frederick Lee Eliot.

Coon, Delia M., comp. "History of Early Pioneer Families of Hood River, Oregon," n.d. OHS.

Eliot, Alexandra Osti. E-mail correspondence with Cynthia Grant Tucker, 2002–6.

Eliot, Alexandra Osti. Interview by Cynthia Grant Tucker, Belmont, Mass., 22 October 2002.

Eliot, Alexandra Osti, and John Marshall. Interview by Cynthia Grant Tucker, Belmont, Mass., 27 April 2003.

Eliot, Christopher Rhodes. Memorial sermon for Dorothea Dix, 24 July 1887, Dorchester, Mass. SL.

———. "Memories and a Memorial: Address before the Cambridge Association of Ministers." Typescript, n.d. SL.

———. "Our Record Is on High," n.d. MHS

Eliot, Henry Ware. "Reminiscences of a Simpleton." Typescript, 1910. WUSL.

Eliot, Margery Howarth. Telephone conversation with Cynthia Grant Tucker, 4 May 1994.

Eliot, Margery Howarth. Telephone interview with Cynthia Grant Tucker, 16 March 1996.

Eliot, Martha May. Twenty-two interviews conducted by Jeannette B. Cheek, Cambridge, Mass., November 1973–May 1974. Schlesinger-Rockefeller Oral History Project. Tapes and transcript, SL.

Eliot, Thomas Lamb. Diaries. Reed William Greenleaf Jr. Diaries. Reed.

———. "Memories of St. Louis in the '70s and '80s." Typescript, 1953. MOHS.

Johnson, Ruth Eliot. Interview by Lorraine McConnell and Ruth P. Nelson, 23 February 1984, Portland, Ore. Audiocassette. PFUU.

May, Eleanor Goddard II, ed. "Selected Excerpts from the Journals of Abby W. May, 1853–1874, Describing the First Twenty-One Years of the Life of Eleanor Goddard May." Typescript 1994. Courtesy of Eleanor Goddard May II.

McSpadden, Kaye. "The Sunday School Revolution." Paper presented at the Unitarian Universalist Church in Lafayette, Indiana, in January 1997, and loaned by its author.

Morris, Carol R. "Frederick May Eliot, President of the American Unitarian Association (1937–1958)." PhD diss., Boston University, 1970.

Parker, Margaret. Interview by Lorraine McConnell, 14 April 1983, Portland, Ore. Audiocassette. PFUU. Preston, Ruth Irish. Diaries. State Historical Society, Iowa City, Iowa.

"Radcliffe College in France," 1918–20 [scrapbooks]. Anna Eveleth Holman Papers, SL.

Robinson, David. "Thomas Lamb Eliot and the New England Tradition in the Northwest." Typescript, n.d. Reed.

Scheck, John F. "Transplanting a Tradition: Thomas Lamb Eliot and the Unitarian Conscience in the Pacific Northwest, 1865–1905." PhD diss., University of Oregon, 1969.

Smith, Theodore Clark. "Camp Reminiscences." Typescript, n.d. Georgesville [Quebec] Historical Society.

Smith-Roberts, Lynn P. "A Carefully Loaded Ship: Our Tradition of Religions Education." Paper presented to the Ohio River Group at the Shrine Center for Renewal, Columbus, Ohio, 30 September 1997. Courtesy of the author.

Wilbur, Earl Morse. "A Father's Reminiscences." Typescript, 1953. Courtesy of Warner A. Eliot.

Wilbur, Earl Morse. "Memories of Eliot Wilbur, 1912–1932." Typescript, 1935. Courtesy of Warner A. Eliot.

PUBLISHED SOURCES

Ackroyd, Peter. T. S. Eliot: A Life. New York: Simon and Schuster, 1984.

"Abigail Adams Eliot: A Tribute." The New England Association of Nursery Education (Spring 1952): 1–25.

Alcott, Louisa May. The Selected Letters. Edited by Joel Myerson, Daniel Shealy, and Madeleine B. Stern. Boston: Little Brown, 1987.

Barclay, Dorothy. "Godmother to the Nation's Youngsters." The New York Times Magazine (6 April 1952): 17, 52–54.

Barrows, Samuel June, and Isabel Chapin Barrows. The Shaybacks in Camp: Ten Summers under Canvas. Boston: Houghton Mifflin, 1887.

Barton, Bruce F. The Man Nobody Knows. Indianapolis: Bobbs-Merrill, 1925.

Bierman, Jessie M. "Martha May Eliot, M.D.: An Introduction." Clinical Pediatrics 5 (September 1966): 571.

Blackwell, Alice Stone. "A Sunday in Camp." Woman's Journal 42 (6 September 1902): 281.

———. "Women in Camp." Woman's Journal 30 (13 July 1890): 1.

Blair, Karen J. The Club Woman as Feminist: True Womanhood Redefined, 1868–1914. New York: Holmes and Meier, 1980.

Blow, Susan, and Henrietta R. Eliot. *The Mottoes and Commentaries of Friedrich Froebel's "Mother Play."* New York: Appleton, 1899.

Brekus, Catherine A. *Strangers and Pilgrims: Female Preaching in America, 1740–1845.* Chapel Hill: University of North Carolina Press, 1998.

Bremner, Robert H. *Children and Youth in America: A Documentary History, Volume 2, 1866–1932.* Cambridge, Mass.: Harvard University Press, 1971.

Bushnell, Horace. *Christian Nurture.* Hartford, Conn.: Edwin Hunt, 1847; New York: Charles Scribner's Sons, 1890.

Cannon, Ida M. *On the Social Frontier of Medicine: Pioneering in Medical Social Service.* Cambridge, Mass.: Harvard University Press, 1952.

Cheek, Jeannette B. "I Don't Know What You Mean by Retirement." *Radcliffe Quarterly* (March 1975): 4–6.

Clarke, Edward H. *Sex in Education; Or, A Fair Chance for the Girls.* Boston: Osgood and Company, 1874.

Cobbe, Frances Power. *The Duties of Women: A Course of Lectures.* London: Williams and Norgate, 1881.

Costin, Lela B. *Two Sisters for Social Justice: A Biography of Grace and Edith Abbott.* Urbana: University of Illinois Press, 1983.

———. "Women and Physicians: The 1930 White House Conference on Children." *Social Service Review* 57 (March/April 1983): 108–14.

Crompton, Arnold. *Unitarianism on the Pacific Coast: The First Sixty Years.* Boston: Beacon, 1957.

Dietz, Jean. "Woman Docto. 79, Fights On to Aid Children." *Boston Sunday Globe* (3 May 1970): 53.

Doherty, Elizabeth M. "Old Girls Club: The Life and Death of Radcliffe's First and Only Secret Society." *Harvard Crimson,* 9 November 2005; http://www.thecrimson.com/article/2005/11/9/old-girls-club-span-stylefont-style-italicwethe.

Douglas, Ann. *The Feminization of American Culture.* New York: Knopf, 1977.

Dunham, Ethel Collins. *Samuel G. Dunham, Alice Collins Dunham, Their Descendants and Antecedents.* Hartford, Conn.: Privately printed, 1955.

Duniway, Abigail Scott. *Path Breaking: An Autobiographical History of the Equal Suffrage Movement in Pacific Coast States.* Portland, Ore.: James, Kerns and Abbott, 1914.

Ehrenreich, Barbara, and Deirdre English. *For Her Own Good: 150 Years of the Experts' Advice to Women.* Garden City, N.Y.: Anchor, 1978.

Eliot, Abigail Adams. "Educating the Parent through the Nursery School." *Childhood Education* 3 (December 1926): 182–90.

———. *A Heart of Grateful Trust.* Edited by Marjorie Gott Manning. Concord, Mass.: Privately printed, 1982.

———. "Two Nursery Schools: Nurseries Working for Health, Education and Family Life." *Child Health Magazine* 5 (March 1924): 97.

Eliot, Charlotte C. *William Greenleaf Eliot: Minister, Educator, Philanthropist.* Boston: Houghton Mifflin, 1904.

Eliot, Henrietta R. "The Adopted Chicken." *St. Nicholas Magazine for Boys and Girls* 4 (February 1877).

————. "An Appeal to Conscience, and 'The Christian Union's' Reply to It." *The Christian Register* 52 (27 December 1873): 1.

————. "Chin Wouy's Wife." *Everybody's Magazine* 10 (January 1904).

————. "Complaint." *Overland Monthly and Out West Magazine* 10 (September 1887).

————. "A Cure for the Toothache." *The Nursery* 28 (September 1880).

————. "For Better, For Worse." *Everybody's Magazine* 11 (August 1904).

————. "From the Bridge." *Everybody's Magazine* 10 (February 1904).

————. *Laura in the Mountains.* Boston: Lothrop, 1905.

————. *Laura's Holidays.* Boston: Lothrop, 1898.

————. "Thistledown." *St. Nicholas Magazine* 5 (November 1880).

————. "Unawares." *Scribner's Monthly* 14 (February 1877).

————. *The Unwelcome Guest and Other Verses.* Portland, Ore.: Privately printed, 1937.

————. "The Violin." *Overland Monthly and Out West Magazine* 9 (June 1887).

————. "Waiting for Day." *Californian* [1–6] (1882).

Eliot, William G. *The Discipline of Sorrow.* Cambridge: Metcalf, 1855.

————. *Early Religious Education Considered as the Divinely Appointed Way to the Regenerate Life.* Boston: Crosby, Nichols, 1855.

————. *The Story of Archer Alexander: From Slavery to Freedom.* Boston: Cupples, Upham, 1885.

Faderman, Lillian. *To Believe in Women: What Lesbians Have Done for America—a History.* Boston: Houghton Mifflin, 1999.

Fahs, Sophia L. *Today's Children and Yesterday's Heritage.* Boston: Beacon, 1952.

Freeman, John R. "Silas W. Holman." *Technology Review* 3 (1901): 6–9.

Gates, Joanne E. *Elizabeth Robins, 1862–1952: Actress, Novelist, Feminist.* Tuscaloosa: University of Alabama Press, 1994.

Gedge, Karin E. *Without Benefit of Clergy: Women and the Pastoral Relationship in Nineteenth-Century American Culture.* New York: Oxford University Press, 2003.

Gleadle, Kathryn. *The Early Feminists: Radical Unitarians and the Emergence of the Women's Rights Movement, 1831–1835.* New York: St. Martin's, 1995.

Gollaher, David L. *Voice for the Mad: The Life of Dorothea Dix.* New York: Free, 1995.

Goodwin, Joan W. *The Remarkable Mrs. Ripley: The Life of Sarah Alden Bradford Ripley.* Boston: Northeastern University Press, 1998.

Halpern, Sydney. *American Pediatrics: The Social Dynamics of Professionalism.* Berkeley and Los Angeles: University of California Press, 1988.

Hilands, Evadne. *A Time to Build: The First Unitarian Society of Portland, Oregon, 1866–1966.* Portland: First Unitarian Society, 1966.

Holman, Anna Eveleth. "Matter." *Radcliffe Quarterly* 18 (October 1934): 223–34.

————. *Poems.* Cambridge, Mass.: Privately printed, 1971.

Holmes, John Haynes. "The Unitarian Ministry: The Problem of Withdrawals Again." *Unity* 68 (December 1911): 229–31.

Horowitz, David A. "Social Morality and Personal Revitalization: Oregon's Ku Klux Klan in the 1920s." *Oregon Historical Quarterly* 90 (1989): 365–84.

Hunt, Marion. "Ethel Collins Dunham." *American National Biography* 7 (New York: Oxford University Press, 1999), 84–86.

———. "'Extraordinarily Interesting and Happy Years': Martha M. Eliot and Pediatrics at Yale, 1921–1935." *Yale Journal of Biology and Medicine* 68 (1995): 159–70.

Jordan, David Starr. *The Human Harvest*. Boston: American Unitarian Association, 1907.

"Kate Stevens Bates." Obituary. *Tacoma Times* (26 November 1941).

Lascarides, Celia V., and Blythe F. Hinitz. *History of Early Childhood Education*. New York: Falmer, 2000.

Leavitt, Judith Walzer. *Brought to Bed: Childbearing in America, 1750–1950*. New York: Oxford University Press, 1986.

Lindley, Susan Hill. "The Ambiguous Feminism of Mary Baker Eddy." *The Journal of Religion* 64 (1984): 318–31.

Lloyd, Jeanne. *The Minister's Double: The Life of Frances Wayland Wood*. Simsbury, Conn.: netLibrary ebook, 1998.

MacColl, E. Kimbark. *Merchants, Money, and Power: The Portland Establishment, 1843–1913*. Portland, Ore: Georgian, 1988.

———. "'The Women to the Rescue.' An Address Delivered at the Annual Meeting of The Parry Center For Children [formerly The Home], 23 September 1980." Portland, Ore.: The Parry Center, 1980. PFUU.

Marsh, Margaret, and Wanda Ronner. *The Empty Cradle: Infertility in America from Colonial Times to the Present*. Baltimore: Johns Hopkins University Press, 1996.

Martin, Theodora Penny. *The Sound of Our Own Voices: Women's Study Clubs, 1860–1910*. Boston: Beacon, 1987.

"Mary May Eliot." *Our Work*. Boston: Bulfinch Place Church (October 1926): 1.

May, Elaine Tyler. *Barren in the Promised Land: Childless Americans and the Pursuit of Happiness*. Cambridge, Mass.: Harvard University Press, 1997.

May, John Franklin, ed. *Descendants of John May of Roxbury, Massachusetts, 1640*, 2nd ed., revised, supplemented, and indexed by John Franklin May. Baltimore: Gateway, 1978.

McPherson, James M. "A Brief for Equality: The Abolitionist Reply to the Racist Myth, 1860–1865." *The New England Quarterly* 45 (1972): 408–16.

Meckel, Richard A. *Save the Babies: American Public Health Reform and the Prevention of Infant Mortality, 1850–1929*. Baltimore: Johns Hopkins University Press, 1990.

Morantz-Sanchez, Regina. *Sympathy and Science: Women Physicians in American Medicine*. New York: Oxford University Press, 1985.

More, Ellen S. *Restoring the Balance: Women Physicians and the Profession of Medicine, 1850–1995*. Cambridge,Mass.: Harvard University Press, 1999.

Morris, Carol R. "The Election of Frederick May Eliot to the Presidency of A.U.A." *Proceedings of the Unitarian Historical Society* 17 (1970–72): 1–45.

"The Mysterious Mr. Eliot: Aspects of T. S. Eliot." Omnibus series. VHS. London: BBC, 1971. Evanston, Ill.: Contemporary Films/McGraw Hill, 1973.

Porter, Maria S. "Recollections of Louisa May Alcott." *New England Magazine* 6 (1892): 13–14.

Rittenhouse, Maud. *Maud: Her Own Journal*. Edited by Richard Lee Strout. New York: Macmillan, 1939.

Robinson, David M. *The Unitarians and the Universalists*. Westport, Conn.: Greenwood, 1985.

Rotundo, E. Anthony. *American Manhood: Transformations in Masculinity from the Revolution to the Modern Era*. New York: Basic, 1993.

Schneider, Dorothy, and Carl J. Schneider. *Into the Breach: American Women Overseas in World War I*. New York: Viking, 1991.

Sklar, Kathryn Kish. *Catherine Beecher: A Study in American Domesticity*. New Haven, Conn.: Yale University Press, 1973.

Smith-Rosenberg, Carroll. "The Hysterical Woman: Sex Roles and Role Conflict in Nineteenth-Century America." *Social Research* 39 (Winter 1972): 652–78.

Soldo, John. *The Tempering of T. S. Eliot, 1888–1915*. New York: Simon and Schuster, 1984.

Stern, Madeleine B. *Louisa May Alcott: A Biography*, rev. ed. Boston: Northeastern University Press, 1999.

———. "Louisa Alcott's Feminist Letters." *Studies in the American Renaissance*, ed. Joel Myerson, 429–52. Boston: Twayne, 1978.

Sweet, Leonard I. *The Minister's Wife: Her Role in Nineteenth-Century Evangelism*. Philadelphia: Temple University Press, 1983.

Swensen, Rolf. "Pilgrims at the Golden Gate: Christian Scientists on the Pacific Coast, 1880–1915." *Pacific Historical Review* 72 (May 2003): 229–63.

Swisher, Walter Samuel. *A History of the Church of the Messiah, St. Louis, 1839–1934*. St. Louis: The Church of the Messiah, 1934.

"Symposium: 'What Should Be Expected of the Minister's Wife in a Modern Church?'" *Unitarian* 4 (June 1909): 227–30.

Traverso, Susan. *Welfare Politics in Boston, 1910–1940*. Amherst: University of Massachusetts Press, 2003.

Tucker, Cynthia Grant. *Prophetic Sisterhood: Liberal Women Ministers of the Frontier, 1880–1930*. Boston: Beacon, 1990.

———. "Women in the Unitarian Universalist Movement." *The Encyclopedia of Women and Religion in North America*. Edited by Rosemary Radford Reuther and Rosemary Keller. Bloomington: Indiana University Press, 2006.

Ungar, Arliss. *With Vision and Courage: Starr King School for the Ministry, the History of Its First Hundred Years, 1904–2004*. Lincoln, Neb.: iUniverse, 2006.

Walsh, Mary Roth. *"Doctors Wanted: No Women Need Apply": Sexual Barriers in the Medical Profession, 1835–1975*. New Haven, Conn.: Yale University Press, 1975.

Wilbur, Earl Morse. *Thomas Lamb Eliot, 1841–1936*. Portland, Ore.: Privately printed [G. M. Allen and Son], 1937.

———. *Pacific Unitarian School for the Ministry: The History of Its First Twenty-Five Years, 1904–1929*. Berkeley: Pacific Unitarian School for the Ministry, 1930.

Wright, Conrad. *The Liberal Christians: Essays on American Unitarian History*. Boston: Beacon, 1970.

———, ed. and coauthor. *A Stream of Light: A Sesquicentennial History of American Unitarianism*. Boston: The Unitarian Universalist Association, 1975.

Ziegler, Valarie H. *Diva Julia: The Public Romance and Private Agony of Julia Ward Howe*. Harrisburg, Pa.: Trinity Press International, 2003.

Index